# Substances
and Universals
in Aristotle's
Metaphysics

ALSO BY THEODORE SCALTSAS

*The Golden Age of Virtue: Aristotle's Ethics*

*Aristotelian Realism* (editor)

*Unity, Identity, and Explanation in Aristotle's Metaphysics*
(co-editor)

# Substances and Universals in Aristotle's Metaphysics

THEODORE SCALTSAS

CORNELL UNIVERSITY PRESS

ITHACA AND LONDON

First printing, Cornell Paperbacks, 2010

First published 1994 by Cornell University Press.

*Library of Congress Cataloging-in-Publication Data*
Scaltsas, T. (Theodore)
    Substances and universals in Aristotle's Metaphysics / Theodore
Scaltsas.
        p.   cm.
    Includes bibliographical references and indexes.
    ISBN: 978-0-8014-7635-8
    1. Aristotle.   Metaphysics.   2. Substance (Philosophy)
3. Universals (Philosophy)   I. Title.
    B434.S32   1994
111'.1—dc20                                         94-8911

Printed in the United States of America

⊗ The paper in this book meets the minimum requirements
of the American National Standard for Information Sciences—
Permanence of Paper for Printed Library Materials, ANSI Z39.48-1984.

*For Patricia*

# Contents

# Acknowledgments

The first draft of this book was written in 1987–88 in the (wonderful!) environment of the Center for Hellenic Studies, Harvard University. I had the opportunity to present the core of the book at a departmental seminar series at the Philosophy Department of the University of Sydney, where I enjoyed and profited from a visiting lectureship during the (southern) autumn semester 1991. In the past ten years, I have had the opportunity to present themes expounded in the book, in different stages of development, on many and diverse philosophical occasions. I am therefore indebted to numerous colleagues for their contributions, of varying size and impact, to the final shape of this work. As I cannot register here my gratitude to all, I mention and wholeheartedly express my thanks to the very few, who, in different ways, have had a more profound influence on the shape and content of this book: John Ackrill, Julia Annas, David Armstrong, David Charles, Russell Dancy, David Furley, Mary Louise Gill, Reinhardt Grossmann, Christopher Kirwan, Anthony Long, Mohan Matthen, Christopher Peacocke, Timothy Sprigge, Sir Peter Strawson, Michael Woods, and collectively the members of the Philosophy Department of the University of Sydney. Deeply felt thanks also extend to Zeph Stewart for making the Center for Hellenic Studies so conducive a setting for research in ancient philosophy. Finally, I would like to thank Jeffrey Carr for copyediting the volume and composing the indexes.

THEODORE SCALTSAS

*Edinburgh*

# Abbreviations

| | |
|---|---|
| *An. Post.* | *Posterior Analytics* |
| *An. Pr.* | *Prior Analytics* |
| *Cael.* | *De Caelo* |
| *Cat.* | *Categories* |
| *DA* | *De Anima* |
| *EN* | *Nicomachean Ethics* |
| *GA* | *De Generatione Animalium* |
| *GC* | *Generation and Corruption* |
| *Int.* | *De Interpretatione* |
| *MA* | *De Motu Animalium* |
| *Meta.* | *Metaphysics* |
| *Meteor.* | *Meteorologica* |
| *PA* | *De Partibus Animalium* |
| *Ph.* | *Physics* |
| *Soph. El.* | *Sophistici Elenchi* |
| *Top.* | *Topics* |

Line references to Aristotle's texts are given to the Oxford Classical Texts edition of Aristotle's works, to the Bude edition of the *Generation and Corruption*, and to Loeb or the *Thesaurus Linguae Graecae* for other texts. Translations of Aristotle's texts are from the Clarendon Aristotle Series, for the texts that have been translated, and from Barnes's edition for the rest, unless otherwise stated. Translations of passages from Plato's *Theaetetus* are McDowell's, and from the *Parmenides* Allen's; translations of other passages from Plato's works are from Hamilton and Cairns's edition.

# Substances and Universals in Aristotle's Metaphysics

# The Theme

A substance is a composite particular. If it is composed of further particulars, will the substance itself be one or many? If composed of universals, can
the substance be particular? Does composition preserve the identity, the
number, or the type of entity the substance's constituents are? Is composition itself an entity in the substance? Are there different types of composition of constituents within one and the same substance? Is the substance
itself identical to some, but not all, of the constituents that make it up?

These are the questions that exercise Aristotle's thought in the central
books of his *Metaphysics*. His answers have been found to be aporetic, if not
contradictory. The text is often ambiguous, and certainly more examples
and richer terminology would have narrowed down the possible interpretations of key passages. Nevertheless, I believe it is possible to extract a
coherent metaphysical theory from these books, a theory that succeeds in
offering satisfactory answers to questions that are as central and legitimate
metaphysical concerns nowadays as they were when Aristotle raised them.

The general problems on which Aristotle focuses are the following.
What type of entity is the matter of a substance? How does the matter
contribute to the particularity of a substance? Is the substance over and
above its matter? If it is—by the form—what type of entity is the form,
and how does *it* contribute to the particularity of the substance? How are
the various constituents of a substance unified into a single entity, and what
determines the identity of the resulting entity?

Central to Aristotle's investigation is a further problem whose resolution
guides most of his metaphysical theory; namely, what a subject is in itself.

This problem was one of the toughest challenges to Plato's Theory of Forms—second only to the Third Man—which, I argue, the theory never resolved. The problem can first be identified in the *Phaedo* and later on in the *Timaeus*, as well as in Aristotle's comments about the Theory of Forms. The problem emerged as follows. When a property belongs to a subject, is the property a feature of the subject, or does it determine the nature of the subject? If *belonging to a subject* determines the *nature* of the subject, then, in the case of a form such as "being a tree," the subject itself would be a tree; but in the case of a form like "being large," the subject would be a large in itself(?). On the other hand, if belonging to a subject does not determine the nature of the subject but is only a *feature* of it, then "being large" would characterize a subject that is not in itself "a large," and inevitably "being a tree" would characterize a subject that is not in itself a tree(?). Thus, if what "belongs to" a subject determines the nature of the subject, the subject will have a nature but no features; if what "belongs to" a subject is a feature of that subject, the subject will have features but no nature. Therefore, the relation of "belonging to a subject" cannot accommodate the difference between the subject's nature and its features.

No way of belonging to a subject can satisfy *both* requirements, which is a problem that Plato confronted in the *Phaedo*. As we will see, the problem is not solved, even by introducing two different ways of belonging to a subject, as a nature and as a feature. Furthermore, it cannot be answered by essentialism, namely, by the realization that there are some properties that the subject cannot lose. A subject may be essentially slender, but this does not turn the subject into "a slender." The resolution of the problem does not call for a distinction between properties a subject may lose and properties it cannot lose; it calls for a distinction between *what* the subject is *in itself* and properties that qualify a subject of that kind. Plato never resolved this difficulty. I argue that Aristotle finally did, but that his solution did not (and could not) rest on the introduction of two kinds of property (natures and features) or two kinds of predication (essential and accidental). Indeed, Aristotle's first attempt at a solution consisted in introducing just these distinctions in the *Categories*, between two types of form—secondary substances and nonsubstances—and between two ways of belonging to a subject—being said of a subject and being in the subject. But his Second Man Argument in his *Metaphysics* (Section 6.3) fatally undermined this proposal by showing that the subject cannot be distinct from its nature, related to it by "the. . . said of . . ." relation, by participation, or any other relation. "Being said of . . .", or "belonging to . . ." a subject metaphysically separates a subject from its nature, placing the subject on the one side and its nature on the other. I call the problem of determining how the nature and the features of a subject relate to it the *nature-feature problem*. Its resolution, according to Aristotle, requires establishing that the nature-feature distinction must be the subject-feature distinction. Aristotle reached the profound realization that for the subject to be something in itself, *the essence cannot belong to the subject, but must be the subject*. The essence cannot belong to a subject (as a set of properties that the subject cannot lose); it cannot belong to it even in a special way of belonging, different from the way that the accidents belong to it. Rather, the essence *is* the substantial subject: "Why should not some *things be essences* from the start?" [1] However, making the essence the subject poses severe metaphysical problems. I have tried to show in the second half of this work that Aristotle does resolve these problems in the central books of his *Metaphysics*.

On the question of particularity, I argue that Aristotle did not derive the particularity of a substance from a primitively particular constituent of it, whether it be the matter, the form, or a bare substratum. Aristotle is committed to the survival of matter even in the most radical transformations; what survives is not necessarily the same *kind* of matter, but it is certainly the same *quantity* of matter—to be explained. The matter of a substance can belong to another substance at a different time, and hence, the particularity of a substance cannot reduce to the particularity of its matter. From that perspective, matter is universal insofar as the same quantity of it can belong to different substances at different times.

The substantial form is introduced by Aristotle to account for the unity of the material components of a substance into a single entity. The central idea is that the form does not unify the components of a substance in the way a relation relates its relata. This is Aristotle's way of establishing that a substance is not a cluster of copresent (even interrelated) components, but a single, unified whole. The form unifies the components of a substance, not be relating them (which would leave their distinctness intact), but by *reidentifying* them, that is, by making them identity-dependent on the whole. It is not *relation* that unites, but the *identity dependence* of the constituents on the whole, in accordance with the principle of the form.

Aristotle's solution to the question of substantial composition applies to any type of analysis of a substance into constituents, whether it is by physical division or division by abstraction. This provides the stepping

---

1. *Meta.* 1031b31, my emphasis.

stone for the individuation account of a substance in terms of the subject and the properties that belong to it. Properties are entities into which we divide a substance by abstraction. The subject is the substantial form that unifies the properties into a whole. The subject does not bond the properties into a whole through a relation, but by reidentifying them according to the principle it stands for. Thus, for example, the abstract entity "red color" is integrated into a substantial whole by becoming identity-dependent on the whole. The form dictates the way in which each property joins the whole, that is, how each property comes to characterize the whole. This means that there is no entity "red color" in the substantial whole; rather, the whole is a red apple, a red wine, and so on. The instantiation of a property involves the fusion of the property with the substance, according to the principle of the form. It is only by abstracting away a property (e.g., "red color") from the substance to which it belongs that the property can be identified and defined. Thus, there is an inverse relation between the *identity* and the *actuality* of a property: The closer we get to the property's *actualized* (instantiated) state, the further we get from the property's *identity*; the closer we get to the property's *identity* (in its definition), the further we get from its *actualized* state.

This inverse relation between the identity and the actuality of a property does not mean that a property makes no contribution to the substance to which it belongs (because the property loses its distinctness in the substantial whole). The case could be compared to the contribution a drop of water makes to a pool of water. When in the pool, there is no distinct entity—no drop; but this does not mean that the incorporation of the drop into the pool of water did not contribute to the constitution of the pool. Similarly, a property's distinctness is lost by its incorporation into a substantial whole, but its incorporation does make a contribution to the constitution of the whole.

The substantial form is the only item whose integration into the whole does not require its reidentification, since all else is reidentified in accordance with the principle of the form. Consequently, the *actualization* of the substantial form, namely, the *composition* of all the properties of the substance into a single whole in accordance with the principle of the form, does not alter *what* the form stands for. My understanding of Aristotle's position is that, whereas the actualization of the form of red *color* results in a red *apple* or red *wine*, the actualization of the form of human being results in a human being. Thus, the substantial form in actuality is the substance itself.

A result that follows from Aristotle's individuation account of substances is that particularity is not a primitive metaphysical notion, but derivative from the unifying function of the form. A *particular* is an *ultimate subject*, where subjecthood consists in the unification—composition—of diverse components into a single whole, and ultimate subjecthood consists in not belonging to another as subject—that is, not being unified into another whole. The subject provides the principle of unification, according to which the distinct entities are reidentified into components of the whole. Substantial wholes of the same kind differ from one another in the components they unify. The components need not be particular, as the particularity of the substance is not borrowed from the particularity of its constituents, but only contribute qualitative difference. Therefore, being a *particular* is being an *ultimate subject* that is *qualitatively different* from other ultimate subjects.

The substantial form that is abstracted from the substances of the same kind is universal. In actuality, the form *is not* a distinct component in the substance, as that would require the form to be bonded to the rest of the components in the substantial whole by a relation, which Aristotle rejects. The concrete substance is not divided into two distinct components, namely, the matter and the form in actuality, or into instantiations of properties (universals or tropes), related to one another by a relation. Rather, the concrete substance is the form in actuality, having assimilated into the whole all the other components by reidentification. What two *similar* substances have in common, for Aristotle, is not a distinct component present in both substances, because being constituted of distinct components would contradict Aristotle's *substantial holism*. Rather, for two substances to be similar is for the same entity to be separable (not physically, but by abstraction) from each of these two substances. Similarity is to be explained in terms of entities that are derived from (by abstraction), rather than contained in, substantial wholes.

Finally, there is *no ontological relation* between the universal substantial form (e.g., human being) and the form in actuality (e.g., Socrates). More generally, for Aristotle, a universal form is not related to its subject by an ontological relation (e.g., by participation, communion, etc.), but it is separable from that subject by abstraction. The *realist* element in Aristotle's account of universals is that the singling out of a form by abstraction is grounded in experience: thoughts about the abstracted universal form derive their *truth conditions* from thoughts about the substance that the form is abstracted from. Thus, the path from the substantial form in actuality (= the concrete substance) to the abstracted form (= the universal) is separation by abstraction, which has no ontological correlate, but is governed by the content of our experience.

The order of exposition of these themes in the book is the following. In

Chapter 1, I examine Aristotle's theory of matter, and more generally his theory of the substratum, by identifying the role that the substratum plays in Aristotle's metaphysical system. I conclude with a positive characterization of the material substratum in radical transformation, determining the nature of matter, and show how the contemporary notion of quantity of matter captures the Aristotelian notion of underlying body (*sōma*). In Appendix 1 I argue that Aristotle's theory of perception does not condemn him, as has been claimed, to an outdated conception of matter. In Appendix 2 I offer an interpretation of *Metaphysics* Z, 3, to show that it does not commit Aristotle to matter as characterless substratum. But I further argue that there is direct evidence in Aristotle's metaphysics that he would be opposed to the notion of an underlying characterless substratum.

In Chapter 2, I survey Aristotle's arguments for positing universals and argue that the operative definition for him is not that of an entity that recurs in different places at the same time, but of an entity that *belongs* to many entities. Chapters 1 and 2 provide the setting for the examination in subsequent chapters of how matter and universals come together to form a single substance in Aristotle's system.

To lead up to this question, I embark in Chapter 3 on the examination of a profound metaphysical problem that surfaced in Plato's metaphysics, which was a guiding force in shaping Aristotle's early ontology, but which was not successfully resolved until Aristotle's mature metaphysical writings. This is the nature-feature problem (already described), which raises the question of the relation between the nature of a subject to the subject itself. The resolution of the nature-feature problem rests on the role that Aristotle gives to the substantial form, namely, its role as the subject. I therefore begin, in Chapter 4, with a detailed analysis of Aristotle's existential arguments for the substantial form. I further compare Aristotle's substantial forms to the closely related structural universals of David Armstrong. I argue that for Aristotle, the substantial form is a nonrelational unifier of the components of a substance. Because there is no relation unifying matter to form, or either of them to the substance, the question arises, In what sense are matter and form present in a substance? I argue that for Aristotle, matter and form are present in a substance in the sense that they can be abstracted away from the substance.

To address the various problems that this position raises, I begin by considering, in Chapter 5, Aristotle's theory of abstraction. In order to comprehend the difficulties that arise with abstract entities and the possible solutions that can be offered, I draw parallels between Aristotle's theory of abstract entities and Kit Fine's theory of arbitrary objects, and I make positive suggestions for the direction Aristotle's theory could take. I further argue that a realist account of matter and form can be offered, even if they are not distinct components in a substance, but only entities that can be abstracted from a substance.

The problem of the particularity of a unified, concrete substance is addressed in Chapter 6, which brings together the themes developed in the preceding chapters. I argue that particularity for Aristotle does not rest on the inclusion of a primitively particular item into the substance. (In Appendix 3, I critically survey the various interpretations of Aristotle that attribute individual forms to him, and in Appendix 4, I offer an interpretation of *Metaphysics* M, 10, arguing that it does not commit Aristotle to individual forms.) Being a particular, for Aristotle, is being an ultimate subject, which is a substantial form in actuality. I present Aristotle's theory of subjecthood and argue that being a subject is being a unifier of the elements that belong to a substance. This is the cornerstone of Aristotle's *substantial holism*: the unification takes place by the reidentification of the elements according to the principle of the substantial form—not by relating the elements into a cluster. The account of particularity I offer in this chapter addresses Kit Fine's paradox on the identity of Aristotelian substances.

In Chapter 7, I use the theory developed to give a reading of *Metaphysics* Z that shows it to be offering a consistent metaphysical theory. I follow the exposition of themes in Z, engaging in close textual examination. Throughout the exposition, I concentrate on the pivotal Aristotelian notion of a self-caused (*kath' hauto*) unity and explain the role it plays in Aristotle's theory of substantial holism. The Conclusion offers a synoptic view of the main themes developed in the book.

# I | Matter

## 1. Physical Continuity in Change

In the introductory chapters of Book I of his *Physics*, Aristotle reviews the accounts of change that had been given by his predecessors, argues against them, and puts forward his own explanation. Change, for Aristotle, involves three principles: two opposites, the form that is lost and its opposite form that is gained, and the substratum. "Something persists, but the contrary does not persist; there is, then, some third thing besides the contraries, viz. the matter" (*Meta.* 1069b7–9). This is so for all change, including accidental alteration and substantial transformation, for example, in the alteration of the color of the skin from pale to tan and in the transformation of blood into embryo. [1] What will concern us in this chapter is not so much the study of Aristotle's theory of change, but his conception of matter as can be derived from his theory of change.

### (A) The Physical Continuity Principle

There are two primary, closely interrelated reasons why Aristotle gives such an analysis of change. We shall call the first the *Physical Continuity Principle*, which requires that there be physical continuity in the processes of

---

1. Charlton (1970) offers a detailed account of Aristotle's position on change in his commentary. A sophisticated discussion of substantial generation and of the *construction model* is offered in Gill 1989, chap. 3.

alteration or generation. If there were spatiotemporal gaps in the physical continuity of the process of the generation of a substance, for example, then the process would be divided into two segments: the destruction into nothing and the generation from nothing. That nothing is created out of nothing is an ancient metaphysical principle that Aristotle adopted in his system. Yet, he had to explain the generation of being from not-being. Aristotle's explanation of this principle parallels Plato's explanation of the attribution of not-being to being. In the *Sophist*, Plato showed that the attribution of not-being to being need not be a monstrosity, if what we understand by not-being is difference in being. Thus, Socrates is *not*, insofar as he is not *large*. Aristotle similarly explained that "that which is not, need not not be altogether: it may not be something definite" (*Ph.* 187a5–6). Transferring this to change, we have that "something comes to be out of what is not, . . . as something which is not" (*Ph.* 191b9–10). Something comes to be, not out of what is nonexistent, but out of what is not such and such. Not-being is the lack of a specific characterization: "A thing can come to be out of the lack, which in itself is something which is not" (*Ph.* 191b15–16); but the lack is in something which *is*. Thus, something comes to be from something else, which lacks some characterization. In this way, although change is from not-being to being, this does not require (or allow) the creation of something from nothing, but only the creation of something from something else lacking a certain form. The processes of alteration and generation contain no spatiotemporal gaps.

(B) The Substratum Principle:
Substantial and Material Substratum

The second principle involved in change, which is closely related to the first, is the *Substratum Principle*. It is a conceptual truth, for Aristotle, that in order to have change, there must be something changing. Thus, "if change proceeds from opposites, . . . there must be something underlying which changes into the contrary state" (*Meta.* 1069b3–6). The challenge that was facing Aristotle was the following. On the one hand, what was changing had to remain physically continuous throughout the change, as a minimal requirement of the Physical Continuity Principle. On the other, it could not be the same *thing* that survived; in generation, the original thing ceases to be and a new thing comes to be. In alteration the same subject survives the loss and gain of opposite forms; for example, Theaetetus grows taller while remaining the same person. But in transformation the loss of form is the loss of the thing in question, as when an egg goes into the making of a cake.

I have argued that Aristotle offered a parallel account of alteration and transformation, which is based on the notion of a substratum predication, where the substratum can be either material or substantial.[2] The main idea in the model is that what must minimally remain the same is not the subject that *possesses* the forms, but the substratum, which *receives* the forms to make up a new whole, the subject. In this way, in transformation, the substratum that remains the same is *material*, and receives a substantial form, to make up the new substance that emerges in the course of the transformation. In alteration, the substratum that remains the same is *substantial* and receives an accidental form to make up an altered substance. But in both cases, the change takes place by a form being received either by a material or by a substantial substratum, where the substratum plus the form make up the compound, that is, the subject:

> I call the man and the not knowing music simple coming to be things, and the knowing music a simple thing which comes to be. When we say that the not knowing music man comes to be a knowing music man, both the coming to be thing and that which comes to be are compound. (*Ph.* 190a1–5)

> Of what we call the simple coming to be things, one remains when it comes to be, and the other does not. The man remains and is a man when he comes to be knowing music, but the not knowing music and the ignorant of music do not remain, either by themselves or as components. (*Ph.* 190a9–13)

> From what has been said, then, it is clear that which comes to be is always composite, and there is one thing which comes to be, and another which comes to be this, and the latter is twofold: either the underlying thing, or the thing which is opposed. By that which is opposed, I mean the ignorant of music, by that which underlies, the man; and shapelessness, formlessness, disarray are opposed, and the bronze, the stone, the gold underlie. (*Ph.* 190b10–17)

Aristotle sees a direct correspondence between, for example, man and gold: they both underlie the change and receive the form to make up the com-

2. Scaltsas 1985b, 218–219 or Scaltsas 1992c, 183–184. On the subject of how the matter receives the substantial form, see also Loux 1991, 109–146, Loux 1979, and Gill 1989, 102–108.

pound, namely, the qualified substance in alteration (e.g., musical man) or the new substance in generation (e.g., the statue). The gold that underlies the generation of the statue is neither a formless lump nor a statue; but, coupled with the opposite forms, the gold makes up the compound of a formless lump of gold at first and later the compound of the statue. Similarly, the man that underlies the alteration is neither nonmusical nor musical; by coupling with the opposite forms he makes up the compound of a nonmusical man at first and later the compound of a musical man.[3] Aristotle retains the distinction between the two types of substrata, the substantial and the material ones, in his later works as well: "we have spoken . . . about the substrate (*hupokeimenon*), of which we have said that it underlies in two senses, either being a 'this'—which is the way in which an animal underlies its attributes—or as the matter underlies the complete reality" (*Meta.* 1038b3–6).[4] What underlies generation is deprived of substantial form, whereas what underlies alteration has a substantial nature, which it retains throughout the alteration.

Aristotle's understanding of change rests on a distinction that can be attained only by abstraction, the distinction between a form and the entity that receives it (e.g. the form of white and a hot piece of iron that receives it).[5] It is essential to realize that any abstraction results in two *abstract* entities: the form that is abstracted, and that which remains, which is the substance minus the abstracted form. In the case of a musical man, if we abstract the form of musicality, the remainder is the man considered without the form of musicality. This does not mean that the remainder is the nonmusical man. A nonmusical man is not an abstraction but a concrete individual. Rather, when a form is abstracted from a subject, the remainder is the subject without that form and without any other form in its place, that is, without the privation of the abstracted form. Thus, in a change in

3. We can also clearly see in *Meta.* 1069b7–14 that Aristotle uses a single model for all change, including both generation and alteration; namely, that of the opposite forms lost and gained and the surviving substratum, which must therefore be material in generation and substantial in transformation.

4. See also *Meta.* 1033a9–10 (the example of man and the privation of health) and 1058b3–6: "Whiteness in man, or blackness, does not make one [i.e., a difference in species], nor is there a difference in species between the white and the black man. . . . For man plays the part of matter."

5. Aristotle distinguishes between a form being separable in account and a concrete substance being separable *simpliciter*, i.e., physically separable, at *Meta.* 1042a29–31; see also *Ph.* 193b33–34.

which a nonmusical man becomes musical, one can determine the component that remains present throughout the change by abstracting away from the changing subject, the man, any forms that are not present in him either at the beginning or at the end of the change. In this case we abstract away the form of nonmusicality and the form of musicality. What remains is the *amusical* man, who is present throughout the process of change: "That which is not opposed remains—the man remains—but the not knowing music or the ignorant of music do not remain, and neither does the compound of the two, the ignorant of music man" (*Ph.* 190a18–21). The amusical man is a *substantial substratum* underlying the change from nonmusical to musical man. Similarly, in the case of generating a statue out of a bronze vase, to determine the item that remains throughout the generation, we need to abstract away the shape of the vase and the shape of the statue. What remains is the bronze that is in the vase in the beginning, and in the statue at the end, of the generation. What remains is not a *lump* of bronze, because being a lump requires having some shape, but it is the bronze stuff without any shape. This is the *material substratum* of the change. The bronze and the amusical man are abstract entities, because they are not physically separate. We describe their nature in detail in Chapter 5.

But there is another sense in which something remains throughout a change. Socrates was nonmusical and is now musical; Socrates survived the change. Now, Socrates is not an abstract entity. He is a physical particular existing separately in the world. Socrates is what changes from being nonmusical to being musical. In fact, Socrates is the only subject of change. That is, the abstract entity that we considered, namely, the substratum "amusical Socrates" that remains the same throughout the change, *does not change*. What changes is the *subject* that possesses the form of nonmusicality to begin with and then loses that form while acquiring the form of musicality. The amusical Socrates neither loses nor acquires any forms, and hence, does not change. The forms of nonmusicality or of musicality *do not belong* to the amusical Socrates, but to Socrates. The amusical Socrates is the substratum that needs to be complemented by an opposite form to make up the subject that undergoes the alteration. It is Socrates that acquires and loses forms, and so, it is Socrates that changes.

In the case of substantial change, there is no subject that survives the change, but only a substratum. Hence, the only entity that survives the change is an abstract one, that is, the one that we individuate by abstracting away the form that is lost and the form that is gained. For example, in the case of the vase that is transformed into a statue, the abstract entity that

survives the transformation is the shapeless bronze, which is the substratum. The bronze is not the subject, because the property of the shape of
the vase or the shape of the statue do not belong to it. Rather, the bronze
combines together with the shape to make up the statue, which is what
Aristotle describes as the composite: "that which comes to be is always
composite" (*Ph.* 190b11). The composite is the subject, and it comprises
the combination of two entities that are individuated by abstraction: the
form (the one that is lost, or the one gained), and the substratum (which
remains the same throughout the change).[6] The statue (= subject) is the
composite of the bronze (= substratum) and the shape (= form).

We can thus understand Aristotle's model of change through the notions
of subject, substratum, and form. The subject is what possesses the form
that is lost or the form that is gained. The substratum does not possess
either form, but it receives either the one or the other form to make up the
subject. Thus, the relation of subject to form is very different from the
relation of substratum to form. It is in this fundamental respect that my
approach to Aristotle's metaphysics differs from Frank Lewis's in his recent
work on the subject.[7] Lewis finds that the same relation obtains between the
subject to its accident and some matter to its form. He says: "The relation of
(metaphysical) predication is defined as . . . : (D3) $x$ is (*metaphysically*)
*predicated of y* (*y* is *subject of x*) if and only if *either x* is an accident of *y* or *x*
supervenes on *y*," where "*x* is an accident of *y*, only if *x* is an accident and *y* is
a (compound material) substance" and "*x* supervenes on *y*, only if *x* is a form
and *y* is matter" (pp. 164–165). The difference between the two metaphysical relations, between an accident belonging to a subject and a form en-
forming a material substratum, will occupy us in depth, especially in
Chapters 4–7.

What is common between accidental and substantial change is that both
can be understood in terms of a remaining substratum (either substantial or
material) that is coupled with a form and later with the opposite form:
"What is most properly matter is the substratum receptive of generation
and corruption; but, in a way, so is that of other changes, since *all substrata
are receptive of contrarieties of one sort or another*" (*GC* 320a2–5, my emphasis).
The difference between accidental and substantial change is that the subject
survives the accidental change but not the substantial one. Socrates is the
subject that is now nonmusical and later musical. But no subject survives

6. "For the knowing music man is composed [σύγκειται] in a way of man and knowing
music" (*Ph.* 190b20–22).
7. F. A. Lewis 1991.

the transformation from vase to statue.[8] Only the (shapeless) bronze remains through it as substratum.[9]

Being separable by abstraction does not mean that the entity is in the mind. Aristotle's ontology of universals is not conceptualist or idealist. On the one hand, he realizes that universals are not separate in the way that substances are separate entities. On the other, he does not want abstract entities to be creations of the mind, independent of what there is in the world. We will see in Chapter 5 that Aristotle's moderate realism with respect to abstract entities combines two factors: a nonrealist and a realist one. The nonrealist factor is that abstract entities are separable only by abstraction. The realist factor is that the isolation of such abstract entities is governed by *truth-conditions* that tie claims about these entities to experience, and hence to what there is in the world.

## (C) The Identity of the Substratum

Is there something more to the sameness of the substratum than physical continuity? Implicitly I have assumed that there is not, and so I would like to come to the examination of this assumption now. The question is, what are the minimal requirements that secure that there is no generation from, and corruption into, nothing in the course of change? Is there need for more than physical continuity? One supposition that would be senseless to attempt to combat is that the world, or a segment of it, is seamlessly destroyed and recreated, for example, that this parcel of matter is destroyed and instantaneously replaced by a qualitatively identical parcel of matter. If that were the case, it might be thought there would, in fact, be destruction

8. Despite the parallel role that the material and the substantial substrata play in change, there is an important difference between them. The material substratum is in a sense *universal*, because it can belong to many substances at different times, but the substantial substratum is not universal, because it cannot belong to more than one substance, even at different times.

9. For further discussion of Aristotle's account of change, see Gill's "construction model" (1989, 94–108, 163–168). For an extensive discussion of form being predicated of matter, see Loux 1991, 109–146. Loux distinguishes between species-predication and form-predication. In species-predication, the subject is the concrete particular, and the predicate expression, which Loux calls a mixed-product expression, designates the infimae species. Thus "George Bush is a man" is an instance of species-predication; the expression "man" here designates a "composite of this formula and this matter taken universally." But "That pack of flesh and bones is a man" is an instance of form-predication, where a parcel of matter is the subject and the predicate is a pure-product expression designating the form. Here the parcel of matter constitutes a particular whose kind is specified by the form (115–120). See also Loux 1979a, 5–11.

into nothing and generation from nothing. But this is not the state of affairs that Aristotle is rejecting in saying that there is no ex nihilo creation (or corruption into nothing). This is not a state of affairs that anyone could sensibly either assert or deny, because it is in principle divorced from experience, and no root to the world could distinguish between its obtaining and not. Furthermore, it would offer no help to posit an underlying continuant that survives in cases of genuine change. The reason is that skeptical doubt applies to it, too. One cannot distinguish experientially between the continuant surviving, on the one hand, and the continuant not surviving but being instantaneously replaced by a qualitatively identical one, on the other. Hence, positing a surviving continuant does not make the skeptical doubt on the continuity of change any more valid.

Could a guarantee against the skeptical doubt be found at level of the properties? Does the parcel of matter remain the same because its properties remain the same? The same skeptical doubt would apply again. How can we ascertain that the properties are not seamlessly replaced by others that are qualitatively identical with them? Again, the doubt is divorced from experientially distinguishable circumstances, and hence it would offer no security toward the continuity of change to posit a continuant whose identity is tied to the sameness of its surviving properties. (Furthermore, this could not have been an Aristotelian solution in any case, because for Aristotle the identity of a property is determined by the subject it belongs to, rather than vice versa.)

Neither the positing of a continuant nor the positing of surviving properties can strengthen the case of physical continuity against the skeptical doubt of generation ex nihilo. Hence, physical continuity is all the security that can be provided against creation ex nihilo, and the sameness of the material substratum will, therefore, rest on physical continuity during the transformation. What is required is that the transformation process constitute a seamless spatiotemporal material worm. Thus, in the transformation of a statue into a vase, that the material substratum of the statue is the same as the material substratum of that vase means that the process is physically continuous. The only requirement for the *numerical oneness* of the material substratum throughout the transformation process is that it remain material and physically continuous.[10] In Section 5, I examine the requirements for materiality.[11]

10. The numerical sameness of matter throughout transformation is a general requirement of Aristotle's theory of matter, deriving from the Physical Continuity Principle. I am therefore in disagreement with S. Cohen's remark that Aristotle "is not led to common matter because he holds a general doctrine that takes him there" (Cohen 1984, 173).

11. Strictly, sameness would require that there be no material input or output in the

## 2. Radical Transformation

To understand the nature of a substratum let's concentrate on transformation and consider the case of radical transformation. In radical transformation neither the initial thing nor anything of the initial *kind* of matter remain at the end, but it has all transformed into a different kind of thing and matter. For Aristotle, the most radical transformations are those where nothing perceptible remains the same: "When, however, the whole changes without anything perceptible remaining as the same substratum, but the way a seed changes entirely into blood, water into air, or air entirely into water, then, when we have this sort of thing, it is a case of generation" (*GC* 319b14–17). Aristotle allows here that no perceptible substratum remains throughout the transformation. Because the Substratum Principle requires that something remain throughout the transformation, and because, as we see in Appendix 2, Aristotle does not allow for a characterless substratum, the question we are facing is: What is the nature of the imperceptible substratum that remains the same in radical transformations?

Aristotle tells us that in the transformation of the elements, for example, of air into water, air does not survive the transformation. The reason is that the process would then be an alteration rather than a transformation, because the initial substance (be it a low-grade nonorganic one), namely, air, would survive, and "being water" would be simply an affection of air (*GC* 332a8–9). So, if air remained, it could remain only as material substratum. Could, then, air just change status and go from being a substantial substratum to being a material substratum? What happens to wood in a generation when a statue is carved out of it? Is that what happens to air when it is transformed into water?

The change from wood to statue is a transformation. Aristotle says: "as there also a thing is not said to be that from which it comes, here the statue is not said to be wood but is said by a verbal change to be not wood but wooden, not bronze but of bronze, not stone but of stone, and the house is said to be not bricks but of bricks" (*Meta.* 1033a16–19). Here, what comes about from the transformation is not wood, but is wooden. Consequently, when he says that wood (*xulon*) is the matter of the casket, and clarifies that the casket is not wood but wooden (*xulinon, Meta.* 1049a22–24), one might

course of the transformation process; i.e., that the transformation be a closed system. In cases where material exchanges take place in the course of the transformation, a slippery slope would be generated with respect to whether the material substratum remains the same, depending on the amounts of matter replaced.

be tempted to conclude that, according to Aristotle, a transformation may turn the initial substance into matter (air into something made of air). That would then certainly allow for water to be air-y, because it is air that is transformed into water.

But this is not what Aristotle is describing. Rather, what happens in this case is that something that is *wooden*, namely, a log, is transformed into something else that is *wooden*, namely, a casket. The initial substantial form (i.e., the low-grade substantial form "log") is destroyed when the statue is created: the statue is not the log of wood it is made from. The log of wood does not survive the transformation, but is destroyed in the process of the creation of the statue. The underlying substratum—the wood in the log— loses the form of the log and receives the form of the casket. [12] The change of form from log to casket constitutes a substantial change because of the important differences between log and casket with respect to shape and function. What remains the same throughout the transformation is a mate- rial substratum, *not* the initial substance (which is the log). So, "wood being transformed into something wooden" does not signal the *demotion* (and survival) of substance to matter (e.g., "log" to something "log-en"), but the *destruction* of substance. The wooden log is destroyed and the wooden casket is generated. Hence, it does not licence the *transformation* of air into some- thing that is air-y, though it does licence the transformation of something air-y (e.g., a cloud) into something air-y (e.g., bubbles in the water).

Let us return, then, to the case of radical transformation: "When . . . the whole changes without anything perceptible remaining as the same sub- stratum, but the way a seed changes entirely into blood, water into air, or air entirely into water, then, when we have this sort of thing, it is a case of generation" (*GC* 319b14–17). Because air does not survive the transforma- tion into water, *it* cannot be the substratum. But water is not even air-y, in the sense in which the casket is wooden. [13] If, then, everything perceptible changes in such transformations, what is it that survives as substratum? The challenging extrapolation of the claim that nothing perceptible survives the change is that no *kind* of matter survives the change. The key issue is not whether there is something perceptible that survives the change, but some- thing stronger, whether the same *kind* of matter remains throughout the

12. I argue that the same thing happens in the case of a brick that is used to build a house. The brick does not survive its integration into the house, but its matter does (Section 4 of Chapter 4).

13. For then it would have to be simultaneously dry and wet, which cannot be (*GC* 332a12–17, using air transforming into fire as an example).

change, whether perceptible or not. If neither the initial object nor the kind of stuff it is made of, survive the transformation, does anything survive it at all?

In the cases where we do not recognize anything remaining the same in the course of a transformation, need we assume that there is an underlying matter that nevertheless survives? Furthermore, does this matter remain the same kind from the beginning to the end of the transformation (e.g., like the substratum remains the same kind in the log-casket transformation, remains wooden)? The answer is to be determined on a priori rather than on empirical grounds. It has to do with the Aristotelian conception of *substratum* and its role in transformation. I will show that Aristotle's account does not require matter to remain the same in kind in radical transformations and will offer the criteria for the numerical sameness of the surviving matter.

## 3. Against Hot, Cold, Wet, and Dry Stuff

The transformation of the elements (fire, air, water, earth) into each other is usually treated separately from transformations at the biological level, such as the transformation of seed into blood, to cite Aristotle's usual example, or blood into flesh. The reason why I am examining them together in the present context, despite the obvious difference of the application of teleological explanations in the case of the biological transformations, is that in neither case is there a recognizable kind of matter that remains the same throughout the transformation. Does Aristotle's account of transformations require an unobservable kind (or kinds) of matter to underlie such radical transformations, or not? I argue that *Aristotle's account does not require matter of any specific kind to underlie radical transformations.* But before doing so, I would like to argue against Montgomery Furth's position that there are, in fact, specific kinds of matter that underlie radical Aristotelian transformations.

I understand the key idea in Furth's solution to be that at the most elemental level, we cannot make a distinction between matter and form. At that level, *matter and form are identical,* not being even *conceptually* distinguishable from one another. This position is opposed to the traditional doctrine of prime matter in the sense of a characterless substratum. If there were such an entity as a bare particular at the (metaphysical) core of a substance, then it would always be in principle possible to make the distinction between matter and form: the bare particular would be the matter that received the forms. But Furth does not think that Aristotle commits himself to a characterless substratum.[14] If one does not attribute to Aristotle the characterless substratum doctrine (as neither Furth nor I do), one is not forced to accept a distinction between matter and form at the most elemental level. Furth rejects the distinction; I will argue that Aristotle did not, by showing that his conception of matter requires the material substratum to survive the most radical transformations, such as organic or elemental transformations.

The elements, fire, air, water, and earth, are characterized, according to Aristotle, by the elemental oppositions: hot, cold, wet, and dry: "The elements all have contrariety with each other on account of their differentiae (*diaphoras*) being contraries. . . . (the one [fire] is dry and hot, the other [water] wet and cold)" (*GC* 331a14–18). The transformation from one of the elements to another takes place by loss and gain of one of the opposites. Thus, "for example, from fire there will be air if one of its properties changes, the former having been hot and dry whilst the latter is hot and wet, so that if the dryness is conquered by wetness, there will be air" (*GC* 331a26–29).

Now, according to Furth, the analysis of the four elements in terms of the four oppositions reaches "what may be called the very deepest-lying 'ultrasimples' of the world . . . the 'ultrasimples,' as such, represent Aristotle's view of that which is the most ultimate matter of things, or 'prime matter' as is sometimes called" (p. 77). What happens in transformations between the elements, for example, fire to earth, with this analysis is the following: "when some Fire changes to some Air, the underlying structure of the change is that in a 'linkage' joining H and D (i.e. in the Fire), the D is replaced by its opposite, the M, while the H remains as the persisting subject (thus the result, H + M, is the Air)" (p. 223). (Here, "H" stands for hot, "D", for dry, "M" for moist.) I argue that this is not Aristotle's position. The significance of understanding Aristotle's analysis of these transformations is derived from the fact that they are the most elemental transformations. Hence, Aristotle's conception of *subject* and of *matter* will inevitably heavily depend on them, which is the reason why they command special attention.

There are several reasons why Furth's analysis of elemental transformations cannot be accepted. First, Aristotle has argued that substance, in the sense of ultimate constituents, does not have opposites. He says: "We may

14. Furth 1988, 188, 226.

also run into the following difficulty if we do not posit some additional nature to underlie the opposites. We never see opposites serving as the reality (*ousia*) of anything, and yet a principle ought not to be something said of some underlying thing. If it is, the principle will itself have a principle, for that which underlies (*hupokeimenon*) is a principle (*archē*), and is thought to be prior to that which is said of it (*katēgoroumenou*)" (*Ph.* 189a27–32). Aristotle says here that an opposite is not *what* something is, that is, its reality and substance. Rather, opposites are *said of* substances. Now, let us assume that an opposite is the principle of which all else is predicated in a thing. Since an opposite is itself said of some underlying reality, it follows that opposites would be ultimate principles (*archai*) that have further ultimate principles; realities whose nature (or reality) is determined by further realities; ultimate substrata that have further substrata underlying them. Hence, opposites cannot be the underlying principles of which all else is predicated in things. Yet, as we saw, according to Furth, "the H remains as the persisting subject" in the course of the elemental transformation from fire to earth. This directly contradicts Aristotle's conclusion that the opposites cannot be the ultimate subject in things. Something else must be the subject which the opposite characterizes.

A further reason why opposites cannot be the subject is that, *qua* subject, they would be substance. But according to Aristotle, substance has no opposite, as nothing is the opposite of a particular thing (*Cat.* 3b24–27). Hence an opposite cannot be substance and, therefore, subject. [15]

Furth must be aware of the direct conflict between his proposal and Aristotle's position, for which reason he presents the subjecthood of the opposites in the elements as a different kind of subjecthood, peculiar to them alone. He says: "But the 'subjecthood' of this sort of *hupokeimenon* is like none of the 'subjects' we have seen hitherto. . . . Instead we have a new and different deep configuration—a subject (*hupokeimenon*), indeed, but a subject in a third way, known as *a 'contrariety' in a new 'linkage,' or with a new 'mate'*" (pp. 224–225). Furth distinguishes this "third type of subject" (p. 225) from the subject in alterations and the subject in transformations

15. We need to distinguish here between being substance qua ultimate substratum and being substance qua form. Aristotle does not allow any subject/substratum in a thing to have opposites, because there are no opposites of numerically single entities. But he does speak of substantial form as being an opposite or a contradictory (*Ph.* 224b28–29, 225a35–b1), because substantial forms, too, have privations (*Ph.* 201a4–5, *GC* 319a14–16, *Meta.* 1065b10–11, 1033a13–15), and privation can be thought of as an opposite (*Ph.* 225b3–4, 229b26, *GC* 332a23–24, *Meta.* 1046b14–15). See also Chap. 2, n. 6. For further discussion of this issue, see Scaltsas 1985b, 235 n. 13, or Scaltsas 1992c, 203 n. 13.

(other than elemental ones). But the Aristotelian arguments he delineated are general, being based on the nature of *opposites* (which are not the realities of anything), and the nature of *subject* (which has no opposite), unrestrictedly. That Furth intends his conception of a subject in the transformations of the elements to be different from the subject in alterations or other transformations is of no assistance toward showing how his position can avoid violating the unqualified Aristotelian conclusions just reviewed.

Furth says that "the 'ultrasimples' [hot, cold, moist, and dry], as such, represent Aristotle's view of that which is the most ultimate matter of things" (p. 77). What this means is that at that level, no division is possible between the form of "being hot," for example, and hot stuff. The division is not possible either physically or conceptually, because there is nothing in the ontology within the hot that underlies heat as subject. Abstraction cannot help us here, because nothing will be left if we abstract away heat from the hot. This means that the hot is *indistinguishably matter and form* at the same time. It is matter that has not become hot but is *primitively* hot and similarly with the cold stuff, the moist stuff, and the dry stuff in the world. The picture that emerges is that the world, according to Aristotle, is composed not of atoms, but of four different kinds of stuff. Aristotle, according to Furth's picture, is not an atomist, but something very close to one, having blobs of stuff as the ultimate constituents rather than discrete atoms. If so, Furth would have to take a stand on the questions that Aristotle raises against the atomists regarding the discreteness of the ultimate constituents. [16]

But Furth, with his third type of subject, also faces philosophical difficulties that are independent of the interpretation of Aristotle. Consider the change from fire to air, in the course of which, according to Furth, the hot is the subject that loses the dry and gains the moist. Now, what is the subject in the air that is created from that transformation? Is the hot the subject for the moist, or the moist the subject for the hot? At the end of the air's generation, the hot is the subject of the moist. At the beginning of the air's destruction, the roles have been reversed, and the moist is the subject of the hot. What then is the subject in the course of the existence of this air, and why? No answer is forthcoming from Furth's theory that would not be arbitrary and that could justify making either of the two elements in the air the subject of the other.

Finally, Furth's account reduces a *metaphysical* relation to a *physical* one.

16. See *Cael.* III.4 and *Ph.* VI. 1–2.

Although there is no more than copresence, or juxtaposition of stuff (e.g., of cold stuff and moist stuff), in water, Furth claims that this relation is a relation of a subject and of what belongs to the subject. Let us consider the subject-form relation in its most general scope, for example, in Socrates (= subject) being wise, or in the wood (= substratum) receiving the form of a statue. What is common there between the subject-form relation and the relation of the cold stuff and moist stuff that are copresent in water? The latter is a physical relation and the former a metaphysical one. In what sense can the former relations extend to the latter? Of what relation is the hot stuff–cold stuff relation a third type, which Furth takes it to be? A physical relation cannot be a species of the subject-form relation. I can find no answer to these questions in Furth's account of ultrasimple materials, nor can I see how some could be provided.

### 4. Quantity of Matter: *Sōma*

One of the considerations that has given rise to the Prime Matter Doctrine [17] is that there are some transformations in which there is no *kind* of matter that is preserved throughout the transformation. We have no difficulty determining what the matter is in the transformation of a bronze statue into a bronze vase, or even in the corruption of an organism when it dies (where, although not flesh, the matter in the corpse still has many of the properties that flesh has). But what of the transformation of blood into flesh or of water into earth? There is no kind of matter that we can detect remaining throughout the transformation. In a sense, what Furth attempted to do is to say that there is always a *kind* of matter that survives in elemental transformations. For example, in the transformation of water into earth, the cold stuff in the water survives as a material substratum. But we saw why Furth's ultrasimple material stuff would not provide us with an acceptable account of what occurs in elemental transformations. I argue in what follows that Aristotle's account does not require a *kind* of matter to survive the transformations.

As we saw, Aristotle's concern in forging a conception of a substratum, either a substantial one or a material one, is to reflect the continuity in the process of alteration or generation of a substance, showing why neither process of change involves creation from nothing. The most challenging

17. I.e., the positing of an underlying characterless substratum.

case is that of the radical transformations where no kind of matter remains the same. Let us then consider what physical continuity requires in the cases of such radical transformations. Even in the most radical transformations, one's intuition of a "closed system," that is, of no matter going in or coming out of the transformation system, is such that we believe that it is the same matter that has survived the transformation. In other words, the matter out of which the new entity is composed is the matter out of which the initial entity was made up. It is important to realize that it is not atomism that gives rise to this intuition, but rather, atomism is one way of paying justice to it. That is, the ultimate material *components* of which any entity is constituted survive the most radical transformations. Aristotle is not an atomist, but atomism is not the only means by which we can pay justice to this intuition of conservation of matter even in the most radical transformations.

When a quantity of blood transforms into flesh, or a quantity of air into water, or a quantity of organic matter into oil, in every case the matter that constitutes the new entity came exclusively from the matter constituting the initial entity. The *kind* of matter changed, but the *quantity* of matter remained the same. The transformation is a closed system, where what we start with is all that goes into the creation of what we end up with, with respect to the quantity of matter involved. No quantity of matter is added to it from without, or subtracted from it, and because the process is continuous (there being no creation from, or extinction into, nothing), the quantity of matter that was there at the end comes from the quantity of matter that was there in the beginning.

Yet, this quantity of matter does not remain the same kind of matter. Throughout the transformation it is in flux with respect to the kind of matter it is, whether because of the amounts of heat, wetness, and coldness it has at each stage, or because of the various ratios of the different ingredients involved in the transformation from blood to flesh at each stage, and so on. But *sameness of kind* is *not* required for physical continuity. So long as the quantity of matter continues in existence, the indeterminacy of the kind of matter it is over the period of transformation in no way threatens its remaining the same *quantity* of matter.

I borrow the term "quantity" of matter from Helen Cartwright's works.[18] Here "quantity" is not being used to indicate measurement of weight or amount. It is not that the quantity of matter remains the same if its weight or amount of mass remain the same, because we can replace all the matter

18. Cartwright 1970, 1972, 1975.

while keeping the weight and amount of mass constant. It is when we do not add, or subtract, any matter in a parcel of matter (as we exert it to radical transformations) that we can say that the quantity of matter has remained the same. Aristotle does not have such a rich terminological repertoire for referring to a quantity of matter. But we shall see that he occasionally uses the term *sōma*, meaning body, as a neutral term to refer to a quantity of matter of unspecified material kind. This, though, is not the only use he makes of this term.

Cartwright uses the notion of a quantity of matter to refer to such entities as the quantity of bronze in a bronze statue or the quantity of wood in a log. This is just the Aristotelian notion of a material substratum, which survives in a transformation (e.g. the transformation from a bronze vase to a bronze statue, or from log to planks). But I will show that we can use the notion of a quantity of matter to understand Aristotle's prime matter, namely, the matter that survives in the most radical transformations.

Aristotle says in the *Metaphysics* that "the old thinkers ranked particular things as substances, such as fire and earth, but not what is common to both, body" (1069a28–30).[19] In *Generation and Corruption* Aristotle holds that "there is no *kind* of body common to everything" (*sōma koinon*, *GC* 320b23, my emphasis) and argues in *GC* II.5, as we have already seen, that there is no common *kind* of matter between all natural bodies (*phusikōn sōmatōn*), including the elements. He also argues in *De Caelo* that it is "impossible that the elements should be generated from some *kind* of body" (*sōmatos tinos*, 305a22–23, my emphasis). So the common body (*koinon sōma*) between fire and earth, for instance, is not a common *kind* of matter, but a common quantity of matter. This common quantity of matter is one kind of matter when it is fire, other kinds in the course of the transformation into earth, and a different one again when it is earth. But it is the same quantity of matter throughout.

We can find this conception of body as quantity of matter in Aristotle's statement about the totality of matter in the universe: "if the totality of body (*sōma*), which is a continuum, is now in this order or disposition and now in that, and if the combination of the whole is a world or heaven, then it will not be the world that comes into being and is destroyed, but only its dispositions" (*Cael.* 280a19–23). Clearly, the totality of matter is not any one kind of matter, but the kind varies with the dispositions. So, the *totality of body* is a *quantity of matter,* namely, the quantity of matter in the universe, and remains the same, though in constant flux with respect to the properties

_____

19. . . . οἶον πῦρ καὶ γῆν, ἀλλ᾽ οὐ τὸ κοινόν σῶμα.

and dispositions that characterize it. The same can be said of a quantity of matter that survives, such as the transformation of egg yoke to chick in the egg. Its properties and dispositions change, and certainly the kind of matter it is changes too, but not the quantity of matter it is.

We will see in the following section that there is further evidence of the presence of the conception of the quantity of matter in Aristotle.

## 5. The Essence of Matter

If there is no kind of matter that survives radical transformations, how can one claim that it is matter that is surviving at all? The answer to this question is that, although the particular physical properties do not remain the same, there are *generic physical properties* that do. In fact we can make this claim stronger: although the particular physical properties cannot remain the same in radical transformations, generic ones must remain the same. I consider the two modal claims separately.

If the particular properties remain the same in radical transformations, the *kind* of matter remains the same, in which case we have seen Aristotle argue that the whole process is an alteration rather than a transformation. The idea here is that if, for example, some quantity of matter remains cold and wet throughout the change, it will remain water, and therefore the process will be an alteration of water rather than its transformation. Hence, the continuity in radical transformations cannot be preserved by the preservation of the particular physical properties of that quantity of matter, as then it will not be transformation but alteration.

That the generic physical properties must remain the same in the quantity of matter that survives radical transformations is derivable directly from the following arguments, which I quote at length. In the first paragraph, we find as clear a description of the notion of a *quantity of matter* as one can give, and the second paragraph provides reasons why the quantity of matter must retain its generic properties:

> The same matter also serves for both a large and a small body. This is evident; for when air is produced from water, *the same matter* has become something different, not by acquiring an addition to it, but has become actually what it was potentially; and, again, water is produced from air in the same way, the change being sometimes from smallness to greatness, and sometimes from greatness to smallness. Similarly, therefore, if air which is large in extent comes to have a smaller bulk, or becomes greater from being smaller, it is the matter which is potentially both that comes to be each of the two.

> For *the same matter* becomes hot from being cold, and cold from being hot,
> because it was potentially both, so too from hot it can become more hot,
> though nothing in the matter has become hot that was not hot when the
> thing was less hot; just as, if the arc or curve of a greater circle becomes that of
> a smaller, whether it remains the same or becomes a different curve, convex-
> ity has not come to exist in anything that was not convex but straight (*for
> differences of degree do not depend on an intermission of the quality*); nor can we get
> any portion of a flame, in which both heat and whiteness are not present. So
> too, then, is the earlier heat related to the later. So that the greatness and
> smallness, also, of the sensible bulk are extended, not by the matter's acquir-
> ing anything new, but because the matter is potentially matter for both
> states; so that the same thing is dense and rare, and the two qualities have *one
> matter*. (*Ph.* 217a26–b11, my emphasis)

When something becomes hotter than it was, nothing has come to acquire
heat—only more heat; when something is curved, and the degree of curva-
ture changes, nothing has acquired convexity; similarly, when something
becomes larger or smaller, not by acquiring new matter or by losing some
matter, nothing acquires size. Generally, the underlying quantity of matter
changes with respect to having a particular size, or convexity, or heat.
Hence, it retains the generic properties of having size, convexity, or heat,
and is in flux with respect to the particular properties, namely, the particular
sizes, curvatures, or heat. The transformations we are describing are changes
from opposites to opposites. They involve changes in degree, which, Aristotle tells us, do not depend on an intermission of the quality. Hence, they
do not involve the acquisition of a generic property, but only a change in the
particular one. Therefore, the matter remains the same with respect to the
generic properties; but it is inconstant with respect to the particular ones, in
the course of the transformation, for which reason it does not remain the
same *kind* of matter, though it remains the same *matter*.

A very important consequence of this Aristotelian position is that *physical
matter* has an *essential nature*. It is an essential nature that is determined only
in terms of *generic physical properties*, specifically, of its having elementary
oppositions to some degree or other. So, if hot-cold is an elementary opposition, then all matter has some degree of it; let us call this generic property
the property of being *thermal*. If wet-dry is an elementary opposition, then
all matter has some degree of it; let us call this generic property the property
of being *hydral*. What Aristotle argued is that changes in degree between
opposites do not involve changes in the generic properties, in the properties

of being thermal and hydral. Because elemental changes are changes between opposites, specifically the four opposites just mentioned, in its most elemental transformations in nature, matter at no point loses its property of being thermal or hydral. Because these are the *most elemental* transformations, matter will always have these properties, and hence, matter is essentially thermal and hydral.

Physical matter will also essentially occupy a place. Aristotle has argued that there can be no transformation in which matter that occupies place transforms into matter which does not occupy space: "if . . . [a body] is in a place and somewhere, it will be one of the elements; and if it is not in a place, nothing can come from it, since that which comes into being and that out of which it comes must needs be together. The elements therefore cannot be generated from something incorporeal nor from a body which is not an element, and the only remaining possibility is that they are generated from one another" (*Cael.* 305a28–32). Because corporeal matter cannot be generated from something incorporeal (which Aristotle here takes to be mathematical entities, which are not in place, 305a26), being in place will be an essential feature of matter. Finally, "every perceptible body possesses the power of acting or of being acted upon, or both of these" (*Cael.* 275b5–6). Thus perceptible matter is essentially empowered with the capacity to produce movement, or to suffer movement, or both. Because the four elements are perceptible, the power to act on, or be acted on, or both, are essential powers of all matter.

There are, therefore, at least the following *essential properties* of physical matter, according to Aristotle: being thermal, being hydral, being spatial, and being a causal agent and/or patient, all of which are *generic properties of matter.*[20]

A serious challenge to the usefulness of Aristotle's theory of matter for twentieth-century metaphysics has recently been forged by Myles Burnyeat, based on his interpretation of Aristotle's theory of perception. In Appendix 1 I offer an analysis of Aristotle's theory of perception and make explicit its consequences for his theory of matter. We now turn to Aristotle's theory of universals.

20. I am therefore in disagreement with Frank Lewis's claim that Aristotle is committed to prime matter, where prime matter is characterless. According to Lewis, "There is prime matter, which, as I have already suggested, is altogether unformed" (1991, 167); "Prime matter appropriately begins the sequence, since it cannot itself be analysed as a compound of form and matter: it is matter pure and simple (p. 168); "we know that prime matter has no matter at all" (p. 169).

## 2 | Universals

### 1. The Rejection of the Platonic Forms

Much of what occupies the core of Aristotle's metaphysical system is a reaction to the problems faced by Plato's Theory of Forms and an attempt to find a way to retain universals without being led to absurdities. For Aristotle, "that is called universal whose nature is to belong to a number of things" (*Meta.* 1038b11–12). A universal recurs in different subjects; it cannot exist separately from the things it belongs to (1040b26–27) but is common to all of them. Aristotle objected to the Theory of Forms because it took universals to be substances: "But those who say the Forms exist, in one respect are right, in saying the Forms exist apart, if they are substances; but in another respect they are not right, because they say the one *in* many is a Form" (1040b27–30); "that which is one cannot be in many things at the same time, but that which is common is present in many things at the same time; so that clearly no universal exists apart from the individuals" (1040b25–27).[1]

Aristotle rejected the existential arguments for the Platonic Forms. But when we look at the arguments that he rejected, we realize that they are objectionable only as existential arguments *for the Forms*, not as existential arguments for universals:

> To each set of substances there answers a Form which has the same name and exists apart from the substances, and so also in the case of all other groups in

1. I agree with Frede and Patzig (1988, 51) that there are no grounds for making a distinction between Aristotle's use of καθόλου and κοινὸν, as Aristotle's free interchange between the terms in the passage referred to shows, or between his use of καθόλου and καθόλου λεγόμενον.

which there is one character common to many things. . . . Of the ways in which we prove that the Forms exist, none is convincing; for from some no inference necessarily follows, and from some it follows that there are Forms of things of which we think there are no Forms. For according to the arguments from the existence of the sciences there will be Forms of all things of which there are sciences, and according to the argument that there is one attribute common to many things there will be Forms even of negations, and according to the argument that there is an object of thought even when the thing has perished, there will be Forms of perishable things; for we can have an image of these. Further, of the more accurate arguments, some lead to Ideas of relations, of which we say there is no independent class, and other involve the difficulty of the "third man." (*Meta.* 990b6–17)

Not all of these arguments will be rejected by Aristotle as existential arguments for universals, but only as proof for the existence of the Forms. Some of these arguments will reappear modified within his own metaphysical system.

But there is a further Platonic argument for the Forms that I believe has been the most influential in Aristotle's thought and that gives shape to the Aristotelian ontology, *the argument from causation*: "In the *Phaedo* the case is stated in this way—that the Forms are causes both of being and of becoming" (*Meta.* 991b3–4). It is true that Aristotle objects to this Platonic argument by showing that the Forms are not sufficient conditions for change because they do not supply the ultimate agents that initiate the changes (991b5). Furthermore, there are not as many Forms as there are kinds of things made, and so the Platonic ontology of Forms would not offer an explanation of the causes that bring about the generation of, for example, a house or a ring (991b6–7). But these objections do not require the rejection of the argument from causation; on the contrary, this argument plays a very significant role in Aristotle's account of universals.

## 2. Existential Arguments for Aristotelian Forms

### (A) The Argument from Being-Becoming

All pre-Socratic philosophers agreed, according to Aristotle, that "opposites are principles" (*Ph.* 188a19).[2] Thus pre-Socratic cosmologists gave

2. Julius Moravcsik has pointed out that the *archē* of a thing was thought of by the early cosmologists as a *constituent* of the thing, but it gradually came to mean a *principle* of the thing (in discussion).

accounts of the things in the world by composing them out of opposites as principles; for instance, Parmenides out of hot and cold, Democritus out of dense and rare (*Ph.* 188a20–22).[3] Aristotle reached the conclusion that opposites are principles of change on the basis of arguments concerning alteration and generation, which he saw as having terminal points that define the change that takes place: "Nothing whatever is by nature such as to do or undergo any chance thing through the agency of any chance thing, nor does anything come to be out of just anything" (188a32–34); rather, everything comes to be and everything passes away into its opposite (188b21–23).[4]

Opposites do not change into one another,[5] and they are not the sole constituents of things in the world. Rather, as we saw, opposites belong to an additional nature that underlies the opposites (189a28–29) and is not itself an opposite. Thus in alteration, something is non-$f$ and comes to be $f$, and in generation something comes to be a $g$ from something which is a non-$g$. For every such pair of opposites, the one is the state of *privation* of the other opposite, where the privation of a form is itself a form.[6] Coming to be out of what is not is coming to be $f$ or $g$ out of that which is characterized by the privation of $f$ or $g$; thus the musical comes from the nonmusical, a house from a pile of bricks, a human being from menstrual fluids.

In accidental and substantial change, therefore, a positive form is lost or gained and a privative form is gained or lost. An ontology of such forms will be an ontology that can provide an account of all change. It will explain what something becomes accidentally, and what that which is generated is. The analysis of *becoming* requires an ontology of *being*, that is, the ontology of the being of the form and the being of the subject that receives it: "the being of pale will be different from the being of that which has received it" (186a28–29). We understand *what* a thing becomes in terms of the *being* of the form that the subject receives. Now, "what a thing is is in every case universal and affirmative" (*An. Post.* 90b4). Therefore the forms that determine what a thing is must be such as to belong to many and be predicable of many; they must be universal.

3. Although, as David Furley points out (1987), "the Atomists banished the traditional 'opposites' from the *elements* altogether. Hot, cold, dry, wet, and other perceptible qualities are relegated to a lower rung on the ontological ladder" (p. 117, my emphasis).

4. I have offered a detailed account of Aristotle's theory of accidental and substantial change in Scaltsas 1985b, pp. 218–226; repr. Scaltsas 1992c, 183–193.

5. *GA* 329b1–2, *Meta.* 1069b6–7.

6. *Ph.* 193b19–20, *Meta.* 1032b1–4 with 1046b8–9, 1058b26–28, 1061a18–20. Aristotle sometimes refers to the form and the privation as a category containing two columns: *GC* 319a14–16, *Ph.* 201b25–26, 201a3–8, *Meta.* 1065b10–13.

### (B) The One over Many

This is a general family of arguments that, as we saw, originates from the Platonic arguments for the existence of Forms.[7] The most fundamental and general criterion for positing universals, which is Plato's inheritance, is the *one over many*: there is a universal for every common feature shared by different substances, such as being musical, white, or human.[8] The family of arguments that are modifications of the one over many in Aristotle's metaphysics consists of the argument from the *objects of thought*, the argument from the *objects of knowledge*, and the argument from the *objects of science*.

A description of the process of abstraction that leads to the recognition of universals is given by Aristotle at the end of the *Posterior Analytics*.[9] Starting from perception, memories of perceived objects are formed, and from many memories the concept of a universal is formed in the mind: "So from perception there comes memory . . . and from memory (when it occurs often in connection with the same thing), *experience*; for memories that are many in number form a single experience. And from *experience*, or from the whole *universal* that has come to rest in the soul (*the one apart from the many*, whatever is one and the same in all those things), <there comes> a principle of skill and of understanding" (*An. Post.* 100a3–8, my emphasis). Although this gives us in outline the mechanism for the conceptualization of universals,[10] it does not address an issue that will play an important role in our investigation in the present work. To describe what this question is, let us consider the example of the universal *white*. Aristotle states that what is required for its conceptualization are multiple perceptions (e.g., of white objects) that result in multiple memories of these objects, from which the conception of the universal *white* follows. The many memories are required in order to make it possible to focus on that feature that is in all those things. Now, regardless of how different the various white objects are, one thing remains invariant, that is, they are all "white objects." We should therefore expect that the abstraction would result in the universal *white object*, rather than the universal *white*. Yet we abstract "whiteness," not "white object."[11] The move from the universal white object to the universal

7. See *Meta.* 990b8–17.

8. Aristotle cites this in relation to the Forms, at *Meta.* 991a2, 1040b29, and 1079a9, among other places.

9. See Cleary (1985) for a discussion of the shortcomings of Aristotle's theory of abstraction as an epistemological, rather than logical, theory (especially pp. 36–45).

10. Detailed analyses of the passage and its context are given in Barnes 1975, 252–256 and Modrak 1987, 161–171. See also Wedin 1988, 146.

11. This problem should not be confused with the question of whether the ultimate

white color is one that cannot be explained by the elimination of differences between the various white objects that we perceive, as all of them are white objects—or, at least, white surfaces. Because it is only white objects that we can perceive, why does not abstraction stop at the conception of the universal white object? What kind of operation is the one that leads us to the conception of white color from white object? This question will occupy us at length in the latter part of this book (Sections 3 of Chapter 5 and 6 of Chapter 6).

### (C)  The Arguments from Thought, Knowledge, and the Sciences

The argument from the objects of thought comes in the context of Aristotle's discussion of the problems whose resolution requires positing entities over and above the many particulars. He says: "If there is nothing apart from individuals, there will be no object of thought, but all things will be objects of sense" (999b1–2). In this passage, Aristotle does not explicitly mention that the object of thought must be a universal. He says that it must be apart from the individuals, which allows that it could be a Platonic Form, which is itself a particular substance, although it is supposed to function as a universal. But the combination of Aristotle's rejection of Platonic Forms and the clear connection between the present passage and the passage from the *Posterior Analytics* that we quoted at length (in which Aristotle states that, starting from perception, the inductive process leads to the understanding of the universal, the one that is over and above the many, *An. Post.* 100a3–8), leaves no doubt that Aristotle must be thinking of a universal in the present passage.

The introduction of universals to account for understanding is of course intimately connected with the introduction of universals to account for knowledge. In fact, Aristotle continues that if there is no object of thought, "there will be no knowledge of anything, unless we say that sensation is knowledge" (*Meta.* 999b3–4); "for the knowledge of anything is universal" (1003a14–15). The reason offered by Aristotle for the need of something over and above the particulars, if there is to be knowledge, is that "all things that we know, we know in so far as they have some unity and identity, and in

---

members of the nonsubstance categories are *particular* or *universal*; e.g., whether in the quality category the lowest level items are particular instances of whiteness or the universal white. Our present question is a debate between two different types of *universal*.

so far as some attribute belongs to them universally" (999a28–29); "how will it be possible to know, if there is not to be something common to a whole set of individuals?" (999b26–27). So it is the one over the many, which is shared by them and predicated of them, that serves as an organizing principle in our cognition of the world, identifying each of the many in terms of that which is common between them. In other words, the many are cognized as instances of the universal.

The scientific acquisition of knowledge is achieved by the derivation of definitions of what things are, which results in the classification of things into species and genera. Insofar as universals are the object of knowledge, they will inevitably be the object of the sciences: "every formula, and every science is of universals and not of particulars" (1059b25–26). In scientific deductions, the propositions are of universal application,[12] and, consequently, so are the definitions, too, "since a definition is either a principle of a demonstration or a demonstration differing in position or a sort of conclusion of a demonstration" (*An. Post.* 75b31–32). This position is also retained in *Metaphysics* Z where Aristotle states that "definition is of the universal and of the form" (1036a28–29).

This, then, is the "one over many" family of arguments that leads Aristotle to posit universals in his ontology. Universals are the object of understanding and of thought, the object of knowledge, and indeed of scientific knowledge, as it is given in derivations of definitions, and structured in stratifications by genera and species.

## 3. The Universality of the Material Substratum

At least some of the time, Plato understands universality in terms of being in different places at the same time (e.g., *Parmenides* 130b1–2), and this conception of recurrence at a time does appear in descriptions of the universal in Aristotle: "it is what is always and everywhere that we call universal" (*An. Post.* 87b32, although here the universal is also required to be eternally instantiated); again he says: "that which is common [*koinon*] is present in many things at the same time" (*Meta.* 1040b25–26). Recurrence at a time is the way that universality has been understood in most philosophical systems and is certainly the way we think of it in contemporary philosophy. But it is not accurate to take this conception of universality to be the

12. *An. Post.* 75b21–22.

primary one in Aristotle. Aristotle defines a *universal* as that which *belongs to many things*: "That is called universal whose nature is to belong to a number of things" (*Meta.* 1038b11–12); "I call a universal that which is by its nature predicated of a number of things" (*Int.* 17a39–40). "By the universal we mean that which is predicated of the individuals" (*Meta.* 1000a1). What is significant about the way Aristotle defines the universal is his focus on the relation of the universal to particulars, that is, that of "belonging." It is not accidental that Aristotle should concentrate on this relation in defining the universal, as he defines particular substance, too, in terms of the relation of belonging: "A *substance*—that which is called a substance most strictly, primarily, and most of all—is that which is neither said of a subject nor in a subject, e.g., the individual man or the individual horse" (*Cat.* 2a11–14). In the *Categories*, these two relations—being said of a subject and being in a subject—are the ways in which an entity may belong to a subject. Thus, the most fundamental entities in Aristotle's ontology, the particular substances, are defined in terms of the notion of belonging to a subject: particular substances do not belong to any subject. It is not surprising then that universals, too, are ontologically characterized by Aristotle in terms of the same notion of belonging to a subject.

The importance of defining universals in terms of belonging to a subject rather than in terms of their multiple instantiation at a time is that the former allows for a broader conception of universals than the latter. If a universal is that which is (or can be) multiply instantiated at a time, universals turn out to be the properties that are abstracted from particulars. But if a universal is that which belongs (in a metaphysical sense) to a particular, universals will include not only what can be multiply instantiated at a time (i.e., properties), but also whatever else can belong to many subjects, even if not at the same time. For example, understanding a universal as that which belongs to different subjects will allow us to think of the form of the vase as a universal, but also, of the material substratum of the vase, namely, the bronze in the vase, as a universal, too, because the bronze in the vase will also belong (at a later time) to the statue into which the vase is transformed. [13] The material substratum will not belong to the

---

13. For example, in the transformation of the lump of bronze into a statue the same quantity of bronze remains throughout: discussing a different point, Aristotle says: "we sometimes speak thus [something coming to be out of something] about things that *do remain*: we say that a statue comes to be out of bronze" (bronze being what remains throughout the transformation, being in the lump first, and in the statue later, *Ph.* 190a24–25, my emphasis).

substance as a predicate, but it will belong to it metaphysically insofar as matter for Aristotle is always the matter *of* a substance.[14] The material substratum is a universal because it belongs to many particulars, though at different times.

In general, what Aristotle's definition of universals allows for is that *universals* are the entities that belong to many particulars, either at a time or through time. Of course, this still sustains the distinction between something that is in different things at the same time (e.g., a universal form) and something that can be in different things only at different times (e.g., matter). Furthermore, the form belongs to the substance in a different way from the way the matter does. Nevertheless, the universality of matter, in the broader sense of "universal," will be a significant consideration when we come to the account of the particularity of substances.

14. In *Metaphysics* Θ Aristotle describes a parallel (but not identity) in the way that the accidents and the matter of a substance belong to the substance: "A casket is not wood but of wood . . . (The subject is called, when music is implanted in it, not music but musical, and the man is not whiteness but white . . . as in the above examples of 'of' something.) Wherever this is so, then, the ultimate subject is a substance; . . . And it is only right that the 'of' something locution should be used with reference both to the matter and to the accidents" (1049a19–b1).

# 3 | The Birth of the Subject

## 1. Plato's Discovery of the Subject

Zeno's paradox was a challenge that every metaphysician of Plato's time had to meet: "If things are many, then it follows that the same things must be both like and unlike; but that is impossible; for unlike things cannot be like or like things unlike" (*Parmenides* 127e1–4). In order to be able to hold that things are many, Plato would have to show that no impossibility followed from that assertion. In the *Phaedo*, Plato is concerned to give an account of the causes for things being the way they are.[1] In one metaphysical move, Plato offers a solution to both Zeno's paradox and the problem of causes by introducing the Forms. The impossibility that follows from the claim that things are many (and hence each of them is both like and unlike) stems from the supposition that the like cannot be unlike. If a thing $x$ is like, it cannot also be unlike because a thing cannot be its opposite. By positing the Forms and participation in them, Plato avoids the (impossible) *identity* of opposites, explaining the phenomenon as the *copresence* of opposites in a subject. $X$ partakes of Forms F and non-F, which entails the copresence of F and non-F in $x$,[2] but not the identity of F and non-F. Thus, Plato can hold that opposites do not mix: "that not only is largeness itself never willing to be

---

1. "It seems to me that if anything else is beautiful besides the beautiful itself, it is beautiful for no reason at all other than that it participates in that beautiful; and the same goes for all of them" (*Phaedo* 100c4–6). David Furley traces the connection between Forms and causation in Plato to Anaxagoras' influence (1989, 63).

2. "Both things are in Simmias, largeness and smallness" (102b5–6).

large and small at the same time, but also that the largeness in us never admits the small" (*Phaedo* 102d6–8).[3] Because participating in a Form F accounts for $x$'s being an $f$, for instance, a flower's being beautiful, the combination of an ontology of Forms and participation in them offers an account of the causes of things being the way they are: "nothing else makes it beautiful except that beautiful itself, whether by its presence or communion or whatever the manner and nature of the relation may be" (*Phaedo* 100d4–6). In this way, Plato's solution to Zeno's paradox offers a theory of causes (or reasons) for things having the properties they have.

Plato gives the same solution to Zeno's paradox in the *Parmenides* (128e6–129b6). Here, too, he insists that, although things may participate in opposite Forms (thereby becoming qualified by opposite characteristics), the Forms themselves cannot partake of their opposites:

> But I find nothing strange, Zeno, if he [someone] shows that things which get a share of both [the like and the unlike] undergo both qualifications, nor if he shows that all things are one by reason of having a share in the one, and that those very same things are also in turn many by reason of having a share of multitude. But if he shows that what it is to be one is many, and the many in turn one, that *will* surprise me. The same is true in like manner of all other things. If someone should show that the kinds of characters in themselves undergo these opposite qualifications, there is reason for surprise. (*Parmenides* 129b3–c3)[4]

I argue that Plato's response to the Zenonian paradox does not fully resolve it. But on the way toward resolving it, Plato lays the foundation for what will constitute its resolution, that is, the *distinction* between *properties that determine the nature of the subject* in the thing and *properties* that do not determine its nature, but *are predicated of the subject.*

3. Although Plato does not state the Zenonian paradox in the *Phaedo* passage under consideration here, it is clear that the solution to it is explicitly given: opposites can be copresent in things that partake of opposite Forms (102b1–6), but opposite Forms or opposite Immanent Forms cannot accept their opposites (see passage just quoted and: "We've agreed then unreservedly on this point: an opposite will never be opposite to itself" [103c7–8]).

4. It is important to realize that the resolution of Zeno's paradox does not rely on the introduction of either relative properties or comparatives. As Allen has pointed out, Plato had already made the breakthrough on these topics in the *Republic*; yet, in the *Parmenides* he is introducing the Theory of the Forms and the relation of participation as a resolution of the paradox. The resolution is metaphysical, not semantic (relying on the distinction between complete and incomplete predicates, and so on). See Allen 1983, 74–77.

The fundamental question we need to address in order to unravel the metaphysical difficulties of Plato's response to Zeno's paradox is: why can two opposites be in a thing, but they cannot be in each other? Plato treats the monstrosity of a Form's being characterized by its opposite as obvious.[5] But Forms may either exclude the presence of other Forms or necessitate it. The latter follows from Plato's *subtler* answer to such a question as "By whose presence in a body, that body will be hot?" (*Phaedo* 105b9). His response is that the body is hot by the presence of Fire (105c2), and this is so because the Form of Fire[6] always brings along with it the Form of the Hot: "not only do the forms that are opposites [e.g., Hot-Cold] not abide each other's attack; but there are, in addition, certain other things that don't abide the opposites' attack" (104c7–9); these are "things that are compelled by whatever occupies them [e.g., Fire] to have not only its own form [Fire], but always the form of some opposite [Hot] as well" (104d1–3). Thus a fire will never accept the Form of the Cold because the Fire in that fire always has with it the Form of the Hot.

In what follows, I will talk of Immanent Forms being in things that partake of Forms. But nothing of what I argue depends on taking Plato to be committed to Immanent Forms. The whole chapter could be rewritten without mention of possession of Immanent Forms, but simply talk of participation in Form F and being *f*.

There are three types of entity, then, that cannot abide the presence of an opposite Form, and there is one that can. First, an opposite Form, and second, an opposite Immanent Form in a thing, never accept their opposites and become their opposites. For example, the Form of the Large will never accept the Form of the Small, thereby becoming small (103c7–8). Similarly, the Immanent Form of the Large in Socrates will never become small by accepting the Small, nor ever behave like, or play the causal role of, the property of being small[7] (102d7–8; see also 102b4–5). Third, snow will

5. *Parmenides* 129b2, c1, c3. Also, 103c7–8.

6. It is a very controversial issue whether Plato commits himself to such Forms as that of Fire or of Soul in the *Phaedo*. In the passage referred to he seems to commit himself to nonopposite Forms unreservedly, but not all passages are consistent with this position. For example, when explaining the same point—of something bringing along with it an opposite Form—earlier on in the text, he says: "there is something else [e.g., fire], too, which is not the same as the form [Hot], but which, *whenever it exists*, always has the character of that form [Hot]" (103e4–5, my emphasis). Because that other thing does not have a continuous existence, it cannot be a Form. As will become clear, it is inessential for my interpretation whether Plato commits himself or not to nonopposite Forms in the *Phaedo*. I assume for continuity of presentation that he does posit nonopposite Forms. For a parallel reading, on either interpretation, of the Final Argument in the *Phaedo*, see Gallop 1975, 203–205.

7. Which would be tantamount to its having become the property of being small.

never accept the Form of the Hot, or fire the Form of the Cold. The reason why not, in this third case, *is not obvious*. The reason why an opposite (Immanent or not) Form will not accept its opposite and become its opposite (by acquiring that opposite qualification) is that it cannot survive that change; the Form of the Hot cannot become cold and still be the Form of the Hot. Plato says: "the small that's in us is not willing ever to come to be, or to be, large. Nor will any other of the opposites, *while still being what it was*, at the same time come to be, and be, its own opposite" (102e6–103a1, my emphasis). We can understand the reason why Plato thought this if we think of a Form F, or an Immanent Form F, as being the source of F-ness, whose presence in a thing makes the thing *f*.[8] For example, the source of heat cannot be cold. But the same reasoning does not apply to entities that are not Forms, as where, as Plato states, "the hot is something different from fire, and the cold is something different from snow" (103d2–3).[9]

A first suggestion as to why fire cannot accept the Cold is that fire always possesses the Hot. We saw that some Forms, such as the Form of Fire, when they occupy something, bring along with it an opposite Form, in this case the Hot (104d1–3). So accepting the Cold would mean that that Fire would have to be hot and cold at the same time. But why could that not be? Socrates is tall and short at the same time: "you do mean then, don't you, that both things are in . . . [Socrates], largeness and smallness? True." (102b5–7). Why could fire not be hot and cold at the same time? Plato does not think that the copresence of opposites in a thing is objectionable. Yet, he thinks that the Cold and the Hot cannot be copresent in a fire. Therefore, his objection to the latter cannot have anything to do with difficulties about the copresence of two opposites in a thing. It must have to do with the only thing that, with Zeno, he finds objectionable, namely, that opposites be their opposites. We saw that Plato repeatedly stated that it cannot be the case that an opposite either becomes or is its opposite, while remaining what it is, while surviving the change.[10] In the case of Socrates, Plato is at pains to show us that the copresence of the Small and the Large in him does not entail either that the Small becomes large (or vice versa) or that Socrates' identity succumbs to the intrusion of the Small or of the Large.[11] Rather, each of the following entities, Socrates, the Small in him, the Large in him, retains its identity in the presence of the other two entities. Hence, if the

8. See Scaltsas 1989a, 69–70.
9. Clearly, what it is to be hot is not what it is to be fire, etc.
10. *Phaedo* 102d6–8, 103c7–8.
11. "Thus I, having admitted and abided smallness, am still what I am, this same individual, only small" (*Phaedo* 102e3–5; also 102b5–7).

Cold cannot be present in Fire, it must be that its presence would violate this condition: its presence would be destructive of the identity of one of the necessary elements in a fire.

If this is the case, because Cold is not opposite to Fire, attribution of Cold to a fire cannot be destructive of the identity of the immanent Form of Fire in that fire. Rather, attribution of Cold to a fire must be destructive of the Form of Hot in the fire. But for this to be the case, the relation of the Hot and the Cold in the fire cannot be the same as the relation of the Small and the Large in Socrates. The Hot-Cold relation in the fire must be of the sort that is *objectionable*; that is, it must be that the Cold would be attributed to the Hot, thereby making the Hot cold. This is the sort of relation that Plato cannot allow: opposites attributed to opposites. But for this relation to emerge, it must be that on Plato's analysis, the special bond between the Form of Fire and the Form of Hot is stronger than simply Fire bringing the Hot along with it when it occupies a body. That would still allow for the presence of Cold in a fire (like the Small in Socrates). Rather, it must be that the bond between the Fire and the Hot in a fire is such that if the cold were to be attributed to the fire, it would be attached to the Fire *and* to the Hot in the fire. That is, the Cold would be attributed to the Hot in the fire, which the Hot could not survive; but without the Hot, the Fire in the fire could not survive, and hence the fire would not survive. Thus, the only way to justify why the Cold and the Hot could not be copresent in a fire while the Small and the Large could be copresent in Socrates is by realizing that in the case of the fire, *the Hot is part of the subject of which the Cold would be attributed*, whereas in the case of Socrates, the Large is not part of the subject of which the Small is attributed. The relation of the Fire and the Hot in a fire is not simply a necessary copresence relation; rather, *the Fire and the Hot in the fire are constituents of the subject that the rest of the properties characterize*. That is why a fire cannot survive the "approach" of the Cold; because the Cold would not simply be copresent with the Hot in the Fire but would *characterize* the Hot, which the Hot cannot endure.

That for Plato the objectionable relation is the incompatibility between the nature of the subject and the nature of the character that attaches to the subject (rather than the relation between two characters that are copresent in a subject) can be seen from the position Plato takes in the *Timaeus*, when he is at pains to show that the substratum has no nature of its own, and so it can accept any character that attaches to it: "If the model is to take every variety of form, then the matter [partaker] in which the model is fashioned will not be duly prepared unless it is formless and free from the impress of any of those shapes which it is hereafter to receive from without. For if the matter were like any of the supervening forms, then whenever any opposite or entirely different nature was stamped upon its surface, it would take the impression badly, because it would intrude its own shape. Wherefore that which is to receive all forms should have no form" (*Timaeus* 50d4–e5). Thus, incompatibilities arise not with the *copresence* of opposites, but when a character *belongs* to a subject whose nature is opposite to the character.

This is the birth of the subject in metaphysics. In the *Phaedo*, this subject is a thing in the world that participates in the Forms. The preparticipation nature of that thing is not discussed in that dialogue (as opposed to the passage from the *Timaeus* just quoted). But participation *can* affect the nature of the subject, as we saw in the case of fire, where the subject of predication is a hot fire, which cannot accept the Cold: "It is not only the opposite [Hot] that doesn't admit its opposite [Cold]; there is also that [Fire] which brings up an opposite [Hot] into whatever [body] it enters itself; and that thing [Fire], the very thing that brings it [the Hot] up, never admits the quality [Cold] opposed to the one that's brought up [Hot]" (105a2–5). It is telling of Plato's conception of the predication relations that he does not say that the body, which partakes in the Form of Fire, will not partake of the Cold; rather, it is the Fire, which brings up the Hot into the body it enters, that will not accept the Cold. Therefore, it is not the body, the original partaker, that alone is the subject; rather, the *subject* is the body, along with the Fire and Hot in it, of which the other properties are predicated. Thus the Cold cannot be admitted. It follows that the formation of the *subject* involves a special bond between the partaker and the Forms of Fire and Hot that will not exist between the partaker and any other of the Forms it partakes in.[12]

Furthermore, it is only the subject that is essentially hot or a fire, not the partaker in the Forms of the Hot or of Fire; that is, it is not the body that partakes of Fire that is essentially hot or a fire. Plato says that "fire, when cold advances, will either get out of the way or perish" (103d10–11). The advance of the Cold will result not in a cold fire, but in the partaking body becoming cold, while Fire gets out of the way or perishes. It is not the partaking body that will get out of the way and perish but the Fire in it.

12. The Theory of the Subtler Causes in the *Phaedo* does not offer us an account of the formation of the subject. Plato's Theory of the Subtler Causes posits a special (necessary copresence) bond between the Forms of Fire and of the Hot: whatever Fire occupies is also occupied by the Form of the Hot. This can explain why the subject is essentially hot if it is essentially a fire, but *not* why it is essentially either hot or a fire.

Similarly with snow; it will not bé the body that will get out of the way or perish (103d7–8) at the advance of the Hot but the Snow in it. Hence, the partaker survives the loss of the Forms of Snow and Cold in it, or of Fire and Hot in it, and therefore it is not essentially bonded to them. On the other hand, the *subject*, which consists of the partaker plus the Forms of Fire and the Hot in it, does not survive the advance of the opposite. It is the *subject*, then, that is essentially hot and a fire.

We have seen the following so far. Plato's Theory of Forms always presupposes a partaker in the world that participates of the Forms. Partaking of a nonopposite Form (e.g., Fire) may necessitate partaking of an opposite Form (e.g., Hot). The partaker, the nonopposite Form, and the opposite Form, comprise a subject (this fire) that is essentially this nonopposite Form (Fire) and this opposite Form (Hot). This subject will not admit of the Form (Cold) that is opposite the opposite Form (Hot) it essentially possesses. The advent of such an opposite Form (Cold) would result in the destruction of the subject (this fire), though not of the original partaker. The existence of the subject requires a special relation between the partaker, on the one hand, and the two Forms (Fire, Hot) on the other; a relation that the partaker does not have with, for example, the Form of the Large. This special relation is responsible for the existence of the subject (this fire). To understand why this fire cannot accept the Cold (although Socrates can accept both the Large and the Small), we must understand the rest of the Forms to be *predicated of the subject*, this fire, not of the partaker. By shifting the locus of predication from the partaker to the subject (which has the nature of being a fire and being hot), we can explain why Plato holds that the Cold cannot belong to the fire (although the Large and the Small can belong to Socrates). The reason is that the Cold would be predicated of the Hot (in the subject), which is disallowed as a Zenonian monstrosity. In the case of Socrates, as neither the Large nor the Small are part of the subject, both can be predicated of the subject and thus be copresent in Socrates.

The general framework of this theory is to be found in Plato's works as late as the *Timaeus*. There, Plato retains the principle that there must be some thing(s) other than Forms that will partake of the Forms.[13] That which partakes retains its nature throughout the partaking. He gives the example of a piece of gold that can receive different shapes while remaining

---

13. "For an image [the Immanent Form—50c4–5] since the reality after which it is modeled does not belong to it, and it exists ever as the fleeting shadow of some other, must be inferred *to be in another* (that is, in space), grasping existence in some way or other, or it could not be at all" (*Timaeus* 52c2–5, my emphasis).

the same thing, gold, and says that that which receives the Forms, the partaker, always retains its own nature (*Timaeus* 50a5–c2). In the *Timaeus* he makes a formal distinction between the two natures of a thing (what I have been calling nature of the partaker and the nature of the subject); the one is given as an answer to the question "what is it?"[14]—here gold—and the other is given as an answer to the question of "what kind" (*toiouton*) this thing is, here a triangle (50a7–b5).[15]

Although Plato needs the distinction between *partaker* and *subject* for the metaphysical claims he makes in the *Phaedo*, it does not follow that his theory can justify that distinction. According to the Theory of Forms (along with the account of the Forms as the causes of things being the way they are), the participation relation holds between the partaker and the Forms it partakes in. Through this relation, the Forms come to occupy, or be present in, the thing that partakes of them, and so the properties the Forms stand for come to belong to the thing that partakes in these Forms.[16] With the theory of the Subtler Reasons, what is being introduced is only a relation between Forms: necessarily, when a Form of some specific kind occupies a partaker, another Form of a specific kind also occupies the partaker. What the Theory of Forms needs, but does not provide, is a different kind of participation relation to explain why, for example, participation in Fire results in the formation of a subject, but participation in the Small does not. Yet, Plato speaks as if it is not just the partaker, but the Fire in the partaker, too, that would *admit* the Cold: "Fire, when cold advances, will either get out of the way or perish; but it will never endure to *admit* the coldness, and

14. τί ποτ' ἐστί;

15. In the *Timaeus* Plato makes explicit what is implicit in the exposition in *Phaedo*, as one can surmise on the basis of Plato's examples. Along with such examples as this fire, this snow, and number 3 in the explanation of the subtler reasons, he also includes the example of fever and illness. (This is ill not because of the presence of Illness—an opposite Form—in it, but because of the presence of Fever in it [*Phaedo* 105c2–4].) Here the partaker is the body and the subject is the feverish body, which is not as substantial as this fire, this snow, or number 3. Plato's treatment of the example of gold in the *Timaeus* may elucidate his lack of discrimination between these examples in the *Phaedo*. Whether it is a golden statue or a golden triangle or a golden lump, is of secondary importance because these have fleeting existences in comparison with the gold that survives the transformations (*Timaeus* 50b2–4). Thus, Plato would not see a major difference in the *Phaedo* between an animate body (for us, a person) or a feverish body (something like a stage in a person's life, for us). The main distinctions are between the partaker, the Immanent Form, and the Form, which, as we have seen, are retained in the *Timaeus*. Subjects are of secondary significance in *Timaeus*, and distinctions between kinds of subjects (for us, substantial or not) are insignificant.

16. *Phaedo* 100c4–8.

still be what it was, namely, fire and also cold" (*Phaedo* 103d10–12, my emphasis). What relation between the partaker and the Form of Fire gives rise to a subject? Plato's metaphysics does not answer this question and is left facing the problem of the *generation* of the subject and the *unity* of the constituents that determine its nature and make up a single individual. Plato does not seem to have identified this problem for what it is, but for Aristotle it will become the pivotal point around which his metaphysics will unfold.

## 2. The "Nature-Feature" Problem

I do not believe that it was an oversight on Plato's part that prevented him from developing an account of the subject as an entity different from the partaker. The reasons for it are related to Zeno's paradox. The problem posed by Zeno's paradox is the incompatibility of the nature of a thing and the nature of a character that is attributed to that thing. How can the large be small if the large is the absence of the small? How can the one be many if the one is the absence of plurality? Plato did not think this to be a pseudo-paradox. He recognized some truth in it that he tried to preserve by positing in his theory that opposite Forms do not accept their opposites. It is impossible for that which is the cause of largeness to be small or for that which is the cause of oneness to be many. This is significant because it goes to the heart of what should be retained of Zeno's position. It tells us that even if Zeno made the mistake of confusing predication for identity,[17] he was still right in thinking that a subject cannot accept any property what-soever. In fact, the *nature of the subject* may require possession of some properties and may exclude possession of other properties. This is the Zenonian truth residue that Plato, as well as Aristotle, preserved in their metaphysics, although in different ways.

Necessary relations, as well as incompatibilities, between properties are determined at the level of the Forms, according to the Theory. It is the Form of Fire that always brings the Form of the Hot in a partaker it occupies and the presence of Fire and the Hot that determines that the Cold cannot be present in the same partaker at the same time. By elevating the necessary relations and incompatibilities to the level of the Forms, Plato was allowing for the partakers in the world to possess opposite properties in them, thereby resolving Zeno's paradox.

17. "The large is small" for "the large is the small."

It is essential for Plato's solution to maintain that by participating in the Forms, *the partaker does not acquire the nature of the Forms.* If it did, then the same incompatibilities that apply at the level of the Forms would duplicate themselves in the worldly objects. If partaking in the Large bestowed on the partaker the nature of the Form of the Large, then the incompatibilities that Zeno warned about would repeat themselves at the level of the things in the world: things could not be both large and small, which is absurd. It is imperative then for Plato that *the relation of participation does not bestow on the partaker the nature of the Form.* Plato's solution requires that *participating* in Forms will provide the ground only for the *copresence* of Immanent Forms in the partaker. If participation in a Form determined the nature of the partaker, then the relation of participation would not offer a solution to Zeno's paradox: just as the Form of the Large cannot be small, so a large thing, too, could not be small, which is Zeno's position. It is therefore part of Plato's solution that participation in Forms does not determine the nature of the partaker, but only engender the copresence of Immanent Forms in the partaker. Even such relations as the necessary presence of the Hot in the partaker when Fire is in the partaker descend to the partaker from the level of the Forms; they are not determined by the nature of the partaker.

But there is a hitch. The very move that freed Plato's ontology from the constraints of Zeno's ontology (allowing a large thing to be also small) is the move that undermined the possibility of explaining why this fire cannot be cold. The Theory of Forms disallows that the Form of the Hot be cold; it demands that the Form of Fire always occupy partakers along with the Form of the Hot; but the Theory cannot tell us why the Form of the Cold cannot occupy the same partaker as the Form of Fire or of the Hot. To resolve this difficulty, Plato relied on the *tacit introduction of a subject*, over and above the partaker in a thing of the world. The nature of the subject, as opposed to the nature of the partaker, *can* be determined by the Immanent Forms in the partaker. In this way, properties that are incompatible with the nature of the subject cannot be present in that thing. Thus, this particular fire cannot be cold because the nature of the subject in it, the hot fire, is incompatible with being cold. We have, then, the duplication, at the world level, of the kind of explanation of combinations and incompatibilities that is operative at the level of the Forms. But that invites back Zeno's paradox. Let us see why.

According to the theory, a partaker can possess in its two opposites because possessing them does not require the opposites' possessing each other. Participation does not determine the nature of the partaker. But Plato also wants to allow for cases in which the presence of some Forms in a partaker prevents the presence of some other Forms in the partaker. This exclusion can readily be explained if the presence of these Forms in the partaker determines the nature of the subject, so that any further Forms predicated of the subject could not include opposites that are incompatible with the nature of the subject. But then, if participation determines the nature of the subject in the partaker, participation will simply duplicate the predication patterns of the world of the Forms in our world. If something partakes of the Large, it acquires the nature of the Large and hence it cannot be small, and so on. It follows that *if participation determines the nature of the subject, opposites cannot be copresent in things in the world* (e.g., Large and Small in Socrates); *if participation does not determine the nature of the subject, opposites can be copresent* (e.g., Cold and Hot in a fire). Both results are unacceptable.

Plato never fully resolved this paradox, and hence, Zeno's paradox either. The passage of the *Timaeus* we examined (*Timaeus* 50d4–e5) explicitly claims that participation in the Forms leaves the nature of the partaker intact, and the attempt to recognize the generation of "such's" as a result of participation in Forms (*Timaeus* 50b4–5) is too embryonic an account of the generation of a subject with a nature for a full-blown answer to the difficulty at hand. [18] But there is evidence in Aristotle that members of the Academy did become sensitive to this problem that the Theory of Forms was facing and tried to remedy it. The evidence is given in a very elliptic but telling passage in the *Metaphysics*. I will argue that Aristotle's attack in this passage is directed against an alternative Platonic position that must have developed in the Academy in order to overcome the difficulty I outlined, according to which, in contrast to Plato, *participation in Forms does imbue the subject with a nature*. Aristotle's objections to this alternative position lead us to his own conception of the relation of the subject to the substantial form that is the subject's nature.

The Aristotelian passage is the following:

> But according to the necessities of the case and the opinions held about the Forms, if they can be shared there must be ideas of substances only [*tōn ousiōn anakaion ideas einai monon*]. For they are not shared incidentally [*ou gar kata sumbebēkos metachontai*] but a thing must share [*metechein*] in its Form as in something not predicated of a subject [*mē kath' hupokeimenou legetai*] (e.g., if a

18. It should not be supposed that the transience of the existence of a golden cube or triangle is the reason why Plato talks of them as "such's" while treating gold as a "this," because gold is, in the long run, just as ephemeral as the cube or the triangle in the world. They are "such's" because Plato cannot offer a metaphysical account of their status as entities.

thing shares in double itself, it shares also in eternal, but incidentally [*kata sumbebēkos*]; for eternal happens to be predicable of the double). [19] (*Meta.* 990b27–34)

The conclusion of the argument is that there will be Forms of substances only, for example, the Form of Man, the Form of Tiger, Forms of Numbers, but not of the Large and of the Hot. [20] If the argument is correct, which I will try to show it is, it should support that conclusion.

Aristotle's tactic in this argument is to dismiss two accounts of the relation of participation in the Forms and conclude that on the remaining alternative, the Forms must all be substantial. The first version of the relation of participation he dismisses is that of a thing partaking of a Form incidentally. He explains what he means by that relation with the example of the Double. Because the Form of the Double is eternal, it might have been thought that to partake of the Double is to also partake of the Eternal. But this is dismissed as an explanation of what participation is. We can see why this is dismissed as a candidate for the relation of participation by looking at the accidental (*kata sumbebēkos*) relation in a different context in Aristotle. He describes this sense of incidental relation in *Metaphysics* Δ, 6, where he explains that the just and the musical can be thought of as being one in the sense that it is the same person who is just and musical

19. The *Meta.* M version of this passage is the following:

> But according to the necessities of the case and the opinions about the forms, if they can be shared in [ἔστι μεθεκτά] there must be Ideas of substances only. For they are not shared in incidentally [οὐ γὰρ κατὰ συμβεβηκὸς μετέχονται], but each Form must be shared in as something not predicated of a subject [ἑκάστου μετέχειν ἢ μὴ καθ' ὑποκειμένου λέγονται]. (E.g., if a thing shares in the double itself, it shares also in the eternal, but incidentally; for the double happens to be eternal.) (*Meta.* 1079a24–30)

20. At the end of the passage, Aristotle repeats the conclusion of the argument by saying: "Therefore the Forms will be substance" (ὥστ' ἔσται οὐσία τὰ εἴδη, 990b34). I have not included it in the quote in note 19, as it is ambiguous. It may mean that each Form is a substance or that each Form is the Form of a substance, as opposed to the Form of a relation, a quantity, a quality, etc. The latter is unambiguously stated in the first mention of the conclusion: "there must be Ideas of substances only" (990b29). Furthermore, if what Aristotle was trying to prove here was that the Forms will be substances, why would he mention that there is no incidental participation in the Forms? How could this show that the Forms are substances? (Finally, the fact that he is using a nonsubstantial Form—the Eternal—in his example, does not show that he is not trying to show that the Forms are all substantial. He could not possibly show what does not happen in participation [e.g., incidental participation] by using an example of substantial Forms, because no substantial Form is characterized by a different substantial predicate in the way that the Double is characterized by being eternal.)

(1015b16–32). So, they are ontologically related by being copresent in the same substance, but there is no ontological effect that their copresence has on each other. In an analogous way, the partaker of the Double is ontologically related to the Eternal, insofar as the partaker participates in an eternal Form, but there is no ontological effect on the partaker from the presence of the Eternal in which the partaker participates.

Having explained what the relation of participation is not, Aristotle tells us what it is in a negative way(!): "a thing must share [*metechein*] in its Form as in something not predicated of a subject [*me kath' hupokeimenou legetai*]" (990b30–31). Clearly, Aristotle is not saying here that, when, for example, a partaker participates in a Form, the partaker is not predicated of the Form.[21] Rather, he is telling us that, *whatever participation is, the result cannot be that the Form is said of the partaker as a subject*. The expression "being said of a subject" (*kath' hupokeimenou legetai*) is used in a technical sense in Aristotle to indicate that an entity is predicable. We find it in the *Categories* (1b4–6), where concrete substances such as Socrates are said not to be predicated of anything, as well as in the *Metaphysics* where it has the same use (1017b10–14). But this cannot be the meaning of the expression in the present context. Suppose that Aristotle were saying here that the Forms cannot be predicated of a subject. Then the conclusion would be that the Forms *are* substances, not that there are Forms *of* substances only, which is the argument's conclusion.[22] So long as Forms are substances, there could be Forms of relations, quantities, qualities, and so on. But Aristotle tells us that the argument shows there are Forms of substances *only*, for example, the Form of Human Being, or Tiger, but not of the Large and of the Beautiful.

To see what Aristotle's reasoning is, we have to briefly introduce a notion that we will examine in detail in Sections 3 of Chapter 6 and 3 of Chapter 7. This is one of the key concepts that will enable us to see how Aristotle explains the unity of the subject and the substantial form in a substance. It

---

21. I take it I do not have to argue this point as there is no context in which the concrete substances are thought of as being predicable of the Forms, and it would be incredible to take Aristotle to be elucidating the concept of participation by telling us something like that. That he is talking of the partaker becoming characterized as an *f* by partaking of the Form F becomes clear in the passage immediately following where he considers that "the Ideas and the particulars that share in them have the same Form" (991a2–3). But more immediately, if Aristotle's elucidation here consisted in his telling us that the partaker is not predicated of the Form, why would it follow from that that there are Forms of substances only? It would be true of *all* Forms that the partaker is not predicated of the Form, whether this is a Form of substance or of relation or of quantity, quality, etc.

22. See note 20.

is the Aristotelian concept of being said *kath' hauto*. In *Metaphysics* Z, 6 (1031b13–14), Aristotle contrasts the notion of being said *kath' hauto* to being said *kat' allo*. Something is said to be *x kat' allo* if it is *x* in virtue of being *y*. For example, Socrates is musical, not on account of being "a musical," but on account of being a person. But he is a person in virtue of nothing else; being a person is what Socrates is in himself (*kath' hauto*). In that sense, being musical is *said of* a subject—the person, who *is* the subject.

The argument Aristotle has been advancing at this stage in Z, 6, has reached its conclusion, that "the Good, then, must be one with the essence of the Good, and the Beautiful with the essence of Beauty, and so with all things which do not depend on something else [i.e., are not *kat' allo*] but are self-subsistent [*kath' hauta*] and primary" (1031b12–14). And then he adds: "For it is enough if this be so, even if there are no Forms; and perhaps all the more if there are Forms" (1031b14–15). Aristotle's last remark means the following: We have just seen that if there are Forms, they must be identical to their essences; more generally, whatever makes a claim to substancehood (primacy, self-subsistency) should be identical to its essence; this must be the case, even if there are no Forms—but all the more if there are Forms. The reason is that the existence of Forms is a threat to the principle just stated, not because Forms themselves violate it—it is not part of the Theory of Forms that the Form of the Good is good by participating in another Form of the Good; this would be the refutation of the Theory of Forms—but because it is part of the Theory of Forms that, if it can explain why Socrates is a human being, it would explain it by denying the very principle Aristotle just argued. This is so because Socrates' being a human being would be explained in terms of participation in the Form of Human Being. But then the partaker—the subject—is different from the essence—the Form of Human Being. Thus, the Theory of Forms would violate the substance-essence identity argued for in Z, 6. So, Aristotle is warning us here that the principle of the substance-essence identity should be observed, especially if one posits the Forms. But how?

Aristotle explains: "if there are Ideas such as some people say there are, the subject/substratum will not be substance; for these must be substances, and not predicable of a subject/substratum; for if they were they would exist only by being participated in"[23] (*Meta.* 1031b15–18, my translation). The

23. εἴπερ εἰσὶν αἱ ἰδέαι οἵας τινές φασιν, οὐκ ἔσται τὸ ὑποκείμενον οὐσία· ταύτας γὰρ οὐσίας μὲν ἀναγκαῖον εἶναι, μὴ καθ᾽ ὑποκειμένου δέ· ἔσονται γὰρ κατὰ μέθεξιν.

problem Aristotle is addressing is the following. If there are Forms, and things in the world participate in them, then the subject—partaker—will be different from its essence—the substantial Form. If the Theory of Forms is to abide by the conclusion that Aristotle has just derived, that the subject should be one with its essence, then, first, the partaker in the Form cannot have a substantial nature of its own. If it did, it would be a substance, and then participation in a Form would predicate the Form of a substance. But then, the Form would not be substance, but would exist only as a predicate of substance (*esontai kata methexin*). Yet, it is the Forms that are substances, so they cannot exist as predicates of substance. Therefore, the partaker in a Form cannot be a substance (*ouk estai to hupokeimenon ousia*), nor can the Form be a predicate of it. If there is to be participation in Forms (as the Theory of Forms requires) that abides by the Z, 6, substance-essence identity principle, the only option is for participation to turn the partakers into substances. Participation, in this sense, far from predicating the Forms of the partakers, would imbue the very nature of the partakers with the substantial nature of the Forms, so that, for example, a partaker in the Form of Man would become a man. Only if participation in a Form does not render the Form a predicate of the partaker, but, rather, affects the very nature of the partaker (by rendering it substantial), will the partaker—now a substance—be one with its essence. (As we saw, this is just the type of participation that Plato rejects in the *Timaeus*.) Therefore, the only way to reconcile participation in Forms with the Z, 6, requirement of substance-essence identity is for the partaker not to be substance, and the Form not to be predicated of it, but for the partaker's nature to become substantial through its participation in the Form.

Alexander's reading of the quoted passage cannot be right in its entirety. The reason is that it cannot support Aristotle's conclusion that, if there are Ideas such as some people say there are, the subject will not be substance. On Alexander's interpretation, what Aristotle is saying is that the subject will not be substance, because a substance cannot underlie another substance; and because Forms are substances, the particular substances (such as Socrates) cannot underlie the Forms; more generally, the Forms, qua substances, cannot be predicated of anything, and so there is no need for Forms (Alexander 450.28–451.6). But this reading does not explain what Aristotle means when he says that if there are Forms, the subject will not be substance. What I mean is that, on Alexander's reading, it makes no difference what the subject will be, because Alexander's conclusion is that the Forms cannot be predicated of anything. On his reading, Aristotle should have said that if there are Forms, there will be no *hupokeimenon*, not

that the *hupokeimenon* will not be substance. Aristotle says in this paren-
thetical note that the subject-essence identity must be the case, *especially* if
there are Forms. Yet, on Alexander's reading, the conclusion is that whether
there are Forms or not makes *no difference* to anything else. This could not be
what Aristotle means here.

Furthermore, Alexander's explanation of the subargument's conclusion,
"for they will be by being participated in" (*esontai kata methexin*, 1031b18),
cannot be what Aristotle intends. Alexander explains it as follows: If a Form
is said of a subject, it will exist in the subject, as "man" does in Socrates and
Callias; but the Form of Man does not exist in us and, hence, it is not
predicated of us; therefore, Forms are not predicated of subjects, and,
consequently, there is no need for Forms (451.3–7). But this does not
explain why Aristotle says that "the *hupokeimenon* will not be substance"
(1031b16–17). Aristotle is not saying that there cannot be a relation
between things in the world and Forms, nor is he rejecting the Theory of
Forms at the mere mention of a thing-Form relation. What he is saying is
that things in the world cannot be substances of which the Forms are
predicated, because substances (i.e., the Forms) are not predicated of anything. But this still allows for the *substantial imperialism* of the Forms we
described (that is, through participation, the Forms take over the very
nature of the partakers, turning them into substances, thereby satisfying
the Z, 6, requirement that a thing be one with its essence). Participation
cannot engender predication, but must directly determine the nature of the
partaker and turn it into a substantial one.

Aquinas' reading of this text (1368–1370)[24] is very similar to Alexander's, taking Aristotle to be arguing for the ontological uselessness of the
Forms, rather than for what Aristotle says at 1031b16–17, that the *hupokeimenon* (i.e., partaker of the Forms) cannot be substance. Aquinas states
explicitly an assumption that is implicit in Alexander, according to which
participation in a Form can only be an inherence relation, namely, predication (1370). But we have seen that Aristotle does consider an alternative
model of the Theory of Forms, according to which, participation in Forms
determines the *nature* of the partaker, rather than predicate an accident
of the partaker. This alternative does allow for a relation between Forms
and things; not of predication, but of nature-determination (which Plato
rejected in the *Timaeus*), through which the partaker's nature becomes
substantial.

A still different reading of the argument is given by W. D. Ross, but

24. Aquinas [1261–1272] 1961.

there are reasons to object to it. He takes it that the subject that Aristotle is talking about is the subject in a Form. He says: "If the Ideas are separate entities, it will not be substratum that is substance; for they are substances which involve no substratum, since if they were predicable of a substratum they would exist merely by being participated in by the substratum."[25] However, this is inconsistent with the text. Aristotle says *ouk estai to hupokeimenon ousia.* Ross takes this to mean "it will not be substratum that is substance." But the Greek should have read *ouk estai hupokeimenon ousia* to mean what Ross understands it to mean, that is, without the definite article *to*—*the* substratum. The presence of the definite article means that it is not in question whether there is a *hupokeimenon* or not. What is in question is whether *the hupokeimenon* is substance or not. Ross explains that it will not be substratum that is substance because they are substances that involve no substratum—observe that in Ross' translation, the two occurrences of the term *substratum* are coreferential, if they refer at all. But the Greek does not allow that there be no substratum, because Aristotle is making a definite reference to the substratum (whose existence Ross denies) and says *about it* that it will not be substance.

Now, if Aristotle is making an unquestionable reference to a *hupokeimenon*—and he is saying about it that *it will not be substance*—then he could not mean the subject in a Form. Because, then, Aristotle would be contradicting himself. He has just concluded that the Form of the Good is identical to the essence of the Good; he could not be saying that there is a *hupokeimenon* in the Good that is not substance and, hence, not identical to the essence, which is substance (1031b2–3). But if Aristotle is not talking of the *hupokeimenon* in a Form, he must be talking of the *hupokeimenon* in things in the world that partake of Forms. And that is just what we would expect, given that this is the challenging case for the Theory of Forms— how can the subject be identical to its essence if the subject is a partaker in the world and its essence is a Form predicated of it? We saw that the solution would have to be that, first, the partaker must not be a substance (i.e., not have a substantial nature of its own), and, second, that participation in a Form must not result in one thing said of another, but must confer to the partaker the nature of the Form (e.g., participation in the Form of Gold must make the partaker be, itself, gold, to use a more Platonic example of substantial nature).

The two passages we have examined in the present Section, *Meta.*

25. Ross 1924, 1:178.

990b27–34 and *Meta.* 1031b15–18, give us adequate grounding for this reading of *esontai gar kata methexin* ("for they will be by being *participated in*," my emphasis) when this expression is contrasted to *me kath' hupokeimenou* (not predicable of a subject), as it is in the 1031b15–18 passage. In the first passage, 990b28–31, participation is contrasted to accidental predication, to being said of a subject, and requires that there will be Ideas of substances only: "if the Forms can be *shared* there must be Ideas of substances only. For they are not *shared* incidentally, but a thing must *share* in its Form as in something not predicated of a subject."[26] In the Z, 6, passage, we learn that the *hupokeimenon* that partakes of the Form must not have a nature of its own—must not be substance. Hence, the *methexis* that Aristotle is contrasting to accidental predication and to being said of a subject and that requires the partaker not to have a nature of its own and the Forms to be Forms of substances only, such *methexis* must be of the kind that confers to the partaker its nature—rather than predicate a property of something with a nature of its own.

The version of the Theory of Forms, then, that Aristotle is discussing in 990b27–31 and 1031b15–18 is the following. There are Forms of substances, such as the form of Man and the Form of Tiger. The result of partaking of these Forms is not the acquisition of a property that is said of a subject as an accident. Rather, the partakers that participate in these Forms are not substances on their own, but acquire their substantial nature by partaking of these Forms. In that way, the result of participating in such a Form is the creation of a substantial subject: a partaker with the nature of a substance. *The relation of participation confers to the partaker a substantial nature.*

The claim I have been leading up to in the present section is that *there was very strong motivation for Platonists to develop this version of the Theory of Forms*, according to which participation endows the partaker with a substantial nature. The motivation is Zeno's paradox! As we saw, Plato's solution was to find some truth in Zeno's paradox and some falsehood. The truth for Plato was that the characters themselves cannot accept their opposites: the Hot cannot be cold. But the falsehood was that things in the world could not possess opposites: Socrates can be both large and small. But that theory left a metaphysical gap: why can't a fire be cold? Plato's solution to Zeno's

26. εἰ ἔστι μεθεκτὰ τὰ εἴδη, τῶν οὐσιῶν ἀναγκαῖον ἰδέας εἶναι μόνον· οὐ γὰρ κατὰ συμβεβηκὸς μετέχονται ἀλλὰ δεῖ ταύτῃ ἑκάστου μετέχειν ἢ μὴ καθ' ὑποκειμένου λέγεται (990b28–31, my emphasis).

paradox does not offer a solution to this question. Plato hinted at a solution by tacitly introducing a subject, over and above the partaker, in the *Phaedo*: it is the hot fire that would accept the cold, not just the partaker. The Fire and the Hot in the fire characterize the nature of the subject. The Cold would not simply be copresent with the Hot in the fire, but would be predicated of the Hot in the fire. But this is not allowed by the Theory of Forms, so the fire cannot be cold. The problem with this solution, as we have seen, is that Plato could not explain the generation of a subject since, according to his theory, participation in a Form did not endow the partaker with a substantial nature. He insisted that the partaker retained its nature, despite participation in any Form. This leaves an explanatory lacuna in the theory that, one would expect, must have prompted his followers to put forward a theory based on an alternative account of participation, according to which *participating in a Form endows the partaker with a substantial nature.* Such an account can account for the generation of a subject (involving the partaker as a constituent) as well as explain why, for instance, this fire cannot be cold. But does it offer us a solution to Zeno's paradox?

The answer is negative, and Aristotle is pointing to it at 990b27–31. If participation does not result in accidental predication, the Forms will all be Forms of substances only. Otherwise, Zeno's paradox will reemerge at the level of things in the world: If there were also such Forms as of the Large and the Small, a partaker that participated in the Large would acquire its nature from that participation; but then it could not partake of the Small as well, because it could not have the substantial nature of the Large and the substantial nature of the Small. Therefore, no partaker could participate both in the Large and the Small, and, hence, nothing in the world could be both large and small. Hence, Zeno would be right!

Some phenomena could be explained by such a theory. Thus, to explain why a fire cannot be cold, participation (in Fire and the Hot) would be taken to determine the nature of the subject in the partaker. Then participation in the Cold would require the Hot (in the subject) to be Cold, which the theory prohibits. Hence, a fire could not be cold. The price is that, if participation determines the nature of the subject, then no partaker could participate in two opposites; therefore, Socrates could not be both large and small. Even worse, no partaker could participate in an opposite at all: there are no things in the world whose substantial nature is to be a large or a soft. Therefore, if participation determines the substantial nature of the subject, then there can be Forms of substances only, such as Man or Elm. But if this limitation of having substantial Forms only is upheld, the theory cannot explain accidental predication (e.g., that this thing is large), let alone explain how Socrates can be both large and small, in order to resolve Zeno's paradox.

We have thus reached an impasse. For a way out, three conditions must be satisfied, which would also resolve Zeno's paradox. First, we need to distinguish between *identity* and *predication*, so as to allow for the *presence* of something in something else, that is, of a property in a thing. Second, we need to distinguish between the *nature* of the subject and the *properties* that are predicated of the subject. Third, we need to distinguish between a *mechanism* for a subject to acquire its *nature* and a *mechanism* for a subject to acquire its *properties*. It would then be possible to allow for opposites to be copresent in a subject, but not predicated of each other, and even to be able to distinguish between opposites that can be copresent in a particular subject and opposites that cannot.

The Theory of Forms satisfies the first, and tacitly the second, condition, but fails to satisfy the third, without which the second condition is undermined. One might think that the third condition can be satisfied by allowing for *two kinds of participation* in Forms: one that endows the partaker with a nature, thereby creating the subject in a thing, and one that accounts for the properties that are predicated of this subject. But, to begin with, such a step could not be taken alone. The theory would need to be supplemented with many principles governing each of the two kinds of participation. For example, it would need a criterion for determining which of the two kinds of participation was applicable in each case of participation and an explanation of why this was so: could opposite Forms contribute toward the determination of the nature of a subject or not? Is it part of the nature of this fire to be hot or not? If yes, when does an opposite become part of the nature of the subject and when not? Furthermore, does participation in any nonopposite Form endow the subject with a nature (e.g., participation in the Form of Fever)? In general, what Plato would need to provide in his theory, which he did not, is an account of *substantial nature* that would explain why participating in this Form results in the determination of the nature of the subject, while participating in that Form results in a property being predicated of a subject.

Furthermore, even if the Theory of Forms was enriched with these distinctions and principles, there would still remain a major problem facing the theory, which it could not resolve without self-denial. That is, the *division of a subject* into a partaker and its nature, held apart by the relation of participation. This division is inherent in the Platonic system, so long as the partaker acquires its nature by participating in a Form. The problem here is not what kind of participation is involved, but the very presupposition of participation, that is, that the partaker is a different entity from what is partaken of. As we will see (Sections 3 of Chapter 6 and 3 of Chapter 7), this division is for Aristotle the fatal drawback in the theory's account of the oneness of a substance.

## 3. Does Participation Presuppose a Partaker?

What is the metaphysical function of a partaker? Could Plato retain the Theory of Forms without being forced to posit partakers, namely, entities whose sole function is to partake of the Forms? Or does the distribution and multiple instantiation of a Form in many different things presuppose distinct partakers to divide the Form into parts or instances? As we have seen (Section 1), Plato retains the partakers in his ontology, even in the later versions of the Theory of Forms. In particular, in the *Timaeus*, the partaker has been reduced to the characterless, empty location, which is qualified by participation in the Forms (51a, 52b). I distinguish four functions that the partakers are (or may be) playing in Plato's metaphysics and briefly consider whether these functions render the partakers an indispensable item in his ontology. First, the partakers of a Form provide a way of partitioning a Form and of distributing the Form to different things. Second, partakers differentiate the many things in the world, answering the problem of the distinctness and particularity of each of these things. Third, they give rise to subjects in the world, to loci around which the Immanent Forms cluster into things. And fourth, the partakers furnish what seems to be a rudimentary mechanism for the formation of a subject with a nature. In what follows I consider whether these metaphysical roles make partakers an indispensable item in Plato's ontology.

First, it should be observed that even Plato must believe that *partakers are not required for the particularity of substances* in general. Forms are the prime realities and substances in Plato's ontology; yet, Forms do not contain partakers in them. In the early conceptions of the Forms, Forms do not participate in each other, and, hence, there is no role for a "partaker" in them. Even in the *Sophist*, where Plato does require Forms to partake of each other,[27] he does not require a partaker in each Form to render the Form unique because no two Forms can be qualitatively identical. Hence, quali-

---

27. The reasons have to do with the possibility of communication (259d) and other problems regarding physical explanation (251c–252e).

tative difference is sufficient for differentiating the Forms from one another. (When qualitatively identical Forms are posited in the Third Man Argument, the Theory is already in fatal trouble.)[28] Nevertheless, an account of the distinctness and separateness of each Form from all other substances would be required in a full-blown theory of Forms as substances.

Not so with things in the world. Things in the world can be qualitatively identical by participating in the very same Forms. But they will still be different from each other, because the partakers in each of these things are different from the partakers in the other things. The reason why the partakers are different is not given by Plato, but at least in the *Timaeus* it can be surmised: they are different locations. The question then arises whether Plato needs to reify partakers. Do they provide for the theory anything more than a spatiotemporal difference? Are they needed for the relation of participation to obtain? Participation need not be a relation between two entities. All that is required is the *instantiation* of a Form at a place and time. This does not call for the reification of a being, the partaker, to accept these properties. It is possible that Plato intends the partaker—especially the *Timaeus* partaker—to contribute just difference to a substance; if so, then, the partaker need not be reified into a being underlying the properties of a substance.

On the other hand, if the partaker plays the role of a *subject*, in the sense of that to which the properties belong, then its function might be reason for its reification in the ontology. In the following chapter I argue that Plato did not see the need for an underlying unifier of properties in a thing. Plato treats things as *clusters* of *copresent* Immanent Forms in the world. If this is so, Plato does not need a partaker in a worldly substance to play any unifying role in the substance.

Finally, we saw in the previous sections of the present chapter that the resolution of Zeno's paradox would require the introduction of a *subject* with a *nature* in a substance. Plato took only initial steps toward the conception of the generation of a subject with a nature in a thing, to which the rest of the properties attach. Does the formation of a subject with a nature require the positing of a partaker to which that nature belongs? In the chapters that follow I show Aristotle's reasons for answering this question negatively: a subject with a substantial nature does not presuppose a partaker underlying that nature.

The *nature-feature* problem we examined in this chapter is pivotal for

28. I have argued (Scaltsas 1992a) that, contra the Sellars (1955) line of interpretations, the premises of the Third Man Argument are committed to a *necessary* falsehood, even if they avoid the Vlastos (1954) contradiction.

understanding the problems that will be addressed by Aristotle in his mature metaphysics. Significantly, the problem is not resolved by the distinction between two types of predicate into natures and features. This distinction could be introduced within the Platonic metaphysics, and it was introduced in Aristotle's *Categories*, but it did not solve the problem. The problem is not how a special group of properties attaches itself inextricably to the subject. This would in fact presuppose the difference between the subject and its nature and merely establish the intimacy between these two distinct entities. The problem is to show how a subject, which is some kind of thing, is that kind of thing *in itself*. It is to show that the *nature-feature* distinction is, in fact, the *subject-feature* distinction.

None of the four reasons for positing partakers that we examined provides compelling grounds for keeping them in the ontology. But not all these reasons emerge clearly and distinctly in Plato's theory, so that it is not easy to determine whether Plato thought them compelling and to what degree he considered the partakers negotiable items of his ontology. Possibly, the minimalist description of a partaker in the *Timaeus*, far from reifying located bare substrata, is Plato's gesture toward ridding his theory of the ontology of partakers. However this may be, these reasons for positing underlying partakers of one sort or another surface in Aristotle's metaphysics. As we see in Appendix 2, Aristotle does not introduce characterless substrata in his ontology. But that is only a negative result. In the remainder of the book I will focus on providing Aristotle's positive accounts of handling the problems of the *particularity* of substances, the *unity* of the various components of a substance into a whole, and of the formation of a *subject* that is a *nature*, showing how the resolution of these metaphysical problems does not lead Aristotle to the positing of any item in the ontology to play the role that the partaker played in Plato's ontology.[29]

29. Before leaving the subject of Plato's partakers, I would like to introduce a note arguing against R. E. Allen's construal of the relation between partakers and Forms and the dangers that he thinks Plato's position is threatened by (1983, 116). Allen argues that if a Form is distributed to many partakers, this will ultimately result in the existential subjugation of the Form to these partakers, because each part of the Form will be unique to the partaker that has it, and hence existentially dependent on the partaker. By why should that be so? It is not true that if a part requires a participant to be identified, the part is unique to the participant. Using Plato's example, we can see that a part of the sail need not be unique to the person that happens to be under it at a time. The same part can be individuated by the presence of a different person under it. Nor is the sail existentially dependent on the persons under it.

For further links between the concept of subject and the Platonic corpus—specifically *Theaetetus*—and for an excellent discussion of further difficulties surrounding the Platonic conception of subject, see Matthen (1986a:166–171).

# 4 | The Substantial Form

## 1. A Substance and Its Parts: Plato's Legacy

Aristotle was not the first philosopher to pose the question of the relation between a substance and its parts, nor was he the first philosopher to give an answer to it. In the context of the search for a definition of knowledge, Plato posed this question in the *Theaetetus*. It appears as part of a complex argument, which is presented as Socrates' Dream (*Theaetetus* 201e–206b). The argument is a reductio ad absurdum, and its structure is the following. The initial hypothesis is that a complex whole is knowable (by the account of its parts), whereas simple elements are not knowable. Then, *either* the whole is identical to its parts *or* the whole is different from its parts. If the whole is identical to its parts, the parts are as knowable as the whole, which contradicts the initial hypothesis. If the whole is not the same as the parts, then *either* the whole has parts, *or* it does not have parts. If it has parts, it will be identical to its parts, which contradicts the supposition that it is not the same as its parts. If it has no parts, it has no account, and so the whole is as unknowable as the simple elements, which contradicts the initial hypothesis.

Twice in the reductio Plato claims that a whole is the same as its parts. The first instance is a hypothesis and the second a proof. In the first instance Plato says: "[Socrates:] do we say that a syllable is both its letters, or all of them if there are more than two? . . . [Theaetetus:] All the letters" (203c4–7). In the second instance, Plato has supposed that the whole is not the same as its parts and, furthermore, that it does have parts (out of which it is constituted, 204a8–10). Here he attains the conclusion that contradicts the hypothesis by providing an argument showing that the whole is identical to its parts. He says the following:

> [S:] Is a sum at all different from all the things? For instance, when we say "one, two, three, four, five, six," or "twice three," or "three times two," or "four plus two," or "three plus two plus one," are we talking about the same thing in all these cases, or something different? [T:] The same thing. [S:] Namely six? [T:] Yes. . . . [S:] So in the case of anything which consists of a number of things, it is the same thing that we're referring to when we speak of the sum and when we speak of all the things? [T:] Evidently. (204b10–d3)

Plato takes this to be conclusive, as is further evident from his summary of this argument, where he says: "it has turned out that all the parts are the same thing as the whole" (205d9–10).

But Plato also briefly considers an alternative to the identity of a thing to the parts that constitute it: "But perhaps . . . a syllable is, not the letters, but some one kind of thing which has come into being out of them: something which has one form of its own, and is different from the letters" (203e3–5). "So the whole doesn't consist of parts" (204e8). A complex would be some absolutely single kind of thing, not divisible into parts (205c2). With astonishing metaphysical intuition he concludes that: "If it's not the case that a complex is its elements, then isn't it necessarily the case that it doesn't have the elements as parts?" (205b1–2). According to Plato then, *a complex will either be identical to its parts or, if it is over and above its constituents, they cannot be parts of the complex.* There is no way, in Plato's conception, for the complex to be constituted from parts, on the one hand, and to be different from the totality of them, on the other.[1] We shall come back to this mereological position when examining the views of a contemporary advocate of it—David Lewis.[2]

Aristotle was acutely aware of the problem of the unity of a substance and of the relation of a substance to its parts, which were so clearly articulated by Plato in Socrates' Dream. Aristotle addresses the problem in *Metaphysics*

---

1. See also my discussion of the contrast between the Platonic and Aristotelian positions on the *composition* of a whole out of its parts (Scaltsas 1990, especially pp. 583–586). Myles Burnyeat has offered a different reading of the Platonic position. He finds that in the Dream, the mereological position introduced by Plato is Euclid's conception of numbers (Burnyeat 1990, 206). Furthermore, Burnyeat concludes that Plato's own position is the rejection of the Euclidian (mereological) composition and aligns with Aristotelian substantial composition (pp. 207–209).

2. For the origins of mereology, see D. Lewis 1991, 72–73.

Z, 17, and takes a different position from the Platonic one, which provides the foundation for his conception of substance. We saw that Plato considered the following possibility in Socrates' Dream: "Perhaps we ought to have laid it down that a syllable is, not the letters, but some one kind of thing which has come into being out of them;[3] something which has one form of its own, and is different from the letters" (*Theaetetus* 203e2–5). Plato argued against this position, claiming that the complex thing is the same as its parts. Aristotle addresses precisely the same question in *Metaphysics* Z, 17, and gives the answer that was rejected by Plato. He therefore owes us a counterargument to the Platonic one, which he indeed provides.

## 2. The Aggregate Argument

When I examined elsewhere the answer that Aristotle gives in *Metaphysics* Z, 17, I concentrated on how this answer provides an existential argument for the substantial form in a substance, showing that a substance is over and above its material parts.[4] This answers why, for instance, these planks are a house and these letters a syllable and provides Aristotle's answer for the unification of the constituents of a substance into a single entity. However, I now realize that the position Aristotle develops in Z, 17, is of much broader application than this. It does not address only the unity of wholes of physical parts. It also addresses the question of the unity of *any* whole that has come together from parts, each of which can be *singled out* independently of the whole (whether or not it can be physically separated from it). Hence, it addresses the question of the unity of a subject with its properties. (Properties cannot exist separately from their subject, but they can be singled out independently of their subject: they are separate, not physically, but in definition.)

The connection between the *part-whole* relation and the *subject-property* relation can be appreciated by first turning to Plato's metaphysics. We saw in Chapter 3 that, although Plato needed an account of the formation of a subject with a determinate nature in order to explain certain modalities in things in the world,[5] he did not have a way of deriving such an account from his theory. The relation of participation in the Forms could explain (if

---

3. ἐξ ἐκείνων ἕν τι γεγονὸς εἶδος.
4. Scaltsas 1985b, 228–230.
5. E.g., that this fire can never become cold.

anything) the presence of a property in a thing, but it could not differentiate between the property *belonging* to the subject (with a nature) and the property *determining the nature* of the subject. In the *Timaeus* the partaker has no nature of its own, in order not to prejudice which Forms the partaker can participate in. Thus, a thing is the partaker plus the (Immanent) Forms in it.

Now, if Plato had argued in Socrates' Dream that a substance is over and above its constituents, he would have faced a problem that his metaphysics was not rich enough to resolve. Participation in Forms could not give him the metaphysical tools with which to justify such a claim. All participation can account for is the attachment of the (Immanent) Forms to a partaker, not the emergence of a nature. Plato can offer no account of how an *eidos* would emerge from the copresence of various items, thereby giving rise to a substance that is not identical to its parts—which is what Plato envisages as an alternative to his position: a whole (e.g., a syllable) being "some one kind of thing which has come into being out of them [the letters]: something which has a form [*eidos*] of its own, and is different from the letters."[6] Platonic participation results just in the attachment of (Immanent) Forms to a partaker. It can explain the copresence of several (Immanent) Forms, but it does not begin to address the transformation of a group of items into a whole that is different from the items. The thing that is generated, therefore, is no more than the copresence of the (Immanent) Forms in a location (which is the partaker). The thing is the sum of its copresent properties.

Plato's stance on the part-whole question is that the whole is identical to the sum of its parts. Having no metaphysical mechanism to generate anything that is over and above the sum of the parts, Plato explicitly opts out for the identity of a thing to the sum of its parts in Socrates' Dream. But he does consider the possibility that "a syllable is, not the letters, but some one kind of thing which has come into being out of them; something which has one form of its own, and is different from the letters" (*Theaetetus* 203e2–5). The fact that Plato does consider the possibility of the creation of a whole that is over and above the constituents that make it up does speak for Plato's sensitivity to the possibility of there being a *subject* that is *generated* in a thing, with a nature that determines what the thing is. But that he does not pursue the possibility of the whole being over and above the parts must be the result of his failure to explain, through his theory of participation, the generation of a subject with a nature in a thing.

6. *Theaetetus* 203e3–5.

It should come as no surprise (although it, in fact, was to me) that when
Aristotle argues in Z, 17, that the substance is over and above its constituents, his solution has wider implications for the unity of a substance. It
should come as no surprise, especially as Aristotle tells us explicitly, in Z,
17, how wide the scope of the question he is answering is. The general
question Aristotle is posing in this chapter is: "why does one thing attach to
another?"[7] This is the most fundamental metaphysical question, as it addresses the very constitution of a substance. The question is about the
metaphysical relation of *belonging to a subject*: "why something is predicable
of something."[8] This includes such questions as why a man is musical, why
a man is such and such an animal, why a noise is thunder, why this flesh and
bones are a man and these bricks a house.

The part-whole relation, which Plato addressed in Socrates' Dream, deals
with the relation of *constitution*: how the parts constitute the whole. Most of
Aristotle's examples fall under that category, and, in fact, the way he frames
the question just before he answers is, as well as the argument he does
develop in answering it, falls under this category, too: "Why the matter is
some individual thing, e.g., why are these materials a house?"[9] Indeed, the
example he considers in giving the answer is a typical example of the
relation of constitution: two letters that constitute a syllable. But there can
be no doubt that he takes the answer he gives to be an answer to the general
question he has been reframing from the beginning of the chapter. The
chapter begins as an investigation into the nature of what substance is, and
it is in this context that the question "Why does one thing attach to
another?" (1041a11) is first framed (e.g., why is "musical" attached to
"man"? [1041a13–14]). Aristotle proceeds to explain that the question is
"why something is predicable of something" (1041a23) and, again, that
"the inquiry is about the predication of one thing of another."[10] What he is
looking for, he continues, is the cause of something being something, not
in the sense of what the efficient cause is (i.e., what made this into that),
but in the sense of what is responsible for this thing's being what it is
(1041a27–32). He is looking for the cause of being,[11] which in some cases
is the same as the final cause of the substance.[12] This cause of being, he

7. διὰ τί ἄλλο ἄλλῳ τινὶ ὑπάρχει, 1041a11.
8. τί ἄρα κατά τινος ζητεῖ διὰ τί ὑπάρχει, 1041a23.
9. τὴν ὕλην ζητεῖ διὰ τί <τί> ἐστιν, 1041b5–6.
10. ἄλλο γὰρ . . . κατ' ἄλλου ἐστὶ τὸ ζητούμενον, 1041a25–26.
11. αἴτιον . . . τοῦ εἶναι, 1041a31–32.
12. τίνος ἕνεκα, 1041a29.

concludes at the end of the chapter, is the *ousia* of each substance (1041b26–31). Clearly, then, the theme of the whole chapter is the role that the *ousia* of each substance plays in the determination of the cause of the substance's being what it is. The answer Aristotle gives addresses all the various forms that the question can—and does—take in this chapter, which go beyond the scope of question of how this matter constitutes this substance; they concern the general metaphysical question of *what it is for something to belong to a subject*, whether it be matter or property. I first examine the argument as given in Aristotle's answer and then show how his answer addresses this general question.

I refer to this argument as the *aggregate argument* [13] (1041b11–31). In outline, it says the following. Consider any complex whole, such that the parts constitute a single whole, not as a heap, but like a syllable is a single whole. Then the whole cannot be identical to the aggregate of its parts. The reason why is that if we disperse the parts, we still have the aggregate of the parts, but we do not have the whole any more. This shows that the whole is over and above the aggregate of the parts. But it cannot be over and above the aggregate of the parts by an element that is like the parts, because then the same argument would apply again. The new aggregate (of the parts plus the extra part that is supposed to turn the original aggregate into a substance) is preserved when its parts are dispersed. But the substance is not preserved when the parts are dispersed. Hence, adding a further element to the original aggregate of elements will not deliver a substance. Rather, what is needed is an extra item that will make the difference between the aggregate of the parts and the substance by turning the aggregate into a single whole. The whole, which does not survive the dispersal of the parts, is the substance. What is lost on dispersal is what unifies the parts into a substance. This unifier is what differentiates a substance from an aggregate of parts. So, Aristotle concludes about it: "It would seem that this is something [*einai ti touto*], and not an element [*stoicheion*], and that it is the cause [*aition*] which makes *this* thing flesh and *that* a syllable. And similarly in all other cases. And this is the substance [*ousia*] of each thing; for this is the primary cause [*aition prōton*] of its being. . . . [the] substance [of natural objects] . . . is not an element [*stoicheion*] but a principle [*archē*]" (1041b25–31). Positing such an entity—the *ousia* or substantial form of a particular substance—is the solution of the problem of the unity of the

---

13. This is the name I used in my discussions in Scaltsas 1985b, 228–230 and Scaltsas 1992c, 196–198. The reasons for the choice will become clear in what follows.

parts of a substance into a single whole. At the same time, however, it introduces a host of questions and problems that I address in the sections and chapters that follow. These questions are the following: Is the substance of a thing a relation, considering it is posited to unify the material parts in the substance? How is it related to the parts in the substance? How is it related to the subject of that substance, how to the essence of the substance and, finally, to the accidental properties of the substance?

### 3. Is the Substantial Form a Relation?

It would be a serious misunderstanding of Aristotle if we took him to be claiming in Z, 17, that the substantial form is a relation. As early as the *Categories*, Aristotle classifies relations under a nonsubstance category, the category of the relative. [14] In *Metaphysics* N, he argues that "the relative is least of all things a real thing or substance, and is posterior to quality and quantity. . . . For there is nothing either great or small, many or few, or, in general, relative, which is many or few, great or small, or relative without being so as something else" (1088a22–29). At *Nicomachean Ethics* 1096a20–22 he says that "that which is *per se* [*kath' hauto*], i.e., substance [*ousia*], is prior in nature to the relative (for the latter is like an offshoot and accident of what is [*tou ontos*])." The argument here must be that, because (as we just saw) the relative needs something to be the relative of, or to be relative to, it cannot ultimately depend on a relative, because then the existential dependence would go on to infinity. It must therefore be dependent on something nonrelative. Because the per se are precisely those things that are what they are in virtue of themselves, [15] as opposed to being so in virtue of some other, [16] they are paradigmatically suited as the termini for the relative's dependence. Because, furthermore, as we will see in Chapter 7, the *kath' hauta* (per se) are the subjects (as opposed to being affections of subjects) in a substance, the relatives that depend on them can be thought of as characterizing them (e.g., "being small" can be thought of as an accident

14. See Ackrill (1963, 78, 98) for his explanation of how relations come under the relative. Ackrill also refers to the distinction Aristotle makes in *Metaphysics* Δ between a relation and the relative: "further, there are the properties in virtue of which the things that have them are called relative, for example, equality is relative because the equal is, and similarity because the similar is" (1021b6–8).

15. καθ' αὐτά, 1031b12–14.

16. κατ' ἄλλο, 1031b12–14.

of man). Thus, far from being substances themselves, the relatives are seen to be accidents of substance. [17]

Aristotle's arguments, then, that relations are not substance rest on the claim that something has a relation qua being something other than that relatum (e.g., *x* is double *y*, in relation to being so high, or so wide, or so heavy). In *Metaphysics* Z, 17, Aristotle claims that the substantial form is what unifies the material parts into a single whole. Does this mean that the substantial form is a relation between the parts it unifies? If that is what Aristotle's solution consists in, then Aristotle is reducing the substance category to the category of relations, which we saw he denies elsewhere in the corpus. I will offer an argument showing why, despite the *unifying* role that the substantial form plays in a substance, it is *not* a relation.

My argument relies on the distinction between an aggregate, a related whole, and a substance. Let us first consider an aggregate. An *aggregate* consists of a number of unrelated items. Borrowing an illustrative example from David Armstrong, we can see that the aggregate of all the soldiers in an army consists of the soldiers, regardless of how they are structured into groups in the army. Thus, Armstrong says, "the aggregate of all armies is identical with the aggregate of all soldiers." [18] Similarly, suppose we divide a class of students into four teams to play volleyball, but only into two teams to play football. Then, the aggregate of the volleyball teams is the same as the aggregate of the football teams, that is, the students in the class. Aggregating different entities together does not unify them into groups or a complex whole. The aggregate is not a single entity; it is the many things that it is the aggregate of: the aggregate of ten soldiers are the ten soldiers. The identity of an aggregate is determined only by the identity of its members, not by the subgroups these members may constitute. Aggregating different entities together does not subjugate their identity to the identity of a further entity, such as a whole. Rather, aggregation of entities has no effect on the identity of these entities.

---

17. Or accidents even of nonsubstance, as Aristotle states at *Meta.* 1088a24–25. Aristotle offers a further argument why relatives are not substance: "An indication that a relative is least of all a substance and a real thing is the fact that relatives alone do not come into being or pass away or change in the way that increase and diminution occur in quantity, alteration in quality, locomotion in place, sheer coming into being and passing away in the case of a real object" (*Meta.* 1088a29–33). Ross (1924, 1:473) explains this as follows: "There is no distinct kind of change which can be called change in respect of relation, as there is change in respect of substance, quality, quantity, and place."

18. Armstrong 1980a, 31.

Second, consider a number of entities related to one another. A *related whole* is different from the aggregate of the very same entities, because the related whole has structure, whereas the aggregate consists of the entities without their interrelation. The difference between a whole of juxtaposed books and the aggregate of the same books is the following: groups of juxtaposed books do not necessarily form a group of juxtaposed books, but aggregates of books always make up an aggregate of books. Thus, although each of the books on the shelves of a library belongs to a series of juxtaposed books, all the library's books do not make up a single series of juxtaposed books. On the contrary, if each shelf has an aggregate of books, all the aggregates of books in the library make up a single aggregate of books.

Third, let us consider a substance that is composed of many material parts. How is it different from the *aggregate* of these parts? And how does it differ from a whole that consists of these parts *related* in a particular way? That the aggregate of the parts of a substance is not the same as the substance was shown in the argument of *Metaphysics* Z, 17: if we disperse the parts, the aggregate survives but the substance does not. The difference, according to Aristotle, is that the parts in the aggregate are unrelated to one another, whereas the parts in the substance are unified into a whole by the substantial form. So the dispersal of the parts does not affect the aggregate, but it destroys the substantial whole. Hence, a substance is not the aggregate of its parts.

Is the substance, then, an interrelated whole? Is there a difference between the parts being unified by the substantial form and the parts being related by a relation? Is the substantial form a relation? My claim is that there is a difference between a substantial form and a relation, which has to do with the identity of the resulting whole. The difference is that the parts that are unified by the substantial form surrender their identity to the substantial form, whereas the items that are related by a relation retain their identity intact. Consider the ten juxtaposed books. The books do not surrender their identity to the related whole. The ten juxtaposed books are many. Their individuality is not threatened by their interrelation. Juxtaposition is predicated of each book without contributing to the individuation of the book. The books do not acquire their identity from the juxtaposition. On the other hand, the items that are united by a substantial form do not retain their identity. Rather, *the identity they have as parts of the substance is derived from the role they play in the substance, which is determined by the substantial form.* This is a theme that we will examine from different perspectives in Aristotle's metaphysical theory, and it probably constitutes the most fundamental claim of Aristotle's substantial realism. A substance is not its many material parts, but a single entity (unlike the related books that, even when related, remain many books).

The material parts from which a substance is made acquire their identity in the substance by the contribution they make to the substance. In the case of a living being, Aristotle says: "The soul of animals (for this is the substance of living beings) is their substance according to the formula, i.e., the form and the essence of a body of a certain kind (at least we shall define each part, if we define it well, not without reference to its function) . . . [the parts] cannot even exist if severed from the whole; for it is not a finger in *any* state that is the finger of a living thing, but the dead finger is a finger only homonymously" (*Meta.* 1035b14–25). What Aristotle says here is that if a component of the whole is severed from the whole, the severed item acquires a different identity from the one it had when integrated in the whole. The severed finger is not a finger; it becomes a finger only as part of the whole functional organism. This passage has usually been related to Aristotle's functionalism and its relevance only been considered when the notion of a functional end is pertinent, that is, when "being integrated into the whole" translates into the acquisition of certain capacities for the performance of a task in which these capacities are used. Thus, the functional contribution of a component to the whole determines the identity of the component in the whole. However, that function unifies the parts into whole by issuing to these parts their identity is an instance of a more general logical truth. In other terms, what is required for the unification of several different entities into a single whole is that there be a principle that determines their integration into the whole by reidentifying them in accordance with the contribution they make to the whole. The contribution of each part could be toward a function performed by the whole, or it could be toward the whole *being what it is*. So long as these merging entities do not keep their identity and individuality when they join the whole, but are reidentified by the principle that determines the contribution their presence makes to the whole, the result will be a single, unified whole rather than a related whole or an aggregate of entities. In the latter two cases the entities retain their individuality and they make up a *whole of many* rather than a unity of one. So, *the unification of a set of entities into a single entity is achieved by the reidentification of these entities on the basis of a principle determining their role in the whole.* With no reidentification, these entities retain their individuality and they remain a plurality of many rather than become a single entity.

The identity of the whole is determined by the principle which unifies the parts from which the whole is composed, by reidentifying these parts. The *reidentification* of the parts as they join the whole marks the difference between a relation and a substantial form. The *relation* does not, unlike the *substantial form*, provide for a new identity of the constituent parts.

Aristotle posits the *ousia* in Z, 17, as that which makes the difference between a substance and the aggregate of the parts from which it is made up. He does not discuss the nature of the *ousia* other than to say that it is a principle [*archē*, 1041b31] and a cause [*aition*, 1041b26]. I propose that we can understand the *ousia* of a substance as the principle that furnishes the criteria for the reidentification of the parts it unifies into a whole. In the *Physics* Aristotle realized that the explanation of a natural phenomenon may rest on the *effects* of the phenomenon. David Furley argued that for Aristotle the phenomena of the frequency of rain in the winter and its rarity in the summer are to be teleologically explained in terms of their *effects* in nature. [19] In the *Metaphysics*, Aristotle realized that the explanation of what a part of a substantial whole is rests on the *effect* of its presence in the whole, that is, the contribution it makes to the whole. This contribution is dictated by the form, which thereby acts as a metaphysical glue for the substantial parts, not by clustering them together or by relating them to one another, but by providing the principle that generates the whole through the reidentification of the merging parts.

## 4. The Threshold Argument

In *Metaphysics*, H, 3, Aristotle offers another argument, which I call the *threshold argument*, that reaches the same conclusion as the aggregate argument of Z, 17. The conclusion is that there is something in a substance that is not one of its component parts, but is a different sort of entity, which is the cause of being—and substance (i.e., the substantial form)—of the particular substance: "but there is something [in man] besides these, if these are matter—something which is neither an element in the whole nor produced by an element [*oute de stoicheion out' ek stoicheiou*][20] but is the

19. David Furley 1985, 177–182.
20. οὔτ' ἐκ στοιχείου should be understood as "nor made out of *many* elements." This is the point also made in *Metaphysics* Z, 17, aggregate argument, when Aristotle says: εἰ μὲν στοιχεῖον . . . εἰ δὲ ἐκ στοιχείου, δῆλον ὅτι οὐχ ἑνὸς ἀλλὰ πλειόνων (1041b22–23, my emphasis).

substance [*hē ousia*]. . . . If then this is the cause of the thing's being [*aition tou einai*], and if the cause of its being is its substance [*ousia*], they cannot be stating the substance itself" (1043b11–14).[21] This conclusion was reached in Z, 17, but through a different argument. The argument here is very compressed. I first offer an analysis of the reasoning in it, which, contrary to Ross, I take to be cogent.[22] I then relate the point the argument turns on to the interpretation I offered of the unifying role of the substantial form.

The way Aristotle introduces the argument indicates where he wants to place the emphasis: "If we consider, we find that the syllable is not constituted from the letters plus composition, nor is the house bricks plus composition" (1043b4–6).[23] Aristotle's argument appeals to our intuitions, by the use of examples, to show us that a substance depends on its form in a way that it does not depend on any of its component parts. The general line of the argument is the following. If a substance is an aggregate of elements (namely, the aggregate containing the substance's parts and form), then the substance will depend on the form in the way it depends on the parts. But it does not depend on the form in the way it depends on the parts. Hence, it is not an aggregate of the parts and the form. Consider, for example, an aggregate of items *a*, *b*, *c*, and *d*. The aggregate *is* items *a–d*, and it does not depend on any one of them differently from the way it depends on any other. But this is not the case with the form of a substance. Consider a threshold. Its position makes it into a threshold (being responsible for the threshold's functional properties): *ho oudos thesei* [*oudos*] (1043b9). However, in the case of the aggregate, none of items *a–d* determines what the aggregate is.[24]

---

21. The text of the last sentence is corrupt. I prefer Ross's rendition of it (which he follows in the translation): εἰ οὖν τοῦτ᾽ αἴτιον τοῦ εἶναι, καὶ οὐσία τοῦτο, αὐτὴν ἂν τὴν οὐσίαν οὐ λέγοιεν, 1043b13–14. This parallels the conclusion of the parallel argument in Z, 17: οὐσία δὲ ἑκάστου μὲν τοῦτο (τοῦτο γὰρ αἴτιον πρῶτον τοῦ εἶναι) (1041b27–28).

22. Ross 1924, 2:231.

23. Barnes's translation (1984) with my amendments.

24. Each item plays a role in the determination of *which* aggregate this is, but not in *what* the aggregate is. We cannot derive what the aggregate is from *any* member of the aggregate. It is for this reason that Aristotle stresses that the threshold is derived from the position οὐκ ἐκ τοῦ οὐδοῦ ἡ θέσις ἀλλὰ μᾶλλον οὗτος ἐξ ἐκείνης (1043b9–10). If the threshold were an aggregate of items, the position being one of them, then the threshold would not be derived from the position any more than item *a* determines *what* the aggregate of *a*, *b*, *c*, *d* is. But what the threshold is *is* derived from the position.

οὐκ ἐκ τοῦ οὐδοῦ ἡ θέσις could mean that the position of the threshold is not made up of the planks that make up the threshold (Ross 1924, 2:231; see next note). But this would be an unusual way of expressing it, as both in this and other contexts Aristotle expresses the thought that the substance form is not made up of elements, not by saying that it is not made up of the substance itself (here the threshold), but by saying that it is not made up of

Hence, the relation of the threshold's position to the threshold is different from the relation of element *a* to the aggregate of *a–d*.[25] Hence, the threshold is not an aggregate of parts plus the position, nor, more generally, is a substance an aggregate of the parts plus the form.[26]

---

στοιχεῖα (1043b12, 1041b19–21—see also 1043b7–8 in one of its readings—see following note). A more plausible reading is the following. If the threshold were an aggregate of constituent parts, including the threshold's form among them, then we should always be able to derive the position from the threshold in the way we can derive its component planks from it. But moving the threshold elsewhere will not make that place the bottom of the door—i.e., we shall not be able to derive the position from the threshold, because it would not be a threshold any more. Hence, the position is not like a member of an aggregate (which would have survived displacement).

25. Ross's attempt to read the word ἐκ with the constitutional meaning even in its occurrences in the sentence of 1043b9–10 cannot be justified by the Aristotelian argument. The sentence is the following: εἰ ὁ οὐδὸς θέσει, οὐκ ἐκ τοῦ οὐδοῦ ἡ θέσις ἀλλὰ μᾶλλον οὗτος ἐξ ἐκείνης. Ross translates and explains in his commentary: " 'The position is not made up out of the threshold' (i.e., out of the material parts of the threshold, cf. l. 7, ἐκ τούτων ὧν ἐστι σύνθεσις), 'but rather the threshold is constituted by the position' " (1924, 2:231). (See notes 24, 25 for a discussion of the first part of this sentence on this reading.) If that were what Aristotle meant here, then he would be telling us that the threshold is made up of the position as a constituent part (as Ross wants to retain the ἐκ in the sense of constitution). But that is precisely what Aristotle denies in the next sentence when he says that the substance of man is οὔτε δὲ στοιχεῖον οὔτ᾽ ἐκ στοιχείου (1043b12). If the threshold were made up out of the position, then the position would be a στοιχεῖον of the threshold. But then, Aristotle would be contradicting himself in these two lines, because on the one hand he denies that the substance of something is a στοιχεῖον in that thing while on the other he affirms that the threshold's substance is a στοιχεῖον out of which the threshold is made up. Clearly Ross's reading cannot be the intended one, and his claim (against Bonitz) that "the use of the ἐκ in two quite different senses is most improbable" cannot sustain his reading it in the constitutive sense in this sentence.

26. In some details, my present reading of this argument differs from the one in my article (Scaltsas 1985b, 230 and n. 69). Regarding the expression ἐκ τούτων at 1043b7, it can be read in two ways, and so can, correspondingly, the whole sentence οὐ γάρ ἐστιν ἡ σύνθεσις οὐδ᾽ ἡ μῖξις ἐκ τούτων ὧν ἐστι σύνθεσις ἤ μῖξις. In the first reading, the sentence is saying that composition and mixing are not themselves items from the bunch (the sort) of items that make up the composition and the mixing, e.g., that composition is not an item from the sort that can be composed, such as bricks or planks. (Bonitz's reading, see Ross 1924, 2:231.) The second reading of ἐκ τούτων parallels the use of ἐκ in the preceding sentence (οὐ φαίνεται δὴ ζητοῦσιν ἡ συλλαβὴ ἐκ τῶν στοιχείων οὖσα καὶ συνθέσεως), as well as its use two sentences below (ἀλλά τι δεῖ εἶναι ὅ παρὰ ταῦτά ἐστιν, εἰ ταῦθ᾽ ὕλη, οὔτε δὲ στοιχεῖον οὔτ᾽ ἐκ στοιχείου). Here the expression connotes constitution, and what the original sentence (1043b7–8) would be telling us on this reading would be that composition and mixing are not made up from the elements that are composed or mixed. If they were so made up, then they might be the same sort of things as the things they are composed of (in the way that a stone is the same sort of thing as the stones that are produced when we break it up). On both readings, the point that Aristotle would be getting across is the following:

In both arguments, the present one and the aggregate argument of Z, 17, Aristotle insists that the substantial form is not a further component part in a substance, but is of a different ontological type from the component parts. In so doing, Aristotle is presenting us with his own theory, but at the same time he is offering a criticism of the Platonic metaphysics. Let us first identify the Platonic problem. Addressed with the question: What is it that unifies a particular substance into a single entity of this or that sort? how would the Platonist respond? Saying that a partaker participates in many Forms (e.g., of the Form of Man, of the Large, the Small, the Just, etc.) will not secure much more than the copresence of all these Forms (or their Immanent Forms) in the partaker. Each item retains its nature (the partaker included) while being copresent with the rest. Hence, the unity of such an agglomeration of elements is no more than the unity of an aggregate of Immanent Forms and of the partaker. Let us apply to it the aggregate argument of Z, 17. Suppose we dispersed the Immanent Forms and the partaker of a given particular substance.[27] We would still have the aggregate of all these items, but not the substance. Hence, the substance is not just the aggregate of the items. There must be another item in the substance, over and above the elements of the aggregate, that is responsible for the presence of the substance.

Suppose the Platonist response is that the partaker is unified into a whole by also participating in the One, which accounts for the unity and oneness of that substance. This would not help, because the Immanent Form of the One in that partaker would simply be another element in the aggregate. If dispersed, the aggregate would be preserved, but the substance would be destroyed. Suppose, then, that the Platonist suggested that all the Imma-

---

Composition and mixing should not be treated as further elements of the same sort as the component parts of the substances that are composed or mixed, because composition and mixing are different sorts of entity from these parts (as the example of the threshold subsequently displays). The recognition of a difference in kind serves as an introduction to the next point Aristotle makes, namely, that the relation between composition or mixing and the substances that have them is different from the relation between an item in an aggregate and the aggregate. (Although Ross reads ἐκ τούτων in the second of the ways suggested, he finds that it makes no sense and that the "reasoning is inconsecutive" in this passage.)

27. Some versions of the Theory of Forms would allow this, particularly if they were designed to account for each human soul as an Immanent Form of the Form Soul (e.g., Socrates' soul, the Immanent Form of Soul in Socrates, could be separated from the rest of Socrates). Ultimately, we will see that it is not just *physical* separation that threatens the oneness of a substance. If the items into which it is divided are even *definitionally separable*, separable as abstract entities, then an account of the substance's unity is still needed. See Section 5 of this chapter.

nent Forms in a particular substance, plus the partaker, are unified into a single entity by participating in a Relational Form that unites them with one another. (Fundamentally, such a Form would be playing the role of a relation of Predication, or of Partaking, because it would be uniting the partaker and the properties into a single whole. As we have seen, Plato does not posit such a Form, nor does he offer a metaphysical account of participation to distinguish it from the mere copresence of partaker and Immanent Form.[28] Again this would be of no help, because participation in the Relational Form would only result in one more Immanent Form being present in the substance, which would be dispersed along with the rest of the elements, and the argument would apply again.

What is needed, in order to impede the further application of the aggregate argument, is a unifier that will *not* be a further element (of the same type as the rest of the elements) in the aggregate (1041b25–26). Plato did not see the need for this unifier, which is further verified by his commitment to the claim that a whole is identical to the parts (see Section 1 on Socrates' dream in the *Theaetetus*)—the very claim that is denied by Aristotle's aggregate and threshold arguments. Platonic metaphysics can only provide participation in more Forms, as an attempt to attribute unity to a substance. But participation in more Forms is nothing other than the addition of more Immanent Forms in cluster of Immanent Forms in the partaker. This will not produce unity in the cluster any more than adding more elements to an aggregate will turn the aggregate into a unified substance (which Aristotle rejected in Z, 17, at 1041b19–25, and again in H, 3, at 1043b12–13).

It is this Platonic predicament that Aristotle is alluding to when he says in *Metaphysics* H, 3: "Nor is man animal and biped, but there must be something besides these, if these are matter [*ei tauth' hulē*]—something which is neither an element in the whole nor produced by an element, but is the substance, which people[29] eliminate and state the matter. If then this is

---

28. Thinking of participation as mere copresence allows Plato to avoid Zeno's paradox in worldly objects. The paradox is avoided, because the Immanent Forms do not affect the nature of the partaker, but simply come to be present in it. (Which is why, as we saw, Plato insists, even as late as in *Timaeus*, that the nature of the receptacle remains intact despite participation in the Forms.) Of course this creates problems for Plato, because he cannot explain why a fire cannot be cold or the Form of the Cold be hot (by participating in the Hot), even though Socrates can be large and small.

29. I agree with Alexander 522.19, that the people referred to by Aristotle are Platonists. Ross (1924, 2:232) thinks that the allusion is general to a common practice of describing a unified whole as merely a sum of parts. But it would be a very strange choice of

the cause of the thing's being, and if the cause of its being is its substance, they cannot be stating the substance itself" (1043b10–14). Aristotle is envisaging that the component parts of a particular substance are the Immanent Forms in it, which would function as the matter of which the substance is composed. But they have to be unified into a single substance, and the unifier, Aristotle says, cannot be a further element of the same kind as them. Hence, what is needed is not further participation in Forms, but an entity of a different type, which will be the cause of the thing's being and its substance.[30]

## 5. The Trope-Overlap Argument

The problem of the unity of a substance remains even if the aggregate is an aggregate of *abstract* components. In the case of the matter and the form of the substance, which are components derived by abstraction, the aggregate argument would be applied as follows: Let us assume that a substance is the aggregate of its matter and form. Now, the matter of a substance (e.g., the wood in a pine tree) can survive in another substance (e.g., a statue). The form of the pine tree (i.e., being a pine tree) also exists in other pine trees.[31] But the original pine tree does not exist after we make the statue out of it. Hence, it is possible for the matter and the form of the pine tree to exist without the tree existing, which means that the pine tree *is not the aggregate* of its matter and form.[32] Furthermore, the tree is not matter plus

example—that man's parts are "biped" and "animal"—if Aristotle wanted to refer to a commonplace belief.

30. Ross does not see that this example is aimed directly at the Platonists for their singular failure to accommodate in their metaphysics an account of the unifying element of each substance (which participation in Forms cannot effect). Ross says that the people (referred to in this passage) who omit mention of the substance form when defining a substance are not the Platonists: "What people? Alexander suggests the Platonists. But a reference to them is out of place. Aristotle is dealing in this chapter with the common tendency to describe a whole as a sum of parts of materials, omitting the principle of unity" (Ross 1924, 2:232). What Ross does not realize is that this is precisely the result of participation in Forms: a whole that is just a sum of parts—without any principle of unity.

31. There is some affinity between the argument I am developing here and one used by David Armstrong (1991). Armstrong's argument has to do with the truth maker for the proposition "*a* is F," which requires more than the existence of *a* and F.

32. As we will see, the solution Aristotle offers is that the substance is not an *aggregate* of matter and form. Rather, form is a principle, and the components that go into the makeup of the substance are potentially what that principle stands for.

form plus some further *element*, because the same argument would apply again. What is required is that one of the items not be an element in the aggregate but a principle that unifies the rest.

It might be thought, however, that if there are *individual forms*, the aggregate argument does not go through. To make the case even stronger, let us assume that a substance's properties cannot exist in other substances—they are tropes, peculiar to the substance they belong to[33]—and they cannot be dispersed, because they cannot survive the loss of the substance. I offer an argument, which I call the *trope-overlap argument*, to show that a substance is over and above the aggregate of its copresent, particular properties (i.e., Aristotelian substances are not bundles of tropes). Let us consider the aggregate of Socrates' properties and assume that all these properties are particular. Not being universal, the properties do not exist in other substances, and therefore the argument presented in the preceding paragraph would not go through.[34] Let us furthermore include among Socrates' properties second-order relations, that is, relations between some first-order properties, for example, the relation of the necessary copresence of color and weight. It follows that the relational properties would not survive the dispersal of the first-order properties (even if that was not necessitated by the nature of the tropes). Hence, the aggregate of Socrates' properties would not survive the dispersal of its members. Therefore, the aggregate argument cannot be applied to the aggregate of Socrates' tropes to show that the aggregate of tropes is different from Socrates.

It is *not dispersal* that will show the difference between this aggregate of copresent, particular properties and Socrates, but *overlap*. For Aristotelian physics let us assume the overlap of a sponge, which is submerged in water, and the water in the location of the sponge. For contemporary physics, we can use the overlap of Socrates and the neutrinos that shower through him all the time. The properties of the water and of the sponge make up an aggregate of copresent properties, as do the properties of the neutrinos and Socrates. (The properties in each aggregate are not necessarily copresent. But then, even the sponge's properties are not all necessarily copresent with one another, as the sponge can survive change.) Consider, then, the aggregate of the properties of the sponge and the water. Why is that aggregate

33. For a development of the individuation of objects in terms of tropes, see Campbell 1990 and Bacon (forthcoming).

34. It was there assumed that the form of "pine tree" of this tree also exists in other pine trees.

two things and not one? Similarly with the aggregate of the properties of
Socrates and of the neutrinos. Why are they not just one substance, but
many? (That we can separate the water from the sponge or Socrates from the
neutrinos cannot help us answer the question. It could be that the initial
aggregate is a single substance that divides into water and sponge, or into
Socrates and neutrinos, very much like an amoeba divides into two. The
possibility of separation is equally compatible with the existence of, initially, only one or of more than one substance. Hence, the possibility of
separation of the aggregate cannot help us answer the question of whether
the aggregate is one substance or many.)

If a substance is an aggregate, then two copresent substances will make
up a single substance (considering that two aggregates make up a single
aggregate). But there is no single substance that the sponge and the water
make up or that Socrates and the neutrinos make up. Hence, the sponge and
the water or Socrates and the neutrinos are not aggregates of properties. In
more general terms, a substance cannot be an aggregate of copresent properties. A substance must differ from an aggregate by something other than a
further element, because this would still leave the substance as an aggregate, only with more elements in it. A substance must differ from an
aggregate by something that will unify the substance in a way that an
aggregate is not unified. The way a substance is unified must explain why
two substances do not make up a single substance, even though two aggregates make up a single aggregate.

We saw that the distinction between an aggregate and a substantial
whole remains even when the constituents of a substance are taken to be the
substance's particular properties—tropes. It follows that the unification of
a substantial whole cannot consist in adding a further property (e.g., a
particular relational or a structural property) to the aggregate of the substance's particular properties. That would simply augment the aggregate of
properties (e.g., by a particular relational property), but not unify it into a
whole.

The aggregate argument, the threshold argument, and the trope-overlap
argument lead us to conclude that the unity of a substance into a single
entity requires the positing of a substantial form. These are existential
arguments that give the reason for positing substantial forms as well as at
least a partial characterization of the type of entity the substantial form is.
But there is much more we have to investigate to uncover the nature of this
entity. The aggregate argument is couched in the general framework of the
question of the unification of material parts by a unifier. But Aristotle's
further allusion to the Platonic account of concrete substances (1043b10–

14) instructs us to conceive of matter in the broadest possible sense—as anything that would play the role of the constituents of a concrete substance, whether it is material stuff or Immanent Forms. The problem that Aristotle is addressing is the general question of a component belonging to a whole, whether the component is conceived of concretely or abstractly. Aristotle tells us in Z, 17, that the question he is addressing is "Why does one thing attach to another? [*dia ti allo allō tini huparchei*]" (1041a11). The foundational weakness of Platonic metaphysics is that it offers no account of the relation of *belonging to a subject*, other than the *copresence* of properties that is the result of participation in Forms. But *copresence produces aggregates, not substances*. It is because of the generality of the question of the unity of a substantial whole (i.e., a component belonging to a subject) that Aristotle treats the question of the relation of "being musical" to "man" (1041a13–14) as the same question as the relation of "being in the clouds" to "sound" (1041a23–25) and "being a house" to "bricks and stones" (1041a25–27). He explains that he is not looking for a cause of what brought all these changes about (i.e., the efficient cause), but for the cause of the being (*aition tou einai*, 1041a31–32) of these unions to answer which is to give the cause of their oneness. It is to give an account of how *predicating one of another results in a single substance*, rather than a related plurality or an aggregate of several items.

It follows that the *ousia* Aristotle posits in the aggregate and the threshold arguments as the cause of the being of a particular substance is the element that is responsible not only for the unity of the *material parts* into a single whole, but for the unity of any type of metaphysical component into which the substance can be analyzed. The trope-overlap argument confirms the need for such a unifier. The substantial form is responsible for *all unity within a substance* of any components whatsoever that *belong* to the substance. In the following chapters I further investigate how this is achieved and what it reveals about the nature of the substantial form.[35]

## 6. Structural Universals and Substantial Forms

So far we have examined the existential arguments for the substantial form. In this section I pursue a defense of the Aristotelian substantial forms against arguments propounded by two contemporary metaphysical realists,

35. For accounts of the existential arguments for the substantial form, see also Witt 1989, 112–126; Gill 1989, 116–120; and Waterlow 1982a, 58–66.

David Armstrong and David Lewis. My purpose is to support Aristotle's existential claim for substantial forms, distinguish them from Armstrong's structural universals, and show that Lewis's alternative treatment of substances does not pay justice to our intuitions about substantial unity.

### (A) Armstrong's Argument against Substantial Forms

David Armstrong argues against Aristotelian substantial forms on different fronts. His main objection is that they serve no metaphysical purpose and, hence, that there is no reason to posit such universals. The principle he advocates is that only the properties that endow particulars with specific causal powers should be allowed into a (realist) ontology.[36] He argues that we do not need to posit a property such as "being an electron," since such a property does not add any causal power to the particular that has it, which that particular does not already possess on account of the other properties it has. Thus, Armstrong says, "Suppose that a particular has all the properties which are required for something to be gold or an electron. Will it not be gold or be an electron? Why postulate some further universal which it must exemplify in order to be gold or an electron?" (1980b, 62). Thus, Armstrong does away with substantial forms in his ontology.

Although Armstrong's theory enables him to account for the causal properties of a particular, it is not clear how he would handle the problem of the unity of the particular, which, as we have seen, was Aristotle's motivation in positing the substantial forms. Armstrong is aware of the need to resolve this problem, and he posits nomic connections. These are second-order properties between first-order properties: "nomic connections between . . . [the] properties [of gold or of an electron] which bind the properties up into a unity" (p. 62). As I have suggested elsewhere,[37] the effect of Armstrong's excising substantial forms from his ontology is moderated by the fact that he allows for nomic connections between properties. There are similarities in the metaphysical role of nomic connections and of the substantial form. Both aim to differentiate a substance from a mere cluster of properties, but they are also different. Specifically, Armstrong explains that "in nomic connection one universal necessitates another. *F-ness* necessitates *G-ness*" (1980b, 149). This establishes a bond of necessary

36. Armstrong (1980b 11). A very interesting discussion of the philosophical origins of the emergence of form is presented in Mourelatos 1984b and 1987.
37. Scaltsas 1985a, 210.

copresence between properties in a substance of a kind that we also encountered in Plato's account of the subtle causes (Section 1 of Chapter 3). But necessary copresence is different from unity, and to that degree Aristotelian substances enjoy a higher degree of unity than Armstrong's substances, because "belonging to a subject" is different from "being copresent."[38] One way in which we can illuminate the difference is by focusing on the difference between a substance and a related whole. Copresent universals, even if they are necessarily copresent, are a related whole, related by the nomic connections. I argue in Chapter 5 that a substance is not an interrelated whole of copresent universals. Rather, a substance results from the unification of the universals by the substantial form into a whole. As we will see, the unity achieved by a substantial form, which will become clear when we discuss the unification of the properties of a substance into a whole, is very different from that secured by the nomic connections.

Armstrong must realize that necessary copresence is not a sufficient condition for the unity of the properties in a substance, because, having rejected substantial forms, he introduces a *Principle of Particularization*:

> Although Essentialist Realism {i.e., Aristotelianism} has been rejected, it does seem that it has an element of truth. . . . It is the truth that for each particular, there exists at least one monadic universal which makes that particular just one, and not more than one, instance of a certain sort. Such a universal will be a "particularizing" universal, making that particular *one* of a kind. Without such a universal, the particular is not restricted to certain definite bounds, it is not "signed to a certain quantity," we do not have a "substance," we do not have *a* particular.[39]

Having rejected substantial forms and then introduced particularizing universals, Armstrong appears to be admitting into the system what he has previously discarded. But there is a difference between the two, and Armstrong explains it as follows: "What will the particularizing universals be? I can see nothing which is *always* available except the *spatio-temporal pattern* possessed by the total or spatio-temporal position of the particular involved" (p. 64). Such a space-time worm, says Armstrong, "need not 'divide its instantiations' in the full-blooded way that, say, *being an electron* yields a number of discrete electrons" (p. 64).

38. Scaltsas 1985a, 210–211.
39. Armstrong 1980b, 64.

As we will see, the individuation of substances according to Aristotle requires that one refer to their spatiotemporal location. But that does not imply that substances are individuated as Quinian spatiotemporal worms.[40] The substantial form provides the identity criteria for the determination of the spatiotemporal limits of a substance, whereas the Principle of Particularization needs external (to it) criteria for the determination of these limits. Therefore, the Principle of Particularization must be supplemented by further criteria in order to demarcate the spatiotemporal extent of a substance. When thus supplemented, the only difference, I believe, that will remain between a substantial form and the Principle of Particularization would be the account of the internal unity of the substance.

### (B) Lewis's Argument against Substantial Forms

One type of universal that Armstrong introduces into his ontology is a structural universal. He defines it as follows: "A property, S, is structural if and only if proper parts of particulars having S have some property or properties, T, . . . not identical with S, and this state of affairs is, at least in part, constitutive of S."[41] He offers as an example the universal "being a hydrogen atom"; a particular hydrogen atom would have a proper part that is an electron and a proper part that is a proton; having such parts is constitutive of being a hydrogen atom. Structural universals are particularizing universals.[42]

Armstrong does not pursue the concept of a structural universal any

40. I am not certain that I have a complete grasp of the content of a particularizing universal, but to the degree that I do understand it, it would seem to me that it would compete with Armstrong's requirement that only properties that endow the particular with causal powers will be admitted into the ontology: "If a particular has a property, that property must endow the particular with some specific causal power" (1980b, 11). Being a spatiotemporal form would not endow that form with causal powers (over and above the powers the thing has on account of its other universals), and hence particularizing universals cannot make a claim in the ontology of scientific realism.

41. Armstrong 1980b, 69.

42. Ibid., p. 70. Armstrong says that a structural universal "need not be a *strongly* particularizing property" (ibid., p. 70). A strongly particularizing property is, for example, "being a man," and a weakly particularizing property is, for example, "being one kilogram of lead" (ibid., 1:117). Particularizing universals such as "having a certain spatio-temporal pattern" are introduced as *weakly* particularizing universals (ibid., 2:64). I wonder whether allowing for structural properties such as "being a hydrogen atom" or "being two electrons," which are strongly particularizing universals (ibid., 2:69–70), is compatible with the rejection of substantial forms qua strongly particularizing universals.

further. It is David Lewis who offers an extensive analysis of three different renditions of what such a universal could be and of the shortcomings of each of the three versions. Of the three, it is the third, the one that Lewis calls the *magical conception of structural universals*, that I wish to examine in detail, as it is the one that corresponds to Aristotelian substantial forms. Lewis describes the structural universals on the magical conception as follows: "On the magical conception, a structural universal has no proper parts.[43] It is this conception on which "simple" must be distinguished from "atomic." A structural universal is never simple; it involves other, simpler, universals. . . . But it is mereologically atomic. The other universals it involves are not present in it as parts. Nor are the other universals set-theoretic constituents of it; it is not a set but an individual.[44] There is no way in which it is composed of them."[45] The example he offers is that of the methane universal. Such a structural universal is over and above the universals it involves (i.e., the universals Hydrogen, Carbon, and Bonded). It is not an aggregate of three universals, not even a group of interrelated universals, but a single, unified entity. This is precisely what we have seen the substantial form to be. Its instances are single, unified wholes, not aggregates, or pluralities of interrelated items.[46] This is just the requirement that Lewis makes of structural universals when he describes them as being *individual* and *atomic*.

The crippling difficulty that Lewis finds with this rendition of the structural universals is a modal one. How can we explain that every instance of the universal Methane *must* consist of instances of Hydrogen, Carbon, and Bonded? If the latter universals were *parts* of the universal methane, then we would have an explanation of why methane's instances involve their instances. But it is essential in this rendition of structural universals that they not be aggregates or collections of parts: they are not a mereological sums of parts, but unified, individual, atomic wholes. The idea here is that the three universals, Hydrogen, Carbon, and Bonded, submit their individuality to the universal methane, and therefore they do not figure in methane

43. Armstrong's definition of structural universals (ibid., 69) did not require that the universal have proper parts, but only that the particular that instantiates the universal have such parts.

44. Here "individual" means a single entity, whether universal or particular. Lewis is contrasting an individual to a set, which, as we will see, Lewis considers to be a plurality.

45. Lewis 1986a, 41.

46. What we showed is that the substance form cannot be a relation, because "being a related whole" is not sufficient for being unified in the way that a substance is unified. Thus, if the substance form is only a related whole, its instances, the substances, would be related wholes rather than substantial unities.

as themselves; so, we cannot explain why methane's instances must involve their instances:

> Therein lies the magic. Why *must* it be that if something instantiates *methane*, then part of it must instantiate *carbon*? . . . on the present conception, this necessary connection is just a brute modal fact. . . . What is it about the universal *carbon* that gets it involved in necessary connections with *methane*? Why *carbon*? Why not some other universal, say *rubidium*? After all, the universal *carbon* has nothing more in common with the universal *methane* than the universal *rubidium* has! They are three distinct atomic individuals, and that is that. . . . Although we understand just what necessary connections are supposed to obtain, we are given no notion how they possibly could. I might say that the magical conception carries an unacceptable price in mystery; or perhaps I would do better to deny that there is any *conception* here at all, as opposed to mere words.[47]

Before coming to Aristotle's defense in view of Lewis's argument against a conception of structural universals as unified wholes (i.e., as substantial forms), it would be helpful to have a broad overview of the alternative positions. Lewis's intuitions on the subject of the whole-part relation agree with Plato's intuitions on the subject. As we have seen (Section 1), Plato identified a whole with its parts. Consistently with this, Plato explicitly rejects the position that a whole is over and above its parts. So does Lewis. He claims that a set is not a whole over and above its parts, but is identical to its parts. What follows from this is that such a whole *has parts*—since it *is* its parts. What it does not have is unity; it is plural, like an aggregate of parts, rather than like an atomic or individual entity.[48] Aristotle, on the other hand, argued that a whole is not identical to its parts. Consistently with this he showed that a whole is *over and above* its parts. Through the *aggregate argument* he showed that the substantial form unites the parts of the whole—the substance—into a single, atomic, though complex, entity. What follows from this is that *a whole* (which is over and above its parts) *does not have its constituents as parts*. This is a point on which all four philosophers, Plato, Lewis, Aristotle, and Armstrong, agree.[49] We saw that this is what Lewis's argument against structural universals as atomic individuals turns

---

47. Lewis 1986a, 41–42.
48. In fact, Lewis proposes that "it might be better to flout grammar and say that the set *are* where its members are" (ibid., p. 32).
49. Scaltsas 1990, 583–585.

on: because they are atomic individuals, they have no parts; so for instance, the universal carbon is not part of methane, in which case how can a carbon atom be part of a methane molecule? This is also what Plato states explicitly in the *Theaetetus* passage we analyzed: "If it is not the case that a *complex* is its elements [i.e., the complex is not identical to its parts], then isn't it necessarily the case that it doesn't have the elements as parts? . . . So . . . a *complex* would be some absolutely single kind of thing, not divisible into parts."[50] I will show in the following section that Aristotle, too, adheres to this position. In general, all four philosophers agree on what the two alternatives are and what the consequences of each alternative are, but they do not all follow the same alternative. Plato and Lewis treat a whole as being identical to its parts; Aristotle and Armstrong treat a whole as being over and above its constituents, which it cannot have as (mereological) parts.

## (C) Wholes and Their Parts in Aristotle

My purpose in the present examination of Aristotle's position of the part-whole relation is to show, first, that Aristotle agrees with Plato and Lewis that if the whole is over and above the parts, the whole does not have parts; second, that Aristotle does have an answer to the modal challenge posed by Lewis to account for the necessary connection between the substantial form and all the universals it involves. I discuss the first issue in this section and the second in the following section.

*(i) The Material Parts of a Substance.* Let us first consider the parts into which a substance can be cut up. We have seen that for Aristotle, when a concrete substance is divided into parts, the parts we get can at best be homonymous with their corresponding counterparts in the uncut substance. Thus, if we sever a finger from a person, the detached finger is only homonymously a finger; that is, it has the name of a finger but not the definition, and hence it is not a finger: "For they [the parts] cannot exist if severed from the whole; for it is not a finger in *any* state that is the finger of a living thing, but the dead finger is a finger only homonymously" (*Meta.* 1035b23–25).[51] The reason why Aristotle claims that the detached finger has a different definition of being from that of the live finger is because it has

---

50. *Theaetetus* 205a12–b2, 205c2, my emphasis.

51. "When things have only a name in common and the definition of being which corresponds to the name is different, they are called *homonymous*" (*Cat.* 1a1–2).

neither the capacities nor the function of the live one. With respect to
capacities, "it is not a hand in *any* state that is a part of man, but the hand
which can fulfill its work, which therefore must be alive; if it is not alive it is
not a part" (*Meta.* 1036b30–32). By being a finger or hand that can fulfill
its work, Aristotle means that, not only must they be alive, but also they
must be attached to the organism in the appropriate way. Having the
function of the live finger requires that the finger be attached to the whole.
That is, even if the detached finger remained alive and did not deteriorate
when detached, it would still not be a finger; the reason is that it would not
have the functional properties of a finger, determined by its relation to the
organism. The functional properties are acquired by the role that the finger
plays in the whole of the organism, which the finger cannot play if it is
detached from the organism. Aristotle says that "the semicircle is defined
by the circle; and so is the finger by the whole body, for a finger is such and
such a part of a man" (1035b9–11). It therefore follows that what a finger is
depends on the relation that the finger has to the whole body. Therefore, a
finger must be incorporated in the body in the appropriate way in order to
perform the function of the finger for that body. Hence, the detached finger
is not a finger and, consequently, not the sort of thing from which a person
is made up. On the contrary, for Lewis "a hand that is in fact part of a body
might have existed on its own . . . and something that is intrinsically just
like the hands that are parts of bodies might exist without being part of a
body."[52]

Of course, the detached finger can be a part of the person, not as a
functional part, but as a material part: the person is constituted of chunks of
matter such as the one that we get by cutting off a finger. In fact, that is how
Aristotle treats such items as the detached finger: "the concrete thing is
*divided* into these parts [of the body] *as its matter*" (1035b21–22, my
emphasis). The aggregate argument directly gives us the reason why such
material components into which the concrete substance can be divided are
not parts of the concrete substance. These material elements do not figure in
the concrete substance because they are united by the substantial form into a
single entity. As we saw with the difference between an aggregate, a related
whole, and a substance, the components into which a substance can be
divided submit their individuality to the whole. That is why the substantial
form does not reduce to a relation, because the relation leaves the individuality of the related parts intact; they do not become one, but remain many

52. Lewis 1986a, 43.

interrelated items. On the other hand, in a substance, we do not have a plurality of related parts, but a single entity that acquires its unity from the substantial form. Thus, the material parts that we get by dividing up a substance come into existence when we divide up the substance, thereby destroying it. They do not exist when the substance exists any more than rain drops exist in a lake: "the parts of animals [are only potentialities] (for none of them exists separately; and when they *are* separated, then they too exist, all of them, merely as matter)" (1040b6–8). So, whereas in the substance, the parts are more than matter by their role in the whole, when separate, they are not these parts, but mere matter.

*(ii) The Functional Parts of a Substance.* Material parts exist potentially in a substance, and they come into existence when functional parts, or any parts of the substance, are separated from it. What, then, of arms and legs and brains that are not detached? Aren't these parts of an animal while the animal is alive? If we call them parts, they are certainly not parts in the sense in which an aggregate or a related whole have parts. The parts of an aggregate or of a related whole are identified independently of the aggregate or of the whole, whereas the functional parts of a substance are defined in terms of the whole substance. Although there can be gradations of signifi-cance of a functional part to the whole, depending on the function of the part and the significance of the function on the whole (e.g., the heart versus nails), all functional parts will require reference to the whole for their identification.

To understand the significance of the fact that a functional part is defined in terms of the whole, we need to draw some distinctions. There are different cases where the definition of $x$ mentions $y$. For example, the definition of an acute angle mentions a right angle. But this does not establish an existential connection between this acute angle and any right angle.[53] Similarly, if the definition of a bulldozer requires mention of large objects, the bulldozer does not existentially depend on these objects. But the relation of an arm to the person it is attached to is not like either of the forementioned relations. The arm *is* existentially dependent on the person. So, the definitional dependence of a functional part on the whole must entail an existential dependence. Similarly, it is not any existential depen-

---

53. At *Meta.* 1034b28–32, Aristotle is discussing the relation of a *part* of a right angle to that right angle, not of an acute angle to right angle. For a discussion of parts mentioned in the definition, see Gill 1989, 126–128.

dence of $x$ on $y$ that captures the dependence of a functional part on the whole. For example, one can be existentially dependent on the match not being struck, without being functionally dependent on it. It is only when *existential* dependence entails *definitional* dependence that we have the kind of dependence of a functional part on the whole. I call the interentailing definitional and existential dependence of a functional part on the whole *identity dependence*. For a part $x$ to be what it is, the whole $y$ must be what it is. It follows that $x$ cannot be related to $y$ in the way that a member of an aggregate is related to the aggregate or a member of a related whole is related to the whole. In both cases the part is identity *independent* of the whole. But in the case of a substance $y$, a part $x$ is identity dependent on $y$. Therefore, $x$, as a functional component of $y$, cannot be related to $y$ as a mereological part of it, because it does not have an independent identity from $y$.

This analysis leads us to a criterion for the distinction between parts and other types of component of substances:

*Mereological-Part Principle:*

If $x$ is a mereological part of $y$, $x$ is identity-independent of $y$.

(In what follows, by "part" I will mean mereological part, unless otherwise stated.) We are not here concerned with the dependence of the whole on the part, but rather the converse. Now, mereological parts are identity-independent of the mereological fusions of these parts. In general, parts of aggregates and parts of related wholes (i.e., the relata) are identity-independent of the wholes. On the contrary, functional parts of wholes are identity-dependent on the wholes and are therefore not mereological parts of them.

A substance, then, for Aristotle, is not composed of mereological parts but of functional parts. This does not mean that we cannot segment it, thereby producing distinct parts from it. It means that these severed parts do not exist *actually* in it. In summary, neither the matter from which the substance originates, nor the matter into which it perishes can be a part of a substance, because they are reidentified by their integration into the substance. On the other hand, whatever exists in the substance is identity-dependent on it and in that sense a functional part of it. Thus, for Aristotle a substance is constructed out of constituents, but these constituents are all unified by the substantial form, becoming identity-dependent on the whole. The unification of the substance, for Aristotle, requires the destruction of the constituents and the creation of a single individual, the substantial whole. It is in this sense that Aristotle is in agreement with Plato, Armstrong, and Lewis that if the substance is over and above its constituents, the substance does not have these constituents as (mereological) parts. But Plato (see Section 1 of this chapter) and Lewis think that the whole is not over and above its constituents; so these constituents are identity-independent of the whole. Lewis's reasons for rejecting the existence of a whole over and above all the parts are given in his modal paradox, which we examined.

## 7. The Aristotelian Solution to David Lewis's Paradox

In simple terms, Lewis's intuition in his modal paradox can be captured by the following example. If one has a whole cake, which is a single, atomic but complex individual, one does not have any cake pieces. If one has all the pieces that were cut up from the cake, one does not have a cake any more but many pieces. One thing that is certain is that one cannot have both the cake and the pieces at the same time. Yet, this is what Aristotelians want to have when they make the modal claim that Methane has a modal connection with *hydrogen*. They treat Methane as a single, atomic individual, which is unified and has no parts. However, they take Methane to have Hydrogen as a part in order to explain why a methane molecule has hydrogen parts in it. It is like wanting the cake whole and cut up into pieces at the same time: wanting the Methane universal to be an atomic individual *and* the Hydrogen universal as a part. To avoid the irrationality, says Lewis, one of the claims must be given up. Because we need to justify the modal connection between Methane and Hydrogen, we have to give up the claim that Methane is an atomic individual. That is, we have to give up the claim that Methane is a substantial form that unifies the constituents into single individual (as opposed to relating a plurality of parts). If a substance is a mereological fusion of parts (rather than an Aristotelian substantial whole), we can see why the substance will have a modal connection with its parts. The existence of the whole does not threaten the individuality of the parts. Rather, the parts exist in the whole as independently identifiable items and, hence, the methane molecule will exist as an aggregate of the hydrogen and carbon atoms in it.

Not so for Aristotle. He is not willing to give up, with Plato and Lewis, the unifying role of the substantial form. A substance is not a plurality of many parts but, rather a single, unified whole. Therefore, an account must be offered within his system that justifies the modal relation between, let's say, Methane and Hydrogen.

This account is offered to us by Aristotle's theory of substratum, which we examined in Chapter 1. According to Aristotle, if we abstract the substantial form away from the substance, what remains is an underlying substratum. This underlying substratum is an abstraction; it *is not* the initial components out of which the substance was created. For example, if we abstract away the substantial form of a bronze statue, the remaining substratum is a *quantity* of bronze, not a *lump* of bronze (like the initial one from which the statue was made).[54] The *quantity* of bronze *receives* the form of the statue, and together they make up the statue. On the contrary, the initial *lump* of bronze is *transformed* into a statue by giving up its form of "being a lump" and becoming a statue.[55] Now, suppose that we initially start with a lump of bronze, a lump of gold, and an ivory piece, out of which we make a single statue. If we abstract the substantial form of the resulting statue, the remaining substratum is not a lump of bronze, a lump of gold, and a piece of ivory. Rather, the substratum is the aggregate of the following abstract entities: the quantity of bronze, the quantity of gold, and the quantity of ivory, from which the statue is constituted. So, the initial lumps give up their identity when they submit to the substantial form and become unified into one entity, the statue. The lumps give up their lumphood, so to speak, before they can become the statue. What the lumps and the statue share is the quantity of matter in them.

It is important to realize that we do not reach the substratum by physical separation of the substance. By that I mean that the substratum is *not* the elements that result from severing the substance. This would be the aggre-

54. The term "quantity of matter" is Cartwright's (1970), but the concept is Aristotle's (see Scaltsas 1985b, 218–219). Cartwright describes the relation of the gold in the ring to the gold as follows: "if . . . the ring is coated with some black substance, then the ring is black and the gold is not. The ring may be more valuable than the gold of which it is made or vice versa. The ring may bear someone's initials or be stuck on someone's finger; the gold . . . does not in such circumstances bear anyone's initials, and it is not stuck on anyone's finger. The ring is circular, the gold is not; the gold has an atomic structure, the ring has no such structure" (Cartwright 1972, 375).

55. That a lump is a "low-grade" substance form does not mean that it is not a form. In Aristotle's system, it is a *privative form*, that is, a form that is either the result of the deterioration of the substance form of a substance or, more generally, the outcome of chance causes in nature that result in an entity that does not belong to any of the substance species. See Chap. 1, n. 15, and Chap. 2, n. 6.

gate of the elements of the substance, not the substratum. Let me use the statue example. The aggregate of the lump of bronze, the lump of gold, and the piece of ivory is neither the statue nor the substratum underlying the statue. The substratum is the aggregate of the *quantities* of bronze, gold, and ivory. When we abstract the substantial form from the statue, we get the three quantities, not the three lumps. The three lumps are each of the three quantities *plus* the form *lump* for each of them. Hence, the substratum is not what we get by destroying the composition of the substance, because what we get then is concrete lumps, not abstract quantities.

There is therefore no sense in which the lump of bronze is in the statue. Only the quantity of bronze in the lump is also in the statue. But we certainly believe that there is a necessary connection between the statue and the lump of bronze, because the one is made out of the other.

Aristotle does provide an explanation for the modal relation between the initial lump of bronze and the bronze statue: the lump of bronze and the bronze statue share the same material substratum, the quantity of bronze that is in both. Aristotle recognized that it is not the presence of the lump of bronze in the statue that is the only possible way of justifying the modal connection between the lump and the statue. That the statue shares a *quantity* of bronze with the lump establishes a modal connection of origin between them.

To answer Lewis's paradox, a further question must be addressed. Is the relation between the hydrogen atom and the methane molecule like the relation of a thing and the substance it becomes? Not necessarily. It all depends on whether a methane molecule is a substance or a related whole. As we have seen, there is a spectrum, on one side of which are substances and on the other side of which are the related wholes and aggregates. Consider the ten juxtaposed books. This is a related whole, not a substance, and as such, the relata retain their individuality in the whole. Now the question about a methane molecule is whether it is like a human being or like the ten juxtaposed books. Lewis has made the tacit assumption that it makes no difference to the identity of a hydrogen atom whether it is part of a molecule or not. This implies that, whatever else he says about the methane molecule, he is making an assumption about it, an assumption that is characteristic of related wholes. That is, incorporation into the whole does not affect the identity of the part. If we agree with Lewis's assumption that the presence of a hydrogen atom in a molecule has no effect on the identity of the hydrogen atom, then the explanation of the modal connection between the hydrogen atom and the methane molecule will be along the lines of the explanation of the presence of a book in the juxtaposition: a relatum of a related whole. What would have to be rejected, which would also resolve the paradox, is that the methane molecule is an atomic individual (i.e., an Aristotelian substance). On the other hand, we may disagree with Lewis and treat the incorporation of a hydrogen atom into the methane molecule like the incorporation of a graft into a living organism. In that case, the explanation of the modal relation between the hydrogen atom and the methane molecule will be different, because, for example, the incorporation of the graft into the whole will reidentify it in terms of the role it plays in that whole. In this case, the claim that will be abandoned, thereby avoiding the paradox, will be that the incorporation of the hydrogen atom into the molecule leaves its identity intact. Rather, the incorporation will give rise to an atomic individual, the methane molecule, and the modal relation between it and the hydrogen atom would be one of origin. I suppose that in the case of the methane molecule, the answer we would give nowadays is that for chemistry it is an atomic individual, whereas for physics it is a related whole.[56] Such an answer would mean that it is not a paradigmatically Aristotelian substance, after all. Each of the par excellence Aristotelian substances, natural organisms, has a single essence.

## 8. Universality Requirements on the Substantial Form

We have so far examined the existential arguments for substantial forms, objections to them, and responses to the objections, as well the central role that the substantial form fulfills in a substance. Although I will return to the examination of the unifying function of the form, in the present section I turn to two further considerations in Aristotle's metaphysics, which will help us understand the nature of the substantial form.[57] These are two fundamental Aristotelian doctrines that require the *universality* of the substantial form: that the form is definable, and that it is knowable.

### (A) The Substantial Form Is Definable

Aristotle says in *Metaphysics* Δ, 8, that "the essence [*to ti ēn einai*], the formula of which is a definition [*horismos*], is also called the substance [*ousia*] of

---

56. Putnam 1993, 339.

57. For an excellent discussion of the modal nature of Aristotelian essence, see Sorabji 1980, Chap. 12.

each thing" (1017b21–23). This position is reconfirmed in *Metaphysics* Z, 4: "definition [*horismos*] and essence [*to ti ēn einai*] in the primary and simple sense belong to substances" (1030b5–6) and in Z, 5, where he concludes that "only substance [*ousia*] is definable. . . . Definition [*horismos*] is the formula of the essence [*to ti ēn einai*], and essence must belong to substances either alone or chiefly and primarily and in the unqualified sense" (1031a1–14). In Z, 10, he explains that by form (*eidos*) he means the essence (*to ti ēn einai*) and that "only the parts of the form are parts of the formula, and the formula is of the universal" (1035b32–1036a1).

Aristotle does not simply assume the universality of the definable and, hence, of substantial form (which is definable in the primary sense), but he offers arguments showing that neither material nor immaterial particular substances are definable. His reason for claiming that material particulars are not definable is that their matter is not definable: "there is no formula of it [i.e., of concrete substance] with its matter, for this [the matter] is indefinite" (1037a27). By this Aristotle means that matter is the seat of the accidental in a substance, which, if it is accidental, is not subject to systematic scientific classification. Aristotle compares matter to the accidents of a substance, describing both of them as indefinite (*aorista*, 1049b1–2), presumably because it is true of both that they have contingent causes. The matter of the concrete substances of a kind could not be defined because of the indefiniteness of the changes it suffers throughout the substances' life span. But definition is not of the changeable and perishable, but of the universal, namely, of that which is the case in all (or most of) the particulars of a kind and is the proper object of scientific investigation (*Meta.* 1027a19–21, 1039b27–1040a2, and, e.g., *An. Post.* Book A, 14).[58]

Aristotle's proof in *Metaphysics* Z, 15, that immaterial substances are not definable applies to the Platonic Forms only. It will not concern us here, for it assumes, first, that particular substances are universals that belong to many (1040a25–27) and, second, that the components of a substance are separate substances (e.g., Animal and Biped of Man, 1040a18–21). Both of these premises are rejected in Aristotle's metaphysics. So such entities do not exist, and therefore there are no such candidates for definition. But, as we will see (Section 1 of Chapter 6), Aristotle does allow for immaterial substances, that is, the first causes of movement in the universe. Thus, in the case of the Prime Mover, his position is that it is particular and is immaterial. I argue (Sections 1–3 of Chapter 6) that this reduces the Prime

58. For a novel explanation of Aristotle's notion of ὡς ἐπὶ τὸ πολὺ (for the most part), see Moravcsik 1994.

Mover to its essence. Because the Prime Mover is particular, it would seem to follow that there is an essence that is not universal. But as an object of definition, it should be universal, according to Aristotle's present contention. Is this an exception to his claim that the object of a definition is universal?

Aristotle does not address this question, nor does he discuss the particularity of the Prime Mover in sufficient detail to extract an argument from it. The Prime Mover is the type of being whose essence could not belong to another substance. There could not be two Prime Movers, for then we could distinguish matter from form in the Prime Mover.[59] If so, generation and corruption of the Prime Mover would be possible, and, therefore, it would not be essentially eternal (see Section 1 of Chapter 6). Being *essentially eternal* requires being *necessarily actualized*—never being in potentiality. It is unclear to me whether it is appropriate for Aristotle to use the notions of actuality and potentiality for a substance that has no matter, for these notions are bound up in Aristotle's system with form coming to be in matter. But I will not pursue this issue any further, mainly because I think that there is very little that Aristotle gives us on the subject of the nature of the Prime Mover, and I do not find it fruitful to pursue this question independently of what he says.[60] One thing is certain, though, that even if the Prime Mover is the exception to the rule of the universality of the object of definition, nothing follows from this about all the other objects of definitions. The reason for this is that the claims about the Prime Mover that seem to force on us its definability, despite its particularity, are not true of other types of substance. So, we leave a question mark in the case of the Prime Mover, and say that in all other cases, the object of definition, that is, the substantial form of a substance, is universal.

In Z, 15, Aristotle argues that definitions are not of particular substances.[61] He says that if we gave a full description of a substance, for example, of the sun, that it is round, and bright, that it goes around the earth, and it is hidden at night, and so on, it would still be the case that all these attributes could be true of another substance (1040a29–b1 along with 1040a9–17). What Aristotle is saying here is that we can imagine another sun, which is numerically different from the actual one, of whom the

59. If there are more prime movers, they have to differ in essence, not in matter. See Section 4 in Chapter 6.

60. For a discussion of Aristotle on God and potentiality, see Sorabji 1983, 280–283. On necessary actualization, see Bogen's and McGuire's discussion of Aristotle on the rotation of the cosmos, *Cael.* I. 12, in Bogen and McGuire 1986–87.

61. 1039b27–30, 1040a6–7, 8–9, b3–4.

description of this sun would be true. In that case, such a description would still be of a universal, which is true of two different substances.

The fact that definition is of essential characteristics entails that the definition of a substance cannot comprise a full description of that substance. Thus, if we include in the definition of the sun the description of its movement and location, we would be committing the mistake of treating its movement and location as essential features of the sun, as if, if the sun stopped moving, it would no longer be a sun (1040a29–33). So, because the definition contains only the essential characteristics of a substance, the definiendum will be a universal, belonging to all the substances of the species.

In Z, 15, Aristotle aims to show that, although definitions are of what is always the case, nevertheless, definitions cannot be of *particular* substances, even if these substances are eternal, such as the Platonic Forms or the sun. As we saw, the argument he offers is that what a definition will describe will always be more universal than the particular substance and will belong to many, that is, to all the members of the species. Now, if what Aristotle believed was that definitions do not refer at all, he would not have exerted so much effort to show that definitions cannot single out particular substances. If definitions do not have a referential function according to Aristotle, there would be no question about definitions succeeding or failing in singling out a particular substance. Yet, Frede and Patzig attribute a *nominalist* position to Aristotle, claiming that definitions do not refer to universals, but are universally true of particular substances. This means that definitions have no referential function, but a different semantic role that would have to be somehow explained by employing a nominalist theory of predication.

Frede and Patzig attribute to Aristotle the position that the substantial form is particular. This is incompatible with Aristotle's claim that the substantial form is definable and, hence, universal. So, they aim to resolve the incompatibility by attributing to Aristotle a nominalist theory of definition. It is not, they say, that definition is *of a universal*; rather, definition is *predicated universally* of many particulars: "Eine Definition immer Definition von etwas Allgemeinem ist, nämlich insofern, als sie *allgemeingültig* ist, d.h. auf jeden Gegenstand derselben Art zutrifft; in diesem Sinne kann die Definition Definition von etwas Allgemeinem sein, ohne daß deshalb der Mensch oder die menschliche Seele etwas Allgemeines sind."[62] Frede and

62. Frede and Patzig 1988, 55, my emphasis. "A definition is always a definition of something universal, that is to say, insofar as it is universally applicable, meaning being true of every object of the same kind; in this sense the definition can be a definition of something universal without the human or the human soul being something universal."

Patzig do not provide the semantic analysis of definitions, that is, what it is to be true of many, but I assume they are employing a nominalist theory of predication, as we understand it in contemporary philosophy, according to which an account in terms of a linguistic entity, the predicate, is true of the referent of the subject. But there are no grounds for attributing such a position to Aristotle. There would be many ways to defend this, drawing from the corpus generally, and I offer one such defense from *Metaphysics* Z.

In Z, 10, Aristotle says that "a definition is a formula, and every formula has parts, and as the formula is to the thing, so is the part of the formula to the part of the thing" (1034b20–22). How could we give this statement, which describes the semantic features of a definition, a nominalist explanation? Somehow, we would have to defend the claim that, although the definition does not make reference to the thing or its parts, the linguistic structure of the definition corresponds, in some way, to the ontological structure of the thing. Even if we could understand this, it would be extremely odd for a philosopher to be putting forward a nominalist theory of definitions, that is entrenched in a superrealist account of language. On the contrary, Aristotle is assuming a correspondence between the definition and what it refers to and between the parts of the definition and the parts of the thing referred to. The thing referred to is a *universal* (for the reasons we have already examined), which Aristotle explicitly states: "by form I mean the essence. . . . Only the parts of the form are parts of the formula, and the formula is of the universal" (1035b32–1036a1). Furthermore, when Aristotle says that "definition is of the universal and of the form," how could we understand this to mean that definition is universally true of particular forms? The only (plausible) reading is that definition is true of the form, which is a universal.

### (B) The Substantial Form Is Knowable

Aristotle holds that "the essence [*to ti ēn einai*] is substance [*ousia*]" (i.e., substantial form) and that "there is knowledge of each thing only when we know its essence [*to ti ēn ekeinō*]" (1031b2–7).[63] He also holds that in the case of things that have "the nature of individuals, they will not be knowable; for the knowledge of anything is universal" (1003a14–15); "all knowl-

---

63. Owen even complains that talking of the essence, or *ousia*, of a thing as a cause might be a mistranslation of *aitia*, for which he would prefer a term suggesting explanation as well (1965a, 82).

edge is of universals and of the 'such' " (1060b20–21; for Aristotle's position on *Metaphysics* M, 10, see Appendix 4). Thus, for Aristotle, because the substantial form is knowable, it is universal. In this section, I offer three reasons that Aristotle gives in order to explain why the knowable is universal and why the particular is not knowable. In the following three chapters I will explain why to know a concrete substance is to know its substantial form.

A concrete particular is not knowable in the strict sense, because, as we have seen, *matter is indeterminate* and, as such, *unknowable*. "Matter is unknowable in itself" (1036a8–9), "for it is indefinite" (1037a27). The reason why matter is unknowable is that it is the seat of the accidental: "The matter . . . which is capable of being otherwise than as it for the most part is, is the cause of the accidental. . . . That there is no science [*epistēmē*] of the accidental is obvious; for all science is either of that which is always or of that which is for the most part" (1027a13–21). Because "sensible substances all have matter" (1042a25–26), it follows that sensible substances are not knowable. This argument would extend to eternal sensible substances as well.

A further reason why sensible substances are unknowable is that they are perishable. Sensible particulars "have matter whose nature is such that they are capable both of being and not being (1039b29–30). But more in general, the objection is that "perishing things are obscure to those who have the relevant knowledge, when they have passed from our perception" (1040a2–4; also 1036a3–7). The reason is that knowledge is of what is always the case: "that of which there is understanding [*epistēmē*] *simpliciter* cannot be otherwise" (*An. Post.* 71b15–16). Hence, whatever is perishable is unknowable in the strict sense. Of such particulars "there is no definition, but they are known by the aid of thought or perception; when they go out of our consciousness, it is not clear whether they exist or not; but they are always stated and cognised by means of the universal formula" (1036a5–8). Hence, if the substantial form were individual, it would perish with the substance it is the form of, and because it is perishable it would not be knowable (which would contradict Aristotle's position that the substantial form is what is cognizable in a substance). As the present argument extends to perishable entities only (material or immaterial), it does not address eternal material substances.

The final reason why knowledge is of the universal is one we have encountered before, that is, the argument from epistemological methodology (Section 2 of Chapter 2). Aristotle says: "how will it be possible to know, if there is not to be something common to a whole set of individuals?" (999b26–27). Only through repeated encounters with instances of *f*-ness or *g*-ness, which are universals belonging to many, can we identify them and come to know them. Hence, the object of our knowledge will be a universal.[64]

Thus, for understanding in the full sense, namely, scientific understanding, which requires systematic classification of the causes of things, the objects of knowledge will be universals and relations between universals. To the extent that concrete substances are subject to chance and accident, they will be the object of perceptual acquaintance and opinion (1039b32–1040a4), but not of knowledge. To the extent that they are subject to lawlike conditions of being and change, the causes of their being and change will be the object of knowledge in the strict sense. As such, the substantial form of a substance is the prime object of knowledge in a substance: "there is knowledge of each thing only when we know its essence" (1031b6–7), where "essence is substance" (1031b2–3) and as an object of knowledge it is universal.

64. See Modrak 1987, 162–168. See Wedin (1988, 118–119) for a discussion of knowledge being of the universal in connection with passages *DA* 417b22–24 and 431b26–432a1.

# 5 | The Unity of Substance

## 1. Abstraction and Separateness

Abstraction is a mental act in which we consider a particular substance without some of its components. For example, we can abstract the form of a bronze statue, thereby isolating mentally the form from the matter. Abstraction is not change. It differs from change in two fundamental respects. First, abstraction is a mental act, not a physical one. When we abstract a component away from a substance, nothing happens to the substance. Abstraction takes place in a mental representation of the substance. Second, abstraction is not the mental representation of physical change. There is a fundamental difference between abstraction and change. Change is understood by Aristotle in terms of the *replacement* of a formal component of a substance by another such component (the replacement of the privative form by the form, or vice versa). Thus, if a statue is dented or bent, its original shape is replaced by a different shape. If it is chipped, its weight and shape are replaced by different weight and shape. Socrates' nonmusicality is replaced by his musicality (see *Ph.* 191a6–19). But this is not the type of loss of component that is involved in abstraction. If a component of a substance is abstracted away, *nothing takes its place* (in our representation of the substance). It leaves behind a vacuum in the constitution of the original substance. That is, what is left of the original substance when we abstract away some component is not a substance. Thus, a statue can change by losing its shape and acquiring a new one, but it cannot *change* by losing shape altogether, being left neither well formed nor deformed. By contrast, we can *abstract* shape altogether from our representation of the statue. Thus, in change the lost components are replaced; in abstraction, they are not.

A substance cannot suffer in reality what it suffers in our representation of it when we abstract a property away from it, because that would leave the substance ontologically incomplete. What this means is that what properties a substance will possess is not arbitrary. Statues must have shape; we cannot physically take away their shape and leave the rest. Properties come in clusters in nature, and we are not in the position to *divide* or decompose these clusters. We can only bring it about that some of these properties in a cluster are replaced by others. Furthermore, what properties cluster together in nature is something we *discover* about reality. It is not within our power to create objects with weight but no shape or with temperature but no size.

That substances come in clusters of properties is captured in Aristotle's system by his notion of the *separateness* of particular substances: "none of the others [nonsubstances] can exist independently [*choriston*] except substance; for everything is predicated of substance as subject." [1] Being separate is not a further property a thing has, like being blue or being short. "Being separate" does not come under any of the categories of being. Rather, it is like "being one," or "being in existence," or "being a substance"; none of these are genera in the categorial hierarchy (*Meta.* 1053b22–24). If Socrates is a man, he is thereby a separate substance. He cannot be a man and not be separate. The clustering of properties into separate substances is the being of these substances. The separateness of a substance is nothing other than the being of the substance. A test that shows that separateness is not a property of a substance is that *we cannot abstract away separateness* from our representation of a substance. Given a representation of a statue, we cannot do with "separateness" what we can do with "shape," that is, abstract it away. We cannot abstract away separateness and retain all other properties of the statue. Similarly, we cannot abstract away just the oneness of a statue and retain all else about it in our representation of it. Ditto with "existing." On the other hand, the separateness of a represented substance will be lost when we abstract away any property of the substance. Thus, what is left after we abstract away the shape of a statue is not the representation of a separate substance.

Aristotle distinguishes ontological separateness from separateness in de-

---

1. *Ph.* 185a31–32, translation from Barnes 1984; see also 1042a29–31.

scription, to show that what we can separate out in description cannot always be separated out physically.[2]

## 2. Types of Abstract Entity

Suppose one is standing on a hillside and is able to discern a way to cross the thickly vegetated forest below. The path to follow is in the forest, but it is not delineated in any way other than in one's mind. The path is not a figment of one's imagination, but, nevertheless, it is traced only in that person's mind. This is the case with items abstracted from substances. They are not figments of the imagination, but are grounded in the substances themselves. What is characteristic of them is that they cannot be separated out but through the operation of abstraction in the person's mind. In Section 4 we will see wherein lies the realist element in the individuation of abstract entities.

There are different kinds of abstract entity in Aristotle's ontology. How many types of abstract entity there are is determined by metaphysical considerations. Separating out entities by abstraction needs to be argued for and to be justified. Such arguments are to be found in Aristotle's accounts of *change* and *individuation* of substances. We have examined in Chapter 1 Aristotle's arguments for positing the substratum. Aristotle needs this type of entity in order to give an account of change—both accidental and substantial change. We have seen that we can distinguish between two types of substrata underlying change: the material substratum and the substantial substratum. (See Section 1 of Chapter 1) When a bronze vase is transformed into a statue, the quantity of brass remains the same as the underlying *material* substratum, while losing the vase form and acquiring the statue form. When Socrates becomes musical he loses nonmusicality and acquires musicality. The "amusical Socrates" remains the same as the underlying *substantial* substratum.

The type of abstraction involved in the two types of change is different. Having examined the role that the substantial form plays in the unification of a substance, we are in a position to offer an analysis of the difference in the two types of abstraction. Consider the *accidental changes* of someone becoming musical or of something becoming red, light, or rough. The Aristo-

2. *Ph.* 193b3–5, 193b34, *Meta.* 1042a28–29.

telian account of the changes involved is that the person lost his or her
nonmusicality and gained musicality and that something lost non-redness,
or heaviness, or smoothness and gained their opposites. These forms are
subsumed within the form that unifies each substance. What must be
appreciated is that the *abstraction* of these entities in the account of change is
the *singling out* of these entities. It is very much like the path that one can
discern from the top of the hill for the return trip. There is no path or road
carved out through the forest, but a path is separated out from its environment in one's representation of the landscape. The individuation of the path
does not involve any physical change, but, nevertheless, an entity comes to
be identified that is not singled out as a physical entity. Similarly with
abstract entities. The abstraction of a color is the singling out of an entity.
Suppose there is a red poppy in the field. Abstracting the color red is the
singling out of a color rather than a flower. When the color is integrated in
the poppy, then it is not that the color is copresent with weight and shape
and size, and so on; rather, these items are unified into a whole by the
substantial form, so that the result is not their copresence, but a red poppy.
The red poppy is not an aggregate of these properties but it is a single
unified entity, where each property contributes to the whole by characterizing the poppy as red, round, or light, and so on. The move from "red
poppy" to "red color" is a move that requires the singling out of the entity
"red color," which is no more separate in the poppy than the way home is in
the forest.

   This is in fact what we would expect from the analysis we offered of the
role of the substantial form in a substance. The color red, such and such a
size, shape, weight, and so on, are distinct abstract entities that can be
singled out independently of each other. This is why they belong to different categories from one another. But this does not mean that the poppy is
a cluster of such properties being copresent. If that were the case, then the
substantial form of the poppy would be a *relation*. It would relate the
various, independently individuated entities to one another, and its role in
the poppy would be similar to the role of "juxtaposition" in the group of
juxtaposed books. Yet, we have seen that there is a fundamental difference
between a relation and a substantial form, namely, the substantial form
unifies by reidentifying the relata, as opposed to relations that relate without threatening the identity of the relata. So, the unification of all these
properties into a single substance requires that they be reidentified through
their integration into the whole. Thus, the integration of the red color into
the poppy does *not relate* the red color to the rest of the properties in the

poppy; rather, it gives rise to a single whole that is a red poppy. The individuation of the red poppy does not involve the individuation of a red color, unlike the individuation of the group of the ten juxtaposed books, which requires the individuation of each book. The red poppy is not a related whole of properties; it is a single entity, not a cluster of many. The poppy is a red *flower*, not red *color* plus such and such a shape, size, weight, and the like.[3] The red color is singled out only by dividing the red poppy up by abstraction.

One of the differences between substantial and accidental change is that the substantial form is unlike all the other forms that can be abstracted away from a substance: the substantial form, as opposed to any other form, is responsible for the unification of all the items in the substance into a whole. This means that, although all other forms are integrated into a whole in accordance with the principle of the substantial form, the substantial form itself is not integrated into the whole by any further principle. The form is the principle of integration and, as such is itself not integrated into the whole by being reidentified. This, as we will see, will be what will allow Aristotle to claim that the substantial form is the subject in a substance (Sections 3 of Chapter 6 and 2 of Chapter 7). That is, the actualization of the substantial form (by its integrating all the other components into a whole) only particularizes it, but does not reidentify it. (For the account of the particularization of the substantial form, see Section 4 in Chapter 7.) The integration of red color in the poppy is not the particularization of red color; the result is not a particular red color, but a red poppy. If the integration of red color resulted merely in its particularization, then the red poppy would not be a substance, but a related whole of individual properties: this red, this roundness, etcetera. But we have seen why that is not what a substance is and how the unification of its components into a whole is achieved

3. "The subject is called, when music is implanted in it, not music but musical, and the man is not whiteness but white, and not ambulation or movement but walking or moving— as in the above examples of 'of' something. . . . And it is only right that the 'of' something locution should be used with reference *both to the matter and to the accidents*" (*Meta.* 1049a30– b1, my emphasis). It is not only that the whiteness does not turn the man into whiteness when it enters him; it is that whiteness does not remain whiteness (= white color), any more than, in the case that is parallel according to Aristotle, the log remains a log in the casket: "a casket is not wood but of wood" (1049a19–20), "the statue is . . . not wood but wooden . . . and the house is said to be not bricks but of bricks (since we should not say without qualification, if we looked at things carefully, even that a statue is produced from wood or a house from bricks, because its coming to be implies *change in that from which it comes*, and not permanence)" (1033a17–22, my emphasis).

through the substantial form. So, all the other components are integrated into the whole by being reidentified; the substantial form joins the whole without reidentification, but only particularization. The integration of red *color* into the whole results in a red *poppy*, but the integration of the substantial form "poppy plant" into a whole results in a *particular* poppy plant. Integration is reidentification for accidental forms, but only particularization for substantial forms.

We have seen, so far, that there are three types of abstract entity that need to be posited to do metaphysical work in Aristotle's account of change: first, the substratum, second the unifying form, and third the nonunifying form. No entity of any of these three types can exist as a physically separate particular; they are separable only by abstraction. That they are *abstract* entities does *not* reveal whether they are *particular or universal*. Particularity will occupy us in Chapter 6.


## 3. The Metaphysics of Abstraction: The Unity of Matter and Form in a Substance

### (A) Arbitrary Objects

We saw in the preceding section that the accounts of the individuation of substances and of the transformation of substances give us the main stock of abstract entities that are required to do metaphysical work in Aristotle's ontology. The possibility of giving an account of the individuation of a substance (i.e., what a substance is and which substance it is), as well as an account of the transformation of substances, rests on our capacity to abstract entities that are not physically separable. The thesis I wish to put forward in this section is that abstraction is the key on the one hand to understanding the fundamental ontological distinctions made in Aristotle's metaphysics and on the other to distinguishing genuine metaphysical problems that he is trying to solve from pseudo-problems that he is not addressing, but that have seemed to interpreters to lurk in the background, threatening his system.

We saw that the main types of abstract entity in Aristotle's ontology are the ones that are required to account for the individuation and the transformation of substances: substantial form, accidental form, and substratum. But these do not provide us with a full explanation of substantial transformation or individuation. To get that, we need an account of the particularity of substances, which presupposes the introduction of the Aristotelian distinction between the potential and the actual. Comprehending this distinction involves an understanding of abstraction and, most important, of the metaphysics of abstraction.

Substances, which are in actuality, are not abstract entities. All the other entities that need to be posited for the individuation and transformation accounts of substances are abstract entities. Can there be relations between abstract entities, given that they are not ontologically separate entities? If there are such relations, do they depend on the properties that the abstract entities possess? What properties do the abstract entities possess? In what sense do these entities exist at all? What determines their life span? To begin answering these question, I will introduce the account given by Kit Fine of arbitrary objects, some elements of which will help us comprehend Aristotle's account of abstract entities.

An arbitrary object is characterized as follows by Fine: "With each arbitrary object is associated an appropriate range of individual objects, its values. . . . An arbitrary object has those properties common to the individual objects in its range."[4] For example, the arbitrary object "tiger" has all the properties that are common to tigers. To refine the criterion, Fine examines such properties as being an individual number, which would be true of each number, but would not be true of arbitrary numbers. Similarly, every tiger is a concrete particular, but an arbitrary tiger is not a concrete particular. To avoid a breakdown of the theory when it comes to such properties, Fine delimits the attribution of properties to arbitrary objects to what he calls *generic* properties (such as being a vertebrate), as opposed to *classical* ones (such as being an individual or a concrete particular). Thus, the principle of property attribution becomes: "for any *generic* condition $\phi(x)$, $\phi(a)$ is true iff $\forall i\, \phi(i)$ is true," where $a$ is the name of an arbitrary object and $\phi$ a predicate variable (p. 64). Being an individual number is thus not attributed to an arbitrary number, because it is not a generic property. On the basis of this principle, Fine offers the identity criteria for arbitrary objects: "$a = b$ iff their ranges are the same" (p. 69).

As Fine points out, arbitrary objects have been discredited by twentieth-century philosophers of logic and metaphysicians under the influence of Frege's criticisms of them.[5] On the intuitive level, Fine mentions what has traditionally been thought to be a problem with arbitrary objects, namely, the supposition that arbitrary objects are on an ontological par with particu-

---

4. Fine 1983, 55.
5. Ibid., p. 55. Fine's list of enemies of arbitrary objects includes Russell, Tarski, Church, Quine, D. Lewis.

lar objects. Fine describes the objection: "An arbitrary number is just another number, an arbitrary man just another man. It therefore appears that one can say the same sorts of things about each. So one is led to the absurd conclusion that one might count with arbitrary numbers or have tea with an arbitrary man." The problem here is not that of (what Fine calls) the classical properties. It is not just that the arbitrary man is not a particular man, but that there are many properties that a man would have that an arbitrary man would not, precisely because not all men have them. Thus Fine says: "This supposition of ontological parity has perhaps two main sources. The first is a certain metaphysical or psychological picture that may have been suggested by the more zealous advocates of arbitrary objects. It is as if an arbitrary man were merely a defective man, one shorn of his peculiar features. . . . So behind every individual man is an arbitrary man" (p. 58). There are several problems here. Arbitrary men are not particular men. They are not full-blown men; they lack many of the characteristics that a particular human being would have. Furthermore, if an arbitrary man is an "incomplete human being," how is he related to a "complete human being"? Is he a component within each man or an incomplete entity on its own? Does he underlie each man as a substratum, or is he like a property while each man is an instantiation?

Fine does not (and could not) address all of these problems within his article. But he does consider one problem that is crucial to the sense in which an arbitrary man is an incomplete man. This problem about arbitrary objects has to do with the attribution of complex properties to them. For example, every number is either even or odd. Hence, it should follow that an arbitrary number, whose range are the even and odd numbers, has the property of being "either even or odd." Yet, such an arbitrary number would be neither even nor odd, because it is not the case that every number is even or that every number is odd. How then could the disjunctive property characterize it if neither disjunct is true of the arbitrary number? Fine's preferred solution to this problem is that the evaluation of the disjunction is different in this case: "It seems to me that we must either deny that $\psi(a) \lor \chi(a)$ is a genuine disjunction or else give up the principle that disjunctions are evaluated directly by a disjunction rule. I, for one, am happy to accept the second alternative."[6] Accepting the second alternative means that the disjunction can be true of an arbitrary object even though neither disjunct is true of it.

6. Ibid., p. 62, where "a" is the name of an arbitrary object, and $\psi$ and $\chi$ are predicate variables.

This solution could, in turn, be applied to the original problem of arbitrary objects. For example, an arbitrary man has, let's say, height, but neither this nor that or the other height. According to Fine's position on disjunctive properties, the arbitrary man will have height, even if he does not have any one specific height, because the disjunction here is evaluated differently. Fine does not give any ontological reasons for a different evaluation of the disjunction other than his commitment to the theory of arbitrary objects, which would be incoherent without the different evaluation. His conclusion is that "it is impossible to achieve complete logical parity between individual and arbitrary objects" (p. 62). But without reverting to ontology to justify a different evaluation of the disjunction, the antirealist can treat the need for a different evaluation of the disjunction as a reason for giving up the theory of arbitrary objects, as Neil Tennant does (1983: 80). He says that Fine's admission that it is impossible to achieve ontological parity between particular and arbitrary objects is an attempt to "play down the importance of the difference: to offer a picture of a progressively diminishing but never disappearing difference in logical behavior upon successive theoretical adjustments and manoeuvres."

In giving Aristotle's theory of abstract entities, I will attempt to be as explicit as possible about the ontological difference between particular and abstract entities and use that difference to justify the variation in the way predicates apply to the two classes of entities.

My purpose here is not to examine the merits of Kit Fine's theory of arbitrary objects or of the solutions he offers concerning the difficulties that surround such entities. My concern is with Aristotle's theory of abstract objects. Fine's theory was presented, first, for purposes of comparison in the exposition of Aristotle's theory and, second, in order to highlight some of the problems that one has to face with any theory of abstract entities. Of the familiar ontologies, the entities that come the closest to Fine's arbitrary objects are Plato's Forms, which are not ontologically dependent on particular entities. I say closest, first, because I do not know what degree of detail Plato would allow in the specification of the properties of the Form of Man, when the Form is taken to be a paradigm. Second, because Platonic Forms are *particular* substances, not recurrent entities. Of Fine's arbitrary objects, we know that an arbitrary man is not a particular man, for an arbitrary man has only generic, not classical, properties, such as being a particular man. But the fact that an arbitrary man is not a particular man does not help us determine whether that arbitrary man *recurs* in particular men. I do not know what Fine's position would be on this issue and, so, how arbitrary objects compare with Platonic Forms with regard to particularity.

But how do abstract entities bear their properties? Is the quantity of brass in the statue brazen? Is Socrates' substantial form a man? For the sake of the subsequent discussion I shall concentrate on these two abstract entities as representative of the Aristotelian material substratum and substantial form. The answer to both these questions may seem straightforward. Yes, a quantity of brass is brazen; no, the substantial form of Socrates is not a man. But this is just where the complications begin. How can something brazen be without shape? If it is brazen, it is made out of brass. Brass occupies space and therefore has shape. Hence, if something is brazen, it has shape. But the quantity of brass in the statue does not have shape. The quantity of brass is an entity that underlies the statue in the sense that it receives the form of the statue to make up the statue. It is present in the lump of brass, the statue, or anything else we make by continuous transformations, starting with an initial substance that is made out of brass. By abstracting the shape away, we separate by abstraction the quantity of brass from the statue, or the lump it is in. Hence, the quantity of brass does not have shape; it can receive shape to make up the substance, but it is not characterized by it.[7] How can it be characterized as being brazen if it does not have a shape?

The situation does not get better when we consider the substantial form of Socrates. Why do we say that it is not a man? The substantial form of Socrates is just what being a man is. It is what it takes for something to be a man. It is that part or aspect of the world that is responsible for Socrates' being a human being. Hence, it is a man.[8]

Of course, at this point, we face the same problem as with the quantity of brass. A quantity of brass is brazen, and that was found to be problematic, because brass has shape, but the quantity of brass does not. Similarly, any man has a specific weight at any one time, and similarly with height, and so on. But the substantial form of Socrates is not characterized by any particular weight or height. How can it be a man? Can we deny that it is a man? Consider the quantity of brass. If the quantity of brass is not brazen, then nothing is brazen, because the quantity of brass is all the brass that there is in the statue. If brass is not brazen, the statue made out of it certainly is not brazen, either. Hence, the quantity of brass in the statue must be brazen. For corresponding reasons, the form of man in Socrates must be a man.

It is clear that there are reasons leading us to say that the entities that are

---

7. See Cartwright 1972, 375, and Chap. 4, n. 53 above.

8. Kirwan says: "Aristotle would have asserted that George's essence is *to be a man* but not that George's essence is *humanity*; rather, it is *man*, which George is, not *humanity*, which George has" (1970–71, 44).

isolated by abstraction from particular substances bear some of the properties of these substances; but then, we also have reasons that urge us to reject this conclusion. Clearly, our intuitions cannot help us settle this issue. In what follows I derive the solution to this problem from Aristotle's ontology, using an argument of his concerning what there is or, better, what there isn't.

### (B) The Unity of Matter and Form in a Substance

In his discussion of the unity of matter and form in a substance, in *Metaphysics* H, 6, Aristotle rejects as a solution to this problem that there is a relation that binds matter to form, resulting in a unified whole, the substance. The problem here is what the ontological relation is between nonsubstantial forms and the subject they belong to, or between matter and form in a substance. Aristotle considers the solution that previous philosophers had given to this problem:

> Owing to the difficulty about unity some speak of participation, and raise the question, what is the cause of participation and what is it to participate; and others speak of communion, as Lycophron says knowledge is a communion of knowing with the soul; and others say life is a composition or connexion of soul with body. Yet the same account applies to all cases; for being healthy will be either a communion or a connexion or a composition of soul and health, and the fact that the bronze is a triangle will be a composition of bronze and triangle, and the fact that a thing is white will be a composition of surface and whiteness. (*Meta.* 1045b7–16)

The items that seem to need to be connected to one another, if particular substances are to be ontologically unified wholes, are such as soul with knowing, soul with health, soul with body, bronze with triangle, surface with whiteness. Some of these are relations between *substantial substratum* and *form* (e.g., soul and knowing, surface and whiteness),[9] whereas others are relations between *material substratum* and *substantial form* (e.g., body and soul, bronze and triangle). The solution that previous philosophers had found in order to account for the healthy soul being one thing, not many,

---

9. Here the substrata are substantial, because receiving the form simply qualifies them, e.g., the soul becomes a knowing soul, and the surface becomes a white surface, rather than determine their identity, as in the case of bronze that receives the form of triangle to result in a bronze triangle.

the living body being one thing, not many, or the bronze triangle being one thing, not many, was *to posit relations relating the substrata to the forms*. The unifying relations that were posited by these philosophers were participation (*methexis*), communion (*sunousia*), composition (*sunthesis*), connexion (*sundesmos*). Aristotle first points out that it makes no difference what such relations are taken to be: "Yet the same account applies to all cases; for being healthy will be either a communion or a connexion or a composition of soul and health" (1045b12–14). That is, the success in solving the problem at hand does not depend on the nature of the posited relation, and, therefore, it makes no difference if connection is taken to be different from communion or composition, among others. All these different positions can be viewed as one and the same proposal when we realize that all of them suggest that the unities in question are attained by the relations that are assumed to relate the forms to the substrata.

Aristotle rejects this solution. The substratum and the form are a unified whole, although not on account of a relation that relates them to one another. For Aristotle, no relation unifies a substratum and a form into a single whole. We realize this, according to Aristotle, once we recognize that the substratum is to the form as the potential is to the actual:

> The reason [that the same account of unity applies to all cases of a substratum and its form] is that people look for a unifying formula, and a difference, between potentiality and actuality. But, as has been said, *the proximate matter and the form are one and the same thing*, the one potentially, the other actually. Therefore, *to ask the cause of their being one is like asking the cause of unity in general*; for each thing is a unity, and *the potential and the actual are somehow one*. Therefore *there is no other cause here* unless there is something which caused the movement from potentiality into actuality. (*Meta.* 1045b16–22, my emphasis)

"The cause of the movement" refers to the agent that causes the matter to receive the form. This is explicitly stated in 1045a27–31: "the question is, what is the cause of the unity of round and bronze? The difficulty disappears, because the one is matter, the other form. What then is the cause of this—the reason why that which was potentially is actually—what except, in the case of things which are generated, the agent?"

What does Aristotle's solution consist in? What does it mean to say that the potential and the actual are one and the same thing, or that they are somehow one? Are we being asked by Aristotle to consider that the quantity of brass in a brazen statue is identical to the substantial form of being a statue? Clearly, this could not be Aristotle's suggestion, as it is so obviously false. The point Aristotle is making is that the material and the formal elements unite into a single entity, the substance, which is unified and one, not an aggregate of many. [10] In fact, the problem of the unity of a substance arises precisely because the material and formal aspects of it are different. Because they are different, if the two together make up a unified whole, it is legitimate to ask what is the cause of their unity.

Aristotle begins this investigation in H, 6, with the observation that he is already committed to a solution regarding the way in which many parts unite into a whole: "In the case of all things which have several parts and in which the whole is not, as it were, a mere heap, but *the totality is something besides the parts*, there is a *cause* of unity" (1045a8–10, my emphasis). This is the problem he addressed in *Metaphysics* Z, 17, of the unity of the parts of a substance. We have seen that his solution was an existential argument for a substantial form in a substance, which is the *cause* of unity of the various parts of the substance. [11] It would *appear* that this is just the problem that these other philosophers Aristotle alludes to in H, 6, are facing, and just the solution they offer: the problem is the unity of items in a substance, and the solution is the *positing of an entity*, such as the communion, or participation, or connexion, or composition between the items that relates them to one another. But this is precisely what Aristotle rejects in H, 6. There is *no relation that unites substratum to form*, such as participation or communion. In fact, there is no cause whatsoever, says Aristotle, of the oneness of the substratum and the form in a substance. (The efficient cause explains *that* their union took place, not *what* their union consists in.) It is important, then, that we distinguish between the Z, 17, and H, 6, problems and solutions that Aristotle offers to them.

Z, 17, provided an existential argument for substantial forms, but H, 6, provides no existential argument for any items in a substance. The problem in Z, 17, was to unite entities of the same type into a single whole. The question that is answered by the aggregate argument is, How can an aggregate of entities be unified into a whole that is over and above the

10. For brevity in the exposition, I will talk of the unity of the material substratum and the substantial form in a substance, when discussing the solution given in H 6, although the same solution is intended by Aristotle for the case of the unity of a substantial substratum and a nonsubstantial form.

11. We explained that the unification takes place through the re-identification of the parts as they are integrated into the whole.

aggregate of these entities—where the whole is not identical to the aggregate of these entities? The answer was that the aggregate is unified by an entity of a different ontological type from them that provides the identity for the new whole. The reason why a new entity needs to be posited to unify the aggregate into a whole (over and above the aggregate) is that the members of the aggregate are of the same ontological type, although they are different from one another, which means that two of them together constitute a plurality of entities of that type. This is the reason why Aristotle insists in the aggregate argument that the entity that is posited to unify the elements of the aggregate will be of a different ontological type. He says that if the unifier is of the same ontological type, "if it is an element [in the aggregate], the same argument will again apply" (1041b20–21). The reason is that if the copresence of such elements constitutes an aggregate, adding one more such element cannot change the aggregate into a unified whole. Whatever keeps the initial elements separate and many will keep them separate and many even after the addition of one more such element. Thus, copresent elements of the same ontological type require an entity of a different type to unify them into a single whole.

But what if the elements are not of the same ontological type? Then, the aggregate argument does not apply to them. There are no a priori grounds for claiming that their copresence will constitute a plurality. The option that is still available in such a case is that their copresence may result in an entity of a different type. They might have what we might call *complementary individualities*. Aristotle's claim that the substratum is not united with the substantial form by a *relation is* the claim that they are complementary entities. Elsewhere, I have offered an explanation of what I here call the complementarity of the matter and the form.[12] The material substratum provides differentiation for the form, whereas the form provides a principle of unity at a time and through time for the matter, so that together they make up a particular. By contrast, in the aggregate argument, the distinct elements in the aggregate do not complement each other because they are the same type of individual. The interdependence of matter and form will be discussed in detail in Section 6 of Chapter 6. For our present purposes it is sufficient to indicate in what sense the two abstract entities, the matter and the form of a substance, may be thought of as being complementary: their copresence does not produce a plurality but an entity of a different type.

12. Scaltsas 1985b, 232–233.

Aristotle says in H, 6, that there is no cause of the unity of the matter and form of a substance (1045b21–22). [13] No relation can unite the matter and the form into a single whole. Aristotle's insight goes deep: if there can be no relation *uniting* them to one another, there cannot be a relation *separating* them from one another. In short, *there is no relation in the world between matter and form in a substance*. But, although the matter and the form cannot be physically separated from each other, they can be separated by abstraction. It therefore follows that *there is no relation in the world corresponding to the mental act of abstraction*. When we separate the substantial form from the matter, this separation is not a state of affairs in the world. The act of abstraction does not have an ontological correlate. But it is through the act of abstraction that we distinguish between matter and form, subject and property, and in general, items within the substance, where the one *belongs to* the other. It follows that in Aristotle's system *there is no ontological correlate for predication*. Substantial forms, nonsubstantial forms, and material substrata are singled out only by abstraction and enjoy no physical separateness. Hence, abstraction is not the recognition of a number of items, but the delineation of these items by division. Abstraction does not mirror physical reality, but individuates what does not enjoy physical separateness. We would therefore not expect the problems regarding the unity of abstracted entities to be solved by positing physical relations between these entities. What is divided by abstraction cannot be united by physical relations (i.e., relations between physically separate entities, such as "connection," "combination," or "mixing"). It is united by reidentification in terms of the substantial form it comes to belong to as subject (see Sections 2 and 5 in Chapter 4, 6 in Chapter 6, and 4–5 in Chapter 7).

## (C) Avoiding the Infinite Regress

We need to clarify a point in order to keep the aggregate argument apart from the argument of H, 6. What we learn from H, 6, is that there is no relation uniting matter to form or a subject to its properties. Yet, we saw in the aggregate argument that the substantial form unites into a whole the material parts of a substance or the properties of a substance, and, in general, any set of items into which the substance can be divided either physically or by abstraction. Although the items into which the substance

---

13. He, of course, allows that there is an efficient cause that brings about the generation of the substance.

can be divided need to be united into a whole *by* the substantial form, the substantial form does not need to be united *to* these items by any relation.

If a relation, $R$, was posited to unite the substantial form to the items that belong to it in a substance, infinite regresses would be generated, because, for the same reasons, a further relation, $R'$ would be required to unite $R$ to its relata, and so on ad infinitum. Why, then, isn't there an infinite regress generated when a substantial form is posited by the aggregate argument to unite the components of a substance into a whole? The answer has been given by Aristotle. A regress would be generated if the substantial form were the same type of item as the ones it united.

But is that not the situation in a substance? Think of a substance as an aggregate of its properties. Adding the substantial form to that aggregate means adding another form, namely, another element to the aggregate. However, positing a further form to unite the aggregate of forms just augments the aggregate, only for the question of unity to appear once again, and so on to infinity. If that was all there was to Aristotle's answer, it would lead to an infinite regress of substantial forms. Yet, we claimed that Aristotle's position does not lead to an infinite regress. The regress is avoided, because the solution to the unity of the aggregate does not consist in the *addition* of a substantial form, which would simply augment the aggregate of forms in a substance; the substantial form does not join the aggregate of forms, but it takes over the aggregate, unifying its elements by reidentifying them according to the principle the substantial form stands for. This is the difference between the substantial form and the rest of the forms that belong to a substance; it is not just copresent with them, but it incorporates them into the whole by depriving them of their independent individuality. Hence, the introduction of the substantial form does not augment the aggregate, and so the question of the unity of the aggregate cannot be asked again, because we do not have an aggregate of items any more, but a unified whole. To turn the whole into an aggregate again, we would have to generate the elements of the aggregate by abstraction from the whole. In other words, far from being a *cluster of properties*, a substance would have to be segmented (by abstraction) to generate a cluster, which would be the destruction (in abstraction) of the substance. Thus, the reason why Aristotle avoids an infinite series of substantial forms for the unity of the elements in a substance is that the substantial form is not an element that joins the rest in the aggregate of forms of the substance, but an individuation principle that reidentifies them. The substantial form is therefore ontologically different not only from the material parts of a substance, but also from all the parts into which the substance can be divided, physical or abstract. The difference consists in its providing an identity principle for the rest of the parts that integrate into a unified substance.

## 4. An Existential Dilemma about Matter and Form

### (A) The Dilemma

Aristotle's solution to the unity of matter and form in a substance entails that no physical relation in the world corresponds to the linguistic act of predication or to the mental act of abstraction. What follows directly from this realization is that typical Aristotelian statements of the form "a substance is a composite of matter and form," or "the matter receives the form to make up the substance" are *statements that have no truth-conditions.* There is nothing in the world that corresponds to a "composition" between matter and form, nor is there any relation such as the "receiving" of form by the matter, since matter and form do not enjoy physical separateness.

Yet, we have in the preceding chapters explained Aristotle's understanding of what it is for Socrates to be a man in terms of Socrates' matter receiving the form of man to make up Socrates. In fact, Aristotle has offered very powerful existential arguments, both for the matter and for the form in a substance, in his accounts of substantial transformation and of the unity of substance. We therefore have very good reason for thinking of a substance as being composed of matter and form.

We are confronted, then, with the following dilemma: (1) there is no relation in Socrates between his matter and his form; (2) hence, the statement "Socrates is a composite of matter and form" has no truth-conditions; (3) yet, that "Socrates is a composite of matter and form" is true. Do we give up (1), (2), or (3)? Do we go back on the conclusion we reached earlier that there is no relation uniting matter to form, thereby opening up the way to an infinite regress? Or on the claim that there is such a thing as matter in Socrates, and such a thing as a substantial form in Socrates, which were hard-won Aristotelian conclusions? Or should we claim that the statement "Socrates is a composite of matter and form" is not true?

Aristotle does not discuss this problem, nor is there any indication of his recognition of the problem, but in what follows I suggest a way of avoiding the inconsistency. At first glance, the third option seems to be the only

Aristotelian one. That is, to claim that the statement "Socrates is a composite of matter and form" is *not entailed* by "Socrates is a man." It must be understood as a statement that is not descriptive of anything in the world and be (nominalistically) explained away by an appropriate reparsing of the statement in language.

Inevitably, this issue relates to the one we raised in Section 3 of Chapter 5: If talk of the relation between matter and form is not descriptive, is any ascription of properties to matter and form descriptive? Does the quantity of brass in the statue have shape, size, without having a specific shape and size? Can it weigh 5 pounds, but be without shape? If, on the other hand, we can talk of the substance being a composite of matter and form, although there is no composition of matter and form, then could we not also talk of the matter having shape, though not a determinate one?

The conclusion that statements about the relation of matter to form in a substance have no truth-conditions is in accord with Aristotle's claim that there is no cause in the world securing the unity of matter and form in a substance; but, at the same time, it leads to a dilemma: Aristotle seems to be committed to both a *realist* and an *antirealist* position toward matter and form in a substance. On the one hand, he offers us *existential arguments* for the existence of the matter and the form in a substance, and on the other he *denies* that there *can be a relation* between them, although they make up a unity, which withdraws their status as entities in the world. The existential argument for the substantial form in a substance is given by the aggregate argument, but the one for the material substratum is given by the physical continuity of substantial transformations. If the matter and the form are in a substance, why can they not be related to each other when they form a unity?

It will not be sufficient to say that no relation obtains between them because the one is potential and the other actual, as no meaning has been given to these terms from which we would *derive* that no relation can obtain between the potential and the actual. (I have discussed elsewhere Aryeh Kosman's influential position on the potential-actual relation in the case of motion and its extension to the case of the matter and form in a substance.)[14] Statements employing the notions of the potential and the actual in relation to the matter and the form are what we are trying to explain and

14. I have detailed my responses to Aryeh Kosman's (1984) interpretation of Aristotelian motion and his application of this interpretation toward resolving the problem of the unity of matter and form in a substance in Scaltsas 1985b, 224–226, and Scaltsas 1992c, 190–193.

make sense of, rather than the explanans. For example, Edward Halper says in explaining Aristotle's solution to the unity of the matter and form in a substance: "Since the identification of form as actuality and matter as potentiality seems to be the only way to account for the unity of the composite, it must be true. No other argument is given to support this identification."[15] He continues: "What causes form and matter to be one? . . . Form is in actuality and matter is potentially, and 'what is potentially and in actuality are somehow one.' . . . Just as form causes unity among the constituents, it causes itself and matter to be one insofar as it is the actuality of the matter" (pp. 190–191). But this does not explain how the unity is achieved. To show the need for further explanation of the potential-actual relation, let me just mention how another commentator uses this relation. Gerald Hughes says that the universal essence, for example, "human being," is the potential and that the enmattered essence, which is particular, is the actual.[16] One may then ask, is the relation of universal essence to a particular essence the same as the relation of matter to form in a substance, for Hughes uses the terms potential-actual for both relations? An answer to this and similar questions cannot be given unless we explain what the potential-actual relation is, rather than take it as primitive and unanalyzable.

## (B) Truth-Conditions for the Individuation of Abstract Entities

So, Aristotle's position on the *unity of substances prima facie* appears to involve an incongruity. On the one hand, he is committed to the *compositeness* of a substance out of matter and form. He provides a powerful argument for the existence of *substantial form* (acting as the unifier of the aggregate of elements within a substance). He further provides an existential argument for *matter* in each substance in his account of the transformation of substances. These arguments commit Aristotle to a *realist* position about matter and form in a substance. On the other hand, Aristotle claims in *Metaphysics* H, 6, that there is *no relation uniting the matter and the form* of a substance into a single entity. But then, if a substance is a *composition* of matter and form and there is nothing in the world corresponding to that relation of "composition," it would seem that we should treat Aristotle's talk about matter and form in a substance non–truth-conditionally. Aristo-

15. Halper 1989, 187–188.
16. Hughes 1979, 124.

telian statements in which reference is made to the matter and form of a substance, such as "these bricks *receive* the form of a house and make up this house" would have to be understood as prompted by this being a brick house, but not as having *truth-conditions* of their own (because no relation of *possession* exists in the world between matter and form). This commits Aristotle to an *antirealist* treatment of matter and form in a substance. Hence the tension in his position.

To show that Aristotle's account of the matter and form in a substance can, with consistency, be claimed to be *realist*, I argue that we can give a *truth-conditional* analysis of talk of matter and form, even though there are no truth-conditions for statements about the composition of the matter and the form in a unified substance.

The starting point in our investigation is the individuation of matter and form in a substance. The question we need to pose and answer is this: What kind of division is the division of a substance into matter and form? Is it like the division of, for example, a brick into two bricks, and, if not, what precisely is the difference? The quick, yet not informative answer is that the division of the brick into two bricks is a physical separation, whereas the division into matter and form is by abstraction. Our concern will be to characterize the type of division involved in the division of a substance into matter and form by abstraction.

What precisely is the difference between the two types of division? I suggest that the difference between physical division and division by abstraction is that *physical division* separates by recomposing, but that the *abstraction* of form and matter does not involve recomposition. The two new rocks that emerge from the division of the original rock, or the two amoebas from the original one, have different shapes, sizes, weights, and so on from the original ones. The division engenders change of properties and recomposition of properties. By contrast, abstracting the form does not involve change of properties and recomposition. The form and the matter that emerge *as a result of the abstraction* have the properties *of the original substance*. They do not each have all the properties of the substance, but whatever properties they have, they inherited from that substance. Thus, if we abstract the form of the amoeba, then the shape and functions and capacities that will characterize the form will be the shape, functions, and capacities of the amoeba. For example, the capacities of the form will not be determined by what the form is capable of doing, but by what the amoeba is capable of doing. This is not the case with the new amoebas that are generated by the splitting of the old amoeba, where the capacities that each of the new amoebas has are determined by what each of them is capable of doing. The matter, too, that is abstracted from the amoeba, will inherit its properties from the amoeba; for instance, the hardness of the matter of the amoeba will be the same as the hardness of the amoeba.

Not all the properties of a substance will be properties of the abstracted form and of the abstracted matter. But my concern here is not to provide detailed criteria of which properties will be included in each of these two types of abstract entity. Rather, I want to elucidate the difference between physical division and division by abstraction and show that it is possible to individuate these entities, remaining faithful to Aristotle's ontological claims about them, without evoking antirealist positions to make sense. I will try to meet these demands by providing a truth-conditional analysis of abstract objects and by using elements from Kit Fine's theory of arbitrary objects. I will concentrate primarily on substantial form, but I will also discuss matter.

Aristotle is a realist and also a severe critic of Platonic realism. According to Aristotle, the forms (e.g., of human being, or elm, or octopus) do not exist *apart* from their instances, in the way that Platonic Forms exist in a different realm from the physical world. Rather, for Aristotle, such forms are existentially dependent on their instances.[17] It follows that whatever method of individuation we offer for such forms, they must come out dependent on the substances that exemplify them.

My contention is that the truth-conditions for thoughts about the matter and form of a substance will be determined by their relation to thoughts about the substance.[18] To show this, we need to introduce a procedure that will relate thoughts about form to thoughts about the substances possessing the form. The operation must give a systematic way of determining the undertaken commitments in having thoughts of the kind in question; for example, here, the operation must determine the conditions a thinker takes to be sufficient for thoughts about substantial forms to obtain. In addition, a thought about a substantial form will be true if and only if some condition, which is determined by the operation in question, obtains. As I suggested, the operation in question, in our case, is abstraction.

We shall define the operation of *abstraction* in terms of a procedure of selecting which (from the totality) of a substance's properties belong to the

17. E.g., *Meta.* 1040b26–27, 1042a22–29.
18. My analysis of the truth-conditions of talk of Aristotelian abstract entities is influenced by Christopher Peacocke's (1986) truth-conditional analysis of talk of *inaccessible objects*.

substantial form. This will require recourse to perceptions of substances and to thoughts involving universal quantification over substances. We saw earlier (Section 3) what Kit Fine's criterion is for the selection of the properties that will characterize each arbitrary object. We will use this criterion to produce a general Aristotelian criterion for property inclusion in substantial forms. According to Fine, an arbitrary object has those properties which are common to the individual objects in its range. [19] We set the following *identity criterion* for substantial forms: the substantial form of a substance will have those properties of the substance which are common to the members of the substance's species. What is important about this criterion is that it derives what properties the substantial form has from the properties that the substances of that species have, which is what we require for the truth-conditional account of talk about the form. Of course, this is only a first approximation toward selecting just the essential characteristics (in Aristotle's sense) of a substance, for inclusion in its form. Such an investigation would require the enrichment of the criterion just given, by introducing a distinction between necessary and essential characteristics, so as to comply with the requirements of scientific classification, determining the content of the definition of the essence of the substance. But such an enrichment of the criterion is not our present concern. [20] Rather, our concern is with the use of such a criterion toward showing that the individuation of the substantial form can receive a realist (truth-conditional) analysis, rather than an antirealist analysis (by reparsing the language) as contemplated earlier on. We therefore use the forementioned criterion as representative of this group of criteria for the content of the essence, allowing for the possibility of refinement in accordance with Aristotle's requirements. [21]

Parallel work to the analysis just offered of the identity criterion for form would determine the identity criterion for *matter*. The range of individuals

19. Fine 1983, 55.

20. For an exposition of this distinction, see Sorabji 1980, 188–206; Gill 1989, 116–120, 132 n. 49; Matthen 1986b, 151–157; Lear 1988, 43–54; and Edel 1982, 389–392.

21. The individuation criterion involves two operations. The first is universal quantification over the substances in a species; the second the abstraction of forms. The first operation, universal quantification, is involved in the selection of the properties to be included in the form. Peacocke (1986) offers a realist defense of this operation. He shows that universal quantification can receive a *truth-conditional* analysis, and so does not commit one to antirealist justification (chap. 3: "Universal Quantification," pp. 28–42, especially p. 40). The second operation, abstraction, is involved in the (nonphysical) separation of the form from the substance. This operation does respect the conditions set out by Peacocke for a truth-conditional analysis of inaccessible objects (ibid., pp. 82–84).

of a quantity of matter would be those that are constituted by that matter. The quantity of matter would have the properties that are common to the individual objects in its range. The guiding principle in the case of matter would be physical continuity in change (see Section 1 of Chapter 1), which would demarcate the relevant range of individuals, in the way that the species demarcated it for the form.[22]

The identity criteria for the form and the matter tie these abstracted entities existentially to the substances from which they are abstracted. This is in keeping with Aristotle's moderate realism and respects his objections to the Platonic positing of universals that exist as substances independently of particulars. The abstracted individuated entities, namely the substantial form and the matter, are existentially *dependent* on substances and do *not* exist as substances.[23]

What is important for our purposes regarding the derivation of the truth-conditions of statements about matter and form from statements about substances is that we do not need to presuppose the physical distinctness of matter and form in a substance in order to talk about them. We can talk of these abstract entities, truly or falsely, without committing ourselves to their physical separability. Thus, if we need to talk about the form unifying the material elements, or about the matter remaining throughout substantial change, as Aristotle does, such talk would not be incompatible either with the abstract status of matter and form or with the realist requirement for talk about these entities. On the other hand, because according to Aristotle there is no relation of composition between matter and form, statements such as "Socrates is a composite of matter and form" would have to be understood in a way that does not commit them to the existence of a relation of composition. I offer such an explanation in Section 6 of Chapter 6.

That the abstracted entities *are not substances* also explains, as mentioned, why the a priori truths about substances do not apply to abstracted entities. There is no contradiction involved in attributing shape to the form of *elm*

22. This would not exclude an interrupted spatiotemporal path of a particular quantity of matter that reassembles at a later time. Simply, the interrupted path would have to be bridged by many smaller paths of physically continuous parts of the original quantity of matter.

23. I am in sympathy with Max Cresswell's description of the existence of abstract entities: "These abstract entities [essences], however, need not be Platonic Forms and need not be like anything in the sensible world. For since individual things have essences, an account of the existence of an *x* which is (*per se*) a φ will be sufficiently given . . . by saying that it is a φ" (Cresswell 1971, 111).

*tree*, without attributing a particular shape to it. Similarly, there is no absurdity in attributing a particular weight and size to the quantity of matter without attributing any particular shape to it. These are requirements to which concrete substances must conform and that the individuation analysis I offered shows not to be applicable in the case of abstract entities. What properties are to be attributed to the abstract entities of matter and form is determined by identity criteria designed for these entities, not for concrete substances. The sole restriction is that the identity criteria for the abstract entities are truth-conditionally grounded on the identity criteria of the substances they are abstracted from.

We started this section with the realization of a realist-antirealist tension. On the one hand, the aggregate argument and the analysis of transformation offered existential arguments for the matter and form in a substance. On the other, the account of unity of a substance required that there be no relation between matter and form in a substance. This suggested that, although we had reason to talk of substances as being composites of matter and form, such talk should not be taken to rest on truth-conditions. It follows that a tension arose between arguments requiring us to give talk of matter and form a realist analysis based on truth-conditions and arguments requiring us to give it an antirealist analysis by reparsing the language. What has been offered in this section is an explanation that, on the one hand, satisfies the requirements of the solution for the unity of substance and on the other gives a realist account of talk of matter and form. The account of the unity of substance that we offered required that there be no physical correlate to the act of abstraction—that is, no relation relating matter to form (see Section 3 of this chapter). This threatened an antirealist account of matter and form. It was this threat that was addressed here, and what was offered was an explanation of the process of *abstraction*, showing that the individuation of matter and form by abstraction is *truth-conditionally* grounded on experience. Therefore, the *Metaphysics* H, 6, solution to the unity of matter and form is not at odds with Aristotle's existential commitment to matter and form in a substance.

# 6 | Particulars

Is there anything that makes an entity into a particular? What is it for anything to be classified as a particular? The particularity question is the pivotal point around which the Aristotelian metaphysical story unfolds. It requires us to address the questions what the subject is in a substance, what the relation of the subject to the essence of the substance is, what is responsible for the unity of a substance as a single whole, and how such a whole relates to its constituent parts.

For Aristotle the class of particular substances does not restrict itself to the material substances. He allows for immaterial substances as well. In fact, he never objects to the Platonic Forms on the grounds that each Form is claimed to be immaterial and particular.[1] Such a combination is not unwelcome in Aristotle's system. (His usual objection is that the Forms are claimed to be both particular substances and universals.) We would therefore expect that particularity does not rest on materiality in Aristotle, which we shall show to be the case in this chapter. Yet two major lines of interpretation have prevailed in the tradition as explanations of the particularity of substances in Aristotle. The first is the bare substratum doctrine, according to which all the properties of a particular substance belong to a propertiless underlying subject that is particular. The second account of particularity assumes the substantial form of a substance to be particular,

---

1. At *Meta.* 1040b27–29 he remarks: "But those who say the Forms exist, in one respect are right, in saying the Forms exist apart, if they are substances." Existing apart is existing as a particular substance.

treating it either as a historical individual or simply as primitively particular.[2] In Appendix 2, I argue against the attribution of the bare substratum doctrine to Aristotle and offer my reading of *Metaphysics* Z, 3. In Appendix 3, I argue against the attribution of individual forms to Aristotle and give an analysis of the Ship of Theseus Paradox. In both cases I further show that the examined positions face philosophical problems that cannot be overcome, resulting in unsatisfactory explanations of substantial particularity. I finally supplement the attack against individual forms in Appendix 4 by offering a reading of *Metaphysics* M, 10, that does not commit Aristotle to individual forms. I present what I understand to be Aristotle's account of particularity in what follows.

## 1. Nonmaterial Substances

"[Callias and Socrates] are different in virtue of their matter (for this is different), but the same in form" (*Meta.* 1034a7–8). This explicit statement almost invariably leads the Aristotelian reader to attribute to Aristotle the position that *matter* is responsible for the *particularity* of substances. This attribution is enhanced by Aristotle's statement that "some things are one in number . . . those whose matter is one . . . things that are one in number are one in species" (1016b31–36). This shows that Aristotle connects the numerical oneness of substances to their matter. My claim in the present chapter is that, although material substances are numerically one on account of their matter, this should *not* be taken to be a *reduction of particularity to materiality*. I shall argue that Aristotle is committed to nonmaterial substances, each of which is numerically one. Furthermore, even in the case of material substances, far from being explanatory, the statement itself that matter is responsible for the numerical oneness of substances needs to be explained. My main objective in this chapter is to offer an explanation of what *particularity* is in Aristotle, given that he does not think particularity presupposes matter in nonmaterial substances, although he thinks it depends on matter in material substances.

In Book Λ of the *Metaphysics*, Aristotle is arguing for the existence of an eternal, unmovable substance, which is the first (unmoved) cause of all

---

2. Independently of the question of whether it is the soul that is responsible for the particularity of substances, it is illuminating to see the historical background of the Greek conception of the soul as a particular, which is given in Furley (1987, 152–158).

movement in the universe. One of the conclusions he reaches about the Prime Mover is that, if it is to cause eternal movement, its substance must be actuality (1071b18–20). For Aristotle, the substance of an object is its actuality.[3] By that, Aristotle wishes to distinguish between entities whose form is substantial, such as a human being, from entities whose form is not a substantial one, such as a lump of bronze. He calls substantial forms actualities and the rest privations.[4] But this could not be what Aristotle is trying to tell us here when he says that the Prime Mover's substance is an actuality; that is, he is not telling us that the Prime Mover is not like a lump of bronze. Such a result would not give him what he is looking for, that is, to establish what the nature of the first mover must be if it causes eternal movement. Nor is Aristotle telling us that the Prime Mover must be in actuality, as opposed to merely in potentiality. First, he could have said so by employing the technical expression he uses for that, namely, the word for actuality in the dative,[5] meaning that something is *in* actuality, rather than the term in the nominative,[6] meaning that something is *an* actuality. But if something is in actuality, this does not guarantee that it will remain in actuality and therefore cause movement that is eternal. Hence, being in actuality is not in itself sufficient for securing that the movement caused by the actual Prime Mover will be eternal, because the actual Prime Mover may cease to be. So what Aristotle must be stating when he says that the substance of the eternal mover will be actuality is that not only is the Prime Mover *an* actuality, not only is it *in* actuality, but also that it can be *only* in actuality.

This is born out by the argument: "if its substance is potentiality . . . there will not be *eternal* movement; for that which is potentially may possibly not be. There must, then, be such a principle whose very substance is actuality" (1071b18–20). To secure eternal being, what is needed is that the Prime Mover not be merely in potentiality, since the potential may possibly not be. But even if it is in actuality, it may cease to be. Hence, what is needed is that the Prime Mover be incapable of being in any other state but in actuality. This must be what Aristotle is expressing by saying that its substance is actuality: it is essential for the Prime Mover to be in actuality.

On the same line of argument, Aristotle continues: "Further, then, these

3. *Meta.* 1043a5–6, 1043a35–36.
4. See note 3 and chap. 2, n. 6.
5. ἐνεργείᾳ.
6. ἐνέργεια.

substances [which are causes of eternal movement] must be without matter; for they must be eternal, at least if anything else is eternal. Therefore they must be actuality" (1071b20–22). Again, the requirement is not simply that they be in actuality, but that they be only in actuality. Only so will their eternity be guarantied. It is for this reason that they cannot contain matter. If a first cause of eternal movement is composed of matter and form, then it is possible for it to suffer substantial transformation: the matter loses the form of the Prime Mover and acquires a different form. If the Prime Mover is composed of matter and form, the possibility of transformation and its corruption will exist, and if it is possible it might be realized,[7] and so there would be no guarantee of their eternity. Hence, a Prime Mover, *qua* eternal, must be incapable of suffering substantial transformation. This is secured if it cannot be divided into matter and form. Therefore, an eternal *Prime Mover* must contain *no element that could function as matter* in substantial transformations.

Aristotle makes use of the conclusion that a Prime Mover is only actuality and is without matter in his proof that there is only one heaven. The proof is not of especial importance for our present concern, except that it rests on the numerical oneness of the nonmaterial Prime Mover. Briefly, it goes as follows: If there were many heavens, each would have its prime mover, and so there would be many prime movers; but to have many items of the same kind, the items must also contain matter to diversify them; but the Prime Mover has no matter—being only actuality; hence there is only one Prime Mover and one heaven that it moves (1074a31–38). Again here we see that being actuality (*entelecheia gar*, 1074a36) cannot mean just that the Prime Mover is an actuality and exists in actuality. Rather, it must mean what it meant in the previous passage, that is, that the Prime Mover is incapable of transforming into anything else. Hence, it must be without matter, because having matter would have enabled it to suffer transformation.[8] Thus Aristotle argues for the uniqueness of heaven from the uniqueness of the Prime Mover.

Aristotle describes the Prime Mover as follows: "the primary essence has

7. Compare, in the same argument, "that which is potentially may possibly not be," 1071b19.

8. It might be thought that this argument requires only that the Prime Mover be without generative-matter. That is, that the Prime Mover can still have matter that is capable of spatial change, although incapable of generation (for such a distinction, see *Meta.* 1042b5–6). The difficulty here is that Aristotle has just produced an argument that the Prime Mover cannot have magnitude. This would exclude matter capable of spatial movement as a constituent of the Prime Mover.

*not matter*; for it is fulfillment. So the unmovable first mover is *one* both in formula and *in number*" (1074a35–37, my emphasis).[9] This passage, on which the argument for the oneness of heaven rests, is extremely significant for understanding the relation between matter and numerical oneness in Aristotle's system. It reveals that for Aristotle, *numerical oneness does not presuppose materiality.* It is important that this claim does not rest on accepting all the arguments about the Prime Mover as being correct ones. Whether they are or not, Aristotle is here explicitly stating that something can be numerically one without being material. It is this independence of numerical oneness from materiality that I want to concentrate on to explore its consequences for Aristotle's metaphysics.

It might be thought that if Aristotle holds that the Prime Mover has no matter but is nevertheless (primitively) numerically one, this is telling proof that he takes the form to be the ground of the numerical oneness of a substance. Thus, the Prime Mover would be numerically one because its substantial form is numerically one. Surprisingly, far from confirming the doctrine of individual forms, we can use the present passage to argue against it. The reason is that if there were individual forms, there could be many different (nonmaterial) Prime Movers, which Aristotle denies here. Aristotle makes the following connection between materiality and plurality in this passage: *numerical plurality within the same kind presupposes materiality.* Aristotle says: "all things that are many in number have matter. (For one and the same formula applies to *many* things, e.g., the formula of man; but Socrates is *one*.)" (1074a33–35). Because numerical plurality within the same kind requires materiality, it follows that numerical plurality within a kind *cannot* be attained if the substances in that kind have only form (and no matter). Therefore, *substantial form is not sufficient for the numerical distinctness between, for example, Socrates and Callias.* What Aristotle is telling us here is that matter is required for such numerical distinctness. But if the substantial form in a substance were particular, matter would not be required for the distinctness of Socrates and Callias. This does not mean that Socrates and Callias could not be material but only that their numerical distinctness would not presuppose their materiality. But Aristotle tells us that it does: "all things that are many in number have matter" (1074a33–34). Therefore, the substantial form is not sufficient for the numerical oneness of the substance, and, hence, *substantial forms are not primitively particular.*

9. τὸ δὲ τί ἦν εἶναι <u>οὐκ ἔχει ὕλην</u> τὸ πρῶτον· ἐντελέχεια γάρ. <u>ἓν</u> ἄρα καὶ λόγῳ καὶ <u>ἀριθμῷ</u> τὸ πρῶτον κινοῦν ἀκίνητον ὄν.

## 2. Particularity and Subjecthood

Because the substantial form is not primitively particular, the question that now confronts us is: If it is neither form nor matter that is responsible for the numerical oneness of the (nonmaterial) Prime Mover, how is the Prime Mover numerically one? To answer this, we first consider what it is to be numerically one. In Aristotle's system, the numerically one items are such entities as Socrates, Callias, this tree, this rock. All these entities are (higher or lower) substances and are characterized by the fact that *they do not belong to any (other substance as) subject.* A concrete substance does not belong to any other substance, but all else in it, or of it, belongs to it. As we have seen, as early as the *Categories*, Aristotle says that a particular, primary substance does not belong to any other substance as species, genus, or as a property: "some are neither in a subject nor said of a subject, for example, the individual man or individual horse—for nothing of this sort is either in a subject or said of a subject"; "a primary substance is neither said of a subject nor in a subject" (*Cat.* 1b3–6, 3a8–9). In *Metaphysics* Z, 3, he says: "substance . . . is that which is not predicated of a subject, but of which all else is predicated" (1029a8–9). Aristotle remains firmly committed to this principle and develops a sophisticated conception of substantial form, so as to combine the roles of substancehood and subjecthood in one.

What follows from the fact that Socrates does not belong to another subject is that *Socrates is the ultimate subject in Socrates.* This means that, whatever is singled out as the ultimate subject in Socrates will have to be identical to Socrates; else, Socrates will belong to an ultimate subject in him other than himself. Prima facie, Aristotle himself seems to be contradicting his own principle in *Metaphysics* Z, 3, when he says that "the predicates other than substance [i.e., substantial form] are predicated of substance, while substance is predicated of matter" (1029a23–24). This would commit Aristotle to the position that the ultimate subject in Socrates is his matter. Since Socrates' matter is different from Socrates, whatever Socrates may turn out to be, he will somehow belong to the ultimate subject within him. This would contradict the Aristotelian position that a particular substance does not belong to any other subject.

Aristotle does give up the position that matter is an ultimate subject (*hupokeimenon*). In Z, 3, he concludes that, although, as ultimate subject, matter should be substance, it is not substance because it does not satisfy other criteria for substancehood, such as separability and individuality (1029a27–28). It would therefore appear that Aristotle is divorcing subjecthood from substancehood in *Metaphysics* Z, allowing that the ultimate subject be the matter and choosing another candidate for substance on different criteria. Thus, we have seen that M. Furth attributes to Aristotle the position that in the *Metaphysics* the subject is the matter and that the substance is the form.[10] Yet, I shall argue, Aristotle does retain the identity of subject and substance in Z (see Section 3). But for the moment we need to note why the Z, 3, threat of division between subject and substance is only apparent. In Appendix 2 I argue that the thought experiment that Aristotle performs in Z, 3, consists of transferring all the descriptive elements in a declarative sentence from the subject term to the predicate term (though Aristotle may not have realized these semantic implications). I suggest that what this reveals is that description is not the only semantic function of the terms of a sentence; specifically, there is the semantic function of referring to something in the world, which is allotted to the subject term. So the Z, 3, thought experiment reveals that there is a division of labor between the subject and the predicate terms in a sentence, corresponding to the referring and the descriptive roles of parts of the sentence. I further suggest that this semantic discovery does not have any ontological implications in itself. It does not tell us anything about what there is in the world, although we cannot know if Aristotle saw that. But if one believed that the thought experiment showed something about the world, it would be showing something about there being a *substratum*, not a *subject*. As we saw in the discussion of abstract entities, abstracting the properties away from the subject gives rise to a substratum. The substratum does *not* possess the abstracted properties; for example, the quantity of bronze in the statue does not possess any particular shape. Therefore, if the thought experiment shows matter to come out the prime candidate as an underlying entity, it is the prime candidate as substratum, not as subject. The role of the subject still remains open in Z, 3, to be filled by one of the other candidates for substance, the form, or the composite of matter and form (1029a29–30).[11]

The substantial form is of course the main candidate for being the subject, given that it stands for what a concrete substance is. But if the substantial form in Socrates is universal, if the form of *human being* in Socrates is the universal form that is in many other human beings, then that universal form cannot at the same time be the subject in Socrates, because Socrates is not a universal. Socrates is a particular, and the subject that

10. Furth 1988, 50, 62, 176, 185, 188.
11. "Form and the compound of form and matter would be thought to be substance."

Socrates is must also be particular. This would seem to suggest that, if the substantial form is subject, the substantial form in Socrates must be particular. But then the following question confronts us: What is the relation of the form to the matter in Socrates? The form is being assumed to be particular independently of the matter. But then, do they each have their own, *distinct* particularity? If they do, is the substance, which is the composite of the two, a plurality rather than a single whole? Identifying the subject with the form, and treating the form as a particular leaves the matter as an unwelcome extra, which somehow appends to the substance. Yet, for Aristotle, material substances are necessarily material, which cannot be justified if the subject (e.g., Socrates) is just the form (without the matter). If Aristotle advocated individual forms, namely, forms of the same kind that differ numerically from one another, he would not have required that things of the same kind be *material* ("all things that are many in number have matter. (For one and the same formula applies to *many* things, e.g., the formula of man; but Socrates is *one*)" *Meta.* 1074a33–35).

Aristotle allows for two kinds of particular substance: immaterial substance, where there can be only one substance per kind, and material substance, where there can be many substances per kind. He does not allow for a third case, for a substance without matter to be numerically different from another substance (of the same kind). But if Aristotle believed (as Frede holds) that substances are primitively individual forms, how could Aristotle claim that from the fact that things of a kind are numerically different it follows that these things are *material*? Yet, Aristotle does claim just that. It follows that the attempt to combine subjecthood and substancehood in the form, in material substances, goes against Aristotle's conception of numerical difference.

Neither the abstracted substantial form of a substance, nor its abstracted matter can be particular, and, hence, neither of them can be the subject that is the substance. The subject will be shown to be the form in actuality, which is the substance itself. In Chapter 7, we will study Aristotle's theory of how the form in actuality is the enmattered form for concrete substances.

### 3. Essence as Subject:
### The "Second Man" Argument

We saw in Chapter 3 that Plato faced the nature-feature problem of explaining through the Theory of Forms how some properties only characterized the subject, whereas others determined the nature of the subject. We also saw that in the *Timaeus* Plato explicitly took the position that participation in Forms does not affect the nature of the subject. This, of course, means that, for instance, being a human being is a property that belongs to a subject that, in itself, is not a human being. Aristotle considered the case of participation determining the nature of the subject and concluded that there could be substantial Forms only, for otherwise there would be such objects in the world as heights, reds, or unjusts.

Aristotle's first response to the nature-feature problem is given in the *Categories*, where he distinguishes between two different ways of belonging to the subject:

> Of things there are: some are *said of* a subject. . . . For example, man is said of a subject, the individual man. . . . Some are in a subject. . . . (By "in a subject" I mean what is in something, not as a part, and cannot exist separately from what it is in.) For example, the individual knowledge-of-grammar is in a subject, the soul. (1a20–26)

> All the other things are either said of the primary substances as subjects or in them as subjects. . . . For example, animal is predicated of man and therefore of individual man. . . . Again, colour is in body and therefore also in an individual body. . . . Thus all the other things are either said of the primary substances as subjects or in them as subjects. (2a34–2b5)

The idea here is that secondary substances, which determine the nature of the primary substances, belong to them in a different way from the way that nonsubstance forms belong to primary substances. But even this distinction between two ways of belonging to a subject still retains one fundamental Platonic position, that the subject is *different* from the being that determines its nature. In Plato this distinction would be between the partaker and the substantial Form it partook in; in the Aristotle of the *Categories* the distinction is between the primary substance and the secondary substance said of it. The Aristotle of the central books of the *Metaphysics* will object to this division of the subject from its nature. This objection is formalized in the "Second Man" Argument in chapter Z, 6.

Aristotle says in *Metaphysics* Z, 6, that "each thing is thought to be not different from its substance, and the essence is said to be the substance of each thing" (1031a17–18). Independently of the motivation for this claim, it is a puzzling one, because as we saw in Chapter 2, first, for Aristotle the essence of a substance is knowable in the strict sense, which requires it to be

universal. Second, the essence of a substance is *what* that substance is, and as
such it is scientifically definable and, hence, universal. But if the essence is
universal, it cannot be the same as the substance, which is particular.
Socrates' essence cannot be both universal (e.g., common to Socrates and
Callias) *and* identical to Socrates and Callias. This is a difficulty for Aristotle's system, which I address in Chapter 7. Our present concern will be
with the motivating argument for the identity claim of a subject and its
essence and the metaphysical significance of this result.[12]

Let us recall the Platonic position presented in the *Timaeus*. There, Plato
assumes that a physical substance results when empty space (i.e., a characterless, particular, receptacle) becomes informed by partaking of the Platonic Forms (50–52). Plato insists that the nature of the receptacle does not
change by participating in the Forms:

> the nature which receives all bodies—that must be always called the same;
> for, inasmuch as she always receives all things, she never departs at all from
> her own nature, and never in any way, or at any time, assumes a form like that
> of the things which enter into her; she is the natural recipient of all impres-
> sions, and is stirred and informed by them, and appears different from time
> to time by reason of them. But the forms which enter into and go out of her
> are the likenesses of eternal realities modeled after their patterns in a wonder-
> ful and mysterious manner. (50b6–c6)

The predicament that results from such an account of substantial composition is that because participation in the Forms does not affect the nature of
the partaker (i.e., the subject), there is no sense in which the subject *is* fire

12. According to some commentators, Aristotle is not claiming here that particular
substance is identical with its essence, but that a universal species form is identical with its
essence. Thus, Asclepius in Hayduck 1888, 392.1–2, 393.23–24, 397.2; Furth 1988,
236; Halper 1989, 88; Loux 1991, 103; and Code 1985, 110–113, who says that "each
properly definable thing [i.e., not a particular such as Socrates, but a *universal* such as the
species man, pp. 112–113] is (strictly speaking) numerically the same as its essence. If each
primary καθ' αὑτό λεγόμενον is definable, then this last statement implies the Z, 6, thesis
[that all things πρῶτα καὶ καθ' αὑτὰ λεγόμενα (primary and called what they are called in
virtue of themselves) are one and the same as their essence (p. 110)]" (p. 113). I also formerly
argued this view in my dissertation (Scaltsas 1983, 180–193). According to others, Aristotle is claiming the identity of particular substance (whether individual form or the
composite) with its essence. Thus, Alexander in Hayduck 1891, 483.18–20, Aquinas
[1261–1272] 1961, 1357; Ross 1924, 2:176; Woods 1974–75:177–179; Hartman 1976,
545; and 1977, 58–59, 62–63, 73; Frede and Patzig 1988, 2:87; and Frede 1990, 126.
Finally, according to J. Lear, Aristotle is claiming that the species form is primary substance
(p. 280), where the species form is neither particular nor universal (1988, 285–286).

or a triangle. The subject will become related to the Form of Fire or Triangle, but, Plato insists, its nature will not be affected by that relation. *What* the subject is will remain the same, regardless of the Forms it participates in. Extrapolating along this line of reasoning, the subject in Socrates (i.e., the ultimate recipient of the forms characterizing Socrates) will not be the human being (if "human being" is one of the forms it *receives*). In its nature, the subject will be a-human. But the subject in Socrates must be the human being, because that is what Socrates is. It follows that the subject in Socrates both is and is not the human being.

A similar problem would be generated if, in place of the Platonic formless receptacle we have Aristotelian matter as the ultimate subject in a substance. The position that Aristotle entertains in *Metaphysics* Z, 3, that the matter is the ultimate subject in a substance, would produce the same problems in the Aristotelian corpus as the *Timaeus* position generates for Plato. In fact, the problems do not even require taking the subject to be characterless, as some take the Z, 3, ultimate matter to be. Whether the substratum is the Platonic formless receptacle, a characterless prime matter, or an Aristotelian elementary matter, the problem remains the same: if the subject is *other* than the forms that determine the substance's essence, then the subject itself will not be *what* these forms stand for. The subject may be related to the forms in one way or another, but in its very own nature it will not be what they are. Thus, if the subject is different from the essence, however it may be related to the essence, the subject itself will not be what the essence stands for; for example, that to which the form "human being" belongs essentially will not, itself, be a human being!

Before coming to the detailed examination of the arguments that establish this result in Z, 6, we should briefly turn to the question of the relation of the present problem to that in the Third Man Argument (TMA). G. E. L. Owen and Michael Woods thought that Aristotle reached his *Metaphysics* Z position as a way of avoiding the TMA by rejecting the Non-Identity Assumption.[13] I hope the preceding discussion has shed enough light on the nature-feature problem to enable us to see that it is a different problem from the one addressed by the Non-Identity Assumption. We see this more clearly when we realize that the nature-feature problem can be resolved without giving up the Non-Identity Assumption. Furthermore, it was within Plato's power to resolve it, but he chose (for reasons we reviewed) to go a different way. Specifically, when in the *Timaeus* Plato opted for the posi-

13. Owen 1965b; Woods 1974–75, 177–179.

tion that participation in a Form does not change the nature of the partaking subject (see quoted passage, 50b6–c6), he could have gone the opposite way and allowed that, in some cases (e.g., in the cases of substantial Forms) participation in a Form determines the nature of the subject. That is, the universal nature that receives all bodies *would depart* from her own nature and *assume* a form like that of the things that enter into her. Thus, participation in the Form of Human Being would turn the very nature of the participating subject into that of a human being. Had Plato made that choice, instead of the opposite one, which he in fact made, then a participating subject would change in its very constitution and become, itself, the nature that was introduced by participation in a (substantial) Form.

What is of interest to us in this case is that this would resolve the nature-feature problem, because the participating subject would relinquish its own nature to the one introduced by participation in the (substantial) Form, so that it would itself become that nature. But this identification of the subject to the nature introduced by participation in the Form need not be incompatible with the Non-Identity Assumption. Plato could allow that the Immanent (substantial) Form become the subject in the thing as a result of participation while retaining the difference between the Form and its instantiations (Immanent Forms). Giving up the Non-Identity Assumption would require a further step: there should be no metaphysical gap not only between the subject and the nature of a thing, but also between a Form and its instantiations, that is, between the universal nature and the nature of a thing. Even if the subject in a thing becomes identical to the Immanent Form as a result of participation, the Immanent Form can still be different from the Form—hence, Non-Identity. But Non-Identity, along with Self-Predication, would generate the Third Man regress. So, the identification of the subject with its nature need not be the identification of the subject with the Form and, hence, need not be the rejection of the Non-Identity Assumption of the Third Man, which is what Owen and Woods have taken it to be. Having resolved the nature-feature problem by the subject-nature identification, one would still be free to tell a further story about the relation of the substance to the universal form. Z, 6's, target is the identification of a thing with its *own nature*, not with the *universal forms*. As we will see, this is required for a substance to be a *kath' hauto* entity, namely, an entity that is what it is in virtue of itself, rather than in virtue of something different from it and related to it.

Aristotle argues for the identity of a substance and its essence in *Metaphysics* Z, 6, through an infinite regress argument as well as five further arguments. We refer to the regress as the "Second Man" Argument (SMA), because it posits a second substance, given a first, namely, the essence of the first substance (unlike the "Third Man" Argument, which posits a third substance, given two similar substances). Aristotle gives the regress argument in the following:

> The absurdity [of the separation of a substance from its essence] would appear also if one were to assign a name to each of the essences; for there would be another essence, besides the original one, e.g., to the essence of horse there will belong a second essence. (1031b28–30)

> If they [i.e., the essence of one and the one] were different, the process would go on to infinity; for we should have the essence of one, and the one, so that in their case also *the same* argument would be found. Clearly, then, each primary and self-subsistent thing is one and the same as its essence. (1032a2–6, my emphasis)

In the case of the essence of horse, an infinite regress is not mentioned, but is alluded to in "the *same* argument would be found." A regress is generated, driven by the principle that an essence has an essence, to which the premises are committed.[14]

---

14. Code thinks that a regress can be derived but that nevertheless Aristotle is not making that point here. Rather, he takes Aristotle to be pointing to an absurdity that is generated by the claim that the essence of horse is different from the essence of the essence of horse (1985, 121). Yet, Code does not offer a satisfactory justification of the absurdity claim. He supplies an argument for Aristotle to show that the essence of horse is identical to the essence of the essence of horse (p. 122). He argues that the definition of the essence of horse will be the same as the definition of the essence of the essence of horse. From this, plus the claim that the essence of something is just what is signified by the definition of the essence, he concludes that essences that share the same definition are one and the same entity. However, this assumes that for essences, qualitative identity entails numerical identity. Frank Lewis agrees with Code and uses this principle in his analysis of the same passage in Z, 6 (Lewis 1985, 161). He formalizes (and strengthens) the claim: "*x* is the definition of *y*, only if *y* = *x*."

Both commentators base their claim on passages in *Topics* A, 7 (Code 1985, 113; Lewis 1985, 174), where Aristotle says that if two things are not the same, they cannot have the same definition (102a13–14). They understand sameness in terms of numerical oneness, because Aristotle says that the term *the same* is used "in a sense agreed on by everyone when applied to what is numerically one" (103a23–24). But this evidence is not sufficient to support the claim that sameness of definition entails numerical identity. They seem to ignore Aristotle's statements in *Metaphysics* to the effect that "some things are one in number, others in species . . . in number those whose matter is one, in species those whose definition is one . . . things that are one in species are not all one in number" (1016b31–36). Further-

It makes no difference whether the substances in question are Platonic Forms (e.g., of the One or of Horse) or physical substances (e.g., a horse or a human being). All that matters is that the initial entity be a substance. Within the context of Z, 6, to be a substance is to be a primary and *kath' hauto* entity. [15] These are the entities that are said to be what they are—and are what they are—in virtue of themselves; they are "substances which have no other substances nor entities prior to them" (1031a28–30); they are "things which do not depend on something else but are self-subsistent and primary" (1031b13–14). In the case of substances, says Aristotle, if the substance is other than its essence, an infinite regress will follow.

Our first concern here will be to establish the premises from which the regress follows. We just saw that the argument concerns substances, namely, things that are what they are in virtue of themselves. For example, a tree is a tree in virtue of itself, but a green thing is not green in virtue of itself, but in virtue of, for example, its being a tree. It is green because it is a tree and trees are green. But it is not a tree because it is some further thing, which in its turn is a tree. There is no further cause to which one can appeal to explain why a tree is a tree, other than the tree's being what it is; it has "no other substances nor entities prior to [it]" (1031a29–30) and does not "depend on something else, but . . . [is] self-subsistent and primary" (1031b13–14). So, an initial assumption of the argument is that there are substances, namely, *f* things that are *f* in virtue of themselves (Existential Premise).

Two further assumptions are that a substance has an essence (Essentialist Premise) and (the premise under contention in the argument) that essences are different from their substances (Non-Identity). Thus, in the case of a horse, its nature of being a horse is different from the horse. [16]

The Non-Identity claim is expressed in three different instances through-

---

more, there is a long tradition of commentators who attribute the opposite view to Aristotle in the doctrine of individual forms. Most recently, Frede argued that Aristotle is committed to individual forms and said about them: "But if it should be demanded that there be something about the form in and by itself which distinguishes it from other forms of the same kind, the answer is that there is no such distinguishing mark, and that there is no need for one" (Frede 1985, 23–24). Hence, the grounds on which commentators attribute individual substantial forms to Aristotle are grounds for denying that Aristotle believed that sameness of definition entails numerical oneness; however, this is the assumption made by Code and Lewis for the justification of the absurdity claim in their reading of Z, 6. For a discussion of further readings of this passage, see Scaltsas 1993a, 126–128.

15. *Meta.* 1031a28, 1031b13–14, 1032a5.

16. This Non-Identity Assumption, as we already saw, concerns the relation of the substance to its essence, leaving open the relation of the essence to the universal form.

out Z, 6, once as a subject of inquiry, and twice as an assumption in the arguments, the last being the Second Man Argument. Aristotle expresses it in terms of difference: "We must inquire whether a thing and its essence are the same or *different* [*heteron*]" (1031a15–16); "if the essence of good is to be *different* [*heteron*] from the Idea of good" (1031a31–32); "if they [the One and its essence] were *different* [*allo*]" (1032a2–3, my emphases). We need assume, therefore, that a substance is a different entity from its essence.

Finally, there is one more assumption that Aristotle is operating on throughout the chapter; it is that the essence of a thing is itself substance. This premise appears three times in the text. First, in the introduction, where he says that "the essence is said to be the substance of each thing" (1031a18), and more directly, in the context of the regress he says "since essence is substance" (1031b31–32). Finally, we can understand the sense in which essence is substance from the third occurrence of this claim in the chapter. Here Aristotle introduces the hypothesis that "essence is substance" (1031b2–3), having just described substances as *kath' hauto* entities with "no other substances nor entities prior to them" (1031a29–30), but being what they are in virtue of themselves. This is the sense in which essences are substances; they do not need to be physically separate, in the way that concrete substances are; rather, they have to satisfy the substance-hood criterion of being *kath' hauto* entities, being what they are in virtue of themselves.

The assumption that essence is substance is vital, because without it Aristotle could not derive the regress. The derivation of the regress requires that an essence be the type of entity that has an essence: "to the essence of horse there will belong a second essence" (1031b30). But it is substances, namely, primary entities with a nature (that are what they are in virtue of themselves rather than being a complex of one thing said of another thing) that paradigmatically have essences (1030a6–13, 1030a29–30, b5–6). So the assumption that essence is substance secures that essences are the kind of entity that have essence, which generates the regress. [17]

We can now state the premises of the Second Man Argument and derive the regress. (The expression "what it is to be an *f*" designates the essence of a

17. Here I disagree with M. Loux who says that in Z, 6 Aristotle is not committed to the premise that "essence is *ousia*," because "that is precisely what Z, 6 is meant to establish" (Loux 1991, 99). But Aristotle must be committed to that premise, in the sense of "*ousia*" just explained, if the regress is to be generated. Being committed to the premise that essence is substance does not entail that the essence of a substance is identical to the substance. All the premise claims is that an essence is the type of entity that has a nature of its own—and is

substance which is an $f$ in virtue of itself.) The operative definition of substance is:

> Definition:  A substance is an entity that is an $f$ in virtue of itself.

**The "Second Man" Argument:**

| | |
|---|---|
| *Existential Premise:* | There are substances. |
| *Essentialist Premise:* | If an $f$ is a substance, there is an $f_1$ = what it is to be an $f$. |
| *Non-Identity:* | The $f$ is different from the $f_1$. |
| *Essence Substantiality:* | The $f_1$ is a substance. |

On the basis of these premises we can now derive the regress. By the Existential Premise, there are substances. By the Essentialist Premise, given an $f$, which is a substance, there is an $f_1$ = what it is to be an $f$. By Non-Identity, the $f_1$ is different from the $f$. By Essence Substantiality, the $f_1$ is a substance. Hence, by the Essentialist Premise, there will be an $f_2$ = what it is to be an $f_1$. By Non-Identity, the $f_2 \neq$ the $f_1$. By Essence Substantiality, the $f_2$ is a substance, and so on ad infinitum. [18]

Aristotle takes this result to establish the conclusion that "Clearly, then, each primary and self-subsistent thing is one and the same as its essence" (1032a4–6). But the question arises, why should this result follow? What exactly is the offending element in the conclusion that forces this result upon us? Is it that Aristotle takes the conclusion to commit us to the actuality of the infinite—for instance, for Bucephalus to be a horse, there should be an infinity of substances, one being the essence of the other? I do not think this is the difficulty at hand. After all, it must have occurred to Aristotle that *every property has a property*, which generates a benign infinite regress. Furthermore, the eternity of each species requires an infinity of members, but this did not prevent Aristotle from committing himself to species eternity. But independently of Aristotle's reasons for rejecting the conclusion of the argument, it is of intrinsic philosophical interest whether

in that sense a substance; this leaves it open whether it is identical to the substance it belongs to or not. It is the latter question that is the target of Z, 6, not the former, as Loux takes it to be.

18. It is of course understood that Aristotle is assuming that if $f_1$ is the essence of $f$, then $f$ is not the essence of $f_1$ (where $f_1 \neq f$). The reason is that it would be metaphysically nonsensical for an essence to belong (as an essence) to what belonged to it (as an essence)! In general, no terms in the series reappear further along the series. The question of metaphysical interest for Aristotle is whether terms recurred consecutively in the series, but this is here denied by the Non-Identity Premise.

the regress of the SMA is a benign or a vicious one and what conclusions one might draw from it, especially if one is not opposed to the actuality of the infinite. I believe that the infinite regress in the SMA is not benign but vicious, and I try to show this. I argue that the premises of the SMA are inconsistent. Aristotle's result is not peculiar to his theory, but it is a metaphysical claim that commands respect in any metaphysical system, [19] warning against any sort of ontological gap between a substance and its nature.

An indication that Aristotle must have associated the result of the SMA with an *impossibility* can be found in the arguments that he offers earlier on in Z, 6, against the substance-essence separation. There are five arguments, not all of which have the same philosophical generality. Aristotle uses as examples of substance the Platonic Forms and assumes that they are different from their essences, which are, themselves, substances. The first three arguments are given in the following:

> If the essence of good is different from the Idea of good, and the essence of animal from the Idea of animal, and the essence of being from the Idea of being, there will, firstly, be other substances and entities and Ideas besides those which are asserted, and secondly, these others will be prior substances if the essence is substance. And if the posterior substances are severed from the prior, [20] there will be no knowledge of the ones and the others will have no being. (1031a31–b4)

I will not dwell on these arguments, because they are too narrowly confined to either the Theory of Forms or Aristotle's epistemology. The first argument concerns the proliferation of substances that results (even within the world of Ideas) from the distinction of substance and essence. The second argument points out that the assumption that a substance has no further substances and principles prior to it is undermined by the distinction of

19. I am thus in full agreement with Loux's conclusion that "the claim that a primary *ousia* and the fundamental essence in virtue of which it is what it is are necessarily one and the same is theory-neutral. It expresses a constraint on any attempt to pick out the ontologically basic things. Commitment to the Identity Thesis, the Aristotle of Z, 6, wants to claim, is a presupposition of doing anything that can genuinely be called metaphysics" (Loux 1991, 94).

20. Barnes (1984) misleadingly translates ἀπολελυμέναι ἀλλήλων as: "And if the posterior substances are severed from one another." The assumption of this argument is not that Platonic Forms are severed from one another, but that they are severed from their essences, as becomes evident both from what precedes and follows this line in the text.

substance and essence. The third argument is that if the substances are different from their essences, then the substances will not be knowable. This latter claim rests on the Aristotelian position that "there is knowledge of each thing only when we know its essence" (1031b6–7), so that if a substance is different from its essence—and its knowable in terms of its essence—the substance will not be knowable. This, of course, is knowledge in the strict, Aristotelian scientific sense.

The fourth argument is again one that is sound only as an argument against the Platonic Forms. It could not hold its ground either within the Aristotelian metaphysics or in the broader philosophical spectrum. Aristotle has explained that "by 'severed' I mean, if the Idea of good has not the essence of good, and the latter has not the property of being good" (1031b4–6). On this basis, Aristotle says that "if the essence of the good is not good, neither will the essence of being be" (1031b8–9). And because the case is the same for all, if the essence of one Form (namely, of the Form of Being) does not exist, neither do the essences of the rest of the Forms: "all the essences alike exist or none of them does; so that if the essence of being is not, neither will any of the others be" (1031b9–10). But even if all other assumptions were agreed to, still the argument rests on there being a Form of Being, which Aristotle was first to deny. Hence, this argument will have no force in the Aristotelian system or any subsequent system in which existence is not a property.

The final argument is the most interesting one. It rests on the explanation that Aristotle provides of the separateness of a substance from its essence: "the Idea of the good has not the essence of good, and the latter [the essence of good] has not the property of being good" (1031b5–6). Aristotle has already derived two consequences from this: that substances will not be knowable, and that essences will not exist. He now wants to show the metaphysical consequence that follows about substances. He says: "Again, that which has not the essence of being good is not good" (1031b11).[21] That is,

21. The Greek sentence here is ἔτι ᾧ μὴ ὑπάρχει ἀγαθῷ εἶναι, οὐκ ἀγαθόν. W. D. Ross's translation, "Again, that which has not the *property* of being good is not good" (my emphasis), is misleading, because it might be read as stating that it is the essence of the good that is deprived of the property of being good. This, in fact, is Alexander's reading of the passage, who takes the argument to be that what is different from the Idea of the good is not good, so that because the essence of the good is different from the Idea of the good, the essence of the good is not good (Alexander 1891, 483.7–12). But this would not be objectionable for the reason that there is no prior understanding that the essence of good is good; only that the Idea of the good is good. Alexander says that ὃ δὲ λέγει, τοιοῦτόν ἐστιν ("Whatever it is called, such it is," 483.9). But it is the Idea of the good, not the essence of

not only will the Idea of the good not be knowable, but, without the essence of good—without being "what it is to be good"—the Idea of good will not be good.[22] However, "good" is just what the Idea of good is. If the paradigmatically good is not good, the theory confronts a contradiction.

That the metaphysical separateness of a substance from its essence leads to contradiction is a warning sign regarding the premises of the SMA. What is common between this version of the Theory of Forms and the premises of the SMA is that in both a substance is different from its essence. Although this would not disallow a substance to be somehow related to its essence, I argue that their difference alone is sufficient to lead to an impossibility and, hence, that the SMA regress is vicious.[23] I further posit that the impossibility is not an epistemic one, as Alan Code has argued, to which Frank Lewis agreed, but a metaphysical one.[24] The key to the discovery of the inconsistency is given to us by Aristotle, but not in Z, 6. In Z, 4, Aristotle defines essence as follows: "The essence of each thing is what it is said to be in virtue of itself."[25] This shows the intimacy between $x$'s essence and $x$ being an $f$ in virtue of itself. *The essence of $x$ is just what $x$ is in virtue of itself.* Therefore, distinguishing $x$ from its essence is distinguishing $x$ from itself.

Aristotle has told us that if substances are severed from their essences, then the Idea of the good will not have the essence of the good, and the essence of the good will not have the property of being good. Furthermore, he declared that the two consequences that follow from this are that substances will not be knowable and essences will not exist. In the third argument—the last quotation—he wants to show that there is a metaphysical consequence that follows about the substances, over and above the epistemological one. That is, not only will the Idea of the good not be

the good, that is said to be the good. Furthermore, it would be strange if Aristotle proved first that the essence of the good does not exist (1031b9–10) and then immediately proceeded to prove that the essence of the good is not good. Ross's position becomes clear in his commentary, where it is evident that the *property* in question (in the quoted passage) is the essence of the good (Ross 1924, 2:178); so he would disagree with Alexander's reading.

22. As Asclepius (in Hayduck 1888) explains: οὐκ ἔστιν ἀγαθὸν ᾧ τινι μὴ ὑπάρχει ἀγαθῷ εἶναι (393.17–18)—whatever does not possess "being good" is not good.

23. A vicious regress is one that is impossible to actualize—i.e., to have the infinitely many steps—because of an impossibility that rests in its premises.

24. Code argues that Aristotle found the series of essences of essences absurd because no essence would be definable, since "one cannot go through an infinite series in thought" (Code 1985, 121). F. A. Lewis agreed (1985, 164).

25. ἐστὶ τὸ τί ἦν εἶναι ἑκάστου ὃ λέγεται καθ᾽ αὑτό (1029b13–14).

knowable, but, without the essence of good, without being "what it is to be good," the Idea of good will not be good. As Asclepius explains, whatever does not possess "being good" is not good."[26] But "good" is just what the Idea of good is. If the paradigmatically good is not good, there is a contradiction in the theory.

The contradiction is not peculiar to the Theory of Forms. If a horse is not what it is to be a horse, it will not be a horse. The reason is that "that which has not the essence of being . . . [a horse] is not [a horse]" (1031b11). But if the separation of a substance (e.g., the horse Bucephalus) from its essence of being a horse results in Bucephalus not being a horse, the horse is not a horse.

Turning to the premises of the SMA, we see that the definition of substance requires an *f*-substance to be an *f in virtue of itself*. But because being an *f* is the substance's essence, it follows that the substance is its essence *in virtue of itself*. But this is just what is being denied by the Non-Identity Premise, which states that an *f*-substance is distinct from what it is to be an *f*. It thus follows that the premises of the SMA require that a substance both be and not be an *f* in virtue of itself, which is a contradiction.

It would be useful, in order to gauge the philosophical significance of Aristotle's result, to look at a contemporary metaphysical system that does separate the substance from its essence. David Armstrong, in his recent book on *Universals* (1989b), has taken up the question of the "Antinomy of Bare Particulars."[27] The reasoning of the antinomy is the following. If *x* is *f*, and *g*, and *h*, *x* cannot be identical to them. Hence, however *x* may be related to *f*, *g*, and *h*, when considered in itself, *x* is a bare particular that has no properties. Therefore *x*, considered in itself, is not *f* but is, and remains, without properties.[28] For instance, Socrates, in himself, is not a human being, which is paradoxical. Amstrong's response to this problem is to introduce the distinction between thin and thick particulars: "The thin particular is *a*, taken apart from its properties (substratum). It is linked to its properties by instantiation, but is not identical with them. . . . The thick particular . . . enfolds both thin particulars and properties, held together by instantiation."[29]

Armstrong's solution is ingenious in that it both retains and overcomes the difficulty that was posed. The question he is addressing is the one that

26. οὐκ ἔστιν ἀγαθὸν ᾧ τινι μὴ ὑπάρχει ἀγαθῷ εἶναι (393.17–18).
27. The problem was presented in John Quilter (1985).
28. Armstrong 1989b, 94–95.
29. Ibid., p. 95.

Aristotle addressed in Z, 6, namely, given that a substance is an *f* in virtue of itself, can the substance be distinct from its essence? Armstrong's answer is to make the essence part of the substance. He allows for an ultimate subject, as described in the antinomy (e.g., for the thin particular Socrates, i.e., Socrates without his properties). Then, the thick particular Socrates is constituted of the thin (in itself, bare) particular Socrates plus the properties it instantiates. So the thick particular (i.e., thin particular plus properties included), in itself, is *f*, because it enfolds the thin particular and its properties held together by instantiation.

The retention of the thin (propertiless) subject in Armstrong's substances has the following consequence. According to the division between thin and thick particular, it is the thin particular that instantiates a property *f* by being related with it through the nexus of instantiation.[30] But the thin particular is not *f*. The thin particular is the substance "taken apart from its properties (substratum)."[31] Rather, the thick particular is what is characterized by the property *f* by containing it in its constitution.[32] It follows that the subject that instantiates a property is not characterized by it and that the subject that is characterized by a property does not instantiate it.

Armstrong's solution is precisely what Aristotle has argued against, because it denies the most fundamental claim about substances, namely, that a substance is what it is in virtue of itself. Armstrong's Socrates is a thick particular that contains within it a further particular, a thin, propertiless particular, which is related to the property of being a human being by the nexus of instantiation. The thin particular is distinct both from the thick particular and from the property of being a human being. In Aristotelian terms, Socrates (the thick particular) is said to be what it is in terms of another thing's[33] (the thin particular's) bearing the property that it does. But this is just what substances are not.

The position that I understand Aristotle to be presenting, which I am putting forward in this book, differs from Armstrong's position in that it does not admit thin particulars, but only thick particulars. This position faces the difficulty, which David Armstrong has put to me in conversation, of explaining how the essence can be both universal (common between

30. It is "linked to its properties by instantiation," ibid., p. 95.
31. Ibid.
32. "The thick particular is a state of affairs. The properties of a thing are 'contained within it' because they are constituents of this state of affairs," ibid.
33. That is, κατ' ἄλλο λέγεται, (Z, 6, 1031b13)—it is said to be what it is in terms of another.

Socrates and Callias) and particular (identical to Socrates, identical to Callias). The answer—what I have been arguing in the second half of the book—lies in the realization that for Socrates and Callias to have a *common nature* is not for them to have a *common component* (that would preclude their both being identical to it). That Socrates and Callias share the same nature means that the same substantial form can be abstracted from both. But as we have seen, abstraction is not the discovery of *components* in a substance, because the division of the substance by abstraction gives rise to components that are not in the substance. There is no essence component in Socrates that is identical to some-essence component in Callias. The moral of Aristotle's claim that the substance is identical to its essence is that the essence in actuality is not a component in the substance, related in some way to the substance; rather, the essence in actuality is the substance itself. This presents the challenge of understanding how the unactualized essence relates to essence in actuality, which is the subject matter of Sections 4 of Chapter 5 and 4–5 of Chapter 7.

Indeed, having argued that a substance is identical to its essence, Aristotle concludes Z, 6, by saying that with regard to "the question whether Socrates and to be Socrates are the same thing . . . we have explained . . . in what sense each thing is the same as its essence and in what sense it is not" (1032a8–11). He has not really explained all that is required yet, but he ultimately does. The final position is that neither essence in actuality nor abstracted essence is a component of Socrates. In actuality, the essence is Socrates. Abstracted, the essence is universal and is neither identical to Socrates nor a component in Socrates (but it is Socrates' because it is derivable from him by division by abstraction). Hence, "to be Socrates" is the same thing as Socrates when the expression designates the essence in actuality, but not the same things as Socrates when it designates the universal essence. We return to this issue in what follows in this chapter and in Section 5 of Chapter 7.

## 4. Particularity of Nonmaterial Substances

It is important to make clear that *being an ultimate subject* does not determine, but *presupposes* a theory of substance. This can be seen from the following thought experiment. Suppose that we developed a theory according to which, contra Aristotle, the full-fledged substances are the Aristotelian species forms rather than the concrete substances. We would of course have to give up the criterion that substance is separate, unless we meant separate by abstraction. But we could still retain the claim that a substance is the ultimate subject, that is, that the species form is the ultimate subject. What would have to change to accommodate this position is the relation of concrete entities to the species forms. Thus, Socrates and Callias would *belong* to the form of man in a metaphysical way. They would not be subjects but would belong to the species form as subject. What follows is that the sort of entity the ultimate subject is will depend on what entities the theory determines to be the substances. But neither notion reduces to the other. There are criteria[34] to be satisfied for something to be the ultimate subject and (partially) independent criteria[35] for something to be a substance. So, neither notion is completely dependent or completely independent of the other. A metaphysical argument needs to be introduced to show that, and to show how, the substance is the subject. This topic is the overarching concern in this and the following chapter.

Determining the *ultimate subject* does determine which entities are the *particulars*. To determine what the ultimate subject is requires determining which entities in the ontology belong to other entities and which belong to none. *The entities that do not belong to any other entities are the particular ones.* A *universal* is that which belongs to many subjects.[36] The ultimate subject itself, by definition, cannot belong to many subjects, because it belongs to none and is therefore not universal, but *particular*. In the non-Aristotelian theory we envisaged in the thought experiment of the preceding paragraph, the species forms, as ultimate subjects would be the particulars. They would not belong to many subjects, for they would themselves be the ultimate subjects, to which all other entities would belong. Thus, *ultimate subjecthood is particularity*, and whatever entities the theory of substance determines to be the ultimate subjects, they will also be the particulars.

The Prime Mover is a substance, in Aristotle's metaphysics. Within its category (or branch of category), it is the entity of which all higher forms are said, and it, itself, is not said of anything else. Nor does it belong to any other substance as a property or constituent. Within its categorial branch, the Prime Mover *is where predication stops*. Thus, it is an ultimate subject and, therefore, a particular. Being a particular does not require its contain-

---

34. Most important, not belonging to anything else, but everything else belonging to it (1028b36–37).

35. E.g., physical separateness, possessing an internal principle or source of growth and development, etc.

36. E.g., *Meta.* 1038b11–12, *Int.* 17a39–40.

ing any special type of component such as matter or a bare substratum. Being a *particular* is being at the bottom of the predicational ladder in a branch of the substance category and being different from the other entities at the same level in the category—which the Prime Mover is on account of its essential properties. Which entities are at the bottom of a substantial branch is determined by the criteria of substancehood, such as being physically separate, having an internal principle of self-development, having the power to reproduce, and the like for the material substances. For entities such as the Prime Mover, the main criterion of substancehood would be being the cause of a single eternal movement without itself being moved (1073a23–25).

We saw that the particulars are the ultimate subjects to which all else belongs and that the ultimate subjects are the lowest level entities in the branches of the category of substance. Thus, *some, at least, of the criteria for being substance have to be independent of the criteria for being subject.* Else, the account would be circular: the particulars and ultimate subjects would be the entities that are the substances, and the substances would be the entities that are the particulars and ultimate subjects. It is therefore essential that some of the criteria for being a substance be independent of being an ultimate subject and, hence, a particular. Otherwise, there would be no way of determining a bottom level in any of the branches of the category of substance (which determines, rather than presupposes, subjecthood and particularity, because it is there that the predicational buck stops).

This is the case with Aristotle's conception of substance. Let us start with the criterion of being physically separate, which is an Aristotelian criterion for material substance (1042a26–31). Now, consider the entity that is a spatiotemporal worm composed of Socrates and his corpse. We can determine that it is physically separate, without determining whether it is an ultimate subject. As a matter of fact, in Aristotelian theory it turns out not to be an ultimate subject, because Socrates is not a phase of this spatiotemporal worm. Rather, Socrates is himself a subject. Not being an ultimate subject, of course, means that this entity is not a particular. In fact, it is two particulars, a human being and its corpse. Consider now a different criterion for being a substance, having an internal principle of self-development. This criterion, too, does not presuppose being an ultimate subject or being numerically unified. Parts of substances have internal movements that determine their development, but they are not ultimate subjects, because they themselves belong, qua constituents, to substances as subjects. Nor are such parts numerically unified, for, as we have seen, they depend on another, the substance they belong to, for their identity.

Some of the criteria for substancehood, then, do not presuppose there being an ultimate subject and, hence, there being a particular. Rather, these criteria combined together determine which entities are the ultimate subjects, which entities do not belong to any other. These entities will be the numerically one particulars. Thus, the criteria of substancehood determine which entities will be the bottom level entities in each branch of the category of substance (e.g., at the level where the entities are physically separate, have an internal source of development, and the power of reproduction[37]). Once this level is determined, all other entities in the branch belong to the bottom-level entities. The bottom-level entities are the ultimate subjects. Thus, being *particular* means being an entity at the bottom level of a branch of the substance category. Its particularity consists in its difference from the other entities at the bottom level of the substance category.

When Aristotle, then, claims that the Prime Mover is *numerically one* and that it contains no matter (1074a35–37), the statement is not problematic. What it means is that the *Prime Mover is an entity at which the predication stops in its branch of the substance category*; it is an ultimate subject in its category branch, and all higher level entities belong to it, although it belongs to no other subject. In the case of the Prime Mover, the question of its difference from the other substances of the same kind does not arise, because there are no other substances of the same kind with it (i.e., being unmoved causes of the type of movement that the Prime Mover initiates). The reason is that the Prime Mover has no matter, and hence it cannot be further differentiated: there are no other entities that are of the same kind as it, but numerically distinct. The Prime Mover differs from all other entities with respect to its essential properties. The Prime Mover is essentially "not moveable either in itself or accidentally, but produces the primary eternal and single [simple spatial] movement" (1073a24–25, 29). The forty-nine "unmovable substances and principles" (1074a15), which are "of the same number as the movements of the stars, and in nature eternal,[38] and in themselves unmovable, and without magnitude, for the reason before mentioned" (1073a37–38), differ in their essence, because each of these substances provides the principle for a different kind of movement. They differ from one another in kind, not in matter. That the Prime Mover has no matter, therefore, does not mean that it is not particular and numerically one. As an ultimate

37. For discussion of this issue, see Waterlow 1982a, 57–58; Gill, 1989, 116–120, 138–144; Loux 1991, 72–90, 168–183; Edel 1982, 231–238.

38. "There must, then, be such a principle, whose very essence is actuality. Furthermore, then, these substances must be without matter, for they must be eternal" (1071b19–21).

subject in its category branch, it is numerically one; as an immaterial subject, it is not the same in species with any other substance.

People are not different in kind from one another. The criteria for being a substance determine that human beings are the substances, not, for example, the form *human being*, or the spatiotemporal worm composed of a human being and his corpse. All human beings are the same kind of substance. Hence, the difference between human beings cannot be a difference in the essential properties that determine their kind. This is why Aristotle says that "all things that are many in number have matter. (For one and the same formula applies to *many* things, e.g., the formula of man; but Socrates is *one*.)" (*Meta.* 1074a33–35). We have already seen that this indicates that Aristotle does not treat the form as being primitively particular, because, then, Socrates would not require matter to distinguish him from other people. What I argue in the present section is that particularity consists in being an ultimate subject. This presupposes a (partially) independent theory of substance to determine which entities are the substances. Some substances are material and some immaterial. Matter's contribution is toward the differentiation between the material substances of the same kind. *Matter does for material substances what essence does for the nonmaterial ones.* The unmoved movers are different because their essences are qualitatively different. The material substances are different because their matter is qualitatively different. This leaves no room either for a theory of individual forms (else, why do humans need matter to be different?) or for a theory of individual material substrata (else, why are immaterial substances particular?). Neither form nor matter introduce primitive particularity for the subject. What form and matter contribute toward particularity is *difference*, not primitive *particularity*. Particularity is ultimate subjecthood. An ultimate subject is where the predication stops in a substance category branch, which is determined by the theory of substance.

## 5. Particularity of Material Substances:
   How Similar Can Different Substances Be?

Matter, then, is not required for the particularity of substances in general. At the same time, "some things are one in number . . . those whose matter is one. . . . Things that are one in number are one in species" (1016b32–36). Here Aristotle is talking of material substances that are the same in kind but numerically different. In the case of the unmoved movers, each such substance is a kind of its own, differing from all other substances in its essence. But when substances are of the same kind, their difference must rest on something other than the form, namely, matter. This is a general, a priori argument that is not restricted in application to *physical* matter, but would apply to any kind of matter. The argument is that if there are substances that are of the same kind, because they differ from one another, they must each consist of more than the form of that kind. Otherwise, they would not differ from each other. "Matter" in this sense refers to whatever in the constitution of such a substance is over and above the form of the kind. It refers to whatever remains when we abstract the substantial form away from the substance. In the case of the First Mover, nothing remains. In the case of physical substances, physical matter remains. Generally, the Aristotelian position is that matter, whatever it may be, differentiates substances of the same kind.

This position does not require matter to play the role of the ultimate subject. In fact, it is important to realize that the position does not require that matter be particular; nor does it reduce the particularity of the substance to that of the matter. All the position requires is that the matter of a substance endow that substance with qualifications that render the substance different from substances of the same kind. For that purpose, any material qualification of the substance, such as "being green," would suffice, if no other substance of that kind could be so qualified either. So, matter must contribute difference, not particularity. (In fact, matter, i.e., the quantity of matter in a substance, is universal in the sense that the same quantity of matter can belong to many substances at different times.) Let us therefore assume that matter will perform this minimal function of diversification. The *matter* in a substance will be the totality of the respects in which the substance differs from another substance of the same kind. These respects are singled out collectively when we abstract the substantial form away from the substance.

I argue in Appendix 2 that Aristotle does not assume matter to be primitively particular and that it would have been explanatorily vacuous (toward gaining an understanding of the particularity of substances) to have done so. No primitively particular element will therefore be assumed to reside in matter; rather, all the respects in which matter contributes to the identity of a substance will be assumed to be universal, that is, to relate to properties of the substance. The question that confronts us is this: If substances of the same kind are supposed to differ with respect to their nonsubstantial properties, is it not possible that two different substances of that kind have the same nonsubstantial properties? If so, how can these substances be different, if they are characterized by the same properties? I confine my examination to physical substances rather than consider what would be possible for any kind of matter (e.g., intelligible matter or other kinds of matter one could conceive of).

For Aristotle qualitatively similar material substances will be different because they will not be in the same location: "two bodies cannot be present in the same place" (*DA* 418b17).[39] As in the Aristotelian conception of substance a body can constitute only one substance, it follows that two material substances cannot be present in the same place. The spatial location, therefore, of material substances will differentiate them.

My concern here is to show that this differentiation does not require the positing of any primitively particular item; most important, that the contribution that the spatial location makes is that of a universal rather than of a particular. Characterizations of spatial location in Aristotle—of the forms that appear in the category of the "where?"—are, for example, "in the Lyceum" (*Cat.* 2a2, 11b14) or "in the market place" (2a2–3). Time characterizations are, for example, "yesterday" or "last year" (2a3). In *Metaphysics* Z, 15, the (impure) property of "going round the earth" is excluded from the definition of the essence of the sun not because it *names* the earth's location,[40] but because it is a *universal* characteristic,[41] and, furthermore, because it is not an essential characteristic of the sun.[42] What is significant for us here is that these characterizations are universal. There is nothing in the characterization "in the Lyceum" that requires it to belong to just one substance any more than the qualification "5 kilograms heavy" is restricted to just one substance (despite the fact that it contains reference to a unique particular, namely, number 5). Restrictions, if any, are introduced by the nature of the material substances rather than the nature of the form "in the

39: Sorabji (1988, 66–76), provides an excellent exposition, and discussion, of Aristotle's arguments from chemical mixture as to why two bodies cannot occupy the same space; so does David Sanford in his arguments for the possibility of two bodies occupying the same space (Sanford 1970).

40. Which shows that Aristotle is not objecting to *impure* attributes—that is, attributes that involve reference to particulars—being included in the definition of the essence of a substance. For a very useful discussion of the distinction between pure-impure attributes and their significance in the individuation accounts of substances, see Loux 1978, 132–137.

41. "They err . . . by the mention of attributes which can belong to another subject; e.g., if another thing with the stated attributes comes into existence, clearly, it will be a sun" (1040a33–34).

42. "They err . . . by adding attributes after whose removal the sun would still exist" (1040a29–31).

Lyceum." The form itself can belong to many subjects at a time, for example, to all the events that overlap in the Lyceum at the same time. So it is for several visual images superimposed on a screen, where the location on the screen characterizes each one of these images at the same time. But it is not possible that different parcels of matter occupy the same location at the same time. This is not because spatial location is the type of entity that cannot characterize more than one individual. Rather, it is because of physical—not metaphysical—restrictions that prohibit the occupation of the same space by different parcels of matter.

What follows is that spatial location will always differentiate one substance from another, at a time. For the purposes of the identity of substances, spatial locations function as universal properties of substances. However, because of the physical nature of matter, a substance cannot share its spatial location with other parcels of matter. It would have been the same if the physical laws of our universe required that each parcel of matter occupy one unique degree of brightness. That is, if parcel $x$ has brightness $b'$, then no other parcel of matter could be $b'$ bright while $x$ was. In that case, although being $b'$ bright would be a universal characterization of that parcel of matter, it would differentiate it from all other parcels of matter. So it is with spatial location. Physical laws prohibit that distinct parcels of matter occupy the same location at the same time—unlike visual images on a screen. Thus, spatial location can always provide the requisite difference for parcels of matter—and hence substances—that exist at the same time.

For the purposes of substantial identity, two physical substances cannot overlap spatially. Even if substances could overlap spatially, they would nevertheless be different, just as the visual images that can overlap spatially do, nevertheless, remain different. Two qualitatively identical visual images that had identical spatial paths on a screen through time, overlapping constantly throughout their life span, would be different; the possibility of having distinct paths would differentiate between them metaphysically, although this would not help us distinguish between them epistemologically at any one time. But that is an epistemological problem, not a metaphysical problem of the particularity of each image with respect to its difference from the other qualitatively identical image. Similarly, even if two qualitatively indistinguishable substances overlapped spatially through time, they would still be different from each other because they *could* have had different spatiotemporal histories from one another.[43]

To summarize, the criteria of substance are what determine what kinds of

43. I first argued this position in Scaltsas 1984.

entities will be the ultimate subjects in the ontology and, hence, the particulars (e.g., whether it will be the species form "human being" or Socrates that will be the ultimate subject and, hence, the particular). Such particulars differ from one another in substantial kind and, within kinds, in their characteristics.[44] Being in a spatial location is one of these characteristics. Only one material substance can be in one spatial location. Hence, the substance's location differentiates that substance from all other substances. But this is not what makes the material substance particular. That the spatial location is itself unique and that it uniquely characterizes that substance does not confer particularity to the substance, but only difference from other substances of the same kind. To be particular is not to be related to a particular but to be an ultimate subject that belongs to no other subjects. If the entity in question is not an ultimate subject, relating it to a particular does not turn the entity itself into a particular; this is how, for example, bundle theorists can claim that a substance is a bundle of universals. Thus, being in a spatial location at a time is not what makes a substance into a particular.

## 6. Substantial Holism

I have been talking of groups of properties characterizing substances and differentiating them from one another. Does that mean that Aristotelian substances are clusters of universals?[45] Earlier I have been arguing against

44. That a characteristic may differentiate an entity from all entities of the same kind does not entail that that entity is a particular. For example, a characteristic may differentiate a universal form from all other universal forms. Ultimate subjecthood is required for particularity.

45. Although Cleary (1985) does not address this question explicitly, what he says about the ontological status of abstract entities in Aristotelian substances—talking of mathematical entities, which is Cleary's concern—allows for the cluster-of-properties conception of substance. Cleary is concerned to show that Aristotle rejected the Platonic separateness of abstract entities as actual substances, emphasizing that for Aristotle abstract entities are separable in thought, although ontologically they belong to a subject:

> we find him [Aristotle] using the characteristic terminology which describes the belonging of attributes to a primary subject. For instance, he says that the mathematician is concerned with the shape of bodies but not qua limit of a physical body. . . . Nor, says Aristotle, does the mathematician consider the attributes which belonged to the physical body *as such* . . . because he separates . . . those aspects which are already separated in thought from change. . . . Since the logical subject of mathematical attributes is not a physical substratum, the mathematician commits no error by intellectually separating them. Of course, the phrase χωριστὰ . . . τῇ νοήσει is itself very ambiguous because χωριστὰ can mean either "separable" or "separated" and

this position. I now bring together the considerations of the unity of a substance and of its particularity.

*Aristotelian substances are not clusters of properties.* The analysis of the aggregate argument (Section 2 of Chapter 4) showed us that the difference beween an aggregate of many components and a unified whole consists in the submission of the identity of the components to the identity of the whole. In the case of related substances (e.g., the juxtaposed books), each book remains the same entity whether juxtaposed to the other books or not. This is distinctly not the case with the components of a substance, which is a unified whole. When a component is separated from the substantial whole, either physically or by abstraction, it is not identical to anything in the whole. The components of a substance are unified into one by the substantial form. The contribution that each item makes to the whole is determined by the form.

The reidentification of the components by the form is what distinguishes Aristotelian *substantial holism* from cluster-of-properties theories. A substance is, for instance, not color plus shape plus weight. It is a colored, shaped, heavy thing. Thus, for example, yellow is not present in a substance in the way that an olive is present in a martini! If it were, a substance would be an aggregate, a cluster of properties, not a unified, single whole. The abstraction of a property from its subject is not like the unearthing of a treasure, but, as we have seen, it is like the amputation of a limb: the amputation of the limb is the destruction of the limb. If the amputated limb is exhibited in a medical museum, the exhibited limb is not a limb. Similarly, we can think of Aristotle's categories of being as an *ontological museum* that, like a medical museum, has to *destroy* what it exhibits in order to exhibit it.[46] The isolation of a property, such as yellow, from its subject gives the property a new identity and definition. If we dissect a human being and we display the parts in a medical museum, the aggregate of these parts will not be sufficient for the existence of that human being. Nor can

------

τῇ νοήσει may be either an instrumental or a locative dative. Obviously, I would prefer to take the phrase as saying that the mathematical aspects of things are separated in thought because this underlines the primacy of the logical situation. (pp. 33–34)

With this metaphysical picture a substance is not a unity, but a plurality, containing different logical subjects and different items that belong to these subjects. I have been arguing that, according to Aristotle, substantial unity requires that a substance be a single subject and that abstract entities are separable from the substance, not separated (by thought) in the substance.

46. Scaltsas 1990, 593–594.

any composition between *these* (separated) parts be sufficient for the existence of the human being. The reason is that these (separated) parts do not
exist in the human being. What is needed to secure the existence of the
human being is not a special bond between the separated parts, but their
subjugation to the substantial form *human being*, which unites them into a
whole by informing them and, hence, reidentifying them. Similarly, what
will secure that *a* is F (e.g., that the lemon is yellow) is not a special bond
between the subject *a* and the property, F-ness (i.e., the lemon and the color
yellow) or a special bond between the properties and relations that can be
abstracted from *a* (i.e., a relation between the color, the weight, etc., of the
lemon). A yellow lemon is neither an aggregate nor a related whole of
properties and relations. The separation by abstraction of properties and
relations (which are definable independently of the lemon) is the singling
out of entities that do not exist in the lemon, just like the physical separation of a human being gives rise to material entities that do not exist in the
human being.[47]

The unification of all the properties by the substantial form into a single
whole makes them identity-dependent on the form (Section 3 of Chapter 5),
which establishes the sense in which the properties *belong* to the form. It is
this identity dependence of the properties on the form that gives the form
the status of the ultimate subject in the substance. However, belonging to
the subject is not a relation, which is why there is no relation of composition
between the unifier and what is unified. A component of the whole belongs
to the substantial form because it is integrated into the whole by the form.
To belong to the subject is to be identity-dependent on the subject, and
*identity dependence* is *not* a relation that relates items in the world *any more than
identity* is such a relation. We cannot construe the predication statement
"this lemon is yellow" as a relational statement between the lemon and
another item, because the other item is identity-dependent on the lemon.[48]

---

47. The realization that abstraction is a kind of separation (from which, items emerge
that do not exist as distinct components in the substance) is the key to understanding the
sense in which the material substratum is in the substance. The substratum is not in the
substance as a distinct component is related to other abstract components in the substance. It
is in the substance in the sense that it can be separated from the substance by abstraction at
any point in the substance's lifetime, but continues beyond that, by being in the lump of
matter that is physically continuous with the substance.

48. Aristotle does tell us that the matter and the accident that come to belong to a
substantial subject surrender their identities to the substantial whole (rather than vice versa):

The statue is not said to be wood but is said by a verbal change to be not wood but wooden, not

A substance differs from all other substances of the same kind by the property components that are unified by the form. No two wholes can be qualitatively identical, because they will differ with respect to their spatio-temporal location and, more generally, by their different histories. None of the components that are unified into a whole confer particularity on the whole. But *the whole is particular*, because *it does not belong* to anything else.[49]

bronze but of bronze, not stone but of stone, and the house is said to be not bricks but of bricks" (*Meta.* 1033a17–20)

(The subject is called, when music is implanted in it, not music but musical, and the man is not whiteness but white . . .—as in the above examples of "of" something.) Wherever this is so, then, the ultimate subject is a substance. . . . And it is only right that the "of" something locution should be used with reference *both to the matter and to the accidents*; for both are indeterminates. We have stated, then, when a thing is to be said to be potentially and when it is not. (1049a30–b3, my emphasis)

It is characteristic that Aristotle sees the incorporation of matter or of an accident into a substantial whole in terms of the actualization of the potentiality of the matter or the accident. Read the last part of the quote with its introduction: "When we call a thing not something else but 'of' that something . . . , that something is always potentially . . . the thing which comes after it in this series" (1049a18–22). See also Chap. 5, n. 3.

49. Understanding Aristotle's substantial holism has required us to explain why the copresence of properties will not suffice as an explanation of the ontological unity of substances (see the trope-overlap argument, Section 5 in Chapter 4). Furthermore, the metaphysics of abstraction (Section 3 in Chapter 5) has led us to understand the sense in which the substratum is "in" a substance, without threatening the ontological unity of the substance. The substratum is in the substance in the sense that it can be abstracted from the substance, rather than in the sense of being a distinct component of the substance. It is in these two respects that my account of substantial unity of Aristotle differs from Mary Louise Gill's account. Gill explains:

[in the cases where the matter survives only potentially], the preexisting matter, though at the outset a separate identifiable stuff, survives at the lower level but only as *a set of properties* that modify the higher construct. And although the same properties are sufficient to determine a simpler body again, once the high-level complex has been destroyed, they do not contribute to the nature of the higher object. . . . The interpretation of horizontal unity as the survival of something potential (generic or indefinite) enables him to accommodate continuity through change, but without prejudice to the vertical unity of the generated whole. . . . In . . . [substantial generations and elemental transformations] horizontal unity is preserved, not by an underlying subject to which properties belong, but by *one or more properties* that belong to the higher object. (Gill 1989, 164, my emphasis)

Gill's claim is that the material substratum survives in the substance as a set of properties, thereby not posing a threat to the vertical unity of the substance by surviving as a second subject in the whole. I think that this account of the role of the matter in a substance needs to be complemented in two ways in order to deliver a full explanation of the horizontal and the vertical unity of a substance. The first has to do with the identity criteria of the material substratum through substantial generation (for my account, see Section 1 of Chapter 1). In order to have "the same quantity of matter" (see Section 4 of Chapter 1), before, during, and after the life span of the substance, we need to know how the *set of properties* that the matter

The whole does not belong to anything else because it is not identity-dependent on anything else.[50]

---

becomes in the substance (according to Gill) is arithmetically the same quantity of matter as the matter from which the substance was generated and into which it degenerates. Second, although avoiding a second subject in the substance does overcome a potential threat to the unity of the substance, we have already seen in the trope-overlap argument that the mere copresence of properties does not secure the unity of a substantial whole. To have an account of the unity of the substantial whole, we need an explanation of why the set of properties make up a unified whole, as opposed to making up a cluster of copresent properties—a plurality of abstract entities. The unity of the substantial definition will not give us this explanation, because the set of properties we are concerned about contains both substantial and accidental properties. What is needed is an explanation of how "belonging to a subject" unifies the properties of a substance into a single whole.

50. Richard Rorty (1973) addresses the question of the unity of definition and the unity of substance in Aristotle. He assumes these two questions to be the same for Aristotle and believes Aristotle's answer to come in three steps: the identification of matter to the genus form; the reduction of the genus form to the species form; the identification of substance to the species form.

> I shall claim that the plausibility of saying that substance is form only appears when this is taken together with the claim that proximate matter and form are identical. I shall be arguing, further, that to understand this latter claim one needs to take Aristotle's claim that genus is matter more seriously than it is usually taken. Roughly I construe Aristotle as saying that the unity of genus and differentia in the definition somehow mirrors the special sort of unity which is the unity of form with proximate matter, and that appreciating this fact clears up the puzzles of Z. (p. 394)

> What I want to argue is that Aristotle thinks that we can get matter into the form by taking the genus, which on anybody's account is a component of the definition, as representing the matter of the composite. (p. 407)

> So the reason why a man is one thing, and why "two-footed animal" is the definition of one thing, is the same: that what looked like two "thises" (or, worse yet, two "suches") was really just one. "Two-footed" doesn't refer to one batch of qualities and "animal" to another. Rather, "animality" is different in horses and in men—there really isn't anything *common* at all, for even what we call "common" is different. The fact that there isn't anything common reflects the fact that the material cause of the substance was not a "this," but just undifferentiated animal goo. We only thought that there was a problem about the unity of definition and the unity of substance because we thought that "two-footed" stood to "animal" as "white" stands to "man"— but the former relation is actualization, which is not, like predication, a dyadic relation between two things but a pseudo-relation between one thing and one non-thing. (p. 416)

I disagree with Rorty on many issues, which I shall not enumerate here, but only sketch the main differences in our accounts. Although Aristotle does say that the genus is like matter, trying to indicate that there is no relation bonding the genus form to species form, any more than there is one bonding matter to form, he certainly does not intend to identify genus to matter. Yet, Rorty assumes him to do so, thereby attaining two things: first, because the genus is part of the definition of the species form, if genus is matter, then matter becomes part of the definition of the species form; and second, because Aristotle says that the genus is nothing over and above the species, matter is conveniently effaced within the definition of the species form. Thus, the material accidents are introduced into the definition of the substantial form without making their presence felt, so as to allow Rorty to further claim

## 7. Kit Fine's Paradox on the Identity
## of Aristotelian Substances

Kit Fine presented the following paradox about the identity of substances in Aristotle's metaphysics.[51] He said that according to Aristotle two substances that belong to the same species will have the same substantial form; thus, Socrates and Callias will have the form of man. This form is a universal, shared by the members of the species of man. It is also possible in Aristotle's metaphysics for two substances to have the same matter. It is easy to realize this possibility with artifacts, as in the case of melting down a brazen vase to create a statue out of the same quantity of brass. But Fine envisages the possibility of two substances sharing the same matter. Thus, millions of years after Socrates died, it is possible for the matter constituting Socrates to be reassembled into a male human being. In that case, this latter person would have the same substantial form and the same matter as Socrates. Because according to Aristotle's metaphysics a substance is a composite of matter and form, and because in this case the matter and the form of Socrates are identical to the matter and the form of the future person, it would follow that that future person is identical to Socrates. But this is absurd. Hence, Fine concludes, Aristotle's account of the individuation of substances is intrinsically fallacious.[52]

---

that the substance is just the substantial form and the unity of the substance is just the unity of the substantial form.

Indeed, there is something similar between genus and matter, insofar as both are further determined by the substantial form, but that is where the similarity ends. Definitely, Aristotle nowhere suggests the replacement of the genus form by matter in the definition of the substantial form, because there are very different roles that the genus and the matter need to play in the individuation and the scientific classification of substances. Furthermore, once matter is introduced into the species form, saying that it does not polarize the species form because it is not a this or a such but only "undifferentiated goo" or a "non-thing" does not explain why it does not pose a threat to the unity of the substance, let alone why it does not need to be related to the substantial form. For a discussion of the unity of definition, see Sheldon Marc Cohen 1981, 234–236.

51. Fine 1994.

52. Charlton (1972) says that for Aristotle: "where we can tell apart two individuals of the same species it is by qualities which qualify their matter rather than the form. This, however, is not to make matter by itself the answer to question (ii) [how we tell one individual from another], and I am not sure that Aristotle thought there must always be an answer to it. Unless he maintained the identity of indiscernibles he must have allowed the possibility of two individuals which really are indiscernible, impossible to tell apart" (p. 240).

Fine formalizes his paradox in a very clear and economical way (p. 14). Let $S_1$ and $S_2$ be the earlier and later substances. Let $F_1$ and $F_2$ be the substantial forms of $S_1$ and $S_2$, respectively and $M_1$ and $M_2$ their matters. The paradox, then, is the following:

(1)    $F_1 = F_2$
(2)    $M_1 = M_2$
(3)    $S_1 = F_1/M_1; F_2 = F_2/M_2$
∴    $S_1 = S_2$

The symbol / represents the composition of matter and form. Because the two substances are different, but the theory finds them identical, Aristotle's theory is wrong.

### (A) Sameness of Matter, Sameness of Form

To avoid the paradox, one of the premises must be abandoned. Some interpretations of Aristotle's metaphysics do not face this paradox. For the long tradition of interpreters that hold the view that Aristotelian substantial forms are not universal, of which Frede is a contemporary proponent, the paradox is avoided by rejecting premise (1). Because the substantial form of each substance is essentially particular, it is not the case that the forms of $S_1$ and $S_2$ are identical. Hence, the conclusion does not follow. But we have seen that, despite the fact that the doctrine of individual forms does allow us to give answers to questions concerning the identity of substances, the answers do not provide us with explanations, as no account is offered of the particularity of the substantial form of each substance. The particularity of the form is problematic; on the one hand the particularity is intrinsic to the form, and on the other the forms of different substances are claimed to have exactly the same specification and definition. Hence, the claim that each form is distinct from the others is at least as puzzling as the paradox that it is called upon to resolve. Even if Aristotle did believe in individual forms—which I argue in Appendix 3 he does not—we, with hindsight, could not answer Kit Fine's paradox in the same way. We would have the responsibility of addressing the paradox by giving a powerful answer.

An alternative way of avoiding the paradox is by a theory of matter that Fine calls the "entrapment" theory. He says that "*Entrapment* then states that, necessarily, things with the same matter and form are the same."[53]

53. Fine 1994, 21.

The idea here is that two substances of the same kind cannot share the same matter at different times; "Entrapment does not allow the matter of anything to be the matter of anything else with the same form."[54] This is the rejection of premise (2) of the paradox. Some Aristotelian commentators might find this theory of matter congenial and even explore the possibility of associating it with Aristotle's theory.[55] I do not find any textual evidence in Aristotle supporting such an interpretation; on the contrary, there are reasons to dissociate the theory from Aristotle's position. Kit Fine does not develop a theory of entrapped matter. He simply describes the position as an alternative way of avoiding the paradox, independently of whether it can be given theoretical credence.

My general objection to an entrapment theory reading of Aristotle is based on two considerations. First, Aristotle's theory of change requires the survival of matter in the course of substantial transformation in order to secure physical continuity in the process of the transformation. If the matter of a substance did not survive the substance's loss, there would be no physical continuity in the transformation, but, rather, destruction into nothing and creation out of nothing. But that is just what would follow if the matter of a substance is entrapped in the substance. Hence, Aristotle would reject this option, being committed to (2) by his doctrine of physical continuity in transformations.

It might be thought that, despite my protestations, my interpretation of Aristotle's theory of the *unity of matter and form* in a substance commits him to the entrapment of matter in form, because my interpretation rests on the realization that the substantial form unites all the components of a substance by reidentifying them through their integration into the whole. It follows that disintegration from the whole, too, reidentifies the components. Thus, the destruction of a substance is the emergence of an entity— matter—that did not exist *in* the substance. It could not exist in the substance, because the substance's components are identity-dependent on the form of the substance, which has now ceased to be. Hence, the matter of the substance is different from the matter that emerges when the substance is destroyed, if my interpretation of internal unity in a substance is correct. The matter, along with all other components of the substance, is entrapped

54. Ibid., 21.
55. I believe that the reading of Aristotle's theory of matter by Mohan Matthen (1986b) develops such an entrapment theory: "there is a sense in which Aristotelian matter is unique to the substance to which it belongs—it comes into being when the substance does, and what remains when a substance is destroyed is not the matter of that substance" (p. 174).

in the substance, being identity-dependent on the form, while the substance exists.

But I am not committed to the entrapment theory of matter by my account of substantial unity. I showed in Chapter 1 that the rejection of generation ex nihilo did not require that the matter from which the substance is made survive in the substance. Suppose that a statue is made out of a log. That the statue is not generated out of nothing does not require that the log survive in the statue. All that is required is that the quantity of matter that can be abstracted from the log be the same as the quantity of matter that can be abstracted from the statue. For these two quantities to be the same, the requirement was that the transformation process be physically continuous, with no spatiotemporal gaps. (Of course the process is assumed to be closed, with no material input or output.)[56] We saw that even in the most radical transformations, we can abstract a quantity of matter that remains the same throughout the transformation (Section 4 of Chapter 1). The physical continuity of the transformation process secures that the quantity of matter at the start of the transformation remains numerically the same throughout.

I should emphasize that on my interpretation of the unity of substance, the quantity of matter that we abstract away from a substance does not exist in the substance. Abstraction is separation of the components of the substance, and separation involves reidentification. Because abstracting the matter away from the substance is the only way of singling out the matter of the substance and abstracting reidentifies (by separating away), the abstracted matter does not exist in the substance. But abstraction is the only way of singling out the matter of the substance. So, when we say that the quantity of matter remains the same throughout a transformation, what remains the same is singled out by abstraction, and in that sense, does not exist in actuality in the substances that are transforming. It is not that some *other* matter exists in these substances. It is that there is no separate component in the substance (i.e., its matter), for a substance is a whole, not an aggregate of matter and the form; and it becomes a whole by the reidentifi-

---

56. The challenge here is to determine what happens in the case where the process is materially closed, with no input or output of matter. We intuitively distinguish sharply between a process that is materially closed and one that involves exchange of matter. In the first, we believe that matter remains the same, whereas in the second it does not. I am here offering the Aristotelian analysis of what this difference comes to, that is, what it means for the matter to remain the same in a sequence of transformations.

cation of the various components by the substantial form, as they are integrated into a whole.

So, in conclusion, the rejection of the ex nihilo creation of the statue requires neither the survival of the log in the statue nor the existence of a quantity of matter as a distinct component first in the log and then in the statue. What it requires is the physical continuity of the transformation process, so that the quantity of matter we abstract from the log will be the same quantity of matter as the one we abstract from the statue. That is what is meant by saying that the matter of the log is the matter of the statue, or that the matter of the blood is the matter of the embryo. If an entrapment theory denies this to avoid the paradox we discussed, it is not Aristotelian or commonsensical, because it pays no justice to our intuitions of the survival of one and the same quantity of matter throughout a transformation. The price we have to pay for these intuitions is that we cannot reject premise (2) and avoid the paradox.

It goes without saying that the interpreters of Aristotle who attribute to him commitment to a *characterless substratum* would be able to reject one of the premises and avoid Fine's paradox. Which premise would be rejected would depend on what they associate the characterless substratum with. If it is a characterless substratum (i.e., prime matter), then premise (2) would be rejected. It it is a characterless logical subject that primitively particularizes the form, premise (1) would be rejected. But these positions would not be resolving the paradox, but only shifting the focus of the paradox, because they would be rejecting the identity of $S_1$ and $S_2$ by assuming an *inexplicable* difference between the matter or form of $S_1$ from the matter or form of $S_2$.

### (B) The Rejection of the "Compositionality Premise"

Our investigation, so far, has shown that we cannot avoid the paradox by rejecting (1) or (2) without thereby committing ourselves to a theory of form or of matter that is just as puzzling as the paradox itself. I shall argue that the problem does not arise from premises (1) and (2), but from premise (3). Premise (3), which we may call the "compositionality premise," says that $S_1 = F_1/M_1$. How are we to understand the symbol /? Does it stand for a relation between $F_1$ and $M_1$? Is Socrates a whole because his form and his matter are bound together through a *relation*? We have seen in Section 2 of Chapter 4 that for Aristotle, a substance is not united into a single whole by a relation between matter and form. He rejected such solutions to the matter-form unity problem—for good reason—being instructed by the problems that the positing of the participation relation created in Plato's Theory of Forms. Nor could the symbol / stand for the *aggregation* of matter and form. Socrates is not the aggregate of his matter and form; otherwise, he would not be a single, unified substance, but a plurality of many items.[57]

It might be thought that we do not need to give an interpretation of the / symbol. But we cannot afford not to, because it would remain a mystery how the substance relates to its matter and form. It is true that one can think of / as a function that maps matters and forms onto substances. But this does not dispel the burden of accounting for how the function does this. Some explanation would be required of how the function is directed from two universals (matter and form) to a particular substance. If the matter, $M_s$ and the form $F_s$ of Socrates are identical to the matter and the form of other substances, what principle determines that $F_s/M_s$ is Socrates and not some other substance? This explanation is required for the truth of premise (3) of the paradox. Without it, premise (3) would be rejected (no mapping would be possible) and the paradox avoided.

I have argued in Section 3 of Chapter 5 that Aristotle's solution to the unity of matter and form in a substance rejects the introduction of a relation binding the two into a unity. Hence, / cannot stand for a relation between matter and form in Aristotle's metaphysics. Moreover, it would be of no help to say something as general as "matter is the potential, form is the actual, and / stands for the relation between the two." This would leave the problem where we found it, because it does not explain wherein lies the solution and how it can avoid the problems that haunt the assumption that a relation binds matter to form.

We separate out the matter and the form of a substance by abstraction. What is common between the log and the statue that is made out of the log is the quantity of matter in the log, which is the same as the quantity of matter in the statue. The quantity of matter of the statue does not exist in the statue as a separate, independent component of the statue. Rather, it is integrated into the whole by being identity-dependent on the whole. The *identity dependence* of the quantity of matter on the whole (when it is in integrated into the whole in accordance with the form) is *not* a relation between the matter and the form or the whole. There is no ontological correlate to identity dependence in the world. That is why the symbol / in

57. Furthermore, the aggregate survives dispersal, whereas Socrates does not, as Aristotle pointed out (*Meta.* Z, 17). So, Socrates cannot be the aggregate of his parts.

$F_s/M_s$ does not stand for anything in the world. The only thing it could indicate in this expression is that matter and form can be abstracted away from Socrates.

But there is an aspect of this separation, by abstraction, of a substance into matter and form that we have not commented on yet, which is important for our present investigation. This is that *nothing in the process of abstraction requires, or guarantees, that the separating out of the matter and the form preserves all the properties of the substance in the one or the other of the two components.* It is not the purpose of abstraction to divide the substance into two items that retain all the properties that belong to the substance. In fact, the process of abstraction is guided by principles of very different intent: the separating out of a form that is common between distinct substances of the same type or of a quantity of matter that is common between the concrete entities in a sequence of transformations. There is no requirement of total property preservation in this process of separation, and, as we shall see, not all the properties of the substance survive in the one or the other of the two items—matter and form. This has an important consequence for the present paradox, because it *rejects* the tacit assumption made in the formulation of the paradox, that *all that is true of a substance is true either of the matter or the form of the substance.*[58]

The position I am arguing is that in the process of abstraction of matter and form, certain of the properties of the substance are lost, in the sense of not belonging either to the matter or to the form. As a consequence, *it is wrong to assume that if two substances are different, their difference must show either in their substantial form or in their matter.* Nothing in the individuation of the substantial form or the matter of a substance is designed or intended to secure such difference preservation. It follows that it is wrong to assume that $S_1 = F_1/M_1$, or $S_2 = F_2/M_2$. Because / carries no ontological significance, and the matter and the form of a substance do not carry all the properties of the substance, "$F/M$" (which refers to matter and form alone) cannot supply what is requisite for the individuation of the substance. It follows that premise (3) of the paradox must be rejected as *false* in Aristotle's metaphysics.

Rejecting premise (3) avoids the paradox that results in the conclusion

---

58. Here is a qualification of this claim, stemming from a remark of a referee. The property of being a composite would belong to $S_r$, in view of $S_r = F_r/M_r$, even though it would not belong to either the form or the matter. But this does not change the point I make in what follows.

that $S_1 = S_2$. It does not answer the question of where the difference between $S_1$ and $S_2$ lies. All it shows is that Aristotle's theory of matter and form does not commit him to treating two substances that have the same matter and the same form as the same substance. It further instructs us not to look for a reduction of the difference between two substances to a difference between their form or their matter, but to look for it in the substances themselves. The difference between two substances that have the same matter and form must lie in their *historical* properties. Neither the substantial form nor the quantity of matter of the substance possess the historical properties of the substance.

In determining why $S_1$ and $S_2$ are not the same substance, the first option that must be dismissed is that $S_1$ and $S_2$ are phases of the same substance in the way, for instance, in which the caterpillar is related to the butterfly. There is no substance whose natural development is to go from a phase of being an old person (e.g., $S_1$) to a phase of being an infant ($S_2$, even if a substance could be spatiotemporally discontinuous). So $S_2$ could not be a phase of a substance in which $S_1$ is an earlier phase. Nor is $S_2$ a recurrence of $S_1$ (in the way that universals recur in particulars at the same or at different times), because substances are particulars that do not recur spatiotemporally. Finally, a reason why $S_1$ could not be the same substance as $S_2$ is that they are *not* spatiotemporally continuous. $S_1$ ceases to be before $S_2$ comes to be. It is constitutive of the conception of a material substance that *there are no spatiotemporal gaps* in the existence of a substance. During the period between $S_1$'s death and $S_2$'s birth, neither $S_1$ nor $S_2$ was in existence. Hence, $S_1$ could not be the same substance as $S_2$. Rather, the birth of $S_2$ is the creation of a new substance.

Does this entail that the time of existence of each of the two substances is essential to them? Can Aristotle's theory allow for $S_1$ to have been born a little earlier or later than he did, or was it necessary for him to be born when he was born? If the latter, then we could not imagine $S_1$ having been born at any other time than at the time that he was born. The time of his coming into existence would become a necessary characteristic of $S_1$. Such a solution to the problem of the differentiation of $S_1$ and $S_2$ is undesirable, because it makes the time of the creation of a substance a necessary characteristic of it, whereas it should be possible to speculate that a substance could have been created at an earlier or later time than it in fact was. Furthermore, nothing in Aristotle's theory of substance suggests that the time of creation is necessary to the substance.

We shall not, then, introduce the time of creation as a necessary characteristic in the individuation of Aristotelian substance just in order to be able to differentiate $S_1$ from $S_2$. It might be thought that the alternative would be to introduce the *difference* in the time of origin between $S_1$ and $S_2$ as a necessary characteristic of $S_1$ and of $S_2$. This would allow $S_1$ and $S_2$ to have come to be at times other than they did, but it would not allow that they come to be at the same time. Yet, this would be paradoxical, because it would require that on his creation, $S_1$ (which came before $S_2$) should have a necessary relation of difference of time of origin to a substance that did not exist yet and had not existed before! Clearly, $S_1$ could not have such a necessary relation to a nonexisting substance. So, this proposal must be rejected.

The solution I would like to propose is that upon creation, $S_2$ is different from $S_1$ because of the spatiotemporal discontinuity between them, and in virtue of this difference, they are necessarily different. $S_2$ *acquires* a necessary relation of difference from $S_1$, when $S_2$ comes to be. This does not bind $S_2$ to the time that it was created; $S_2$, as well as $S_1$, could have existed at different times, so long as it was not the same time, since they are made out of the same matter. $S_2$ is different from $S_1$ because $S_2$ came to be at a different time from $S_1$. Either of them could have been created at a different time than they were created, but $S_2$ could not have been $S_1$, because $S_2$ was created at a different time from $S_1$. In fact, we can imagine that $S_2$ might have been born when $S_1$ was born, and $S_1$ when $S_2$ was born. No inconsistency is involved in such speculation. The reason has to do with the identity of objects across possible worlds. Saul Kripke argued that the identity of objects in possible worlds is not determined by *comparing* them to objects in the actual world. Thus, we would not consider a possible world that contained a person born when $S_1$ was born, as having the same matter and form as $S_1$ and *then* endeavor to determine the identity of that person. Rather, the identities of objects in possible worlds are *stipulated*, not discovered.[59] Thus, we would stipulate that $S_2$ exists in a possible world and consider that in that world, $S_2$ is born at the time as $S_1$ was born in the actual world. In other words, $S_2$ travels across possible worlds carrying its identity card along and, with it, its difference from $S_1$.

So, $S_2$ is composed of the same matter as $S_1$ and has the same substantial form as $S_1$, but $S_2$ has a different spatiotemporal origin from $S_1$. Their

59. Kripke 1972, 44.

spatiotemporal origins are not properties of their matter or of their form, but properties of the substances themselves. Nor are their origins necessary to them, but because they were created at different times, the two substances are different, and hence necessarily different. $S_2$ could not have been $S_1$, even if $S_2$ had been created at the time that $S_1$ was in fact created.[60]

60. I have discussed the question of the relation of the origin to the identity of substances, which are made out of the same matter and have the same form, but exist at different times, in Scaltsas 1981.

# 7 | The Zeta Contradictions

## 1. The Contradictions

The tensions that torment the reader of *Metaphysics* Book Z relate to the way in which Aristotle characterizes the substantial form. The whole of Book Z is a study of the concept of substance. On the one hand Aristotle investigates what work substance is expected to do in the metaphysical system, and on the other he considers one by one the candidates that might fit that role and hence contest the title of "substance." In the course of the various arguments for, or against, the different candidates for substance, Aristotle makes several claims about substance that appear to be contradictory. This, of course, has attracted special attention to Book Z, presenting an exegetical challenge that has prompted very different proposals and explanations. These vary from interpretations that treat the contradictions as irreparable to suggestions that they can be overcome even if the end result is not a satisfactory theory of substance. Enormous ingenuity has fueled the debates on Z, and so no one interpretation can expect to outshine the others and establish itself as the conclusive one.

My interest here is not to produce or even to attempt to produce the final word on Z. Rather, I want to present a coherent story of how I understand a theory of substance to emerge from Book Z. I concluded with this reading of Z as being philosophically the most heuristic understanding of it, finding no other interpretations more compelling than this one. I do not, by that, mean that suddenly, Z reads like a textbook or that every passage in it will receive the only interpretation it can afford. That a coherent story can be told will not stop the interpreter who prefers to find inconsistencies from doing so or the interpreter who finds consistency at the cost of interpretations that attribute to Aristotle positions lacking explanatory value. In short, my interpretation does not exhaust the possibilities of Z, but I hope that it does bring out the philosophical richness contained in the book.

The fundamental distinction in Book Z is between substance as a *separate entity* and substance as *what* a separate entity is. The former can be a concrete substance such as Socrates or a tree, or it can be a nonmaterial substance such as the First Mover or a Platonic Form, if there are such entities. The latter, what a separate entity is, is the essence or the substantial form of a separate substance. Part of the difficulty of Z is to establish whether the various arguments or statements about substance concern separate substance or the substantial form. The debate is exacerbated by the terminological problem of the ambiguous use of the term *ousia* for both separate substance and substantial form.

The second point of tension in Z is whether the substantial form is particular, just as separate substance is, or universal. This is a problem on its own, especially as Aristotle seems to make contradictory claims about it, asserting in certain contexts that the substantial form is universal and in others that it is particular.[1] But this question also has important implications for other logical features of substance, especially for whether substance is definable and knowable. According to Aristotle's theory of definition and knowledge, only universals are defined and known, at least in the strict sense of definition and knowledge.[2] But if substance is particular, especially if both separate substance and the substantial form are particular, then neither are, strictly speaking, definable and knowable. But substance is the par excellence object of definition and knowledge (see Section 2 of Chapter 2)![3]

On the other hand, if the substantial form is universal—which would resolve the epistemological problem—what is its relation to the separate substance whose form it is? The substantial form stands for *what* the substance is, but *which* substance it is is determined by the identity of the whole substance. Is there a logical gap between the *what* and the *which* of a substance, the first being universal and the second particular? How does the

1. For universality claims, see Section 2 of Chapter 2. For particularity claims, see, e.g., *Meta.* 1040b17.
2. See Section 2 in Chapter 2.
3. E.g., "definition and essence in the primary and simple sense belong to substances" (1030b5–6); "to *know* each thing . . . is to know its essence" (1031b20–21).

*particularity* of the substance depend on and relate to the *nature* of the substance?

Finally, if the substantial form is particular, how does its particularity relate to the particularity of the matter, with which it makes up the concrete substance? Whose particularity does the substance possess? If the substance *is* (just) the substantial form, as what does the substance's matter append to the substance? On the other hand, if the concrete substance is both matter and form, both of them being particular, how does a single particular—the substance—emerge from two particulars—matter and form? If the substantial form is universal and the matter is particular, whose identity does the concrete substance possess, and how is this identity generated? How is the matter related to the form, and how do these two produce a unified, single entity, the separate substance?

Clearly, some of these problems have occupied us for a large part of the present book. With the help of what Aristotle says in Books H and Θ, I will now try to show how such issues all come together in a theory of substance that allows us to understand the position Aristotle is expounding in Book Z. I will first briefly sketch how the main ideas of the theory come together before going through the detailed examination of the passages in Z that provide the arguments for it.

## 2. The Consistent Zeta Picture

I want to argue that one of the *greatest achievements* of the central books of the *Metaphysics* is the derivation of *which* substance something is from *what substance* it is. Aristotle showed that the *substantial form*, that is, what the substance is, is the *subject* that that substance is. The challenge he faced was, on the one hand, to retain the substantial form as that which is definable and knowable. This required the substantial form to be universal. The lesson he derived from the Platonic legacy was that the substantial form should *not* be *related* to the subject. This required the *identification* of the substantial form with the subject, which is a separate substance. I claim that Aristotle resolved this dilemma successfully. His resolution consists on the one hand in distinguishing between the substantial form *as* an actuality determining what a substance is and the substantial form *in* actuality, i.e., being in-mattered; and on the other in not treating the matter as primitively particular (which would import a subject other than the substantial form) while recognizing the role the matter plays toward the particularization of the form.

The key idea is that the form in actuality unifies the nonsubstantial properties. We have already examined in detail the metaphysics of this unification, which explains why a substance is a single whole (Sections 2 and 5 of Chapter 4), why the items belong to the substantial form as subject (Section 3 of Chapter 5), and why the whole is a substantial particular (Sections 4–5 of Chapter 6). In this unification, the form acquires a distinct identity without the importation of any element that is particular prior to, and independently of, the form. The form in actuality is the *only* particular, and this is not achieved either by merging with a primitively particular item or by merging with an item that would change the form's nature; in other terms, nonsubstantial properties, including spatiotemporal location, do not contribute primitive particularity[4] or change the nature of the form by coming to belong to it. The nonsubstantial properties differentiate the form without changing its being into a different kind of being. Thus, the *substantial form in actuality is particular*, but the *substantial form in abstraction is universal*. The form in actuality is not reidentified, but it is particular, by unifying the nonsubstantial forms into a single whole. In actuality, the substantial form is the subject of all the nonsubstantial forms, and, as we have seen, ultimate subjecthood is particularity.[5]

What is definable is the substantial form in abstraction, namely, the substantial form in its potential state rather than the form in actuality; what is particular is the substantial form in actuality that has incorporated the nonsubstantial properties, thereby giving rise to a whole that defies definition. The reason why the form in abstraction stands for the nature of the actualized substance is that the form in actuality is not *reidentified*. *Being in actuality* means being incorporated into a substantial whole. All other items become reidentified by the substantial form as they are incorporated into the whole. The substantial form alone remains what it is, because it is *in terms* of its *own* principle of organization that the other items become what they are when unified into a whole. That is why the substantial form in actuality is not different with respect to what it is, so that the emerging *subject*, namely, the form with all the nonsubstantial properties that belong

4. Spatiotemporal location contributes to the differentiation of a substance, but does not of its own secure the substance's particularity; see Section 5 in Chapter 6.

5. I am sympathetic to Chris Shields's (1990) discussion of the generation of form in Aristotle, as several elements in his discussion of such generation can be incorporated in an account of the actualization of form.

it and differentiate it from other subjects, does not change with respect to what it is, but only acquires number. All other items that become integrated into a substantial whole change both with respect to their being and number, and, hence, they cannot be the subjects in the general substance, because the integration into the whole transforms them. Thus, the substantial form in actuality becomes the subject by unifying all the components into a whole. The substantial form in actuality is therefore the substance itself, not a component within the substance.[6] So, we understand in what way the substantial form satisfies the requirements of *universality* and of *particularity*, as well as the requirements of standing for *what* a substance is and for *which* substance it is, when we understand its unifying role in a substance and the effect it has on the form itself and on the items the form unifies.

### 3. Self-Caused Unities

One lesson that one can learn from the demise of the Platonic Theory of Forms is that there should be no distinction between a subject and what the subject is. Dress this any way you like: *distinguishing the subject from its essence leads to absurdity.* Aristotle learned that lesson, and he taught it to us in *Metaphysics* Z, 4–6, thereby laying a metaphysical foundation that one can ignore only at the system's peril.

One major goal of Z, 4–6, is to determine what must be the case if something is what it is in virtue of itself. Aristotle is investigating what is involved in being *ho legetai kath' hauto*, that which is called [what it is] in virtue of itself. This expression is very significant for understanding both the problem that is being addressed by Aristotle and the solution he gives to it. The covering notion is the general causal notion of *to kath' ho* ("that in virtue of which"), which Aristotle explores in the earlier part of the *Metaphysics* at Δ, 18. He says of it that "in general 'that in virtue of which' will be found in the same number of senses as 'cause' " (1022a19–20). So, when he

---

6. The actualization of the substantial form is captured by Aristotle, as we have seen (Section 1 of Chapter 6), by his distinction between something being an actuality and being in actuality. The abstract universal form is *an* actuality that has the potential of being actualized into the particular substance, which is the form *in* actuality. On this issue, I am in disagreement with A. R. Lacey who says: "Pure form is . . . free from potentiality" (1965, 66–67). The abstract form is not free from potentiality, even though it is an actuality, because it is not *in* actuality.

introduces, in the same chapter, the expression *kath' hauto* ("in virtue of itself," 1022a25), he is introducing the notion of that for which a thing is *itself* a cause. To be what something is *kath' hauto* relates *what* something is to *that* thing by saying that the thing is what it is in virtue of itself. For short, I refer to *kath' hauto* entities as *self-caused*, meaning that they are what they are in virtue of themselves. As we will see, this notion will function as the very *denial* of the most fundamental presupposition of Plato's Theory of Forms, that a thing is what it is not in virtue of itself, but in virtue of participating (*metechein*) in a Form that gives it its being and substance.[7]

In Z, 4–6, Aristotle surveys all types of unity that fail to be self-caused. All of them have one thing in common: they are instances of *something being said of something else*. This is the very seed of metaphysical division that undermined the Platonic Forms and would undermine any theory that allowed for it. The first test that Aristotle applies in order to determine whether $x$ is the cause of $y$ and, hence, whether $xy$ is a self-caused unity, is to test whether being $y$ stems from being $x$. If not, then the cause of $y$ cannot be found in what it is to be $x$, and therefore their combination is not a self-caused unity. $X$ is $y$ in virtue of itself if to be $x$ is to be $y$.

But this test presupposes something even *more fundamental*, namely, that $x$ and to be $x$ are a self-caused unity. Otherwise, even if "to be $x$" is "to be $y$," an $xy$ will not be a self-caused unity, because there will be a break between $x$ and being $x$ as well as between $y$ and being $y$. This will be the culmination of the investigation in Z, 6, when Aristotle will conclude that the ultimate requirement for being a self-caused unity is that the *subject* be the same with its *essence*:

$x$ is a self-caused unity iff $x$ is the same with what it is to be $x$.

As we saw, this is to be understood as claiming the identity of a substance with the essence in actuality. (That is, the essence in actuality is not a component within the concrete substance, but the substance itself.) If this condition is not fulfilled, then nothing will be what it is in virtue of itself. Furthermore, it would reintroduce the problems of the Third Man and

7. Already in Δ, 18, Aristotle lists a Platonic type of explanation as a case of "that in virtue of which," but not as a case of "in virtue of itself": "that in virtue of which a man is good is the good itself" (1022a15–16). This indicates Aristotle's awareness of introducing a type of explanation, self-causation, which is not achieved in Platonic metaphysics, although the intention was there. (As the Third Man regress was never overcome, even the Good itself is good in virtue of some further Form of the Good.)

other monstrosities that we have already been warned against. In Greek, the linguistic test for self-caused unity is performed by use of the dative. The dative construction—*to* . . . [dative] *einai* (i.e., to be)—picks out what it is to be that thing (which is denoted via the dative). Thus, the ultimate test for being a self-caused unity is that *a* be the same as *to a* [dative] *einai*.

### (A) *Metaphysics* Z, 4

The survey begins with accidental unities, such as a person that is musical (1029b14–16). Here the objection is that the person is not musical in virtue of herself or himself: "The essence of each thing is what it is said to be in virtue of itself. For being you is not being musical; for you are not musical in virtue of yourself" (1029b13–15). A person can be a person without being musical. To be a person is not to be musical. Hence, the cause of being musical lies outside being a person, and so "musical person" is not a self-caused unity.

The next stage in Aristotle's investigation in Z, 4, connects with the notions of self-caused unity that we find in Book Δ of the *Metaphysics*. In Δ, 18, Aristotle distinguishes between two groups of uses of the expressions *kath' hauto* ("in virtue of itself"). The one is where *x* is *y* in virtue of itself because *x* is the only cause of *y* (1022a32–36). Aristotle's example is that man (*x*) is man (*y*) in virtue of himself. Similarly, a substance, being self-subsistent, separate, and existentially independent from other substances, can have no other cause for its being[8] but itself. Therefore, it is its own (and only) cause, and in that sense it is itself in virtue of itself. Although these cases do point to the self-causing aspect of the *kath' hauto* unities, they are not especially illuminating, because they hardly say more than that a thing is its own cause in the sense of being self-subsistent.

However, the second group of cases is very interesting. Aristotle lists three cases in descending order of *kath' hauto* candidacy, which will turn out to be the reverse order in which he considers them in Z, 4–6. What is fascinating is that what is the most straightforward and prime case of self-caused unity in Δ, 18, will turn out to be the most difficult to argue for and establish in Z, 6: that the subject is not *other* than its essence and that it *is* its essence in virtue of itself. In Δ, 18, Aristotle says that the expression "in virtue of itself" applies to the following cases:

8. This is to be distinguished from its coming to be, for which, of course, the cause will be different, i.e., the efficient cause.

(1) the essence of each thing, e.g., Callias is in virtue of himself Callias and the essence of Callias;

(2) whatever is present in "what" [something is], e.g., Callias is in virtue of himself an animal. For animal is present in the formula that defines him; Callias is a particular animal.

(3) Whatever attribute a thing receives in itself directly or in one of its parts, e.g., a surface is white in virtue of itself. (1022a25–31)

By contrast, in Z, 4–6, Aristotle will start with the cases of a subject receiving an attribute directly, or firstly, for instance, as surface receives white, and will dismiss them as proper cases of self-causation. Aristotle sees that there is an enormous difference between different kinds of subject-form relation, and only one of them qualifies as a proper case of self-causation, the case where *the subject is the form*, where it is the substantial form.

In Z, 4, Aristotle will dismiss ontological unities falling under case (3) as a proper instance of self-causation, and in Z, 5, he will discount a case of definitional unity, which would appear to be an instance of (2) (i.e., what belongs to the definition of a thing, but in fact does not). I contend that there is something common between the two cases Aristotle will reject that initially recommends them as self-caused unities and that what Aristotle does is to expose their failing, for which he will discard them as self-caused unities. It is common to have an aspect of the subject-form relation that resembles the genus-species relation—recommending it as a self-caused unity—but he will also show that it fails to be like it in one respect.

The first case, then, that is dismissed is the metaphysical unity, such as white and surface. Such unities have been singled out by Aristotle as being of special importance, because the subject is not just any subject that the color white might characterize, but it is the first subject, the subject in which white would be found if it is found anywhere at all. That is what Aristotle describes as being directly in that subject, or being received first by that subject.[9] The aspect of this relation that is like the genus-species relation is that if something is white, it is a surface that is white, just as if something is a human being, it is an animal that is a human being. Close as this similarity between surface and white may be, it is not what is required for a self-caused unity, which requires that the *subject* be the cause of what the subject is. Yet, in this case "being a surface is not being white" (1029b17–18). Therefore, the subject—the surface—cannot be the cause

9. ἐν αὐτῷ δέδεκται πρώτῳ (1022a30).

of the presence of white in it, and hence their unity is not a self-caused unity. It might be objected that, similarly, "being an animal is not being a man." But here, it is not the genus that is the subject but the species; and "being a man" *is* "being an animal," whereas in the surface-white relation, the surface is the subject, [10] and "being a surface" is not "being white."

Of course, it would not help to claim that "being a white surface" is said of surface in virtue of itself, because this is not what is understood by self-causation. What is understood by self-causation is the bond between a subject and what that subject is when we analyze what it is (not by repeating its name, e.g., that surface is surface) without going in circles: "The formula, therefore, in which the term itself is not present but its meaning is expressed, this is the formula of the essence of each thing"; "the essence of each thing is what it is said to be in virtue of itself" (1029b19–20, 13–14). So, the prime case of self-causation is the relation between the subject and what the subject is, that is, its essence. So even if a form is always instantiated in a particular type of subject, this will not suffice for self-causation, in case the subject could be found without the form.

The failure of "white surface" to qualify as a self-caused unity is very important in Aristotle's metaphysics, because it is the same failing that will disqualify the forms in the nonsubstance categories from being counted as such unities. Just like white, which, if instantiated, is instantiated in surface, similarly, *all the nonsubstantial forms, when instantiated, are instantiated in a subject.* So, "since there are compounds in relation to the other categories, too (for there is a substrate for each category, e.g., for quality, quantity, time, place, and motion), we must inquire whether there is a formula of the essence of each of them, i.e., whether to these compounds also there belongs an essence" (1029b22–27) and, hence, whether they are self-caused unities.

What raises the question whether the items in the nonsubstance categories are candidates for self-caused unities is that being instantiated is being a unity. Thus, "bitter" will always be found in something wet, such as a juice or a sauce. Is this bond the type of unity that is captured by self-causation? We have already seen that this kind of bond will not qualify "white surface" as a case of self-causation, because, although white is always found in surface, to be surface is not to be white. Hence, the subject, surface, is not the cause of the white in it. The same objection applies to all nonsubstantial

---

10. Aristotle rejects the possibility that, for example, in the case of a white log, the white is the subject of the log; rather, it is the log that is the subject of white (*An. Post.* 83a1–14).

forms. Even if there is a type of subject in which a nonsubstantial form is always found, such as bitterness in liquid, it will still be the case that to be liquid is not to be bitter. Hence, the subject, liquid, is not the cause of its being bitter, and so "bitter liquid" is not an instance of self-causation.

We saw that the requirement stated at the beginning of Z, 4, for self-caused unity is that the form predicated of the subject be what the subject is, in the sense in which the essence of the subject is what the subject is. Only then is the subject the true cause of the predicated form. Aristotle returns to this requirement after discussing the case of the unities involving nonsubstantial forms, where he concludes that such combinations fail this requirement. The presence of a nonsubstantial form in the subject in which it is instantiated is not caused by the nature of the subject. Hence, such combinations are cases of "one thing said of another," and they are contrasted to the cases of the presence of what the subject is (i.e., its essence) in the subject, which are not cases of one thing said of another, but of a primary unity:

> For the essence is what something is; but when one thing is said of another, that is not what a "this" is, e.g., white man is not what a "this" is, since being a "this" belongs only to substances. Therefore there is an essence only of those things whose formula is a definition. But we have a definition not where we have a word and a formula identical in meaning . . . but where there is a formula of something primary; and primary things are those which do not involve *one thing's being said of another.* Nothing, then, which is not a species of a genus will have an essence—only species have it, for in these the subject is not thought to participate in the attribute and to have it as an affection, nor to have it by accident. (1030a3–14, my emphasis)

Being an animal is not an attribute or an accident of human being. Rather, it is what being a human being is, and therefore it is by virtue of being a human being that it is an animal. Such cases, where the subject is the cause for the presence of the forms that are mentioned in its defintion, are the par excellence cases of self-caused unity, and Aristotle calls such a subject *primary* and a "this"; it is contrasted to combinations of one thing said of another, which would strictly be "these" rather than a "this."

We have seen, then, that neither combinations that cross categories, such as white surface, where the white is always instantiated in a surface, nor bitter liquid, where the bitter is always instantiated in a liquid, will qualify as self-caused unities, because the presence of white or bitter does not emanate from the subject. On the contrary, combinations that stay within a branch of a category, such as species-genus combinations, will qualify for being self-caused, because the predicated form is just what the subject is. This would prima facie treat a unity in the substance category (e.g., human being) on a par with a unity in a nonsubstantial category (e.g., white). Animal is in the nature of human being, just as color is in the very nature of white. Aristotle realizes this and is willing to allow that there is a sense in which nonsubstance subjects can be self-caused unities, bearing their genera in virtue of what these subjects essentially are, such as white being a color by virtue of what it is. But he still wishes to distinguish between substantial and nonsubstantial subjects and to treat the substantial ones as the most representative self-caused unities. The reason is important, and we should recognize a significant and heuristic intuition in this Aristotelian distinction: "Essence will belong, just as the 'what' does,[11] primarily and in the simple sense to substance, and in a secondary way to the other categories also—not essence simply, but the essence of a quality or of a quantity" (1030a29–32). Definition, essence, and the "what" do not belong to the nonsubstance species (e.g., to white) in a *secondary* sense only because nonsubstances do not fit the species-genus format. In fact, they do, so they are not lacking in this respect in comparison to substances. The sense is secondary because there has to be a *subject shift* before one asks the "what is it?" question of nonsubstances, which there need not be in the case in substances. By this I mean the following. We cannot find the definition of a nonsubstance, its essence, or what it is, when we look at a nonsubstance as it is instantiated in the world. The "white surface" does not have a definition or essence, for the reasons that we exposed. Yet, this is just where white is to be found in the world. To get a definition and an essence when we ask the "what is it?" question, we need to *abstract* white and treat it as a subject in its own right, asking the "what is it?" question of *it*. It is this subject shift that marks the secondary sense in which nonsubstances have a definition or essence. Nonsubstances, as found in nature, do not have definition or essence. In abstraction, when the nonsubstances become the subject themselves, they do have a definition and essence; but they never have this role of a subject when they are in actuality.

The intention here is that substances *do* have a definition and an essence

11. "But . . . all 'definition,' like 'what a thing is,' has several meanings; 'what a thing is' in one sense means substance and a 'this,' in another one or other of the predicates, quantity, quality, and the like. For as 'is' is predicable of all things, not however in the same sense, but of one sort of thing primarily and of others in a secondary way, so too the 'what' belongs simply to substance, but in a limited sense to the other categories. For even of a quality we might ask what it is, so that a quality also is a 'what'—not simply, however" (1030a17–25).

when they *are* in actuality. The challenge for Aristotle is to show that *no subject shift is required in the case of substances* in order to reach *that which has a definition and an essence.* This challenge is taken up in Z, 6.

### (B) *Metaphysics* Z, 5

Going from Z, 4, to Z, 5, we encounter a further challenge. There are certain items that do not exhibit a subject shift of the kind that white does. We saw that as we move from the "white surface" to the "white color," the subject shifts from surface, which is white, to white, which is a color. But there are certain items that cannot be described apart from the subject in which they are actualized. These are unities such as "male animal," where the animal is male in virtue of itself (*kath' hauto*, 1030b21–23). About them, Aristotle says that "such attributes are those in which is involved either the *formula* or the *name* of the subject of the particular attribute, and which cannot be explained without this; e.g., white can be explained apart from man, but not female apart from animal" (1030b23–26). In other words, a subject shift is not possible here (as it is from man, who is white, to white, which is a color), because any explanation of "female" reintroduces the subject, animal, which is female. Aristotle says that "there is no essence and definition of any of these things, or if there is, in another sense" (1030b26–27). What exactly is the problem with such unities?

One such unity that Aristotle considers in Z, 5, is the snub, which is defined as a concave nose. A nose is snub, from which follows that the definition of the term *snub* contains reference to the subject that is snub, namely, the nose. "Snubness is compounded out of the two [concavity and nose] by the presence of the one in the other" (1030b17–18). So, the snub is a concave nose. Why is this not a self-caused unity? We saw in Z, 4, that the unity "white surface" is not a self-caused unity. The reason was that being a surface did not require being white, because there could be surfaces that are not white. Hence, when a surface is white, it is not white in virtue of being a surface. But this is not the case here. Aristotle makes this explicit when he says that "it is not by accident that the nose has the attribute either of concavity or of snubness, but in virtue of its nature; nor do they attach to it as whiteness does to Callias, or to man (because Callias, who happens to be a man, is white)" (1030b18–21). So, the problem in the case of the snub is not the same as in the case of white surface, because a nose is concave in virtue of itself and its nature. Then, why is the snub, that is, a "concave nose," not a self-caused unity?

Aristotle describes such unities as being "one thing in another"

(1030b18), being "not simple but coupled" (b15–16), describable "by an addition" (b16). But none of these reasons helps understand how "concave nose" is different from, for example, rational animal. If man is rational animal, doesn't that make man the same as "concave nose," because in both cases the attribute is true of the subject in virtue of the subject itself? Yet, such unities as "rational animal" are the paradigmatically self-caused unities. To find the difference, we need to return to a requirement made by Aristotle for the specification of the essence of a self-caused unity in Z, 4. There he said that "The formula . . . in which the term itself is not present, but its meaning is expressed, this is the formula of the essence of each thing" (1029b19–20). This criterion does distinguish between the two unities in question and justifies Aristotle's claims of unities such as the snub being one thing in another. The snub, namely, "concave nose," is not a unity like "rational animal," but a unity like "rational man." In the latter, *although it is true that man is rational in virtue of the nature of man*, "rational man" does not possess the unity of an essence or definition, because the term itself is present in the definition of that term. This repetition of the term is what plagues such terms as *the snub* or *male*, which cannot be explained without mention of the subject that possesses them. "Rational man" is not the definition or essence of man or of anything else any more than "concave nose" is the definition or essence of nose or anything else.

A further problem with such expressions as "snub," says Aristotle, is that their redundancy gives rise to an iteration. Consider the snub. If "it is impossible to speak of snubness apart from the thing of which, in its own right, it is an attribute" (1030b30–31), the snub is a nose that is snub; hence, it is a nose that is a nose that is snub, and so on ad infinitum (1030b28–35). The argument is not valid,[12] but it does help us understand

---

12. Aristotle says: "if snub and concave are not the same (because it is impossible to speak of snubness apart from the thing, of which, in its own right, it is an attribute, for snubness is concavity *in the nose*), either it is impossible properly to say 'snub nose' or the same thing will have been said twice, concave nose nose; for snub nose will be concave nose nose. And so it is absurd that such things should have an essence; if they have, there will be an infinite regress; for in snub nose yet another nose will be involved" (1030b30–1031a1). There are several hypotheses one can try out on the logic of this passage, but none can deliver a regress that is consistent with all that is claimed in the passage. Generally, we can understand the difference with the foregoing cases of unities, if we think of the following comparison: snub is like white being "paleness in surface"; then "white surface" would be "surface that has paleness in surface." Aristotle's complaint seems to be that of *subject-redundancy*. This is different from the complaint of the *subject-shift* from surface (which is white) to white (which is a color), since, in the present example, white is color *in a surface*; hence, surface remains the subject, and so there is no subject shift.

why Aristotle thinks that terms such as "the snub" involve more than one mention of the subject of the attribute. [13]

From this discussion, Aristotle draws a general conclusion. To understand the conclusion we need to consider why it is that prima facie such terms as "female" or "snub" make a claim to being self-caused unities. It is that one and the same term designates both the subject and the affection of the subject. Thus, a "female" would be, for example, an offspring-bearing animal. In Z, 4, Aristotle stipulated that the term *cloak* means "white man" (1029b23–28). Such a combination is not self-caused, because being white is not what it is to be a man. But now we have a further reason why this would not qualify as a self-caused unity. That is, even if "cloak" meant "rational man," it would not define the essence of the subject, man, because it includes a term that refers to the subject itself. In other terms, the definiens, cloak (= rational man), includes reference to the definiendum, man. This fault is diagnosed with precision in Z, 5, and is described by Aristotle as involving an account *by addition*. [14]

So, the Z, 5, objection is much stronger and broader than the objection that to be a surface is not to be white. This latter objection will not work with such a combination as the concave nose, because to be a nose is to be concave: "it is not by accident that the nose has the attribute . . . of concavity, but in virtue of its nature" (1030b18–20). What the Z, 5, objection tells us is that what disqualifies a combination of a subject and its attribute from being a self-caused unity is *independent* of whether the attribute is part of the nature of the subject. Whether it is or it is not, there is a fault that disqualifies the combination from being a single nature—that the subject is mentioned as part of the combination. The lesson we can derive from the Z, 5, restriction on self-caused unities is that *unity* is in the essence of the subject, not in the subject *having* an essence.

We can now understand why Aristotle generalizes the case of the snub to all the nonsubstance categories: "Clearly then only substances are definable. For if the other categories are definable, it must be by addition" (1031a1–

13. 1030b23–26, if they don't involve more than one subject: "for in snub nose yet another nose will be involved" (1030b35–1031a1).

14. ἐκ προσθέσεως; Aristotle gives two definitions of this phenomenon. In the first, he says that terms that describe something by an addition are those that describe "the presence of the one thing in the other" (1030b18). E.g., the snub means the presence of snubness in the nose. But if the snub is a snub nose, then, if this expression is meaningful at all, it repeats the same thing: snub nose nose. Hence, terms by addition mention the same thing twice, which is the second definition: " 'by addition' I mean the expressions in which we have to say the same thing twice" (1031a4–5).

3). The reason is that Aristotle is here considering nonsubstances *in actuality* (e.g., white surface rather than the abstracted color white, which does have a definition, but in a secondary sense). Nonsubstances in actuality always qualify a substance or a part of a substance. Thus, if we attempt to define an actual "white," "male," "kilo," we would always have to analyze them in terms of a (substantial) subject *having* an attribute. Whether the attribute is part of the nature of the subject or not, the selected combination will not be a single unified nature, because it will stand for a subject *having* an accident or an essence. Essences, such as "rational animal" for human being, *are* self-caused unities, because they are not instances of a subject being characterized by a form. The genus (e.g., animal) is not a subject for the differentiae (1037b18–19, 1038a3–6).

It follows that the nonsubstance in actuality (e.g., this white) will always be a combination of the form: such and such a substance (or part of a substance) being white. Therefore, the description of a nonsubstance in actuality will involve mention of something other than itself, namely, mention of the substance in which it is actualized. Hence, it will always have the format of a form in a subject (e.g., concavity in the nose, 1030b32) that cannot express a unified nature, for the reason I gave. It follows that descriptions of actual nonsubstances will never be self-caused unities. Thus, only essences, depicted by definitions of substances, will be the par excellence self-caused unities, standing for what the subject is rather than for a subject having a nature.

### (C) *Metaphysics* Z, 6

Elsewhere I tried to show that when Aristotle says in Z, 6, that each thing (*hekaston*) is the same with its essence and that some things (*enia*) are directly their essences, he did not mean concrete substances such as Socrates and Callias, but, rather, species such as man or tiger. [15] Thus, because the thing that is identical to its essence is the species form, which is universal, the essence, too, will be universal. But I now believe that that approach is not the correct one. Even if Aristotle does not refer to concrete substances such as Socrates and Callias in his examples, we need not assume that his examples are exhaustive. What is more important than the examples and the terminology in which the argument is couched is the *scope* of the argument. The scope of the argument is global and applies to any type of

15. Scaltsas 1983, 179–193.

subject that makes a claim to being a substance and, hence, an ultimate subject that has a nature of its own. Whether such a substance is material or immaterial, being a substance means that nothing else, but the substance itself can be the cause of its nature, and therefore, *no ontological division* between the *subject* (which the substance is) and the *nature* of the subject (its essence) can be allowed.

We have seen so far that a self-caused unity must satisfy two criteria: (1) A self-caused unity is what it is in virtue of itself; (2) A self-caused unity is not a combination of a subject possessing a property. With reference to (1), we saw that in Z, 4, Aristotle tackled the issue of unities of the form $xy$, where the requirement was that $x$ be $y$ in virtue of what $x$ is. It was pointed out there that we still had to face the question of whether $x$ is what it is to be $x$ in virtue of itself. We further saw in Z, 5, that even if $x$ is $y$ in virtue of what $x$ is (e.g., an animal being female in virtue of itself), still $xy$ cannot be a unity if it comprises a subject of which a form is predicated. Thus, a self-caused unity must be what it is in virtue of itself, although it is not being related to what it is as subject to property. The only meeting point for these two requirements is that in a *paradigmatic self-caused unity*, the subject is not different from what it is. Hence, essence must *not* be *predicated* of the subject, but must *be* the subject!

To understand the nature of the problem Aristotle is concerned with here, we need to turn to the predicament faced in Plato's Theory of Forms. We shall follow Aristotle's guidance through the problem, as offered in Z, 6. The entities that he is focusing on are the substances that are what they are in virtue of themselves. It makes no difference whether they are concrete things in the world, immaterial substances, or Platonic Forms. What characterizes any substance is that its nature is not determined by another, different entity, but that it is itself the very source of what that substance is. This principle is violated if one assumes that a subject acquires its nature by participation in a Form. This is characteristic of the Theory of Forms, according to which a substantial subject, whether a thing or a Form, becomes what it is by participating in a Form. [16]

16. Aristotle is not necessarily considering a version that Plato held himself at any point in his lifetime, but a position that was either held by members of the Academy or was a consequence of the doctrine of participation in Forms. He describes the position: "But in the case of the so-called in-virtue-of-themselves things [*kath' hauta*], is a thing necessarily the same as its essence? E.g., if there are some substances which have no other substances nor entities prior to them—substances such as some assert the Ideas to be? If the essence of good is to be different from the Idea of good, and the essence of animal from the Idea of animal, and the essence of being from the Idea of being . . ." (1031a28–32).

We have already examined the absurdities that follow from the separation of the substantial subject from its essence (Section 3 of Chapter 6). From these, Aristotle concludes that "the good, then, must be one with the essence of good" (1031b11–12), and that "it is not by accident that the essence of one, and the one, are one" (1032a1–2). That is, the substance must be the same entity with what the substance is. If the substantial subject and the essence were different entities, paradoxes follow, because if what it is to be the subject is different from the subject, then it cannot be what it is to be the subject. *There is no metaphysical glue that will make one entity what it is to be another entity and keep the two entities distinct.*

The generality of Aristotle's arguments dictates the generality of their conclusions. He began the chapter by stating that "each thing is thought to be not different from its substance, and the essence is said to be the substance of each thing" (1031a17–18). He argued that in the case of the things that are what they are in virtue of themselves (*kath' auta*, 1031a28, b13) and primary—not said to be what they are in virtue of something else (1031b13–14)—"each thing . . . and its essence are one and the same in no merely accidental way . . . and to know each thing . . . is to know its essence" (1031b19–21). "Not only are a thing and its essence one, but the formula of them is also the same" (1031b32–1032a1); and he concludes, "Clearly, then, each primary and in-virtue-of-itself [*kath' hauto*] thing is one and the same as its essence" (1032a4–6). Thus, the ultimate requirement for being a *self-caused unity* is the *identity of the cause with the effect*. In that respect, the notions of cause and effect will not serve us if we take them in the material sense, because that conception does not allow for an identity between cause and effect. But considering causation in the Aristotelian *formal* sense, we can understand the notion of a *kath' hauto* entity as an entity in which there is no division between the subject and its essence.

### (D) *Metaphysics* Z, 13

We have seen that a claim to substancehood in Aristotle's system is a claim to being a particular entity, a single, unified subject that exists independently of other substances. In Z, 4–6, Aristotle argued that the two candidates for substancehood, namely, the subject and the essence of a substance, are the same, thereby showing that there is no internal division between *that* which is *x* and *what x* is. It follows a fortiori that if any other item that belongs to a substance made a claim to substancehood, it would pose the same type of threat to the unity of a substance as the division between subject and essence would. In Z, 13, Aristotle undertakes to show that *universals* cannot enjoy the type of distinctness that belongs to substances. This is directly opposed to the Platonic position, in which the Forms are the par excellence substances and are at the same time the universals that belong to many particulars. [17]

Aristotle provides three arguments to show that no universal is distinct in the ways that substances are. The first reaches the conclusion that no universal exists as the *essence* of a substance. The second concludes that no universal exists as *a distinct component of the essence* of the substance. The third concludes that no universal exists as *a distinct component of the substance*. In all three cases, the *particularity* that a claim to being a substance requires is incompatible with the *universality* of the universal in question. What is significant for the whole argument, which becomes explicit in the third stage of the argument, is that Aristotle is showing in Z, 13, that no universal can be an *actual* substance. No universal can be substance in complete actuality, either as a *distinct* component within substances or existing by itself as a *separate* substance. [18]

*(i) The Universal as Essence.* In the first argument of Z, 13 (1038b8–17), the universal is shown not to be substance in the sense of being the essence (*ti ēn einai*, 1038b14 and 17) of a substance, because the essence of a substance is peculiar to that substance, whereas the universal belongs to many substances: "That is called universal which naturally belongs to more than one thing. Of which individual then will this be the substance? Either of all or of none" (1038b11–13). It cannot be the substance of all, because "the substance of each thing is peculiar to that thing" (1038b10). It cannot be the substance of one of the many things to which it belongs, because then, says Aristotle, "this one [thing] will be the others, also; for things whose substance is one and whose essence is one are themselves one" (1038b13–15). Strictly, the latter conclusion does not follow. The claim was not that the universal will be the essence of every single thing to which it belongs,

17. That Aristotle sees the Platonic Forms as being committed to this discrepancy is made clear in the following passage: "But those who say the Forms exist, in one respect are right, in saying the Forms exist apart, if they are substances; but in another respect they are not right, because they say the one *in* many is a Form" (1040b27–30).

18. Much discussion has been directed at the analysis of *Metaphysics* Z, 13, in recent years, not all of which can be considered here. For the interested reader, I shall mention some of the main alternatives, apart from the ancient scholiasts: Ross 1924, 2:208–211; Woods 1967 and 1991a; Code 1978; Teloh 1979a; Hughes 1979; Frede and Patzig 1988, 241–263; Halper 1989, 118–132; and Loux 1991, 197–235.

but only of one of these things. What follows is not that all these things will have the same essence, but, rather, that the essence of one thing will be present in many other things. To get Aristotle's conclusion, we need the extra step that an *essence* (of any thing) cannot be present as an *attribute* in another thing, but, rather, that if it is present in another thing, it is present in the character of an essence. This, of course, is a fundamental truth in Aristotelian (and all nonextreme relativist) metaphysics. Without it, one would be allowing that some human beings are essentially human, whereas other types of substances are human beings accidentally. Assuming that the essence of one thing cannot be present as an accident in another thing (e.g., that the form of human being cannot be present as an accident in any substance), if a universal belongs to many and is present in one of them as its essence, it will be present in all of them as their respective essences. Because it is the same universal in all and the essence of a substance is peculiar to that substance, the essences of all these things will be one and the same, and therefore these things will be one and the same thing. Hence, the universal cannot be the essence of just one of the things it is in, either.

A further reason why a universal is not substance is that a universal is always predicated of a subject, whereas a substance is not (1038b15–16). Rather, substance is the subject of which the rest are predicated. Aristotle does not provide an argument why the universal must always be predicated of a subject. But the reason must be that a universal belongs to many. If it belonged to many in the sense of being the many (i.e., being the subject in each of them), the many would be the same thing. Hence, it must belong to the many, not by being a subject in each of them, but by being predicated of a subject.

This argument has a broader scope than the previous one, as it does not presuppose that the universal is substance in the specific sense of being the essence of something. This breadth of scope is exploited in the second argument of Z, 13.

*(ii) The Universal as a Distinct Component of Essence.* In the second argument of Z, 13 (1038b16–34), Aristotle is concerned to show that the universals involved in the essence of a substance are not existentially *distinct* components in the essence. The argument has two parts. In the first part, Aristotle argues that, starting with the supposition that a universal is inherent—is an existentially distinct component—in the essence of a substance, it follows that the universal is substance. But that the universal is substance was refuted in the first stage of the Z, 13, argument. Hence, the

universal cannot inhere in the essence as an existentially distinct component. The second part derives a further absurdity from the claim that the
universal inheres as a distinct entity in the essence of a substance.

Part One: 1038b16–29. In this section, Aristotle argues in three sub-
arguments that the inhering universal will be a substance.

1. (1038b16–19). It will be a substance, because the universal, qua
distinct entity in the essence of a substance, will have a formula (*logos*,
1038b19). But as something definable, it will be substance in the sense of
being the essence of something. And if the claim that the universal inheres
in the essence leads to the conclusion that it will be substance, this concludes the argument, because the substantiality of the universal has already
been refuted in the first stage of the Z, 13, argument.

This argument is not valid. Aristotle has shown that it is items that have
*definition*, not just a formula, that are substances (1030a6–7). But here
Aristotle is claiming that this inhering universal will have a formula, not a
definition. From this, it does not follow that the item would be a substance.

2. (1938b19–23). Aristotle must be aware of the weakness of this argument, and the reason that he is not concerned to strengthen it is that he
immediately proceeds to show that, even if the universal does not have a
formula (let alone a definition), it will still be substance (1038b19–23).
The reason he offers is that the universal will be the substance of some item,
just as man is the substance—essence—of a particular man (1038b21–22).
The rationale here is that the universal will be peculiar to some item,
namely, a form (*eidos*, 1038b23), that must be the item initially assumed to
inhere in the essence of a substance. Aristotle is claiming here that the
universal in question will be the essence of that item. Thus, to use his
example, if the universal Animal inheres as a distinct item in the essence of
man (1038b18), then *what* that distinct item (in the essence of man) will be
is Animal. [19] Animal will pick out the essence of that distinct item in the
way that Man picks out the essence of a man. Hence, the universal (Animal)
will be substance, in the sense of being the essence of that distinct item, and
"the same thing will happen again"; because the hypothesis leads to the

19. It is not the fact that "animal" will be peculiar (*idion*, 1038b23) to that item that
gives "animal" the status of the essence of that item, because something can be peculiar to a
substance without being its essence (*Top.* 101b19–23). In this case, the item that has been
singled out as inhering in the essence of a substance, has been picked out *as itself being* the
universal "animal." Hence, *what* that item is is "animal." This rational is also found in Z, 14
(1039b9–10): "the animal in each species will be the substance of each species; for it is not
said [what it is] in virtue of something else." (Compare 1030a10–11.) This is a weak
principle of substancehood, mirroring the principle according to which every item of the
categories makes a claim to having definition (1030a29–32).

conclusion that the universal is substance, in the sense of being the essence of a distinct entity, the hypothesis must be rejected, as it was shown in the first subargument of Z, 13, that the universal is not substance in this sense.

Thus, whether the *inhering (enuparchon)* universal has a formula or not, it would have to be substance in the sense of being the essence of something, which it cannot be, as shown in the first argument (1038b8–17).

3. The last section (1038b23–29) of Part One of the second argument again provides reasons why, if the universal inheres as a distinct component in the essence of a substance, it will itself be substance. Aristotle says that if substance (here, the essence of some substance) is composed of distinct items, these items must be substances. Otherwise, the components of a substance would be nonsubstances, and, hence, nonsubstances would be prior to substances. But nonsubstances are not prior to substances, in formula, in time, or generation. If nonsubstances were prior to substances, they would also be separate, which they are not. Hence, if a substance had distinct components, they would be substances, and therefore the universal as such a component would be substance. But we saw in the first argument of Z, 13 (1038b9–17), that universals are not substances; so, the universal cannot be a distinct component of substance.

Part Two: 1038b29–30. If a universal (e.g., Animal) is a distinct component of the essence of a substance (e.g., of Socrates), then on the same principle, the essence of Socrates will be a distinct component in Socrates (*enuparxei*, 1038b29, doubles *enuparchei*, 1038b18, in the initial premise of this argument in Z, 13). But then, Animal will be the essence of two entities; it will be the essence of the distinct component, animal, inhering in the essence of Socrates; and it will be (in part) the essence of the essence of Socrates. The reason, again (which we encountered in (2) of the first part of this argument, 1038b20–23), would be that Animal would be *what* these distinct components in Socrates are; that is, what the distinct component, Animal, is, and (in part) what the distinct component, Man, is in Socrates. This would contradict the claim made in the first argument of Z, 13—see item (i)—that required the essence of a thing to be peculiar to it and, so, would not allow an entity to be the essence of two distinct substances. Hence, again a universal cannot be a distinct component of the essence of a substance.

*(iii) The Universal as a Separate Substance.* If the universal is a separate, particular substance, existentially independent of other substances,[20] then

---

20. If it exists apart from the many particulars and indicates a "this" (*tode ti*) (1038b32–1039a1).

a Third Man Argument (TMA) follows. It is possible that Aristotle is here referring to the Platonic TMA, which presupposed the separateness of universals. But he might be thinking of an infinite regress similar to the Second Man Argument (SMA) at 1032a2–3, which we discussed in Section 3 of Chapter 6. There, it was envisaged that the essence of substance *a* is a distinct entity and that, as such, it would itself have an essence, which would also be distinct from it, and so on to infinity. Here, too, if a universal is a separate substance, the universals that are in its essence (e.g., the genera) will also be separate substances, and so will the universals in them, ad infinitum. Hence, the universal cannot be a separate substance.

The conclusion that Aristotle arrives at from the first three arguments of Z, 13, is: "in general it follows, if man and such things are substances, that none of the elements in their formulae is the substance of anything, nor does it exist apart from the species or in anything else; I mean, for instance, that no animal exists apart from the particular animals, nor does any other of the elements present in the formulae exist apart. . . . It is plain that no universal attribute is a substance, and this is plain also from the fact that no common predicate indicates a "this," but rather a "such" (1038b30–1039a2).

*(iv) The Components of a Substance Are Not Actualities.* This conclusion is the culmination of the line of thinking that began with Z, 4, specifying the requirements for the internal unity of a substance. Until now, we had examined the requirements of the unity of essence.[21] Now, Aristotle turns to the unity of a substance as a whole and tells us that "*a substance cannot consist of substances present in actuality*" (1039a3–4, my emphasis).[22] The

21. With the exception of the TMA just considered, which has the same generality as the present argument.

22. Gerald Hughes takes the position that "Essences . . . are substances just when they are the essences of actual individuals; in this case, essences are not universals and are not predicated of the individuals whose essences they are. Taken as universals, essences are no more than the potentiality of there being substances; this potentiality is identical in definition with the relevant set of individuals, but is identical with them in no other way" (1979, 124). But Hughes does not explain what the relation of the potential to the actual is, i.e., what the relation of the universal essence is to the actualized essence. Furthermore, he does not explain what the relation of the actualized essence is to the concrete substance. He only says that "the essence of Socrates is not a potential entity, it is the actuality of his flesh and bones" (p. 124). But how is the actuality of Socrates' flesh and bones related to the flesh and bones? I have argued in this book that the relation between the potential and the actual and the relation of the actuality of a substance to the components that constitute the substance are based on the unifying role of the substantial form, which is achieved by the reidentification of the components that enter into the actualized whole in terms of the form.

components of a substance exist in it in potentiality, like the two halves of a line or anything that is generated from a synthesis of distinct units (1039a4–14). Aristotle has not told us so far in Z how these actualities (which come together to make up a substance) will be unified into a whole; but he is telling us in Z, 13, that *if they remain as actualities, the result will not be a single actuality, but a plurality of actualities.* Thus, Z, 13, prepares the ground for the aggregate argument that will be offered in Z, 17. There, we have seen, he shows that the substantial form of a substance unifies the various elements that go into the makeup of the substance by reidentifying these elements through their role in the whole, which is determined by the form. This allows him to claim in H, 6, that the matter and the form in a substance are somehow one (Section 3 of Chapter 5).

Furthermore, Aristotle says that "no substance can consist of universals because a universal indicates a 'such,' not a 'this'" (1039a15–16). He thus arrives at the aporia that, if substance does not consist of actual substances or of universals, "every substance is incomposite" (1039a17–18) and, hence, not definable (a18–19). Aristotle does not explain here what precisely the objection is. His meaning depends on how we interpret the expression "this"—*tode ti*. If *tode ti* means "concrete particular" (e.g., as in 1033a31), then "such"—*toionde*—must mean universal. In this case, we can understand the difficulty along the lines he explains it in 1087a21–22: "if the principles must be universal, what is derived from them must also be universal." Hence, the objection would be that whatever consists of universals is itself a universal, which (concrete) substance is not.[23] If on the other hand, *tode ti* means "of a particular kind" (where the kind is designated by a *sortal term,* providing a count principle, e.g., "horse," as, for example, in 1042a27–29), then *toionde* must mean "qualified in some way" (where the qualification is nonsortal). In this case, the objection is that a cluster of universals will not comprise a substance of any sort. In both cases, the difficulty lies with the composition of a concrete substance out of what is nonsubstance in one way or another. The difficulty is left as an aporia in this chapter, to be resolved in subsequent chapters, when Aristotle tackles the

---

23. This should be distinguished from the difficulty mentioned in 1003a7–9: "If they [the first principles] are universal, they will not be substances; for everything that is common indicates not a 'this' [*tode ti*] but a 'such' [*toionde*], but substance is a 'this.'" Here the complaint is not that the thing *composed* of the principles will not be substance, but that the principles themselves will not be substance. The difference is vital, because, here Aristotle takes no position on *composition,* whereas in the 1087a21–22 passage his complaint is a complaint about composition.

problem of the *composition* of a concrete substance directly (i.e., Z, 17, and H, 6; see Sections 2 and 4 of Chapter 4 and 3 of Chapter 5).

Before closing this section, I would like to address an apparent contradiction in Z, 13. At 1038b24–25, Aristotle says that "it is impossible and absurd that the 'this,' i.e., the substance, if it consists of parts, should not consist of substances nor of what is a 'this'." And a few lines after this he says that "it is impossible that a substance consist of substances present in it actually" (1039a3–4). Although these statements seem to contradict one another, our analysis of the constitution of a substantial whole shows that the contradiction is only apparent. The difference is that for Aristotle a substance is not the sum of its parts. In fact, *a substance has no parts*, that is, items that can be individuated independently of the whole. On the contrary, any part or aspect of a substance is what it is in virtue of its presence in the whole. The parts that can be separated out from a substance (whether physically or by abstraction) exist in the substance only potentially, not actually, and the separation gives birth to an entity that did not exist in the whole: "even of the things that are thought to be substances, most are only potentialities—e.g., the parts of animals (for none of them exists separately; and when they *are* separated, then they too exist, all of them, merely as matter)" (1040b5–8). Separation into parts is the *creation* of these parts, although on the whole, they do not exist, except potentially. But because separation from the whole deprives them of their role in the whole, when separate, they exist only as matter. By being separated, they lose their identifying form, which stems from their contribution to the whole. Similarly with the parts that go into production of a substance. They cease to exist once integrated into a whole. Thus, Aristotle's position is that a substance does not consist of (distinct, independently identifiable) parts. Rather, it is a unified whole. But if it consisted of parts (which is the Platonic position,[24] Section 1 of Chapter 4), that is, if a substance were a plurality of many, then these (mereological) parts would be substances themselves. Thus, there is no contradiction in the two statements I quoted.

## 4. Potentiality Entails Homonymy

A latent theme in the parallel discussion of identity dependence, potentiality, and homonymy is that potentiality entails homonymy. If *x* is poten-

---

24. I have argued (Scaltsas 1990, 583–584) that this is the position put forward by Plato in Socrates' Dream in *Theaetetus*.

tially a *y* then *x* is homonymously a *y*, because, although we can say that *x* is a *y* (e.g., these bricks are a house),[25] *x* is not actually a *y*, but only potentially so. In that sense, an account of what *x* actually is would not be an account of what a *y* is. So *x* is only homonymously a *y*. The potential here may be a log or a lump of bronze, or it may be an abstract entity such as biological matter of low organization, a material substratum (e.g., the wood in the log that is potentially Hermes), or the body in a human being. (Aristotle does see a parallel between the relation of the body to the human being it constitutes and the bricks to the house they constitute.)[26] More in general, anything that constitutes a substance (whether pieces of concrete matter, bundles of properties, or clusters of opposites) is *homonymously* the substance. For the substance to exist in actuality, these constituents must merge by becoming reidentified in accordance with the principle of the substantial form.[27]

Suppose it is objected that there are always entities in an actual substance that are only homonymously that substance, that there *actually* exists in the substance an aggregate of components whose nature is independent of what the substance is, such as the first elements—earth, water, fire, and air. My claim is that Aristotle would then conclude that there would be *no substance*. What there would be is the aggregate of components,[28] having (*per impossibile*) the substantial form as their accident. If it were counterclaimed that both the aggregate of components and the substance are actual and copresent, only at different levels of internal structure, then these two actualities would be *related* to one another by a relation other than fulfillment of potentiality, because it cannot be the case that the lower level is *actually* one thing, the upper level is *actually* another thing, and that the upper level is *also* the actuality of the lower level. The lower-level thing cannot be two actualities. So, adding levels of composition between what constitutes and what it constitutes cannot allow for two distinct actualities—what constitutes, and what it constitutes—to comprise one and the same substance.

---

25. *Meta.* 1041b6.

26. "The question is *why* the matter is some individual thing, e.g., why are these materials a house? Because that which was the essence of a house is present. And why is this individual thing, or this body in this state, a man? Therefore what we seek is the cause, i.e., the form, by reasons of which the matter is some definite thing; and this is the substance of the thing" (*Meta.* 1041b5–9).

27. See Chap. 5, n. 3, and Chap. 6, n. 48, for Aristotle's association of potentiality with the re-identification of the substantial constituents, whether it is matter or it is accidents, that merge into the substantial whole.

28. σωρός (*Meta.* 1040b8–10).

Rather, two such actualities would have to be related by the kind of relation that Aristotle dismissed when he rejected participation, communion, composition, connection, and any other kind of metaphysical bridge between what constitutes and what it constitutes.[29] He rejected them because the totality would be a related whole of distinct actualities, not a substance.

We have already seen that the unity of a substance is threatened not only by distinct *concrete* components, but equally by distinct *abstract* components. To individuate a component by abstracting it from the substance is to divide the substance. This division has the same effect as physical division: the entity that emerges—the abstract entity—is not present in the substance. The abstract entity that emerges is not an actual component of the substance any more than a severed arm is an actual arm. Separation from the substance destroys the identity dependence on what the substantial whole is. Thus, the abstracted entity emerges with an identity of its own, very much like the severed arm, or the drop of water that is separated from the water in the glass. In general, any process by which we divide the substance up into distinct components is a process of generating entities that are independent of the form of the substance; hence, they are entities that do not exist in the substance.[30]

We have seen that this does not mean that the components of a substance that can be separated out only by abstraction are simply creations of our mind and that therefore Aristotle is not a realist about universals (Sections 2 and 4B of Chapter 5). Aristotle has told us that universals do not exist as separate entities apart from substances and that substances do not contain distinct components in actuality (whose identity is independent of the substantial whole). Putting the two together gives us the position that universals exist only as (identity-dependent) components of substances in the world. It is as if salt could exist only in solution in the universe.[31] Universals exist, but only fused into substances in the world.

29. *Meta.* 1045b7–16.

30. Frank Lewis and Mary Louise Gill develop a notion of concurrent matter within the substance, which survives potentially in the substance. See Lewis (1994) for a discussion of the contribution that the ingredients in potentiality make to the substance (p. 275), and Mary Louise Gill (1989), who attributes a conception of lower concurrent matter to Aristotle, where matter survives only potentially as material properties in the substance (p. 164). Mohan Matthen develops a parallel between the way form is predicated of matter and the way nonsubstance attributes are predicated of a substance (Matthen 1986a, 162, 172–174).

31. There are obvious limitations, of course, to this analogy, but I introduce it in the hope that it is suggestive.

## 5. Is the Substantial Form of a Substance Numerically One?

The knowability and definability of the substantial form, as well as its being common to the members of the same species, require the form to be *universal* (Section 2 of Chapter 2). Nevertheless, when we consider Socrates live and in full actuality, is not his substantial form numerically one? When Socrates exists in full actuality, what else can his own form be but as particular as Socrates himself is? These are challenging questions, and they test one's intuitions severely, because one has the inclination to say that, if Socrates is particular, his form, being in full actuality when Socrates exists, is also *particular*. This is an intuition that is further fed by the thought that if Socrates ceases to be, his substantial form ceases to be, but the form of "being a man" does not cease to be. Therefore, Socrates' form must be unique, peculiar to him, alone. Is, then, the substantial form, when in full actuality in a substance, particular?

It has been the project of the whole book to give an answer to this question by showing that its *presuppositions* are *false*. This realization rests on understanding Aristotle's position on the *particularity* of a substance and the *unity* of a substance. My claim is that according to Aristotle it would lead to a *contradiction* to take the substantial form of a substance to be a distinct component, existing in actuality in the substance, *whether the form is taken to be universal or particular*. If we claimed that when Socrates exists, the substantial form in him is an actual, distinct component in him, this would contradict Aristotle's conclusion that the subject is the substantial form. Socrates is the concrete substance, that is, the subject that belongs to nothing else, but to which all else belongs. But if his substantial form or essence is a distinct component in Socrates, then the subject (Socrates) will be different from the form and essence (the form of "human being" in him). But, as I have tried to show in the present chapter, a good part of Book Z is devoted to arguing that there can be no distinction between the subject and its essence in a substance. This is probably the most significant contribution that Aristotle made toward avoiding the problems of the Third Man regress that confronted Plato's Theory of Forms. A substance, and what a substance is, must be one and the same.

The picture becomes much more complicated if one believes, as for example, Frede and Patzig do, that the form and the matter are independently particular.[32] Then, there are three particulars to contend with: the

32. Frede and Patzig 1988, 2:57.

matter, the form, and the composite of the two. How can the primitive particularities of the matter and the form combine to make up a third particular? It makes no difference whether we say that the matter (or the form) is only potential, so long as we take it to be particular independently of the form (and vice versa). The *independence* of the particularity of the matter from that of the form (and vice versa) is a kind of *actuality*; that is, the matter (or the form) is particular on its own, not potentially particular. But then, the substance, that is, the composite of the two, will not be one, but many.

It is because of his awareness of this insuperable problem for the unity of a substance (see Appendix 2, Sections 2 and 3) that Aristotle explicitly argues in Z, 13, that there are no components of a substance existing in it *in actuality*. A substance is a single, unified whole. This means that to single out a component in a substance is to separate it out, either physically or by abstraction, from the rest. We saw that such a separation does not leave the identity of that component intact. For all the other components, whether material parts, functional parts, or properties, such a separation from the whole involves their reidentification. When in the whole, they are unified *into* a whole by being identity-dependent on the whole, in accordance with the contribution they make to the whole. This contribution is determined by the substantial form. Hence, all components that go into the makeup of a substance are unified by being reidentified in accordance to the substantial form. By unifying them, the substantial form does not, itself, become reidentified, for then there would be some further first principle (*aition prōton, archē*, 1041b28–31) in terms of which that form would be reidentified. By unifying them, the substantial form changes only in number. The unification of all the components that go into the makeup of a substance results in a single whole that is distinct from all other such wholes and that belongs to no other whole; it is therefore a particular. So, being in actuality is for the substantial form to unify all the components of a substance into a single particular.[33] That particular contains no components in actuality; it

---

33. I believe that Michael Loux expressed a similar view in the following: "Kinds are universals whose instantiations are fully articulated substances. Nor is a kind just another constituent of a substance; being an instantiation of a kind is just what each of them is" (Loux 1974, 783). I have tried to show that the individuation of objects is even more complex. Loux says that "the individuation of objects presupposes a kind of magic in our theory: our theory must somehow accomplish the impossible and convert what is one thing into many things. But when we hold that every object falls under a kind, the connection between universals and particulars ceases to be a mystery. Since kinds have numerically different instantiations, the various objects belonging to a kind are, in virtue of being its instantia-

is single and unified.[34] Thus, *the form in actuality is the substance itself, which is one and the same with the subject.*

The answer we can therefore give to the question of whether the substantial form is particular or universal is the following. On the one hand, when abstracted away from a substance, *the substantial form is universal*, because it is separated from the elements that particularize it. The (abstracted) universal form is immaterial, definable, knowable, and common to all the substances of the kind. Furthermore, it is eternal, not as a separate substance (in the way that planets are eternal), but because the species is eternal.[35] A substantial form does not exist in the world as a separate entity, but as an entity that can be separated out from a concrete substance by abstraction. So it depends on the continuation of the species for its existence; if no such concrete substances exist in the world, neither does the form.

On the other hand, when the substantial form is in actuality, it is not a distinct component in the substance, for there are no such components. The substantial form in actuality cannot be differentiated from—and related to—the matter in a substance.[36] Rather, *the substantial form in actuality is the concrete substance itself, which is particular.* As such, it is material and is not definable and knowable in the primary sense. Some material substances perish, whereas others, such as the planets, are eternal.[37]

---

tions, numerically diverse" (p. 783). I have offered Aristotle's theory of abstraction and his theory of the unifying role played by the substantial form toward understanding how the many become one and vice versa. These theories might be seen as the "second sailing" on the instantiation of substance kinds, which circumvents the magic.

34. Sarah Waterlow Broadie says the following on unity: "The *per se* unity of the whole [organism] is not diminished by its being composed of different things, for the actually present components are not substances, while the substantial components are not as such actually present" (Waterlow 1982a, 89). I agree with Waterlow that the substantial components are not actually present in an organism. But I have argued that the nonsubstances are also a threat to the unity of a substance (Section 5 of Chapter 4) and offered the metaphysics of abstraction to explain why a substance is unified, despite the fact that we can abstract away from it such entities as properties, material substrata, and the substantial form.

35. *GA* 731b32–732a2.

36. Yet, this would seem to be necessary in the case of Frede's analysis, according to which the form does not contain the matter, and so the form (which is the substance) would have to be related to the matter by a relation (Frede 1990, 126; see n. 38 below).

37. Wilfrid Sellars has moved in a similar direction, although his position is different from mine. He says: "Thus Aristotle can say that the form of *this shoe* is, in a certain sense, the shoe itself. For, to follow up the above line of thought, the form of *this shoe* is the shoe itself *qua* footcovering made of *some* appropriate kind of matter. The form is *in this disjunctive sense* (indicated by 'some') more 'abstract' than the shoe, but it is not for this reason a *universal*. Furthermore, the form, in this 'abstract' (disjunctive) way includes the whole being of the

In conclusion, this, I propose, is the final Aristotelian answer to "whether
Socrates and to be Socrates are the same thing" and "in what sense each thing
is the same as its essence and in what sense it is not" (1032a4–11). Socrates is
the same thing with "what it is to be Socrates" in actuality. Socrates is not the
same thing with "what it is to be Socrates" in abstraction. There is no third
entity, namely, an immaterial substantial form that is a distinct component
in Socrates.[38]

---

individual shoe" (Sellars 1957, 698). It is very difficult to understand what role matter plays
in a substance according to Sellars' Aristotle, as the form is itself particular and also includes
the whole being of the substance. It is further difficult to see what it means for a *material*
substance to have its *whole* being included in an *abstract* entity.

38. I therefore seem to be in disagreement with Frede (1990, 126) who says that
"Composite substances are not straightforwardly identical with their essence or form. . . . If
we insist that in a way the composite is not distinct from its form, because, in a way, what it
really is is its form, taken in that way *it* [*the composite*] *will be distinct from the matter, insofar as
the form is distinct from the matter*" (my emphasis). In my view, that what the composite really is
is its form does not mean that the composite identifies with its form at the cost of distinctness
from its own matter; this describes a failure rather than the success of the form as the cause of
substantial unity. The success story is that the form does indeed mould the matter into the
composite without being remoulded itself, so that the composite turns out to be just what
the form is. In actuality, the form is the composite; it is not distinct from the matter it
unifies.

# Conclusion: Revisiting the Zeta Contradictions

There is one fundamental issue on which Book Z of the *Metaphysics* appears to offer contradictory answers: Is the essence of a substance particular or is it universal? We saw that at the end of Z, 6, Aristotle allows that in a sense the essence is identical to the concrete substance, and in a sense it is not (1032a7–11). The tensions that surround this position are created by the following Aristotelian commitments. The essence of a particular substance, which depicts *what* the substance is, is the species form, which belongs to all the members of the species and is passed down from generation to generation. This form is the par excellence knowable and definable entity, and what is knowable and definable (in the strict sense) is universal.

On the other hand, the essence that stands for *what* a substance is must be the subject in that substance; otherwise, if the subject is different from its essence, the subject itself will not be what the essence stands for. The reason is that there is no metaphysical glue that can bond together two distinct entities, the subject and the essence, so that *what* the subject is will be the essence, and *who or which* the essence is will be the subject. Rather, metaphysical absurdities follow from the attempt to separate the subject from the essence in a substance by relating them to each other.

However, a concrete substance is particular and material; hence, the subject is particular and material. Therefore, if, in order to avoid the subject-essence separation, the subject is identified with the essence, the essence must be particular and material. Yet, the essence is precisely the non-material aspect of a substance. It is what is common to all the substances of the same kind and, hence, universal. The essence is the object of scientific study, classification, and definition, which matter could not be, for matter itself is indeterminate and can constitute any number of kinds of thing.

Furthermore, suppose the essence of a substance to be particular. If the matter is also particular, then the substance will not be one, but a plurality of two related, particular entities.

Finally, suppose that the essence is universal and the matter particular. Matter's particularity could not be the kind of particularity requisite for a substance, because the same matter belongs to many substances (e.g., the same quantity of bronze belongs to many artifacts that are created out of it, whereas a substance belongs to nothing). If matter is particular, in the sense in which substance is particular, it could not belong to many substances.

I have tried to show that Aristotle did resolve these tensions and that he did offer an answer to these questions that does not commit him to contradictory positions.

The key ideas for the resolution of these problems are the aggregate argument in Z, 17, the oneness of the potential and the actual in H, 6, and the metaphysics of abstraction—by which substances are divided into abstract components. The aggregate argument showed that the unity of a substance requires something over and above the elements from which the substance is made up in order to unify these elements into a whole. A plurality of elements that have independent identities is unified into a single whole, because their incorporation into a whole reidentifies these items in terms of a single principle. The *principle* of reidentification of the elements that are unified into a substance is the *substantial form*, which determines the role that each element will play in the whole.

A substance is a unified whole. As the unification is achieved by the reidentification of the components in terms of the principle of the form, there are no distinct entities in the substantial whole. Any "parts" of a substance will be identity-dependent on the whole, but a substance can be divided up into components—physical or abstract—that are not identity-dependent on the whole. Division separates them from the whole and generates entities that are not present in the whole.

It is Aristotle's most mature metaphysical realization that the unity of a substance is incompatible with the actuality of distinct components in the substance. It has the most profound effect on the understanding of universality and similarity, and most important, on the understanding of what it is to be a component of a substance. Any division of the substance into components that are identifiable independently of the substantial whole is a generation of components that are not present in the substantial whole.

Hence, it is in principle impossible to extract distinct entities from a substantial whole that exist in the whole. It follows that *similarity* between substances cannot consist in the presence of a distinct (abstract) component in different substances. Rather, it consists in the *derivation* of the same distinct entity out of different substances. It is the possibility of the derivation of the same entity, rather than the presence of the same entity, that characterizes similarity between substances. That Socrates and Callias are both white does not mean that they both possess the entity "white color," but that the entity "white color" can be abstracted away from both of them. Similarly, that they are both human beings does not mean that they both possess the distinct form "human being" in them, but that this form can be abstracted away from both of them. For Plato the problem was how a universal could be in many different substances. For Aristotle *the universal could not be even in a single substance*, for the distinctness of the universal would destroy the unity of the whole. But this does not mean that there is no universality, similarity, or composition; it only means that they are not to be understood in terms of the presence of distinct components in the whole, but, rather, in terms of the derivation of distinct components from the whole by abstraction.

The substantial form determines *what* the substance is. As an ultimate unifier of the substantial whole, it is the ultimate subject in the whole. It is the principle in terms of which the rest of the components of the whole are reidentified as they are incorporated into the whole. Because it is such a principle, the incorporation of the substantial form into the whole does not change what the form stands for, but only contributes to the numerical difference of the form from other instantiations of it. Thus, the substantial form in actuality is not reidentified; rather, the instantiated substantial form is a particular substance. Hence, neither the universal form nor the instantiated form are distinct components in a substance. Socrates is identical to the instantiated substantial form, but different from the universal form—which is not a component in Socrates but is derivable from Socrates by abstraction.

No element in a substance is *primitively particular*. By not introducing primitively particular items for the particularity of the substance, Aristotle avoids the division between the *which* and the *what*. The substantial form in actuality is the *unification* (by reidentification) of all the elements that go into the make up of a substance. The unified whole is *particular* insofar as it belongs to none of them as subject and is different from all other unified wholes. *Only the whole substance is particular*, being an ultimate subject (i.e., unifier), and it contains no primitively particular items within it, either formal or material. Substantial wholes are the only sources of particularity in the ontology.

Finally, determining what is common between Socrates and all other human beings singles out Socrates' form by abstraction, that abstracted entity is universal because it belongs to many substances. However, "belonging to a substance" is not a relation in the world, because *abstraction* does not have an ontological correlate. To *belong to a substance* is to be derivable from the substance by abstraction. (This process is truth-conditionally governed by being grounded on the experientially given.) Therefore, the substantial form, all other universals, and the material substratum, are not inherent in the substance as distinct entities, but are singled out by dividing the substance by abstraction. The *unification* of all these components into a substantial whole that renders the form into a substantial *subject* is the form *in actuality*.

# Live Matter

Is Aristotelian matter different from matter as we understand it in contemporary philosophy? This is an important issue with serious ramifications for the overall appraisal of Aristotle's metaphysics. A negative answer to this question has found supporters among Aristotelians in recent years, after the wide circulation of Myles Burnyeat's article "Is an Aristotelian Philosophy of Mind Credible?" (1992). The general claim is that Aristotle did not conceive of biological matter as being inanimate, by contrast to our own conception of matter, which we have inherited from the sharp Cartesian division between material substance and mental substance. Rather, the claim continues, for Aristotle *perceptual powers*, as well as other mental powers, are *primitive properties* of biological matter. Perceptual powers are as primitive as the weight or the warmth of biological matter. It follows that, if we are committed to this Aristotelian conception of matter, we cannot even state the mind-body problem as this problem is understood in contemporary philosophy. The contemporary conception of the problem allows for the possibility of dualism in advanced biological organisms; that is, that the organism consists of inanimate material substance and of mental substance. This possibility does not exist if matter is what this interpretation attributes to Aristotle, because according to it, there is only one type of substance, which primitively has physical and mental properties. The difference between this conception of matter and the contemporary one *does not* require the truth of dualism. It only requires the possibility of its truth, which is allowed by the contemporary conception of inanimate biological matter, but precluded by the putative Aristotelian one.

I will argue that Aristotle's theory of perception does not compel us to attribute this conception of biological matter to him. His theory of perception does allow, for example, that perceptual powers be *emergent* properties of matter. In other words, even if perceptual powers are *irreducible* to physical properties, such irreducibly mental powers need not be taken to be primitive powers of matter. Rather, they may be powers that emerge only when matter is organized in a particular way, according to a specific principle or mean (*archē* or *mesotēta*, DA 424b1–2). Hence, Aristotle's theory allows that there be a quantity of matter underlying the corruption of a live organism into a corpse. (This is also relevant for the entrapment theory of Aristotelian matter proposed by Kit Fine [see Section 7.A in Chapter 6].)

To show this, I turn to the chapter in Aristotle's *De Anima* that has been the basis of the interpretation of biological matter as primitively sentient, Chapter 12 in Book B, which I examine in detail, offering an interpretation of it. My goal is to explain the type of change that *perception* is for Aristotle and characterize it. I distinguish between three types of effect that perceptible forms (e.g., color, sound, smell, etc.) have on things: (1) Their effect on a sense organ; (2) their effect on the medium of a sense organ; (3) their effect on nonsentient things.

## 1. Perceptual Experience

### (A) Receiving the Form, but Not the Matter

*De Anima* B, 12, begins with what appears to be the definition of perception: "with regard to all sense-perception, we must take it that the sense is that which can receive perceptible forms without their matter" (424a17–19). There are two points that Aristotle is interested in making in this initial characterization of perception. Let us turn to the illustration he offers. The sense receives the perceptible form of the object without its matter "as wax receives the imprint of the ring without the iron or gold, and it takes the imprint which is of gold or bronze, but not *qua* gold or bronze" (424a19–21). That the wax receives the imprint of gold, but not qua gold, points to a fundamental feature of the perceptual process, namely, *selectivity of information*. The information about the shape of the ring is received by the wax, not whether the ring was golden, of silver, or of bronze. Similarly, the perceptual process is a *selective* processing of information about the world. That we perceive an object does not entail that we become aware of every aspect of that object, but only of certain aspects of the object. [1] Each sense perception is selective about the aspects of an object it responds to, and it is these aspects that we become aware of through that perceptual experience.

But that sense-perception receives the form without the matter of the perceived object has a second, very significant implication, apart from the selectivity of processed information. It seems to point to something that sense-perception cannot do. I do not think that the fact that the sense organ receives form without matter shows that there is some ultimate aspect of the object, namely, its material aspect, that we cannot perceive. There is nothing in what Aristotle says about perception to commit him to the position that we are blind to the material aspects of the object. What I believe he is telling us by saying that the sense receives the form without the matter is that the *way* in which the sense organ receives the form of the perceived object is different from the way in which an object receives a form when it suffers *physical* change. In both cases, change is change in form, but *the kind of change is different*. To see the difference, let us contrast receiving form perceptually (without the matter), to receiving form with the matter, for example, perceiving the weight of an apple, to eating the apple. The sense-organs *receive* the form of the weight and size of the apple, and we become aware of the apple. But by eating it, we become larger and heavier; we *change* with respect to our weight and size. Now, to change with respect to weight and size is to *receive* new forms of weight and size. The difference, then, between receiving a form as a result of perceiving, and receiving a form as a result of eating lies in the *way* in which the forms are received. The perceived form does not change us physically; it does not make us larger, heavier, circular, pink, or loud. But the reception of form by receiving matter does change us physically; we become characterized by the form, not aware of it. This is the difference that Aristotle is getting at in describing perception as the reception of form without matter, that is, nonphysical reception of form. [2]

1. "The sense is affected by that which has colour or flavour or sound, but by these, not insofar as they are what each of them is spoken of as being, but insofar as they are things of a certain kind and in accordance with their principle" (*DA* 424a22–24).

2. It might be thought that Aristotle introduces a further *kind* of change when he says that it is not the thunderbolt that splits the wood, but the air accompanying the thunderbolt (424b10–12). But such a change is no different from the ones mentioned, i.e., physically receiving a new form: the form of the air, i.e., the hardness of the (fast-moving) air, deforms the wood. The case of air splitting the wood is a case of a tangible form—hardness—affecting a body. It is entirely parallel to the air swelling the sail of a boat or tearing down the

But the criterion of receiving form without matter goes only halfway toward securing nonphysical reception of form. Consider the wax example that Aristotle offers to illustrate receiving form without matter. It shows that something can receive shape without changing in size or weight, as it would if more matter was added to it. But *it fails to show that perception is not physical change.* After all, the wax changes form physically. To give a full account of the *way* the sense organ receives the perceptible form, Aristotle will take two more explanatory steps. First, he will make it explicit that in perception, the reception of form without matter does not result in physical change; second, he will offer a positive account of the type of change that becoming aware of a form comprises. I examine these two issues in the following two Sections respectively.

### (B) Receiving the Form, but Not in the Matter

To perceive is to receive the perceptible form without the matter of the perceived object. But, although the wax receives the form without matter, the wax does not perceive. Aristotle needs to explain why, and he does so while also explaining why plants do not perceive. I shall argue for an alternative reading of this passage from that which it receives by the translators and interpreters of this chapter.

Aristotle considers the effect that perceptible forms have on animate, yet nonsentient, beings: "It is also clear why plants do not perceive, although they have a part of the soul and are affected by tangible objects; for they are cooled and warmed. The reason is that they do not have a mean, nor a first principle of a kind such as to receive the forms of objects of perception; rather *paschein meta tes hules*" (*DA* 424a32–b3).[3] I have left out the translation of the last phrase of this passage, because its meaning is what is contested here. The phrase has been systematically translated as saying that the plants are warmed by receiving the matter of the heat source. The term *hulē* in the phrase in question is taken to refer to the matter of the *cause* of the change. Thus, Hamlyn, in the *Clarendon Aristotle Series*, translates "they are affected by the matter as well,"[4] which J. L. Ackrill retained in his new edition of Aristotle's works.[5] W. S. Hett, in the Loeb edition, construes it

---

walls of a hut; these are effects that are to be understood along the same lines as the effect of an axe splitting wood or a stone falling on earth, which Aristotle explains as perceptible form affecting inanimate body (424b12).

3. πάσχειν μετὰ τῆς ὕλης.
4. Hamlyn 1977, 43.
5. Ackrill 1987, 186.

as follows: "[they] are affected by the matter at the same time as the form."[6] J. Smith, in W. D. Ross's edition translates as follows: the plants have no principle capable of taking the forms of sensible objects "without their matter; in the case of plants the affection is an affection by form-and-matter together."[7] Finally, R. D. Hicks has rendered it as follows: "when they [plants] are acted upon, the matter acts upon them as well."[8]

There are three objections to this rendition of the text. First, it would be amazing if Aristotle believed that the wax can receive the form of the ring without the matter of the ring, but a plant cannot receive the heat of a source without the matter of the source. Commentators who attribute this position to Aristotle do not compare it to the wax example. For instance, Ross says in his commentary that "plants cannot be affected except by the form and the matter together of that which they absorb."[9] Why? If inanimate objects can receive form without matter, there is no reason why animate ones cannot. It makes no sense to take Aristotle to be denying this on entirely arbitrary grounds.

Second, it is unquestionable, and must have been for Aristotle, too, that in some cases, form can be transferred to plants without matter. For example, when a stone scratches the stem of a plant. Now, roughness of surface is a tangible form, just like heat.[10] Why then can one tangible form—roughness—transfer to plants without matter, but another tangible form—heat—cannot? It certainly could not be the nature of the plants that prohibited transfer of form without matter, as this evidently happens in the case of scratching.

Third, Aristotle explicitly claims that tangible forms *do* affect bodies (424b12). Here it is the tangible *forms*, not the matter they are in, that produce the effect. Aristotle makes this clear by contrasting them to the case of the thunderbolt, where it is not the light, but the matter the light is in, namely, the air, that splits the wood (424b10–12). By contrast to that, it is the tangible forms themselves, for example, heat, that affect bodies. Now, if Aristotle claims that tangible forms can affect inanimate bodies, why would he deny that they can affect nonsentient bodies, such as a plant? If a dead tree can be warmed up near a fire, so can a live one, and it would be very implausible to assume that Aristotle denies this.

6. Hett 1935, 137.
7. Ross 1931.
8. Hicks 1907, 105.
9. Ross 1961, 266.
10. Heat is classified as a tangible form in the text under examination (see *tōn haptōn*, 424a34–b1). See also, "in the object of *touch* there are many pairs of opposites, *hot* and cold, dry and wet, rough and smooth" (422b25–27, my emphasis).

It follows that it would not make sense to take Aristotle to be saying in
424b3 that the plants cannot be affected by the form of heat alone, but they
"are affected by the matter [of the heat source] as well." Rather, what he
must be is saying is that the plants do not have a means or first principle to
receive the perceptible forms, but *"they are affected with the matter"*; that is,
they receive the perceptible form *in their matter*, rather than in a perceptual
principle or means, since they do not possess such a principle or means. The
word *"meta"* in *"paschein meta tes hules"* does not mean "together with," but
"with," as in "it burns with the wood that it's made of." It points to the
vehicle of patience: it is the matter of the plant that suffers the change, by
receiving the form. The plant receives the form of heat in its matter, just as
the wood that is split by the thunderbolt receives the form of the moving air
in its matter (by splitting). The point Aristotle is making is that, because
the plant does not have a principle of perception that can be affected by the
form of heat, the only effect that heat can have on the plant is on its matter,
by heating it.

Philoponus interprets the expression πάσχειν μετὰ τῆς ὕλης as suffering the effect of the perceptible forms physically, through bodily change.
He says "the expression μετὰ τῆς ὕλης means that they [the plants] suffer as
matter," because it is their matter, which is inanimate, that is affected by
the perceptible forms (Hayduck 1897, 440). Philoponus does mention that
there are some interpreters who have understood this expression as referring
to the matter of the perceptible form, rather than to the matter of the plant.
He gives examples that make this position plausible, such as dyes that color
bodies, steam that makes the material aromatic, and Aristotle's example of
the thunderbolt splitting the tree with the force of the air that the thunderbolt is in (pp. 440–441). Of course, Aristotle mentions the example of the
thunderbolt to contrast it to the case of perceptible forms themselves (without their matter) affecting other bodies; so it can hardly be taken as evidence
that Aristotle means this (the thunderbolt example) to be the only way that
perceptible forms can affect nonsentient beings.

Philoponus finally says that in the case of heat and cold, and only in their
case, the perceptible form can affect material bodies around them, e.g., by
heating or cooling something at a distance. He explains that this is so
because only these two properties have the creative cause of generation and
corruption. It may be that Philoponus is introducing this position as a
partial vindication of the Aristotelian claim that all perceptible forms can
affect the nonsentient beings in their matter. But in any case, there is no
doubt that Philoponus takes the Aristotelian position to be that all perceptible forms affect nonsentient beings, because he describes Aristotle's posi-

tion by using the term αἰσθητῶν (440.21, 24—the term that Aristotle uses, too, in the passage under examination, 424b2), which refers to perceptible forms in general, not just heat and cold.

R. D. Hicks opposes Philoponus' reading of the passage by urging that we understand the expression μετὰ τῆς ὕλης in contrast to the expression ἄνευ τῆς ὕλης at 424a18–19 (Hicks 1907, 419). There, Aristotle said that perception is the reception of the perceptible forms without receiving the matter they are in. The idea then that Hicks is promoting is that, by contrast to sentient beings, plants can receive the perceptible form only if accompanied by the matter as well. But we have seen that Aristotle allows that inanimate beings can receive perceptible forms without matter, e.g., wax receives the form of the ring without its matter. Furthermore, we have seen that Aristotle explicitly argues that inanimate bodies receive perceptible forms (i.e., without matter, 424b12, 14–15). And no one would entertain that Aristotle believes that the ring can imprint its shape on the wax, but not on the trunk of a tree. Yet, Hicks finds no reason to be alarmed by such a hypothesis: "nor does anything Aristotle says justify us in assimilating what takes place in plants to the case where τὸ πάσχον, as well as τὸ ποιοῦν, is lifeless" (p. 419). We remarked already, however, that what can happen to the matter of a dead plant can certainly happen to a live one (i.e., receive form without matter). Aristotle does not need to put that in writing! Far from contrasting 424b3 (μετὰ τῆς ὕλης) to 424a18–19 (ἄνευ τῆς ὕλης), I have argued that we should realize that the former complements the latter by making it explicit that perception is the reception of form, but not in the way that an object receives form in its matter (as the wax does).[11]

We can conclude, then, that what Aristotle is telling us about plants is

---

11. I first presented this interpretation of this passage when I read a paper at the Center for Hellenic Studies (Washington, D.C.), in May 1988. Zeph Stewart, director of the Center, noted that in Hicks's commentary, reference was made to Philoponus reading the passage in the same way and that Hicks disagreed with it. I am grateful to Zeph Stewart for this valuable reference.

W. D. Ross takes the same position as Hicks and justifies it in the same way, by contrasting the expression μετὰ τῆς ὕλης to the one at 424a18–19, ἄνευ τῆς ὕλης (Ross 1961, 265), which we have already discussed. But then Ross says something surprising: "What they [plants] cannot do is to be affected by the form alone, in other words, to perceive" (p. 266). But the whole point of the arguments Aristotle offers in the second part of B, 12, is to show that inanimate bodies are affected by perceptible forms—not by the matter the forms are in. (The contrast between the thunderbolt and the tangible forms is that in the first it is the matter of the thunderbolt that splits the wood, but in the second, it is the tangible form itself that affects the body [424b10–12].) How can Ross then say that being "affected by the form alone" is perceiving? Wood is affected by a tangible form alone, and so is wax, but they do not perceive.

that they receive the perceptible form *in* their matter, rather than in a sense organ. This is the contrast between our capacity to sense heat and a plant's capacity to be warmed up. The plant receives the form of heat in the way that the wax receives the shape of the ring: Both suffer a respective change. Both changes are physical changes; they are not instances of perception. For perception, it is necessary that there be a *means* and a *principle*, which are the receptors of the form. The plants (and the wax) "do not have a mean, nor a first principle of a kind such as to receive the forms of objects of perception; rather, they suffer *with* their matter" (*DA* 424b1–3). On the contrary, perception is not physical change, but requires a completely different type of reception of form. [12]

So far, we have discussed two criteria and mentioned a third criterion of what perceptual experience is for Aristotle. The first criterion is that *perceiving is receiving the form without the matter.* I have argued that Aristotle's illustration of this point is misleading. Although the wax receives the form of the ring without the matter of the ring, the change that the wax suffers is *in* its matter—physical change. Perceptual experience is not material change for Aristotle. (When the sense organ perceives a circle, it does not become circular in the way that wax changes in shape when it receives the ring imprint.) I suggested that we understand the expression "receiving form without matter" as signaling a different way of receiving form (from receiving form physically) but not as telling us what this way of receiving form is. [13] Thus, perceiving the shape of the ring *is not* receiving its imprint in the way that the wax receives the imprint of the ring, because the latter is

12. Burnyeat agrees with the general position presented in this conclusion, but disagrees about what this different type of reception of form is. He says that "receiving the warmth of a warm thing without its matter means becoming warm without really becoming warm, i.e., it means registering, noticing or perceiving the warmth without actually becoming warm" (1992, 24)—where the mentalistic terms are unanalyzable primitives. In what follows I argue that Aristotle did treat this different kind of reception of form as being further analyzable.

Sorabji presents an alternative interpretation of the different type of reception of form, arguing, in contrast to Burnyeat, that the whole process of reception of form remains physiological. He first presented this position in Sorabji (1971) and has provided further arguments in an exceptionally comprehensive and thorough study of Aristotelian sense perception in Sorabji (1992).

13. Contrast W. D. Ross, who is treating this criterion as sufficient for perceiving: "What they [plants] cannot do is to be affected by the form alone, in other words, to perceive" (Ross 1961, 266). Here Ross treats receiving form without matter as sufficient for perception, failing to distinguish between receiving form in the matter and receiving form in the principle of the sense-organ.

physical change. The perception of the shape of the ring and the impression of the ring onto the wax have this in common: receiving form without matter; but they are two different *types* of change, two different *types* of receiving form.

The difference in the two ways of receiving form is made explicit in the second criterion of perception: *in perception, the form is not received in the matter of the sentient being.* The point of this criterion is to establish the difference between physical and perceptual reception of form. This description prevents any misunderstanding that could be caused by the wax example. According to the first criterion, plants should be able to perceive warmth, because they receive heat without the matter of the heat source. But Aristotle clarifies that this is not perception, because the plants receive the form in their matter. [14]

The first criterion, then, tells us that perception involves transference of form without transference of matter. The second tells us that the perceived form is not received by the matter of the sentient being. The second criterion restricts the first by excluding cases of *physical* transference of form (e.g., the transference of the shape of the ring onto the wax, or of heat into the plant). We now turn to the third way of characterizing perception.

### (C)  Receiving the Form in the Principle of the Sense Organ

I should at the outset say that Aristotle has not satisfactorily answered the question of what perceptual experience is. Nor has anyone else, as we still do not have a fully adequate account of perceptual events and of their difference from physical events, although there has been much progress on this subject in recent years. One can hardly, therefore, expect anything more than a rudimentary beginning in the writings of Aristotle on a subject that has resisted explanation for almost two and a half millennia since Aristotle wrote. For this reason, my concern here will not be how illuminat-

---

14. We shold not think that the distinction Aristotle is drawing here is between receiving the form in the matter as opposed to receiving the form in the form. Receiving the form in the matter means changing in *form*. Saying that plants receive the form in their matter simply is saying that plants suffer physical change, i.e., change in their physical form. The intended contrast is between this kind of change and perception, where the result is the *experience* of the received form. This still allows that physical change may also be involved in perception (which receiving the form in the form does not), but it demands that there be more to perception than physical change.

ing Aristotle's account of perceptual experience is or whether it contains insights that could be of use in contemporary analyses of it, but, rather, to give a general characterization of the direction that Aristotle follows on this issue and to identify the contemporary theories with which Aristotle's position would be compatible.

To have the capacity to perceive for Aristotle is to "have a means [*mesotēta*] . . . [or] a first principle [*archē*] of a kind such as to receive the forms of objects of perception" (*DA* 424b1–2). He does not explain what it is to receive a form in the principle of the sense organ, but he does the next best thing, he gives an example of something with a principle and a means. The example is that of a lyre, in which the tension of the chords secures their consonance (*sumphōnia*) and correct pitch (*tonos*, 424a31–32). We will come to the reasons why Aristotle introduces this example in what follows. What is relevant for the present purposes is that this example gives us a rudimentary model of what Aristotle has in mind when talking of a sense organ having a principle. We can think of the sense organ as a lyre whose chords are tuned in accordance with a principle of consonance and correct pitch. The lyre model will provide a way of understanding what it is to receive the form in the principle rather than in the matter.[15] Although this will not give us an explanation of what perception is, it will reveal Aristotle's general metaphysical stance on the mind-body problem.

What the lyre model provides is the possibility of explaining that more than physical change occurs in perception. Striking the strings of a lyre does produce a physical change, namely, the movement of the strings, but that is not all that occurs. What *more*, or what *other*, occurs depends on the relation between the movement of the strings and the concordant chord. I am not talking here of the relation between the chord and the experience one has of the sound, but, rather, of the movement of the strings when the chord is struck and the harmonious sound that is produced, which results from the consonance and pitch of the strings. Not any tuning of the strings will secure a harmonious sound when the strings are plucked. An explanation would therefore need to be provided of what harmony is and how the harmonious sound is related to the state and the movement of the strings.

Aristotle does not discuss this further, but various aspects of his metaphysical theory, including his doctrine of material versus formal cause and his doctrine of final cause and teleology,[16] would allow one to develop

---

15. ἔχειν μεσότητα . . . [καὶ] τοιαύτην ἀρχὴν οἵαν τὰ εἴδη δέχεσθαι τῶν αἰσθητῶν (*DA* 424b1–2).

16. See Furley 1985; Gotthelf 1988; Kullmann 1977–78; Lennox 1982; Nussbaum 1978, 74–99; and Witt 1989, 79–100.

various themes as interpretations of the lyre model. The lesson I want to derive from it is that the harmony in the sound of the lyre is not a primitive, inexplicable property of the lyre. On the contrary, it is an *emergent* property of the lyre and can be explained in terms of the tuning of the lyre. What is important is that, however we explain the harmony of the sound (e.g., functionally, teleologically, etc.), the harmony will be an emergent property of the lyre. Even assuming that the harmony is *irreducible* to physical properties, the harmony will still be an emergent property of the lyre, which the lyre acquired when its strings came to be in a particular state of tension. Therefore, the perceptual organ, by analogy to the lyre, will possess the principle and means as a result of the material organization of the organ. The principle or the organ (and therefore the perceptual experience), like the tuning of the lyre, may be irreducible to physical properties, but it would still be an *emergent* property of the sense organ. The *irreducibility* of the perceptual experience should be kept apart from its *primitiveness*, which is rejected by Aristotle through the lyre model. [17]

That the form is received by the principle of the sense organ tells us that perception is not just physical change in the sense organ. *Perception* is the change brought about by the form when it is received in the sense organ, which is in an emergent state, just as the harmonious sound is the reception of the movement in the strings, which are in the emergent state of consonance. This still leaves the characterization of the emergent state open (and it remains an open question in contemporary philosophy, too). But it clearly does not treat the state of the sense organ as a primitive capacity of biological matter, any more than the consonance of the strings is a primitive capacity of the matter of the lyre.

We have therefore described, so far, the following three requirements for perception in Aristotle's analysis. In perception: (1) The form of the perceived object is received without the matter of the perceived object; (2) the form of the perceived object is not received by the matter of the sense organ; (3) the form of the perceived object is received by the principle of the sense organ. We have understood these three requirements as securing that the reception of form in the principle of the sense organ is not physical reception of form. Furthermore, we used the lyre model offered by Aristotle to show that the irreducibility of the perceptual experience does not establish its primitiveness in the matter of the sense organ. The principle of the sense organ should be understood as an emergent state in the sense organ, rather

17. I am not, therefore, in agreement with Aryeh Kosman's conclusion that Aristotle is an identity theorist, reducing perception to material change (Kosman 1975, 518).

than as a primitive capacity of the matter of the sense organ. It follows that Aristotle's account of perceptual experience is compatible with an understanding of the mind-body problem in one of the modes in which we frame the problem in contemporary philosophy.

## 2. Transmitting the Form through the Sense Medium

Aristotle has argued in the chapters preceding B, 12, that perception is possible only if the perceptible form is transferred to the sense organ through a *medium*: "For seeing takes place when that which can perceive is affected by something. Now it is impossible for it to be affected by the actual colour which is seen; it remains for it to be affected by what is intervening, so that there must be something intervening. . . . The same account applies to both sound and smell. For none of these produces sense-perception when it touches the sense-organ, but the intervening medium is moved by smell and sound, and each of the sense-organs by this in turn. And when one puts the sounding or smelling object on the sense-organ, it produces no perception. The same applies to touch and taste" (*DA* 419a17–31); "We perceive all things surely through a medium" (423b7). Because a medium (e.g., air, water) is required for perceptible forms (e.g., colors, sounds, smells, etc.) to have an effect on the sense organ, it follows that colors, sounds, smells, and so on must have the capacity to affect the medium. Yet, in the second part of B, 12 (424b3–18), Aristotle questions whether perceptible forms can affect inanimate matter, and if they can, whether all perceptible forms can. This is alarming, because if perceptible forms cannot affect inanimate matter (e.g., air, water), then they could not be transferred by the sense media to the sense organs. Aristotle's whole theory of perception would collapse. Surprisingly, although Aristotle raises the question of whether perceptible forms can affect inanimate objects (in the second part of B, 12), he does not register any worry for a negative answer to this question for his theory of perception. Even when he states that some forms *cannot* affect inanimate matter (which he later qualifies), he makes no connection to his doctrine of the sense media, which he has just finished presenting. To understand this apparent discrepancy in his theory I first examine his arguments in the second part of B, 12, and then draw some telling conclusions about the nature of the transmission of forms through the sense media.

### (A)  Can Perceptible Forms Affect Inanimate Matter?

Aristotle addresses the question directly in the case of inanimate bodies (e.g., air, water, and the forms of smell, color, sound, light, and darkness) and initially takes the position that these forms do not have any effect on inanimate objects; furthermore, that they affect sentient beings only in relation to *sentient* beings, and not in any other way (e.g., in relation to material objects [*DA* 424b3–11]). The argument he offers is that "if the object of smell is smell, then smell must produce, if anything, *smelling*" (424b5–6, my emphasis). This is a very important argument for the nature of secondary properties, whose implications we cannot examine in the present context. Its significance lies in the fact that Aristotle recognizes a *definitional dependency* of the powers of objects (e.g., smell, colour, sound, etc.) on the *sensation* they produce in sentient beings. That is, if these powers of objects are to be defined, they will be defined as causal agents of the sensation they produce in the sentient agent. Hence, *the nature of the powers in the objects will be defined in terms of the experience of the agent*. Even when Aristotle eventually argues that perceptible forms can affect inanimate matter, the *effect* of (some of) the forms on inanimate matter is still definable *only* in terms of the empowerment of inanimate matter to produce experiences in sentient beings (e.g., the effect of a scent on air is to make it odorous).

Important, not all perceptible forms have a definitional dependence on the experience of the agent, according to Aristotle. We can derive this from the following. He says that "tangible objects and flavours do affect bodies" (424b11). The argument he offers is that, if the objects of taste and touch do not have any effect on inanimate bodies, "by what could soulless things be affected and altered?" (424b13). Here Aristotle must be thinking of such changes as causing an object to move by impact with another object, or denting an object, or scratching an object, or curing meat or fish in brine, or causing milk to curdle by mixing it with certain juices, and so on. It follows that the weight, the hardness, the roughness, of an object, as well as the salinity and the like of a juice, are powers of objects that can be defined *independently* of the experience they cause in a sentient being, in terms of the physical changes they bring about in other inanimate objects.

So the initial position is that some perceptible forms cannot, while others can, affect inanimate bodies. But then, Aristotle has second thoughts about the ability of the first group of perceptible forms to affect inanimate beings. He returns to the example of smell and sound and considers whether it is possible that a smell have an effect on inanimate bodies (424b14–16). Registering that sound and smell cannot affect *all* nonsentient bodies, he wants to allow for a possible effect of these perceptible forms on *some* inanimate objects. He says: "Or is it the case that not every body is affected by smell and sound, and those which are affected are indeterminate and inconstant, like air (for air smells, as if it had been affected)?" (424b14–16). So a scent makes air odorous; that is, it makes air such that a sentient being could smell it. This effect is standardly assumed to be the effect that a scent has on air qua medium of the sense of smell. But this must be wrong. My reason for claiming this is the following. Aristotle has argued that every sense organ receives the perceptible forms through its medium—for example, air or water. Hence, each perceptible form must be able to affect the medium of a sense organ. It follows that in B, 12, Aristotle cannot be questioning whether perceptible forms can affect inanimate objects, because he has just established that they *do* affect the medium of their respective sense organ. Rather, I argue that in B, 12, Aristotle is examining a *different* type of effect of perceptible forms on inanimate objects. To understand it, we must distinguish between air *becoming* colored and air *transmitting* the form of the color to the sense-organ (as a transparent medium), for example. It is the first, rather than the second, type of change that Aristotle is considering in the second part of B, 12.

### (B) Encoding Perceptible Forms in the Movements of the Medium

We have just seen why there must be a difference for Aristotle between the *transmission* of a perceptible form through a medium and the *acquisition* of that form by the medium. In this section I offer further reasons why I claim that Aristotle does not hold the view that the medium embodies the form, for instance, that the jelly of the eye gets red when we perceive red. This view has a long history and has in recent years received strong support in Richard Sorabji's writings on the subject.[18]

First, a commonsense argument. Everyday experience shows us that the flame of a candle makes the air around it hot; a rose makes the air around it scented; the setting sun makes the sky pink. According to Aristotle, the perceptible form is transmitted to the sense organ through the medium, and perception is the reception of the form by the principle of the sense

18. Sorabji 1971 and 1992.

organ. If this requires the medium to embody, and be characterized by, the form it is transmitting (as in the examples we just mentioned), then flesh should harden when it touches something hard and transmits that form to the sense organ.[19] Similarly, it must get rough, when touching a rough surface, and sharp, when touching an edge, and liquidy when we touch water, while the air must become green when we see a tree, and round when we see a circle.[20] Clearly Aristotle could not commit himself to such a non-commonsensical account of perception.

There is a further reason why the medium cannot embody the form it transmits according to Aristotle. He holds that no perception is generated when a body possessing the perceptible form comes in direct contact with the sense organ. So if the medium possessed the form, no perception would result from the contact of the medium with the sense organ:

> When one puts the sounding or smelling object on the sense-organ, it produces no perception. The same applies to touch and taste. (419a28–31)

> For seeing takes place when that which can perceive is affected by something. Now *it is impossible for it to be affected by the actual colour which is seen.* (419a17–20, my emphasis)

> None of these [sound, smell, etc.] produces sense-perception when it *touches* the sense-organ. (419a26–28, my emphasis)

> That what is placed upon the sense-organ itself should be imperceptible is common to all animals. (421b17–18)

> We do not perceive that which is placed on the sense organ. (423b24–25)

So, it is impossible for the sense organ to be affected by direct contact with the color it sees. Aristotle could not, then, with consistency, explain the perception of a color by holding that the medium transmits the color to the sense organ by *becoming* colored itself. It is not the color, or a colored body, that he wants to bring in contact with the sense organ (since he holds that such contact does not result in perception). But making the medium pink would only result in the color pink *touching* the sense organ, and Aristotle

---

19. Flesh is the medium of touch: "the body must be the naturally adhering medium for that which can perceive by touch, and its perceptions take place through it" (423a15–16).

20. Burnyeat makes a similar point: "it is one thing to say that it takes a strong hard hand to appreciate the delicate softness of the hand it is holding, quite another to suggest that the strong hard hand softens as it holds the other, or that a hand that touches the pavement literally becomes itself as hard as concrete" (Burnyeat 1992:20).

tells us this is *not* how the perception of the color is achieved. Hence, even if the medium comes to possess the form of the perceived object, this cannot be part of the explanation of the perception of that form by the sense organ. Even if the air becomes colored, or the flesh hot, this cannot explain the transmission of the color, or of heat, to the sense organ.

Finally, Aristotle states explicitly that the transmission of a form through a medium is fundamentally different from the embodiment of the form. While discussing taste, he distinguishes transmitting from embodying a form: "The body in which the flavour resides, the object of taste, is in moisture as its matter . . . Hence, even if we lived in water we should perceive a sweet object thrown into it; but the perception would not have come to us through a medium but because of the mixture of the object with the moisture, just as in a drink. But colour is not seen in this way as the result of admixture, nor through effluences" (422a10–15). The distinction is clear: the acquisition of the flavor by the water is not the transmission of the flavor through a medium. If we are in the water and we taste the sourness of lemon juice, which has been poured into the water, the sourness of the juice is not transmitted to us through the water as *medium*; rather, the water has *become* sour through the mixture, just like a lemonade. Hence, the *transmission* of perceptible form through the sense medium is radically different from the *acquisition* of the form.[21]

How, then, is the perceptible form transmitted to the sense organ, if not by the medium becoming characterized by the form of the object? Let us turn to Aristotle's descriptions of the process:

> The colour *sets in motion* the transparent, e.g., air, and the sense-organ is moved in turn by this when it is continuous. (419a13–15, my emphasis)

> The intervening medium is *moved* by smell and sound, and each of the sense organs by this in turn. (419a27–28, my emphasis)

> the air . . . produces hearing, when it is *moved* as a single, continuous mass. (419b34–35, my emphasis)

> It seems in general that just as air and water are to sight, hearing, and smell, so the flesh and the tongue are to their sense-organ as each of those is. . . . Hence the flesh is the medium for that which can perceive by touch. (423b17–26)

---

21. In this context, Aristotle uses this difference to argue that the water does not function as a medium of the sense of taste, even if flavors reach us through the water. Later on he argues that flesh—the tongue—is the medium of taste (423b17).

What kind of movement is the movement of the medium, such that on the one hand the perceptible form is transmitted to the sense organ through the medium while on the other the form is not embodied in the medium? Aristotle's account of perception through a medium calls for a model that allows for the *transmission* of the form, without requiring the *presence* of the form in the medium.

Aristotle's theory need not be committed to the unacceptable consequences that flesh becomes hard when feeling a hard surface, nor, on the other hand, to deny that the air becomes scented in the proximity of a rose. Furthermore, he does not need to reject his conclusion that perception does not arise from direct contact between a colored surface or a sounding bell and the sense organ. Nor does he have to give up the distinction between mixing flavors in a drink and transmitting flavors through a sense medium. In this section, I offer an interpretation of Aristotle's theory of the transmission of a perceptible form through a sense medium that shows that the distinction between transmission and embodiment of form can be sustained on Aristotle's own model for this distinction. My proposal is that the perceptible form is transmitted through the medium, being encoded in the *movement* of the medium, rather than being embodied in the medium. Thus, transmission does not entail embodiment. The model I am guided by in understanding the encoding of form in a medium is found in Aristotle's explanation of human procreation, where the human form is transmitted by its being encoded in the movements in the sperm.

In procreation the human form is transmitted through the sperm, which shapes the menstrual fluid into an embryo.[22] The sperm is *not* a human being, nor is the human form *present* in it. Yet, the sperm *transmits* human form to the menstrual fluids, and thus the embryo is created. My suggestion is that the transmission of a perceptible form to a sense organ through its medium can be understood along the same lines. The sense medium corresponds to the sperm, and the creation of an embryo to the perception of a form by the sense organ. Just as the sperm is not a human being, but it transmits the form of a human being, thus the medium is not hard or sharp or pink, but it transmits these forms to the sense organ.

I should stress at the outset that the fact that the form is transmitted encoded through the medium in no way clashes with Aristotle's requirement that the form is received by the sense organ in actuality: "Perceiving is

22. "What the male contributes to the generation is the form and the efficient cause, while the female contributes the material" (*GA* 729a10–11). More in general, see *GA* 1.18–21 and 734b–735a.

a form of being affected; hence, that which acts makes that part, which is potentially as it is, such as it is itself actually" (424a1–2). Just as the parent's form is received by the menstrual fluids in actuality, thereby shaping the embryo, thus the perceived object's form is received by the sense organ in actuality, thereby giving rise to the perception.

What is required for perception is that the medium be *moved* by the perceptible form so as to *transmit* the perceptible form to the sense organ. But this is just what happens in the sperm's case: the sperm is moved by the heat in the blood of the parent, and it in turn moves the menstrual fluids. The sperm is the medium via which the movements of the father's blood are carried to the menstrual fluids in the mother, where they shape the embryo. Thus, the human form is transmitted through the sperm, as medium, without being in the sperm at any point or making the sperm into a human being. The human form is *encoded* in the movement of the sperm, which is caused by the progenitor. Similarly, the perceptual medium transmits the form from the perceptible object to the sense organ without becoming qualified by that form. The perceptible form is *encoded* in the movement of the medium, which is caused by the perceptible object. The encoding of the form in the medium is a *physical* change, just like the encoding of the human form in the sperm; perception does not occur in the medium.

Now, a sperm cannot embody the human form. Similarly, a medium may not be appropriate for embodying the perceptible form. Thus, flesh is able to transmit the movements encoding the hardness of a surface, but flesh cannot become hard. On the other hand, it may be possible that a medium is appropriate *both* for receiving the encoded form and for embodying that form. Thus, air may transmit the movements encoding the form of a noise and may make a noise itself when it blows violently against a surface. Finally, the two may be combined: the air in the sky *becomes* pink from the sun; but it also *transmits* to the sense organ the form of the color of the sun, encoded in the air's movements. The fact that in some cases the medium may also embody the form it is transmitting to the sense organ should not mislead us into thinking that it is the embodiment of the form that is essential for perception; rather, it is the encoding of the form in the movement of the medium that allows the form to be transmitted to the sense organ. Otherwise, the medium would be just another colored, or hard, or sonorous thing whose contact with the sense organ could produce no perception, according to Aristotle.[23]

The difference, then, is this. When we see a tree, the air around the tree

23. 419a26–31, 419a17–20, 421b17–18, 423b20–25.

does not become green. Rather, we see the green of the tree because "the colour sets in motion the transparent, e.g., air, and the sense-organ is moved in turn by this" (419a13–15). In some cases, as in the case of a scent, the medium cannot but be affected by the source, and so it becomes scented. But it is not the contact of the scent with the sense organ that produces the perception: "when one puts the . . . smelling object on the sense-organ, it produces no perception" (419a28–30). Rather, it is the movement caused by the scent in the air that encodes the form and transmits it to the sense organ. There is no inconsistency in Aristotle's holding that in some cases, the medium cannot help but become characterized by the form. In fact, this can explain such phenomena as the following. Whereas there is no question in our minds that it is the tree (not the air) that we see, when we perceive the green, we would hesitate to claim that it is the rose that we smell, when we smell the air near a rose, although the rose is the origin of the scent. We would be especially hesitant when we smell the air after the rose has been removed.[24] When the air becomes scented, *the air is not acting as a medium, but as a perceptible object itself.* It becomes the source of the form, not the medium of its transmission.

We can therefore conclude by summarizing the characterization of perception according to Aristotle's analysis. We have already encountered the first three requirements, and have now argued for the fourth.

In *perception*:

1. The form of the perceived object is received without the matter of the perceived object.
2. The form of the perceived object is not received by the matter of the sense organ.
3. The form of the perceived object is received in the principle of the sense organ.
4. The form of the perceived object is transmitted to the sense organ by being encoded in the movement of the medium.

## 3. Does the Sense Organ Become Warmer When Perceiving Heat?

Does anything in us have to get warmer for us to feel heat? The answer to this question is connected to several themes in Aristotle's discussion of perception, which I would like to compare and set apart. First, does the

24. We would say that the air smells like a rose, rather than that we smell a rose.

sense organ get warmer when we sense heat? Second, does the medium, our
flesh, get warmer when we sense heat? And third, if the medium or the
sense organ becomes warm when we perceive heat, is there more to perceiving heat than its becoming warm?

We saw that Aristotle requires that the sense organ receive the perceptible form in actuality: "perceiving is a form of being affected; hence, that
which acts makes that part, which is potentially as it is, such as it is itself
actually" (424a1–2). The reason why Aristotle requires this is not entirely
clear. One of his motivations is clear: if the form is received by the sense
organ in actuality, then his theory can explain the perceptual phenomenon
of *blind spots*, of not being able to sense the temperature of a body if it is the
same temperature as us. Aristotle says: "For this reason we do not perceive
anything which is equally as hot or cold, or hard or soft, but rather, excesses
of these, the sense being a sort of mean between the opposites present in
objects of perception. . . . And just as that which is to perceive white and
black must be neither of them actually, although both potentially (and
similarly too for the other senses), so in the case of touch that which is to
perceive such must be neither hot nor cold" (424a2–10). I take this to
require that the sense organ receives the perceptible forms in actuality and
suffers physical change by receiving these forms, by becoming white, or
hot, or soft. This position is the main motivation for Sorabji's holding that,
for example, literal coloration takes place in the sense organ when one is
perceiving a color.[25] Burnyeat criticizes Sorabji by pointing out that, if it is
the sense organ that embodies the form when perceiving it, then the
explanation will not be very satisfactory for the phenomenon of blind spots
(e.g., in the case of touch, according to this explanation, it would not be the
temperature or hardness of the flesh that will be relevant in explaining why
we fail to perceive this as warm or that as soft but the temperature and
hardness of the heart, the sense organ of touch).[26] It is not clear whether this
is a problem faced by Sorabji's interpretation or by Aristotle's theory. But I
will not pursue this question any further here, as I wish to point out a much
more serious problem that Aristotle's explanation of blind spots creates for
his theory of perception. Yet, I want to mention that on Burnyeat's interpretation of Aristotle's theory, no explanation of blind spots can be given, a
serious problem for the interpretation. The reason is the following: Perceiving, on Burnyeat's interpretation, is possible because of our (primitive)

25. Sorabji 1992, 214–215.
26. Burnyeat 1992, 20–21.

capacity to become *aware* of forms; this primitive capacity is independent of the physiology of the matter it is in; hence, we should be able to perceive all the perceptible forms; but this leaves no room for the phenomenon of blind spots.

We saw that the quoted passage seems to require that the sense organ embody the form it perceives. I shall argue that, as important as this position is for Aristotle's handling of blind spots, it is far from conclusive evidence that this is the final picture that Aristotle would want to preserve in his account of perception. There is a problem. The problem is revealed if we consider the perception of heat. If the sense organ perceives heat by becoming actually hotter than it was, then if the sense organ was exposed to a heat source, it should sense heat. But Aristotle says that it does not: "when one puts the sounding or smelling object on the sense organ, it produces no perception. The same applies to touch and taste" (419a21–31). An inconsistency therefore follows in Aristotle's explanation of perception, from the claim that the sense organ perceives by embodying the form it receives through the medium; contact with a hot body should produce perception in the sense organ, but Aristotle denies that it does. On the other hand, if the sense organ does not embody the form it receives from the medium, then Aristotle's solution to the blind spot problem would have to be abandoned. So, clearly, there is a discrepancy here in Aristotle's theory on this point, and so the claim that the sense organ embodies, in actuality, the form it receives, cannot be taken to be a conclusive position.

A further problem arises from Aristotle's distinction between receiving a form in the matter and receiving the form in the principle of the sense organ. We have seen (Section 1C of this appendix) that receiving the form in the principle of the sense organ is not a physical change, in contrast to receiving the form in the matter. But becoming warmer is a physical change: it is receiving the form of heat in the matter. Therefore, even if the sense organ gets warmer when it perceives heat, this cannot be what perceiving heat consists in, because the organ would be receiving form in the matter rather than in its principle. So, Aristotle's solution to the blind spot problem is also incompatible with the requirements he set for perception in B, 12.

Of course, to solve the blind spot problem in a way compatible with the rest of his theory of perception, he would have to develop in detail his distinction between receiving the form in the matter and receiving the form in the principle of the sense organ. Only by showing how the principle of the sense organ depends on the physiology of the sense organ (e.g., as the tuning of the lyre depends on the tension of the strings) could he determine why the principle of the sense organ is not sensitive to certain forms. Between the two positions, between his solution to the blind spot problem and his doctrine of receiving the form in the principle of the sense organ, the latter is the important one, because it can be compatible with a theory that can cope with mental events. If perception is claimed to be just physical change, as the solution to the blind spot problem requires, then there is no hope of accounting for the experiential aspect of perception or for perceptual representation.

Aristotle does address the question of whether perception involves more than physical change, at the end of B, 12. Although this passage has received much attention by commentators, I believe very little philosophical weight rests on it, because however we read his statement, the problems that the two alternative (and incompatible) readings purport to solve still remain in the theory. It is the problems that demand and dictate the solution, not brief, general statements of the sort with which Aristotle ends B, 12, with. Either way we read the statement, some of the problems I itemized will remain unsolved.

At the end of the *De Anima* B, 12, Aristotle establishes that even perceptible forms such as smell and sound can affect *some* inanimate bodies, for example, the bodies that are indeterminate and inconstant, such as air or water. So, he concludes, "air smells, as if it had been affected" by smell (424b16). And he continues: "What then is smelling apart from being affected? Or is smelling *also* perceiving, whereas the air when affected quickly becomes an object of perception?" (424b16–18, my emphasis). The word "also"—"*kai*" in Greek—is the bone of contention. The term has not been included in all renditions of the Greek text. It is in the *Oxford Classical Texts*, W. D. Ross's edition, without any notes in the apparatus, as well as in R. D. Hicks's edition;[27] but it has been omitted in the Loeb edition by Hett, as well as in the *Thesaurus Linguae Graecae*.[28] Aryeh Kosman has argued that the "*kai*" is an addition by the scribe, and Myles Burnyeat as well as other commentators have agreed with him; Sorabji omits it, but his interpretation does not rest on the omission.[29]

27. Hicks 1907, 106.

28. In the compact disk edition of the Greek texts.

29. Kosman (1975, 510), who also gives an informative account of the history of the term in the manuscripts, pp. 509–511; see also Kahn 1966; Burnyeat 1992, 25; Sorabji 1992, 219–220.

Having taken the position that the "*kai*" does not belong to the text, for Burnyeat it reads as follows: "What then is smelling apart from being affected? Or is smelling perceiving" (424b16–17), which he interprets as follows: smelling is not the air becoming odorous *plus* something more, but it is directly a primitive capacity of organic matter to be affected by smell, to perceive smell.[30]

I want to argue that whether the "*kai*" is a corruption of the original text or not, the text does not require perception to be a primitive capacity of matter.[31] Let us first assume that the "*kai*" belongs to the text: "Or is smelling *also* perceiving?" (424b17) What Aristotle would be saying here is that smelling is not only the air being affected by the scent, but *also* the *perceiving* of the scent. That is, smelling involves in addition the transmission of the form of the scent through the medium of smell and its reception by the principle of the sense organ. The medium of smell is air or water (419a32–33). As we have seen, there is no inconsistency in the claim that the air can at the same time be both, a source of smell and the medium of smell.

Let us now suppose that the "*kai*" is an addition to the text. "Smelling is perceiving, whereas the air when affected quickly becomes an object of perception" (424b17–18). We can understand Aristotle as saying that, whereas the air becomes scented by receiving the form of the smell in its matter, thereby being physically changed, smelling is not such a physical change. Rather, smelling is perceiving, and we have just seen (in B, 12) that perceiving is the reception of the form of a scent by the principle of the sense organ of smell.

Either way we read the line, we are not forced to treat perception as a primitive capacity of biological matter. Rather, it is the reception of the perceptible form by the principle of the sense organ, which we understood in terms of Aristotle's lyre analogy to be an emergent, rather than a primitive, capacity of biological matter. Therefore, within Aristotelian metaphysics, we can construe the mind-body problem in terms of inanimate matter and emergent capacities of the matter. As we have seen, that the capacities may be irreducible to physical ones, just as the consonance of the strings is (for it is not reducible to the tension of the strings, although it presupposes it), does not mean that they are primitive capacities of matter.

30. Burnyeat 1992, 25.
31. Kosman (1975, 518) argues that Aristotle is committed to a materialist conception of perception (along the mind-body identity theory lines), on the basis of his position on the origin of the *kai*.

## APPENDIX 2
# Against Bare Substrata

One can easily see the attraction of the position according to which the particularity of a substance is relegated to an ultimate, underlying logical subject, which is characterless and particular.[1] Being primitively particular, it accounts for the particularity of the substance, restricting the universality of the properties that belong to it. Being characterless, no problems of incompatibility arise between its nature and the properties that determine the substance's nature. Sometimes, the nature of the underlying subject is described as pure potentiality, indicating that any property can belong to it. Clearly nothing is incompatible with pure potentiality, which makes such substrata very convenient metaphysical posits.

As the notion of a bare particular is conceptually problematic, I had in the past resisted attributing it to Aristotle by focusing on the passages that were traditionally taken to show Aristotle as committed to it and showing that they do not provide clear evidence for such a commitment on his part. I discuss only *Metaphysics* Z, 3, which is the strongest evidence that supporters of the bare substratum theory adduce in support of their position.[2] Then, I offer direct evidence, which I have now found in Aristotle's arguments on numbers, that Aristotle rejects the notion of a characterless particular component of a substance.

1. Charlton (1970, 129) has a representative selection of passages from Zeller (1897) describing such a position. But the position is still popular and alive, and one frequently comes across it in discussions of Aristotelian prime matter, as, e.g., in Suppes 1974, 29–30; Dancy 1978; Loux 1991, 9; and F. Lewis 1991, 1267–1269.
   2. Charlton (1970, 129–145) discusses many other passages.

## 1. Ontology or Semantics? *Metaphysics* Z, 3

The passage that has received the greatest attention in attempts to show that Aristotle is committed to a characterless substratum is *Metaphysics* Z, 3, where Aristotle begins his search for what substance is. The candidate for substance he considers in Z, 3 is the substratum of which the properties of a substance are predicated. The reason why the substratum suggests itself as the prime candidate for being substance is the *principle of subjecthood*. This is a principle that is first encountered in the *Categories* and is never given up by Aristotle, according to which substance is the ultimate subject, of which all else is predicated, and that is not itself predicated of any. He says in the *Categories*, "that which is called a substance most strictly, primarily, and most of all, is that which is neither said of a subject, nor in a subject" (2a11–13), and "all other things are either said of primary substances or in them as subjects" (2a34–35). Here in *Metaphysics* Z, 3, Aristotle says that "the primary subject is thought to be in the truest sense substance" (1029a1–2); "substance . . . is that which is not predicated of a subject, but of which all else is predicated" (1029a8–9). And in Z, 13, he repeats that "substance means that which is not predicable of a subject" (1038b15–16).

That substance is the ultimate subject is a principle that Aristotle never abandons. But *what* that subject, and hence substance, is changes. In the *Categories* it is "the individual man or the individual horse" (2a13–14), that is, the concrete particular. In *Metaphysics* Z, 3, three candidates for being the subject in a particular substance are put forward: the matter, the form, and the composite of the two (1029a2–5). But it is matter that is considered to be the ultimate subject in Z, 3 (1029a23–24), of which all else is predicated, and consequently, the prime candidate for being substance (1029a10, 26–27). Yet, in opposition to the interpretation put forward recently by M. Furth,[3] and possibly, if I understand her correctly, by M. L. Gill,[4] I argue that Aristotle finally shows that it is not matter, but the substantial form, that is the *ultimate* subject in a substance.

The question I address here is whether Aristotle commits himself in Z, 3, to a characterless substratum functioning as the ultimate subject in a substance. The subject in a substance is described as follows: "the subject is that

---

3. Furth 1988, 50, 62, 176, 185, 188.

4. Gill says "the stripping [of layers of forms] finally exposes a *subject* that, although something in its own right, is not composed of a form realized in a distinct matter—in other words, a subject that is not a composite. Aristotle adopts . . . [this] alternative. There is an ultimate matter, and the matter is something in its own right" (1988, 40, my emphasis).

of which other things are predicated, while it is itself not predicated of anything else" (1028b36–37). To discover what sort of entity the subject is, Aristotle goes through the following thought experiment. He abstracts from a concrete substance all the characteristics it possesses, anything that could be predicated of it. "When all else is taken away, evidently nothing but matter remains" (1029a11–12). "By matter, I mean that which in itself {*kath' hauten*} is neither a particular thing nor of a certain quantity nor assigned to any other of the categories by which being is determined" (1029a20–21).

What kind of test is this, and what does it establish? It is the abstracting away of properties from the subject. We can describe what Aristotle performs in the thought experiment as the transferring of all the *descriptive* elements from the subject term to the predicate term in a declarative sentence and testing to see if anything resists transferral. This would show if there is anything more in a substance than the properties in terms of which the substances is described. What results is the discovery that: "There is something of which each of these is predicated, so that its being is different from that of each of the predicates; for the predicates other than substance are predicated of substance, while substance is predicated of matter. Therefore the ultimate substratum is of itself neither a particular thing nor of a particular quantity nor otherwise positively characterised; nor yet negatively, for negations also will belong to it only by accident" (1029a21–26). This is an existential statement, and the question that faces us is whether it is supported by an existential argument. I claim that it is not. What Aristotle is engaging in here is a semantic exploration into the different roles of the *subject*, and the *predicate*, terms in a sentence. What he has uncovered is that *referring* to something in the world is not a semantic role that can be transferred from the subject term to the predicate term. So ultimately, after all descriptive elements in the subject term have been transferred to the predicate term, the sentence will have the form: "there is something which is an *f, g, h.* . . ." No further transferral of semantic function from the subject term to the predicate term is possible. The referring expression does *not describe*, or if it does, only with a minimal amount of information that can be given about anything: that it is a subject of predication (i.e., something which is).[5] What the subject term does is to *refer* to the thing that is described by the predicate expression, and this is a semantic function that cannot be performed by the predicate expression.

This is not an existential argument for the existence of a bare substratum,

5. I have argued this interpretation of Z, 3, in Scaltsas 1985b, 219–222.

but a semantic argument for the division of labor between the subject and predicate terms of a sentence. Yet, this does not address the question of whether Aristotle took it to be an existential argument for bare substrata or not. Let me begin by saying that, although it is a semantic argument, I do not believe Aristotle saw it as such. But this does not mean he saw it as an ontological argument. He certainly does not accept the direct conclusion that follows from his argument, that is, that matter, qua ultimate subject, is substance: "For those who adopt this point of view [given in the quote from 1029a21–26], then, it follows that matter is substance. But this is impossible" (1029a26–27). The conclusion is rejected because more criteria for substancehood are introduced, namely, separability and individuality (1029a27–28), that matter, especially bare matter, does not satisfy. So this thought experiment of Z, 3, does not lead to the discovery of substance for Aristotle. As he rejects its conclusion, it is difficult to judge whether Aristotle saw further results of an existential nature following from the argument.

Whether it is a discovery of matter as characterless substratum cannot be judged from the aporetic nature of Z, 3, alone. But there is direct evidence elsewhere showing that Aristotle would object to the bare substratum as a senseless notion, leading to irrationalities.

## 2. Characterless Particulars Do Not Differ from One Another

In this section I want to introduce evidence showing that Aristotle would reject the bare substratum doctrine and with it the account of the particularity of a substance that rests on an underlying propertyless particular. The evidence is found in his arguments against a version of the Platonic Forms according to which Forms, and numbers too, are made up of units (*Meta.* 991b21–27).

If it is supposed, says Aristotle, that the units in each number, for instance, 10,000, are different from each other and that they are also different from the units of all other numbers, "numerous absurdities will follow" (991b24). The question of a difference in kind between the units does not arise because they cannot be different from one another, being that they are characterless units:[6] "for in what will they differ, as they are without quality? This is not a plausible view, nor can it be consistently

---

6. ἀπαθεῖς μονάδες.

thought out." (b26–27). Clearly, Aristotle sees the claim that there can be *different characterless particulars* as a source of irrationalities. Yet, this is the very notion on which the tradition rests the proposal for the resolution of the particularity of substances.[7]

The particularity of the alleged characterless substratum is primitive. It has to be primitive because the substratum has no nature from which its *difference* from other substrata could be derived. Because it has no nature of its own, no transformation from one kind of substance to another can change it. The substratum is capable of receiving any properties that any sequence of transformations may bring its way. It can underlie the nature of any substance as the subject of that substance's properties. Hence, the substratum is pure potentiality in the sense that, in itself, it must not be this kind or that kind. It must be characterless (*apathes*). But if it is characterless, it cannot be different, as Aristotle explicitly states. To be different, the substrata in question would have to differ *in some respect*, which would answer Aristotle's question of: in what (*tini*) will they differ? But they do not have different respects or properties. Hence, characterless units cannot be different. It follows that, according to Aristotle, the particularity of a substance cannot rest on an underlying characterless substratum.

### 3. Characterless Particulars Do Not Combine and Divide

Another difficulty with the supposition of an underlying characterless substratum is its *compositionality*. Let us suppose that we have a bronze vase and a bronze statue that we melt down and use to construct a bronze tray. How many substrata does the bronze tray consist of? The substratum theory would explain the particularity of the tray in terms of a single characterless subject underlying all the properties of the tray. Thus Zeller says: "Becoming in general . . . presupposes some Being . . . which underlies as their subject the changing properties and conditions, and maintains itself in them. This substratum cannot itself have a commencement; and . . . it is imperishable also."[8] But if each substratum survives any transformation of the substance it underlies (which is the existential claim for substrata as pure potentialities), then the substratum underlying the statue and the one

---

7. Zeller 1897, 342; Solmsen 1958; Robinson 1974; Williams 1982, 211–219.
8. In Charlton 1970, 129.

underlying the vase survive the destruction of the statue and the vase.[9] Therefore, they both exist in the tray. Is the substratum of the tray the same as either of these two substrata or different? If the same, on what grounds is it the same with one of the two, and why this one and not the other? If different, is it independent of them or is it composed of the two of them? If it is composed, then it must have at least some structural properties that determine its nature, which is inconsistent with the hypothesis of the characterlessness of substrata. If it is not composed, what role do the other two substrata play in the tray? How is it that when the statue is transformed into a vase we have the same substratum—though not the same substance— remaining throughout, but when the vase and the statue are transformed into a tray, their substrata become useless and a new substratum comes into existence? Clearly, absurdities abound.

Aristotle did not present the problems of *compositionality* of substrata in so many words. But he was aware of such difficulties as follows from his arguments against the conception of numbers as composed of different units. If the ideal 10, says Aristotle at *Meta.* 1082a1−11, is the composition of two 5s, the two 5s cannot be identical. If they differ, the units they are composed of must differ (presumably because the two 5s are specifically the same, and so their difference must be in their components). If the component units differ, then there are more than two 5s in 10, because, as Ross explains,[10] the units of the two 5s (in different combinations) will compose further 5s. If there are more than two 5s in the ideal 10, Aristotle asks: "what sort of 10 will consist of them? For there is no other 10 in the 10 but itself" (a10−11). Therefore, Aristotle did not think that a whole (here, number 5) can be composed of qualitatively indistinguishable but numerically different unit components. It follows that he would have the same objections to any account of the composition of a characterless substratum (e.g., the tray's) in terms of component characterless substrata (here, the statue's and the vase's).

For an example that is analogous to the case Aristotle is discussing, let us

---

9. Zeller in fact believes that all the different substrata resolve themselves into one and the same substratum: "since everything which perishes resolves itself finally into the same substratum. . . . This will be . . . the Subject . . . or substratum . . . which is receptive of them [the thinkable predicates] all" (Charlton 1970, 129). I submit that I cannot understand how it can, then, be the substratum in each substance that is responsible for the particularity of each substance. It should follow from Zeller's stance that all substances are, ultimately, mere modifications of one and the same subject, which receives them all.

10. Ross 1924, 438.

consider melting down two pennies in order to create a twopence coin. What is the relation of the substrata of the two pennies to the substratum of the twopence coin? Just as the 5s in Aristotle's discussion attain their respective identity from their numerically different units, so the five dimes attain theirs from their numerically different substrata (on the characterless substratum theory). Aristotle concluded with the absurdity that there will be more than two 5s in 10, which will make up more than one 10. Similarly here, there will be more than one substratum in the twopence coin, which will make up more than one coin. It would be irrational to suppose that a philosopher who registers these complaints about the compositional problems of 10 from its units would not register complaints similar to the ones listed in this and the previous paragraph about the composition of the characterless substratum of a new substance out of the characterless substrata of the substances it was constructed from.

At its core, the problem is that *characterless, primitively particular substrata are not additive.* Yet, substances are produced from the fission and fusion of other substances. Hence, the characterless substratum hypothesis would lead to absurdities, which Aristotle would have recognized if he had entertained that hypothesis toward an account of substantial particularity.

The arguments offered in the preceding two sections against the characterless substratum apply whether the substratum is taken to be material or formal. Because it is characterless, and is qualified only by its role as the ultimate substratum, it makes no difference whether we call it matter or form. Aristotle would reject *prime form*, that is, a characterless form that is primitively particular and is the ultimate subject of predication in a substance, for the very same reasons that he would reject a material bare substratum.

# Against Individual Forms

## 1. Form as Efficient Cause

My general line of argument in any attempt to account for the particularity of a substance through the particularity of the substantial form, when the form is treated as a historical individual, is that this answer only pushes the question one step back without answering it. I first discuss the account that Irving Block gave of the substantial form as a historical individual (even though he did not explicitly address the question of what is responsible for the particularity of a substance), because his position is representative of a line of interpretation that one frequently encounters in current discussions of the problem of particularity. [1] Block's position is that the substantial form of a particular substance is particular; furthermore, that the substantial form is a combination of, or is at one and the same time, the formal and the efficient cause of the substance. Insofar as the efficient cause shaped *this* matter into *this* substance, the efficient cause is particular. Block says: "There [in *Metaphysics* Z, 17] it is said that the *to ti ēn einai* is more than the definition or the *infimæ species* of a thing, which is the way that *to ti ēn einai* is described in the Topics. . . . In Z ch. 17 the substance of a thing is said to be the organizing principle—an *archē*—that moulds this flesh and blood into a particular man, Socrates. . . . The *to ti ēn einai*, in other words, is not a quasi-logical concept as *ti esti*—it is a *metaphysical* principle—a combination of efficient and formal cause." [2] I will discuss the identification of the

1. See Matthen 1986a, 152, 158–162, 172–176.
2. Block 1978, 62.

efficient and the formal causes in the following section. My concern here is
to show that Block's position does not give us an answer to the question of
the particularity of a substance.

For Aristotle the efficient cause is particular: "the individual is the source
of the individuals. For while man is the cause of man universally, there *is* no
universal man; but Peleus is the cause of Achilles, and your father of you,
and this particular *b* of this particular *ba*, though *b* in general is the cause of
*ba* taken without qualification" (1071a20–24).[3] Thus, Block is right in
assuming the substantial form to be particular, because he assumes the
substantial form to be the efficient cause in the substance. But such an
assumption does not provide an explanation of why the substance is particular. Most important, it does not even tell us whether it is the particularity of
the form that is responsible for the particularity of the substance, or the
particularity of the substance for that of the form. The only thing we know
is that, if the substantial form is the efficient cause, it must be particular.
But how? Primitively? Because it is in-mattered? Or because it belongs to a
particular substance?

For Block, the substantial form is the dynamic motion that unifies the
actualized substance: "I think it is that the *archē*, or the organizing principle
of Z ch. 17, is more than just a static form or structure. It is a dynamic
motion. . . . Substance here is more than a unifying principle; it is an
organic full completion and realization and the only objects in the world
that possess such a motion of this kind are organic living things. . . . Soul is
the only true substance in Aristotle, the organizing principle that makes
this matter . . . into a single thing moving towards or away from the full-
grown maturity which is its *telos* or end."[4] That the form is motion, a
particular motion, does not tell us what it is for it to be particular or why it
is particular. Saying that it is *actualized* is just introducing a term for what
we need to explain. It is not itself an explanation of the particularity of the
motion in question. The substantial form is in matter: "Potentiality is the
matter in which the motion of *energeia* attempts to attain its perfected,
completed form, as an acorn grows into the full oak" (p. 63). Does that

---

3. Even when he discusses the case of artifacts and says that in their case the efficient
cause is not in the artifact but in the mind of the craftsman, we have to assume that this
efficient cause is not a universal, e.g., something like the blueprint of a house or a statue, but
the particular thoughts and decisions of the craftsmen that lead to the construction of this
house or statue: "the principle that organized *these* bricks into *this* house is not one and the
same with the house but outside of it in the mind of the builder" (ibid., p. 62).

4. Ibid., p. 63.

explain its particularity? If it does, then the particularity of the form is derivative from the particularity of matter, which itself would have to be explained. Or is it the opposite, and the particularity of the form accounts for the particularity of the material potentiality?

Block does not address the question of particularity in his paper, but he does take a position on it, according to which the substantial form, which is both the formal and the efficient cause in the substance, is particular. I have tried to indicate that, even if such a position is buttressed by Aristotelian texts that claim the efficient cause to be particular, it carries with it an explanatory gap. The gap needs to be filled by offering an account of what is being claimed by treating the form as a particular and whence its particularity is derived.[5]

5. Jennifer Whiting (1986) aligns herself with the proponents of individual forms. But at times she talks as if there are individual forms in substances and at other times as if the individual forms are the concrete substances.

> It *cannot* be the difference *in matter* which accounts for their [i.e., the statues of Hermes, and subsequently Discobolus, which have been made from the same piece of bronze at consecutive times] *numerical distinctness*. Nor, by hypothesis, can it be a difference of species form which explains this difference. This suggests that diachronic individuation requires appeal to individual forms. (Whiting 1986, 365–366, my emphasis)

> So Aristotle can say that the soul in particular (and individual forms in general) are accidentally one in movement and indivisible in place and time. . . . But this just means that the individual forms will be one in number and thus individuals *on account of the matter* in which they are embodied. This in turn explains why Aristotle says that Socrates and Callias are different on account of their matter. (p. 371, my emphasis)

> There are two salient possibilities. . . . On either account, we must think of form not as something abstract and immaterial (or more precisely, not as a universal realised in a particular piece of matter), but rather as a concrete thing constituted by or identified with some matter. (p. 372)

> There remains one further objection to this account of form as the principle of individuation. This is that individual forms don't explain anything, but simply presuppose what (i.e., individuality) they are supposed to explain. (p. 373)

The first passage suggests that matter does not have anything to do with the numerical difference between the two statues and that, rather, it is the primitive numerical difference of the forms that accounts for their difference; but the second passage says that the forms are individual on account of the matter in which they are embodied. Furthermore, in the third passage, the form is identified with the concrete, material substance. But then, this is a very different doctrine from the doctrine of individual forms, which seems to be the one in the fourth passage, i.e., that the forms are primitively (inexplicably) numerically one and that they, in turn, account for the numerical oneness of the concrete substance (which is different from the forms).

I am not entirely clear what Whiting's position is. In addition, as she says in her paper, questions remain regarding the relation of matter to form; however, questions must also be addressed regarding the relation of the individual forms to the universal form, common to members of the whole species.

## 2. The Hylomorphic Conception of Substantial Form

An interpretation of the substantial form that follows the same general line as Block's reading of Aristotle on this subject is Alan Code's interpretation. His thesis is that the nature of every sublunary natural body is its efficient cause, its substantial form, and its essence: "Aristotle treats this efficient cause [the nature and *archē kinēseōs*] as the *substance* of the body to which it belongs per se, and this in turn he identifies with the form (*eidos*), or essence of the physical object. The form is a primary substance, and as such is a primitive, irreducible causal agent. . . . For Aristotle, then, each kind of (sublunary) natural body, whether animate or not, is endowed with a nature (i.e., a form) that belongs essentially to all (and only) bodies of that kind, and which is *causally responsible for that kind's natural motions and changes.*"[6] My main objection to Code's interpretation is that he conflates a physical with a metaphysical relation. The efficient cause is a physical cause that gives rise to motions and changes in physical things. The relation of the efficient cause to that which it generates, for example, of the craftsman to the artifact, or of the semen to the embryo in formation, is a *physical relation.* On the other hand, the formal cause and essence of a substance are described by Aristotle (in the passage Code refers to) as "the form or substance, which is the *end* of the process of becoming."[7] The end of the process of becoming cannot have a physical relation to the substance that is being generated; whatever that relation may be, it will be *metaphysical*, not physical. The end toward which a process is aiming does not have physical causal powers. Even less can it give rise to that process in the physical sense, because the end of the process does not exist when the generation begins. Rather, it is a cause in the sense that we can *explain* what occurs as the generation takes its course, on the premise that it is aiming toward that goal. Code wants one and the same entity to be both the physical cause of the process and what explains what occurs in that process; but these two roles cannot be satisfied by the same entity.

Nor does Aristotle say that they can. In the passage on which Code bases his interpretation, Aristotle explicitly distinguishes between the sense of "nature" (*phusis*) as efficient cause and the sense of it as the formal-final

---

6. Code 1987:52, my emphasis.
7. 1015a10–11, my emphasis.

cause—*eidos* and end toward which the process is moving.[8] At the end of the passage under consideration, Aristotle concludes as follows: "From what has been said, then, it follows that nature in the primary and strict sense is the substance of things which have in themselves, as such, a source of movement; for the matter is called the nature because it is qualified to receive this, and processes of becoming and growing are called nature because they are movements proceeding from this. And this nature [or substance] is the source of movement of natural objects, being present in them somehow, either potentially or actually."[9] Far from identifying the efficient with the final cause, Aristotle is not even decided in this passage whether he wants to talk of the cause being present in actuality or only in potentiality. He says that it is present *somehow*, either *potentially* or *actually*. As an efficient cause it would be present actually, bringing about physical changes; as a final cause it would be present potentially, being the end toward which processes and changes in the thing are aiming. It is true that Aristotle is gesturing toward a combination of roles that he wants the substance of thing to play, but precisely because he realizes the ontological demands made on the substance by these roles, he withholds judgment, not committing himself as to whether the substance is present in the thing in actuality or only in potentiality.

Yet, Code takes Aristotle to be identifying the two senses of nature, and on this he builds his hylomorphic account of substantial form: "Since according to the Aristotelian conception of soul, the soul of a living thing is its nature, form, or essence, it follows that this conception presupposes a physics according to which physical bodies are endowed with natures that *cause* (and *explain*) their *natural changes* and *motions.*"[10] Soul, according to Code, is an efficient cause, a causal agent that brings about physical change

---

8. *Meta.* 1014b18–22, with b35–1015a11. The first is ὅθεν ἡ κίνησις ἡ πρώτη, and for the second he says ἔτι δ' αλλον τρόπον λέγεται ἡ φύσις ἡ τῶν φύσει ὄντων οὐσία, οἷον οἱ λέγοντες τὴν φύσιν εἶναι τὴν πρώτην σύνθεσιν (my emphasis) and continues to call it εἶδος, μορφήν, οὐσίαν, and τέλος τῆς γενέσεως, none of which either suggests or allows a hylomorphic account of the nature of a substance.

9. *Meta.* 1015a13–19. The translation is from Barnes (1984), with some amendments of my own. The Greek text is the following:

ἐκ δὴ τῶν εἰρημένων ἡ πρώτη φύσις καὶ κυρίως λεγομένη ἐστὶν ἡ οὐσία ἡ τῶν ἐχόντων ἀρχὴν κινήσεως ἐν αὐτοῖς ᾗ αὐτά· ἡ γὰρ ὕλη τῷ ταύτης δεκτικὴ εἶναι λέγεται φύσις, καὶ αἱ γενέσεις καὶ τὸ φύεσθαι τῷ ἀπὸ ταύτης εἶναι κινήσεις. Καὶ ἡ ἀρχὴ τῆς κινήσεως τῶν φύσει ὄντων αὕτη ἐστίν, ἐνυπάρχοντά πως ἢ δυνάμει ἢ ἐντελεχείᾳ.

10. Code 1987, 53, my emphasis.

and motion in the concrete substance. To understand this hylomorphic model of substantial form that Code attributes to Aristotle, we can think of the substantial form as the DNA macro-molecules of an organism. These are the efficient cause that give rise to the changes that take place in the human being in the course of his or her development. In that sense, they are the seat of the potentialities that are gradually actualized in the course of that person's lifetime. Let us suppose that we can even explain what a person is by giving a full account of his or her DNA structure. However, it would be a mistake to think that this shows that there is *an* entity that is both the efficient and the final cause. Rather, when we give an account of the DNA structure, we explain it *in terms of* the ends that will be fulfilled; that is, we explain the efficient cause in terms of the final cause, which has not been realized yet. Unless we make reference to the final cause, the description of the DNA will not reveal any potentialities and, hence, any causal powers for the individual's development. The DNA molecules are what they are only when understood in terms of the *end* toward which they contribute. The DNA molecules are *not* that end, but they aim toward it through the contribution they make toward the development of the substance. The distinction between efficient and final cause is *presupposed* in order to understand the DNA molecules as the efficient cause of change toward the end of the development. It would simply be a conflation to identify the end in term of which the explanation is given, with the efficient cause that acts toward that end.

Code's account of Aristotelian soul renders the soul as something of a *physical ghost* in the machine: a physical cause that is the end to be realized. On the one hand, he talks of the soul as the form of the concrete substance: "[Bucephalus'] equine soul is the form of that organic body";[11] but on the other, he treats it as the physical efficient cause: "In the semen it [the soul] is . . . the active principle, or *efficient* cause, for generation."[12] And he insists that the relation is a physical relation: "For Aristotle . . . each kind of . . . natural body . . . is endowed with a nature (i.e., a form) that belongs essentially to all (and only) bodies of that kind, and which is causally[13] responsible for that kind's *natural motions* and *changes*."[14] So in the end, one

11. Ibid., p. 56.

12. Ibid., my emphasis.

13. "Causally" has been explained as meaning "the efficient cause (ἀρχή κινήσεως)" (ibid., p. 6).

14. Ibid., p. 56, my emphasis. Also, "The soul is, for Aristotle, a primitive causal principle that is internal to that of which it is the soul, and is an efficient cause of natural changes" (ibid., p. 55).

and the same item is both the essence of the substance and its efficient cause, which is physically responsible for the changes and motions of the substance. As we just saw, it is extremely hard to understand how one entity could satisfy both roles. Furthermore, Code seems to think that both roles involve only physical relations in Aristotle's system; he repeatedly directs our attention to the fact that the dual role of the "nature" of the substance (as essence and efficient cause) comes under Aristotle's science of physics, not under his metaphysics:[15] "Aristotle's hylomorphic conception of soul is inextricably intertwined with this physics, and makes no sense without it."[16] I argue at length in Chapters 4–6 that the metaphysical role of the essence (as a unifying principle in the substance) cannot be reduced to physical causation.

In the present context, what I wanted to point to is that it is this reduction of essence to efficient cause, and of the metaphysical to the physical, which Code attributes to Aristotle, that lies at the heart of Code's conclusion that his paper "begins with some of the general considerations which show how and why this idea about soul is conceptually inseparable from Aristotelian physics, and then sketches out some of the reasons why such a view is not possible after the 17th century scientific revolution."[17] I would like to go further than Code and say that such a view and reduction are not possible. Aristotle does not abandon his metaphysical conception of the soul (or essence) over a hylomorphic one, which makes his conception of soul paradigmatically suitable for contemporary conceptions of the mind-body problem.

## 3. Substantial Form as an Identifiable Particular

According to Aristotle, the substantial form is not sufficient for the numerical distinctness between, for instance, Socrates and Callias. I present his argument in Section 1 of Chapter 6 and do not introduce it here.

Michael Frede holds that substantial forms in Aristotle's metaphysics are particular. He furthermore holds that the identity of a substance is derived from the identity of the substantial form. The particularity of the substance reduces to the particularity of the form.[18] I first discuss a passage that I

15. Ibid., pp. 51, 52, 53, etc.
16. Ibid., p. 53.
17. Ibid., p. 51.
18. This is opposed to the account offered by Charlotte Witt, who is also a proponent of individual forms, but who derives the numerical oneness of the form from that of the

believe is (frequently) wrongly taken to be Frede's account of the particularity of the substantial form and show that no account of particularity is given in that passage. Then I examine Frede's argument for the particularity of Aristotelian substantial forms and raise some objections to it.

A misleading passage in Frede's "Substance in Aristotle's *Metaphysics*" is, I believe, the reason for the misinterpretation of Frede's position: [19]

> Substantial forms, then, as ultimate subjects and as substances are particular. But we may still ask how they manage to be particular given that their specification, down to the smallest detail, is exactly the same for all things of the same kind. To answer this question, though, we have to get clearer as to what it is that is asked. If the question is how we manage to identify particular forms at a time the answer is simple: they differ from each other by being realized in different matter (cf. 1034a6–8; 1016b33) and by being the ultimate subject of different properties. A particular form can be identified through time by its continuous history of being realized now in this and now in that matter, of now being the subject of these and then being the subject of those properties. [20]

On a first reading, one gets the impression that Frede is advocating that the substantial form is a *historical particular* that owes its particularity either to the matter it enforms or to the properties that it has at different times. We should first observe that if that were Frede's position, then the particularity of a substance would not reduce to the particularity of the substantial form, but, conversely, that it would reduce the particularity of the substantial form to that of the substance (as a historical particular) or its matter. [21] Yet,

---

substance: "Individual substances explain the differences between two essences of the same kind (e.g., two human essences) in a manner analogous to the way in which matter accounts for the differences between two individual substances of the same kind (e.g., two human beings). . . . I invoke individual substances to explain how one essence differs from another essence of the same kind (e.g., Socrates' essence from Callias' essence)" (Witt 1989, 179). This is a very different conception of individual forms, because their numerical oneness is *not primitive* but derivative from the oneness of the substances.

19. As one hears it quoted in philosophical discussions and meetings.

20. Frede 1985, 23.

21. Matthen puts forward a position about individual forms, where the particularity of the form rests on the spatiotemporal location: "It is important to note that the notion of individual attributes outlined above is perfectly compatible with there being two individual attributes that are qualitatively identical but numerically (i.e., spatio-temporally) distinct. . . . It follows that there will be individual forms, but it does not follow that these will be qualitatively different. . . . There will . . . be a pair of numerically distinct forms for every pair of individual substances (1986a, 162).

as we will see when we examine another passage of Frede's paper, he holds that for Aristotle the substantial form, not the matter, is the source of particularity of the substance. Hence, he could not, with consistency, hold that the particularity of the form reduces to that of the matter, or to the substance as a historical particular.

The misleading aspect of the passage is due to the fact that, although Frede starts by asking a metaphysical question, he reverts to an epistemological question. The *metaphysical question* is: How does a substance form manage to be particular given that its specification is universal? This is a question that concerns how substantial forms *are* what they are. The *epistemological question* is: How do we manage to identify particular forms? This question concerns *our recognition* of substantial forms. How we are able to identify particular forms does not need to involve what makes these forms particular. For example, I can identify a particular book by its features of being large and green. If in a particular context it is the only large green book, these features would be sufficient for selecting the book. But certainly it is not its being large and green that makes it a particular book. Thus, criteria that are sufficient for distinguishing one book from another are not necessarily criteria that explain why this is a particular book. The reason for the difference is that when we are interested in recognizing a particular substance, we *assume* its particularity and look for a feature that sets it apart from other particular substances. But if we are interested in offering an account of the particularity of a substance, no particularity is assumed. Although Frede does move from the metaphysical to the epistemological questions in the quoted passage, I do not think that he conflates the two. I take Frede's discussion to be about the epistemological concern of how we *identify* substantial forms, already assuming that they are particular. The identification can rest either on the matter they are in or on their history, because we have perceptual access to such information. This answer is not proposed by Frede to be a *solution* to the metaphysical question that his paragraph starts with, nor should it be so taken, as it does not offer us an account of what the particularity of the substantial form amounts to, but only tells us how, given *particular* substantial forms, we can tell them apart from one another.

My claim that according to Frede, it is *not* the matter that *makes* a form individual, but that the form is individual on its own (while the matter and the accidental properties serve the epistemological purpose of enabling us to *distinguish* between forms), is confirmed by the position put forward by Frede and Patzig in their commentary of *Metaphysics* Z. There they make it clear that they disagree with interpreters who think that it is the matter that is responsible for the particularity of a concrete substance, while the form is universal. Rather, while discussing 1037a6–7, they say "In diesem Fall ist klar, daß auch an dieser Stelle eine individuelle Form des Einzelmenschen vorausgesetzt wird."[22] And again, they claim that according to Aristotle, the matter serves an epistemological purpose, enabling us to distinguish one object from another, without that indicating that the form is not being treated as a particular by Aristotle: "Aristoteles will darauf verweisen, daß wir zwei Gegenstände einer Art dadurch unterscheiden können, daß wir auf die unterschiedliche Materie und die Unterschiede verweisen, die sich aus der Verbindung der Form mit dieser Materie ergeben. . . . die Rede, und die Art und Weise, wie Aristoteles sich dort ausdrückt . . . spricht eher dafür, daß es sich um eine individuelle Form handelt."[23] Of course, this does not explain why, if both the matter and the form are particular, it should be through the matter, rather than through the form, that we are able to distinguish between the different substances. What is it that makes the particularity of the matter cognitively accessible to us, as opposed to the particularity of the form of a substance?

Frede's account of the particularity of substances is given in a different passage of his paper. There he discusses the Ship of Theseus example in order to derive some general conclusions regarding the particularity of substances. The original ship is continuously repaired until all its planks are new; let the ship with the new planks be called *Theoris I*; then *Theoris II* is built according to the original plan from all the old planks. Frede explains that the ship with the new planks is identical to the original ship, because the form of the ship has remained one and the same. He argues as follows:

> It will be objected that, if the two ships are faithfully built according to the same specifications, they will have just one and the same disposition [form]. There will be over a period of time some one thing, namely, the Theoris I, which has that disposition and there will be, for an overlapping period of time, another thing, namely, Theoris II, which has the very same disposition. But according to our theory, though it is true that as long as each ship is

22. Frede and Patzig 1988, 1:57. "In this case it is clear that in this passage again an individual form of an individual human is presupposed."

23. Ibid., p. 56. "Aristotle wants to point to the fact that we can discriminate two objects of one kind by pointing to the different matter and to the differences that result from the combination of the form and this matter. . . . [T]he language, and the way and manner in which Aristotle expresses himself there, . . . argues rather for it being an individual form."

in existence there is always something [the matter] which is thus disposed, it is *not* necessary that that which is thus disposed be the same throughout the time of the ship's existence. Hence the identity of what is thus disposed [the matter] is not a *sufficient condition* for the identity of the ship; neither is it a necessary condition, *as we can see from the case of the old ship with the new planks.* And since one of the two factors [the matter or the form] is to account for the identity of the ship [i.e., of the old ship which is identical to Theoris I], it has to be the disposition [the form]. And so we have to distinguish the disposition of the two ships, though their specification may be exactly the same.[24]

As we will see, Frede is resting the position of individual forms that he attributes to Aristotle on results that he assumes have been reached in contemporary metaphysics about the identity of the ship of Theseus. I will argue that there are strong reasons to doubt these positions.

Frede's argument in this passage is the following: First he *assumes* the identity of the original ship and Theoris I, which is the ship that results after replacing all the planks in the original ship. That Frede assumes this identity is evident from the fact that he refers to Theoris I as "the old ship with new planks." Theoris I is different from Theoris II—the ship that is constructed out of the dismantled original planks—but they are the same in form. According to the theory Frede is attributing to Aristotle, a particular substance does not have to have the same matter in order to remain in existence. Since a substance could have different matters throughout its existence (the old ship which then acquires new planks), the identity of any one of these matters could not be all that the substance is. There must be something different about the identity of the substance, other than the identity of its matter, if the substance can remain the same when its matter is changed. The identity of the matter cannot be all that is required for the substance's identity. Hence, the identity of the matter is *not* a *sufficient condition* for the identity of the substance.[25] Furthermore, because Theoris I is the same ship as the original one, although it now has new planks, the identity of the matter is *not necessary* for the identity of the substance. But because *the identity of the ship depends either on the identity of the matter or on the*

24. Frede 1985, 22; the second and third emphases are mine.
25. This argument will not work with something that is disjunctively defined, e.g., "game." Here, something is a game if it is $x, y, z$ or has characteristics $r, s, t$. That something can be a game without being $x, y, z$, does not show that $x, y, z$ are not sufficient for being a game.

*identity of the form*, and because the matter is neither necessary nor sufficient for the identity of the ship, it follows that the identity of the ship must depend on the identity of the form. Hence, the form of Theoris I, although qualitatively identical to the form of Theoris II (i.e., their respective forms are specified in exactly the same way), is numerically different from it and is numerically identical to the form of the original ship.[26]

Frede's argument needs only the assumptions he makes. The first is that the original ship is the same ship as Theoris I, the ship with the new planks. Frede does not argue this position, but this is the received view in contemporary metaphysics, which, I take it, he relies on.[27] His second assumption is that "one of the two factors [i.e., either the matter or the form] is to account for the identity of the ship." On the basis of these two assumptions, one can immediately conclude that it is the form that is to account for the identity of the ship. The reason is that the matter of the original ship (i.e., the original planks) is different from the matter of Theoris I (i.e., from the new planks). Because the ship remains the same, but the matter is different, it must be the form that accounts for its identity. It follows that Theoris II does not need to come into the picture at all, for Frede's argument. His two assumptions are sufficient for the conclusion he reaches, that the form of the ship is responsible for its numerical identity.

In the following two sections, I will offer reasons for not accepting the two assumptions made by Frede. First, I argue that there is not good reason

26. A point of clarification. Frede claims that because it is not necessary that a particular substance have the same matter throughout its existence, it follows that the identity of the matter is not a sufficient condition for the identity of the substance. I take Frede to be saying here that the identity of the substance does not reduce to the identity of the matter. Otherwise, an objection could be raised to his claim. Let us consider the example of someone's library. It is true that it does not need to retain the same books in order to remain the same library. But it is also certainly true that so long as it retains the same books, it remains the same library. It might change location or arrangement, but it remains the same library if the books are the same. Thus, the books' remaining the same is a sufficient condition for the library's remaining the same. (I am here treating the library as one entity, not as an aggregate of books or as so many juxtaposed books. I am also not considering the case where it ceases being a library by becoming part of another library.) This does not show that the identity of the library reduces to the identity of the books. But the identity of the books, which has remained the same, does settle the issue of whether it is the same library in the beginning and in the end. So the identity of the matter is not sufficient for telling us *what* the substance is, but it can be sufficient for telling us that the identity of the substance has remained *the same*.

27. Wiggins (1980) says: "coincidence under the concept *ship* has to be the makings of a sufficient condition of being the same ship" (p. 92); see further his discussion of this topic, pp. 92–96. See also B. Smart 1972, 148, and 1973, 24–27.

for assuming Theoris I to be identical to the original ship. Second, I show (in these sections and in my discussion of Kit Fine's paradox, in Section 7 of Chapter 6), that we cannot assume, nor does Aristotle assume, that the identity of a substance is determined either by the identity of the matter or by the identity of its form.

### (A) Does Theseus' Ship Remain the Same?

As we saw, Frede's argument rests on the assumption that Theoris I (the ship with the new planks) is identical to the original ship. I offer a version of the ship of Theseus example that challenges this assumption and, therefore, undermines the fundamental assumption in Frede's argument.[28]

Let us suppose that there are two ships that sail from Piraeus to Delos and back. The one ship, *Athena*, carries the holy relics that have to be presented at the temple in Delos once a year, and the other ship, *Hermes*, is the accompanying ship. The two ships have the same structure. One year, in the course of the voyage, the two captains decide to amuse themselves by exchanging the planks of the two ships (but not the content). By the time they get back to Piraeus all of the planks have been exchanged. When they arrive at the harbour, the citizens of Athens are shocked to observe that the holy relics are on *Hermes*, not on *Athena*! The captains are put on trial and plead in their defense that the relics are, in fact, on *Athena*, not on *Hermes*. They argue that the ship on which the relics were on their return is the ship that has remained spatiotemporally continuous and structurally the same as *Athena*. It is true, they confess, that the planks it is composed of are the ones that originally belonged to *Hermes*, but the change of the *identity of the parts* is overridden by the criterion of the *continuity and qualitative sameness of the form* of the ship. But the Athenians won't have it! They look and see that the relics are on *Hermes*, not on *Athena*. The captains might as well try to convince them that whenever a ship is disassembled at the shipyards for repairs, when it is assembled again it is not the same ship but a new one, because temporarily its form did not exist. Outrageous! Yet, that is all that happened to *Hermes*. It was taken apart and assembled again. How could it possibly not be the same ship? The form of the new *Hermes* is qualitatively identical with the form of the original *Hermes*, and the parts it is made out of are the very same as those of the original ship. What more do the captains

---

28. I have presented this version of the ship of Theseus example in Scaltsas 1980. Michael Wedin expresses similar intuitions (1991, 383).

want in order to realize that it is the same ship? The *continuity* plus *sameness of form* are clearly overridden by the combination of the *qualitative identity of form* plus *identity of parts*. What took place in the course of the journey is the disassembling of each ship and their reassembling in different locations; not the replacement of each ship's planks by different planks. The captains are condemned!

What follows from this analysis is that, when sameness of form is preserved, if we consider the criterion of the *continuity of form* on the one hand and of the *identity of parts* on the other, it is not clear that the continuity of form carries the weight for the determination of the identity of the substance. The intuition in the case of the two ships is that *Hermes* is reassembled in a different location, rather than that *Athena* had its planks replaced. This shows that despite the fact that a ship form is spatiotemporally continuous in the course of a journey (as *Athena* is gradually disassembled and *Hermes* assembled in its place), there is no reason compelling us to take it to be the form of one and the same ship. Frede's argument for the existence of individual forms relies on the *assumption* that the final ship carrying the relics is *Athena*, which was the ship that originally carried the relics. Frede offered no arguments for this claim but assumed it on the grounds of the received contemporary view concerning the identity of the ship of Theseus. But we saw in the version of the paradox I offered that the received view can find no more intuitive support than the competing view. This intuition is also borne out in Derek Parfit's *spectrum arguments*, which can be used in support of my claim.[29] Hence, Frede cannot argue from the *assumption* that

29. Parfit develops three *sorites* arguments—the physical spectrum, the psychological spectrum, and the combined spectrum arguments—in his *Reasons and Persons* to investigate whether personal identity depends on physical continuity or on psychological continuity. In the *physical spectrum* argument, Parfit considers a surgeon gradually replacing Parfit's body cells by duplicates, while *psychological continuity is retained*. Parfit wonders whether the emergent replica would be Parfit—on account of the psychological continuity—or whether after a critical percentage point in the cell replacement, Parfit's identity would be lost and a new individual would emerge. He argues that there is no hard fact of identity either way: "I do not know whether the resulting person will be me, or will be someone else who is merely exactly like me. But this is not, here, a real question, which must have an answer. It does not describe two different possibilities, one of which must be true. It is here an empty question. There is not a real difference here between the resulting person's being *me,* and his being *someone else.* This is why, even though I do not know whether I am about to die, I know everything" (Parfit 1984, 235).

In the *psychological spectrum*, Parfit considers a surgeon gradually changing his brain structure, while physical continuity is retained, so that Parfit gradually loses his memories and acquires apparent memories that fit the life of Napoleon. Would the resulting person be

the original ship is the same as *Theoris* I (in his example); but without this assumption he cannot show that it is the form that carries the identity of the ship, and hence that the form must be numerically one—whatever its specification may be.

### (B) What Can Make the Organization of a Substance Particular?

Frede's general line of approach to Aristotelian substantial forms is the following. We have to explain why Aristotle claims that the substantial form is the subject in a substance.[30] He suggests that we think of the substantial form as the organization of the substance or the disposition displayed by the matter of the substance.[31] The substance has to remain organized in the requisite sort of way so long as it persists. Therefore, Frede continues, the organization must remain the same throughout the existence of the substance.[32] The matter that belongs to the substance can be different at different times, and so can properties such as temperature or the size of the substance.[33] From these Frede concludes: "If we then analyze an ordinary physical object into matter, form, and properties, *the only item which in the case of animate objects has to stay the same as long as we can talk about the same thing is, on this account, form.* And this may give some plausibility to the assumption that it is really the form which is the thing we are talking about when we at different times say different things about an object. For what the object ultimately amounts to is this form which at different times takes on different matter and different properties."[34] Frede's rationale is the following: If the object remains the same, there must be an item in the object that

---

Parfit—on account of the physical continuity—and if not, at what point did the identity change occur? Parfit argues that there need not be an answer to this question: "we do not believe that, in these cases, there must be an answer, which must be either Yes or No. We believe that, in these cases, this is an empty question. Even without answering the question, we know everything" (Parfit 1984, 233).

Parfit's argument is that, neither physical continuity nor psychological continuity can be shown to be sufficient for the preservation of the person's identity. Similarly in our case, neither physical nor formal continuity can be assumed to be sufficient for the preservation of the object's identity.

30. Frede 1985, 20.
31. Ibid., p. 21.
32. "So what has to stay the same as long as a particular animate object exists is just that organization or disposition to behave in a way characteristic of the kind" (ibid., p. 21).
33. Ibid.
34. Ibid., my emphasis.

remains the same throughout its existence. As this item is neither the matter nor the particular properties the object has, and as the organization of the object does remain so long as the object exists, it must be the organization of the object that is the particular that accounts for the identity of the substance.

I do not find the reasoning in this argument compelling. For the object to remain the same it is *not* necessary that there be a particular item in the object that remains numerically the same, accounting for the identity of the object. This could not be the only possible answer to the question of the particularity of a substance, because, ultimately, it would lead to an infinite regress: a particular is particular because it contains a particular, and so on. Therefore, Frede cannot justify his conclusion that the form of a substance must be numerically one. To avoid the infinite regress, Frede takes the position that the form will be primitively particular. That is, the form's numerical identity is not relegated to some numerically single item in the form: "But if it should be demanded that there be something about the form in and by itself which distinguishes it from other forms of the same kind, the answer is that there is no such distinguishing mark, and that *there is no need for one*. It just is not the case that individuals are the individuals they are in virtue of some intrinsic essential distinguishing mark."[35] In other words, we do not need an item that is peculiar to the form in order for the form to be particular. But then Frede cannot also sustain his previous argument, according to which if substance remains numerically the same, there must be an item in it that remains numerically the same, namely, the form.

I believe that Frede is aware of these difficulties with his position, as he takes a step that I can explain only as a way of defusing the tension between his account of the particularity of a substance and the particularity of the form of a substance. The step is to treat the form of a substance as the substance itself. In this way he avoids commitment to the principle that would give rise to an infinite regress (by embedding particular items within particular items in order to account for their numerical identity). If the substance is the form, then there is only one answer to the particularity question: the substance is primitively particular, just as the form is (see preceding quote). Frede is not very happy with this solution, because it requires identifying a material substance to its substantial form, rather than to the totality of the form, the matter, and the properties of the substance. That is why Frede speaks of the form-substance identity merely as being plausible: "this may give some plausibility to the assumption that it is

---

35. Ibid., pp. 23–24, my emphasis.

really the form which is the thing we are talking about when we at different times say different things about an object. For what the object ultimately amounts to is this form which at different times takes on different matter and different properties."[36] I find it difficult to understand the identification of a material substance with its substantial form (to the exclusion of the substance's matter and properties), so I will not explore this option further. (As we have already seen, Frede's comment that "A particular form can be *identified* through time by its continuous history of being realized now in this and now in that matter, of now being the subject of these and then being the subject of those properties"[37] is answering the *epistemological* question of how we identify a particular form. It is not answering the *metaphysical* question of "how they [the substantial forms] manage to *be* particular?"[38] I think that Frede realizes this, because this is the reason why he says that there is nothing that *makes* the forms particular. He could not, with consistency, also claim that the matter and the history of the particular substance *make* the form particular.)

Independently of the problems facing the form-substance identification (to the exclusion of its matter and properties), there are the difficulties of treating the forms (and substances) as being *primitively* particular. Frede insists that the particular substantial forms in two men or, more generally, in substances of the same kind, have a specification, which "down to the smallest detail, is exactly the same for all things of the same kind."[39] Yet, the forms of different substances of the same kind are different: "Substantial forms, then, as ultimate subjects and as substances are particular."[40] They are different without any distinguishing mark differentiating them from one another, because "there is no such distinguishing mark, and . . . there is no need for one."[41] Thus, substantial forms are primitively and inexplicably particular. Why? How is this different from positing a bare particular underlying all the properties in a substance, being primitively and inexplicably particular? I believe that Frede's solution to the question of the particularity of forms, and derivatively (in Frede's account) of substances, is the same solution as the traditional account of the bare *substratum*, whose shortcomings I examined.[42]

36. Ibid., p. 21.
37. Ibid., pp. 34–35, my emphasis.
38. Ibid., p. 23.
39. Ibid.
40. Ibid.
41. Ibid., p. 24.
42. For a critical discussion of the thesis of the particularity of form in Frede and Patzig 1988, see Wedin 1991.

A further argument against attributing individual forms to Aristotle is that if he allowed for individual forms, he would not think that if different things are of the same kind they are material. If he allowed for individual forms, things of the same kind could differ by their form. Yet, Aristotle does claim that if within the same kind there are different things, these things are material (*Meta.* 1074a33–35). I discuss this point extensively in Section 2 of Chapter 6.

Furthermore, if the substantial form is particular, then the substance would be many: the form and the composite of form plus matter. Aristotle makes effectively the same point when he says the following: "if we can actually posit the common predicate as a single 'this,' Socrates will be several animals—himself and man and animal, if each of these indicates a 'this' and a single thing" (1003a9–12). In our case, if substantial forms were individual, then Socrates' form would be one thing, and the composite of matter and form (which is Socrates) would be a second, thus making Socrates a plurality. To avoid the plurality of substance (while advocating the particularity of form), one can claim that an Aristotelian substance is not the composite of matter and form, but only the form. Frede has made this claim, which I discuss in Section 2 of Chapter 6.

For further arguments for the universality of Aristotelian substantial forms, see Section 8 of Chapter 4.[43]

## 4. Against Substance Being the Form without the Matter

(a) Edwin Hartman has put forward the view in his work *Substance, Body and Soul,*[44] that for Aristotle, the essence of each particular is identical with that particular, but not to the composite of matter and form. I find this view difficult to comprehend. In effect, it means that the particular substance is identical with its substantial form or essence, but not to the composite of the form with the matter. One would have thought that that would require the substantial form to be primitively particular. But this is not what Hartman proposes. Rather, he says that the substantial form is universal, but it is made particular by the matter. So, the form, which is universal in

43. Loux gives an analysis of what it is to be for an individual according to Aristotle, from which he derives reasons why Aristotle does not condone individual forms in his metaphysics (1991, 225–235).
44. Hartman (1977).

itself, is particularized by the matter, and as a particular it is somehow identical to the particular substance, without that making the particular substance identical to the form plus the matter, but only to the form as particularized by the matter. In order to avoid inadvertently misrepresenting Hartman's position, I quote the key passages here:

> the relation between each substance and its essence is identity. A substance is a material object, but not a combination of form and matter. (p. 57)

> Aristotle is indeed committed to individual form. When he says that substance is form, he cannot very well mean that the object of his search is the universal. (pp. 61–62)

> To say that your essence is different from mine is not to say that you and I have different essential properties . . . that distinguish us each from all others. . . . Your essence is to be distinguished from mine in just the way in which you are to be distinguished from me, since each person is identical to his essence: we are to be distinguished in that we have different matter. (pp. 63–64)

> The very existence of a particular essence requires that there be some matter constituting it. (p. 64)

> . . . substance is not this form plus this matter. (p. 66)

> When Aristotle does say a substance is form and matter, he can only mean that (for example) Callias is associated with some matter of the appropriate sort at all times. It does not follow that he is identical with something more than his essence, for his identity with his essence does not excuse him from necessarily having matter. (p. 68)

> On the alleged new view, a substance is not . . . identical with a material object, which is a combination of form and matter. So the thing's form is not the same as the thing, because the thing is matter plus form. But what is the force of the "plus"? . . . Perhaps the defender of the distinction would say that the "plus" just indicates that substances require some sort of matter, that the individual form cannot exist alone; but that is, as I have argued, quite compatible with the view that the form is the thing in a clear and pertinent way in which the matter is not. Perhaps the resistance to identifying a material object with its form comes of a mistaken impression that the identity of substance and form makes substances matterless; but it does not, nor does it make them accidentless. A substance *is* an essence (a form); it *has* accident (matter). (p. 71)

The positions that Hartman commits himself to come to the following. Substance is not a composite of matter and form. Rather, it is the form, which is particularized by the matter; but this does not make the form, or substance, material; the form only *has* matter.

One cannot have it both ways. One cannot treat the universal entity as being identical with its instantiation in matter. But that is just what Hartman wants. That is, to identify the universal with its instantiation and thereby resolve the Aristotelian problem of the relation of a concrete substance to its essence. But that cannot be done. *Universals do not become particulars by being related to particulars any more than particulars become universals by being related to universals.* A universal that is related (by whatever such a relation might be) to a particular (e.g., to this bit of matter) remains a universal. Universals are not particularized by being tied down by a leash to a particular. The only way to particularize a universal is to create a new entity, distinct from the universal; an entity that is particular. Otherwise the universal will remain universal, however it might be related to a particular. Hartman believes that the universal form of a substance can remain what it is and that the matter of the substance will stick to it as a label that particularizes the form, but does not change the type of entity the form is. This is impossible. Either the label is doing metaphysical work toward changing the universal into a particular, in which case it will no more be a label, but part of the content of the new entity, or the label does no such metaphysical work, but only names the universal for what it is—a universal. Hartman's attempt to distinguish between *being* the form and *having* the matter is an attempt aimed at using the matter as such a double agent: do the metaphysical work to convert the universal into a particular, but treat that as an external, labeling change, rather than as a change of the very constitution of the "labeled" universal. I examine the metaphysics involved in the transition from universal to particular in great detail in Chapters 5–7.

But there are further problems in Hartman's position with respect to the particularity of the form. He says:

> The identification of substance and essence is a step towards solving some problems of identity through time. (p. 58)

> What, then, does it mean to say that this river before you is the same as the one you swam in last week? Not that the water is the same, indeed, in this case it certainly is not. All that need have remained from time $t_1$ to time $t_2$ is the form or essence. I mean this particular form, not a universal. . . . It [the

river] is here because the essence that was here last week is here, not because the particular water is still here . . . it makes sense to say that *what the thing is is a particular form* rather than a particular parcel of matter. (p. 60)

Once Aristotle has developed a notion of form that is virtually indistinguishable from essence, it stands to reason that the matter will be in the same position as accident with respect to change. (p. 61, my emphasis)

But, once again, Hartman cannot have it both ways. He cannot claim here that the matter does not remain the same, but only the form does, in the course of change, while earlier on he said that what particularizes the form is the matter ("Your essence is to be distinguished from mine in just the way in which you are to be distinguished from me, since each person is identical to his essence: we are to be distinguished in that we have different matter," pp. 63–64). What does the particularity of the form consist in? It seems that for Hartman it is not primitive, but it depends on the matter it enforms. Yet, the particularity of the matter may change (as in the case of the changing water) without that affecting the particularity of the form. Somehow, according to Hartman, the form remains, not only qualitatively the same, but numerically the same. How? We do not find an answer in Hartman's position.

(b) Robert Heinaman has argued that the resolution to the tenth aporia in the early books of the *Metaphysics* requires Aristotle to posit particular substantial forms in substances.[45] The tenth aporia is whether the principles of perishable and imperishable things are the same or different. Heinaman argues that Aristotle's way out of the aporia is that the principles of perishable and imperishable things are different. The principles of perishable things are perishable, but without perishing into elements, so that the principles do not have further principles prior to them (pp. 250–251). From this, Heinaman concludes that the substantial form is not the species form, and hence a universal, but an individual form that comes to be and perishes for every natural substance (pp. 269–270), without being generated or being resolved into elements.[46]

Before coming to the details of Heinaman's argument, I would like to note at the outset that one cannot expect the decision on whether substan-

45. The life span of the substantial form is determined by the life span of the substance (Heinaman 1979, 269).
46. This would seem to commit Aristotle to generation ex nihilo and destruction into nothing, which his metaphysics aims to deny. See *Ph.* 191b13–14.

tial forms are particular or universal to rest on what resolves the tenth aporia, because the notion of a principle (*archē*) is so broad in Aristotle that any number of substantial constituents qualify for the job, modulo the appropriate qualifications. Furthermore, if individual perishable forms could be posited for perishable substances (e.g., a tree), corresponding forms could be individuated in imperishable substances (e.g., the sun). Hence, contrary to the hypothesis, the principles of perishable and imperishable substances would be the same. In general, very different problems and arguments from those of the tenth aporia will determine, first, what the substantial form of a substance is, and second, why perishable things perish and imperishable ones do not.

My objection to the details of Heinaman's argument is that he takes what Aristotle explicitly applies to universal forms to be Aristotle's claim about individual forms. Heinaman uses Aristotle's claim that forms are and are not without being generated or destroyed as an indication that the substantial forms of living things are not their universal species forms, but entities that perish, that is, their souls (pp. 269–270). But there is no indication that Aristotle is speaking of *perishable* forms. In fact, the very passage that Heinaman quotes, 1044b21–29,[47] is about universal forms, which are imperishable; furthermore, this is explicit in *Metaphysics Z*, 15: "Since substance is of two kinds, the concrete and the formula (I mean that one kind of substance is the formula taken with the matter, while another kind is the formula in its generality), substances in the former sense are capable of destruction . . . for there is no destruction of the formula in the sense that it is ever in course of being destroyed; for there is no generation of it (the being of house is not generated, but only the being of *this* house), but without generation and destruction formulae are and are not" (1039b20–26). Here it is indisputable that Aristotle says that the universal forms are and are not without generation and destruction. So, Aristotle's discussion of something being or not being without generation and destruction is no indication that he is talking of something individual: universals are and are not without generation and destruction. Hence, even if substantial forms are and are not without generation and destruction, this is no indication that they are individual rather than universal. On the contrary, the quotation indicates that substantial forms must be universal, and it contrasts them to the being of the particular substance.

47. "Since some things are and are not, without coming to be and ceasing to be, e.g., points . . . and in general forms [εἴδη] (for it is not white that comes to be, but the wood comes to be white . . .)" (1044b21–23).

In general, the difference between the perishable and imperishable substances cannot be given by simply allowing that the principles of the perishable things be perishable. There are many more factors that enter into the analysis of each kind of substance, which require the solutions to be different from case to case. For example, the sun is imperishable (1073a34–35), and so is the First Mover. The First Mover's imperishability requires it to be immaterial (see Section 1 of Chapter 6). This cannot be the case with the sun. Thus, no one solution can apply to all cases of imperishables across the board.

# The Argument of *Metaphysics* M, 10

In what follows, I present my reading of *Metaphysics* M, 10, and discuss Julia Annas's alternative reading of it. [1] The logical steps of M, 10, are the following. Suppose that substances are separate (just as concrete particulars are) and that substances are composed of elements and principles. Then,

DILEMMA: Let substances be similar because of entities that exist apart from the similar substances. What are the elements and principles of substances (1086b16–20, 1087a4–7)?

(A) If the elements and principles of substances are particulars, not universals, then

(i) The elements will be all the beings there are (because similarity would be impossible).

(ii) The elements will not be knowable.

(B) If the elements and principles of substances are universals, then

(i) Either the substances composed of them are also universal, in which case they will not be substances.

(ii) Or, if the substances are particular, that which is *prior* to substance, that is, its universal elements and principles, will not be substance (*qua* universal).

RESOLUTION: Rejection of the two assumptions of the Dilemma by allowing that:

(A) Knowledge is of the particular.

(B) Similarity is primitive, nonexplicable.

1. Julia Annas 1976.

Then the principles of a separate substance can be particular. (But now the *principles* of a separate substance are doing *no* work toward *explaining* either similarity or knowability of substance, because separate substances, *qua* particulars, will be primitively similar and directly knowable.)

It is important to realize that the *resolution* of the two problems that generate the dilemma, namely, the similarity between separate substances and their knowability, *does not require the positing of any principles of substances at all*. It is not the case that individual forms resolve any problem in M, 10. In fact, individual forms are not introduced at all, simply because there is no metaphysical or epistemological work they can do toward the resolution of the dilemma. When Aristotle proposes that particular things can be similar (*homoiai*) without there being any separate entity causing their similarity (1087a7–10), he does not revoke what he has just claimed, that is, that similar substances share the same form (*to auto eidos*, 1087a5–6). (The two expressions—"similar" and "having the same form"—are being used interchangeably.) Rather, he is simply asserting that similar things are similar without there being a separate entity that causally grounds their similarity. This leaves similarity unexplained: having the same form is not explained in terms of ontological commitments in the system. Now, positing individual forms in each substance would contribute nothing toward explaining the substances' similarity. Nor would it help, in any way, to say that distinct individual forms are the same in form or have the same definition. "Having the same form or definition" is precisely what is in need of explanation. Unless the ontological commitments of such statements are made explicit, they do not explain anything. Aristotle's proposal in M, 10, is that no analysis of the ontological commitments of these expressions is necessary (1087a7–10), that is, that similarity is a primitive in the ontology.

It follows from this analysis that there is a fundamental disagreement between my interpretation of M, 10, and the one offered by Julia Annas— as much as I have profited from her many, very insightful, observations regarding problems that arise from Aristotle's commitments in this chapter. Annas interprets the chapter as follows. She takes Aristotle to be claiming that the reason why similarity between substances cannot be explained is the *separateness* of the common form, rather than the *particularity* of the common form.[2] But when Aristotle presents the difficulty

2. "According to him [Aristotle] the trouble lies in accepting the Platonist premise that over and above the individuals sharing a common form there is a separate extra entity, the Form. The Platonists assume that the only satisfactory way to explain the fact that things

about similarity, he states explicitly that it is the *nonuniversality* of the principles of substances that stands in the way of there being similar substances; he says: "If they [the elements and principles of substances] are individual and *not universal*, then there will be as many existing things as elements"—that is, there will be no similar substances.[3] Even if by "individual" he means separate particulars, the explanation he supplies ("and not universal") leaves no doubt that it is the fact that individuals are not universals that is causing the problem. It is nonuniversality that is incompatible with belonging to many substances and, hence, that leaves no room for similar substances. Thus, what is being denied is that *particular*, rather than separate, principles can explain similarity. It follows that individual forms, being nonuniversal, can provide no explanation of similarity between different substances.

Aristotle says that "if there is nothing to stop there being many As and Bs (as with the elements of speech) without there being an original A and an original B over and above the many then . . . there will be infinitely many similar syllables" (1087a7–10). The different As and Bs in the syllables represent the different elements (*stoicheia*) of substances (1086b22–24). Aristotle's saying, in the quote, that the As and Bs in syllables are different—many—does not commit him to individual forms any more than claiming that the bricks in different walls are different commits one to holding that the forms of the different walls are different. Aristotle may have held, at this point, that the letters of a syllable and the bricks of a wall are particular, but the form of the syllable and the form of the wall are universal.[4] So, the fact that Aristotle speaks of particular elements in substances in no way commits him to the particularity of the substantial forms of these substances. So, neither Aristotle's treatment of similarity as a primitive nor his allowing for particular elements in substances provide any indication of his allowing for individual forms in substances. Yet, Annas,[5]

---

share a common form and common name is to posit another thing over and above them, the Form. But if one accepts that a separate Form is necessary to explain this fact, then one is in a dilemma: one's basic particulars cannot have principle or elements" (Annas 1976, 189–190).

   3. εἰ μὲν γὰρ καθ᾽ ἕκαστον καὶ μὴ καθόλου (1086b20–22, my emphasis).

   4. This would not be incompatible with his claim that "if principles must be universal, so must what comes from them be universal" (1087a21–22), since here at least some of the elements into which the substance is analysed—letters, bricks—are taken to be particular. So the substance would not be composed just of universals.

   5. Things can be one in kind and share a common form without there being an extra entity over and above them to explain the fact of their sharing a common form. There can be many elements or letters of the same kind, e.g., many As, without this implying either that there is a Form A or a mysterious universal. . . . It is wrong to assume that things cannot share a

as well as Frede and Patzig,[6] assume that Aristotle commits himself to
individual forms in M, 10.

---

common form without there being another thing to explain this. . . . Here he seems to agree that
basic particulars (individual men, horses, etc.) can have forms, as long as these are not taken to
be separate from the things they are the forms of, like Platonic Forms; and further, *these forms* can
be regarded as first principles of the individuals they are the forms of, and are *individuals*. . . .
The *claim* that these non-separable forms are nevertheless individuals enables Aristotle to *escape*
the present dilemma. (Annas 1976, 190, my emphasis)

I do not know why Annas believes that Aristotle claims that there are individual forms in
substances. I have argued that nothing Aristotle says in M, 10, suggests any commitment to
individual forms, nor could the introduction of individual forms solve any of the problems
that are addressed in this chapter.

6. Frede and Patzig also believe that Aristotle finds himself committed to individual
forms in M, 10, which, according to them, is what forces Aristotle to allow that knowledge
is of the particular, in this chapter:

Nach Aristoteles das Wissen immer Wissen vom Allgemeinen ist. . . . Dieser Einwand trifft
aber wiederum nicht unsere Interpretation, sondern legt eine Schwierigkeit dar, die sich für die
aristotelische Theorie selbst ergibt und deren Aristoteles sich auch bewusst ist. Er formuliert
sie . . . und will sie schliesslich (M, 10, 1087a15–25) dahingehend auflösen, daß tatsächliches
Wissen immer Wissen vom Einzelnen ist, während allgemeines Wissen Wissen "der Möglich-
keit" nach ist. Damit revidiert er jedenfalls an dieser Stelle . . . seine Auffassung vom Wissen
grundlegend, was nicht anders zu erklären ist, als daß er sich zu dieser Folgerung eben durch die
Annahme gezwungen sah, die primären ousiai, d.h. aber die Formen, seien individuell und
nicht allgemein. (1988, 1:56)

"According to Aristotle knowledge is always knowledge of the universal. . . . This objection
however again does not affect our interpretation but describes a difficulty which arises for the
Aristotelian theory itself, and which Aristotle himself is aware of. He formulates it . . . and
eventually (M, 10, 1087a15–25) wants to dissolve it so that actual knowledge always is
knowledge of the particular, whereas universal knowledge is knowledge of the potential. Thus
he in any case revises in this passage . . . his understanding of knowledge fundamentally, which
cannot be explained otherwise than that he saw himself forced to this conclusion exactly by the
assumption that the primary substances, i.e. the forms, would be particular and not universal."

This is not the reason why Aristotle allows for particulars to be the objects of knowledge. It is
not the case that Aristotle commits himself to individual forms and then is forced to allow
that knowledge is of the particular. As we have seen, Aristotle does not introduce individual
forms in M, 10, nor would their introduction have served any purpose. Rather, what forces
Aristotle to allow particulars to be the object of knowledge is his conception of *composition*;
i.e., that "If principles must be universal, so must what comes from them be universal"
(1087a21–22). His commitment to this principle in M, 10, does not allow him to account
for the particularity of substances if their principles are universal. But if the knowability of
substances requires them to have universal principles, then substances would be composed of
universals, and they would themselves be universal.

Furthermore, I do not understand why Frede and Patzig introduce the notion of *primary*
substance in their discussion of M, 10. It is knowledge of *separate* substances that concerns
Aristotle here. So long as he holds knowledge to be of the universal, he is forced to relegate
knowledge of separate substance to knowledge of its universal principles. But once he allows
for particulars to be knowable, separate substances become the objects of knowledge themselves.

Now, it should be stressed that the reason why Aristotle momentarily allows for the very antirealist move of treating similarity as a primitive is that in M, 10, he has no way of accounting how a particular can be composed out of universals. He says that "if the principles must be universal, so must what comes from them be universal" (1087a21–22). If he had a way around this, then he would have solved the metaphysical and epistemological problems in one fell swoop,[7] without having to resort to the unsatisfactory, halfway, solution that he introduces by allotting the universal to potential knowledge and the particular to actual knowledge.[8] But I have argued (in Sections 1–4 of Chapter 1, 2 of Chapter 4, 3 of Chapter 5, 5–6 of Chapter 6, and in Appendix 2) that he does finally show that particulars are *compositions* of universals (even if some of them are impure universals involving reference to particular spatiotemporal locations). And this is precisely what allows him to retain his position that knowledge is of the universal in Book Z.[9]

In fact, in M, 10, Aristotle seems to be operating still with a Platonic, rather than an Aristotelian, conception of composition. As we have seen, *Platonic composition* is mereological, treating a whole as an aggregate of the parts (Section 1 of Chapter 4). On the other hand, *Aristotelian composition* is nonmereological insofar as the whole is different from the aggregate of the parts. The parts are unified into a single whole by the substantial form. This is not the M, 10, picture. In the first part of the chapter Aristotle seems to be allowing for two possibilities. He allows that "if the principles *are* universal, either the substances that come from them are universal, ‹or› nonsubstance will be prior to substance" (1086b37–1087a1). The first alternative assumes that what we put in is what we get out: universals in, universals out. The second alternative comprises the possibility that, although composed of universals (= nonsubstance), the substance itself is a particular.[10] So here, the composition of universals does not produce a universal, as it would if it were mereological composition, but a particular. But at the end of the chapter Aristotle claims that "if principles must be universal, so must what comes from them be universal" (1087a21–22). This does not even allow for the possibility that the emergent whole be a

7. In view of the fact that he systematically propounds in his works that knowledge is of the universal.

8. 1087a15–21. See Annas (1976, 191) for an analysis of the drawbacks of this epistemological solution and why it does not finally rid him of the need for positing universals.

9. *Meta.* 1036a8, 1040a23–25.

10. Just as a substance ought to be; but in that case nonsubstance, i.e., the universal, will be prior to substance, i.e., the composed particular (because the universal is prior qua element of the product and is nonsubstance qua nonparticular).

different type of entity from the constituents. So, although mentioned, the nonmereological type of composition is not finally countenanced. This is why Aristotle feels compelled to allow for knowledge of the particular, so as to give up universals as components of substances (because a particular substance cannot be *composed* out of universals). That Aristotle starts with a listing of two possible types of composition but finally drops the non-mereological one by the end of the chapter, mirrors the progression we encountered in the *Theaetetus*. As we have seen, Plato mentions there the possibility of the (nonmereological) emergence of a single entity, which is different from the aggregate of the constituents that compose it,[11] but finally argues for mereological composition, which only allows aggregation of the parts, not composition of a different entity out of them.

Nowhere in M, 10, is there a hint of the sophistication of the unifying function of the substantial form that characterizes Aristotle's final metaphysical picture. According to his final position, a substance is over and above its universal constituents. Universals belong to the substance, but belonging is not a relation in the substance. Rather, the universals belong to the substantial whole by being unified into that whole. They are unified through their reidentification in accordance to the principle of the form, which determines the role each universal plays in the whole; that is, *the form determines how the substantial whole is characterized by each universal*. The composition of universals by the substantial form does not produce a universal; on the contrary, the resulting entity is a whole that belongs to no other whole, and hence, is a substance.

It should not be thought that because substances are composed of universals, this entails that substances are bundles of properties. Far from it. *Substances are neither bundles of universal nor bundles of particular properties*, as no distinct entities of any kind exist in Aristotelian substances. *Universals are in substances only potentially*, because their individuation requires abstraction, that is, separation from the whole. A substance has *no* parts of *any* kind *in actuality*. Dividing the substance up (either physically or by abstraction) into entities that are identifiable independently of the whole gives rise to entities that do not exist in the substance. It is a mistake to think that a universal joins a substantial whole by becoming particular (i.e., a particular property). A universal joins a substantial whole by *losing* its separateness and distinctness. One can speak of particular properties, or particular essences, and Aristotle does, but not because they exist as distinct items in a "sub-

---

11. "But perhaps . . . a syllable is, not the letters, but some one kind of thing which has come into being out of them: something which has one form of its own, and is different from the letters" (*Theaetetus* 203e3–5).

stantial aggregate or cluster." Aristotle's theory in its most sophisticated arguments of his *Metaphysics* Z does not allow for the "aggregate" or "cluster" view of substances. In this context, all that talk of particular essences or properties can convey is that one substance is *sufficient* for the existence of a property or an essence. In other words, a single red substance is all that is necessary for there to be the universal "red," and a single human being for there to be the universal "human being." Multiple instantiation is not required for the existence of a universal.[12] However, strictly speaking, it is not a particular red property or a particular human essence that is inherent in the substance; all there is is a substance that is red or a substance that is human, from which we can abstract away the universals "red" or "human being" (Section 6 of Chapter 6).

Finally, the substantial forms that are necessarily in actuality and numerically one cannot belong to, and be the substantial forms of, many substances. In the case of immaterial substances we have seen that there is only a single—numerically one—substance per kind (e.g. only one unmovable mover for this kind of movement, and only one for that kind of movement). We saw why, in the case of eternal substances, the substantial form is not actualized in matter, but is directly actual. In fact, the only possible state for such a form is the actualized one. (We cannot even abstract such forms from their actuality, in the way we can abstract the form of "human being" from Socrates.) It follows that such an actualized, numerically one, substantial form could not be the substantial form of another substance. But that is just what the Platonists are committed to, when they claim that a Form, which is an immaterial actual substance, is the substantial form of other substances. How could a numerically single form belong to, or be, many substances? The Platonist will have to give up the claim that either the Forms are actual substances or that they are the substantial forms of other substances. No entity can be both numerically single (that is, substance in actuality) and belong to many subjects. This is the import of Aristotle's argument against Platonic Forms in Z, 16, 1040b16–32. He concludes by saying that "no universal term is the name of a substance, and no substance is composed of substances" (1041a3–5). The two points are connected. If universals were substances, they would be actual, and hence, the substances they belonged to would be composed of substances and be pluralities of many substances, rather than unified substantial wholes.

12. But it is necessary, according to Aristotle, in order to come to *know* the universal (*An. Post.* 100a3–b5).

# Bibliography

Ackrill, John L. 1963. *Aristotle's "Categories" and "De Interpretatione."* Clarendon Aristotle Series. Oxford: Clarendon Press.

——. 1965. "Aristotle's Distinction between *Energeia* and *Kinesis.*" In Bambrough 1965, 121–141.

——. 1972–73. "Aristotle's Definitions of *Psuche.*" *Proceedings of the Aristotelian Society.* 73:119–133.

——. 1981. "Aristotle's Theory of Definition: Some Questions of *Posterior Analytics* II 8–10." In *Aristotle on Science: The Posterior Analytics. Studia Aristotelica* 9:359–384.

——, ed. 1987. *A New Aristotle Reader.* Princeton: Princeton University Press.

Albritton, R. G. 1957. "Symposium: Forms of Particular Substances in Aristotle's *Metaphysics.*" *Journal of Philosophy* 54:699–708.

Alexander of Aphrodisias. Σχόλια εἰς τό Ζ τῶν μετά τα Φυσικά. In Hayduck 1891.

Allen, R. E. 1983. *Plato's Parmenides.* Oxford: Basil Blackwell.

Annas, Julia. 1974. "Individuals in Aristotle's *Categories*: Two Queries." *Phronesis* 19: 146–152.

——. 1976. *Aristotle's "Metaphysics"—Books* M *and* N. Oxford: Clarendon Press.

Anscombe, G. E. M. 1953. "Symposium: The Principle of Individuation." *Proceedings of the Aristotelian Society,* Supp. Vol. 27:83–96.

Anscombe, G. E. M., and P. T. Geach. 1973. *Three Philosophers.* Oxford: Basil Blackwell.

Anton, J. P. 1968. "The Aristotelian Doctrine of *Homonyma* in the *Categories* and Its Platonic Antecedents." *Journal of the History of Philosophy* 6:315–326.

Aquinas, Thomas. (1261–1272) 1961. *Commentary on the Metaphysics of Aristotle.* 2 vols. Translated by J. P. Rowan. Library of Living Catholic Thought. Chicago: Henry Regnery.

Armstrong, D. M. 1973. *Belief, Truth, and Knowledge.* Cambridge: Cambridge University Press.

———. 1980a. *Universals and Scientific Realism: Nominalism and Realism*. Cambridge: Cambridge University Press.

———. 1980b. *Universals and Scientific Realism: A Theory of Universals*. Cambridge: Cambridge University Press.

———. 1983. *What Is a Law of Nature?* Cambridge: Cambridge University Press.

———. 1989a. *A Combinatorial Theory of Possibility*. Cambridge: Cambridge University Press.

———. 1989b. *Universals: An Opinionated Introduction*. Boulder: Westview Press.

———. 1991. "Classes Are States of Affairs." *Mind* 100:189–200.

Armstrong, D. M., and N. Malcolm. 1984. *Consciousness & Causality—A Debate on the Nature of Mind*. Oxford: Basil Blackwell.

Asclepius. Σχόλια εἰς τό Ζ τῆς μετά τα Φυσικά 'Αριστοτέλους Πραγματείας. In Hayduck 1888.

Aune, Bruce. 1985. *"Metaphysics": The Elements*. Oxford: Basil Blackwell.

Ayers, M. R. 1974. "Individuals without Sortals." *Candian Journal of Philosophy* 4:113–148.

———. 1981. "Locke versus Aristotle on Natural Kinds." *Journal of Philosophy* 78:247–272.

Bacon, John. Forthcoming. *The Alphabet of Being*.

Balme, D. M. 1962. "Development of Biology in Aristotle and Theophrastus: Theory of Spontaneous Generation." *Phronesis* 7:91–104.

———. 1972. *Aristotle's "De Partibus Animalium" 1 and "De Generatione Animalium."* Clarendon Aristotle Series. Oxford: Clarendon Press.

———. 1987. "Aristotle's Biology Was Not Essentialist." *Archiv für Geschichte der Philosophie* 62:1–12.

Bambrough, Renford. 1971–72. "Objectivity and Objects." *Proceedings of the Aristotelian Society* 72:65–81.

———, ed. 1965. *New Essays on Plato and Aristotle*. London: Routledge & Kegan Paul.

Barcan Marcus, Ruth. 1971. "Essential Attribution." *The Journal of Philosophy* 68:187–202.

Barnes, Jonathan. 1970. "Property in Aristotle's *Topics*." *Archiv für Geschichte der Philosophie* 45:136–155.

———. 1971–72. "Aristotle's Concept of Mind." *Proceedings of the Aristotelian Society* 72:101–114. Repr. in Barnes, Schofield, and Sorabji 1979, vol. 4:32–41.

———. 1975. *Aristotle's "Posterior Analytics."* Clarendon Aristotle Series. Oxford: Clarendon Press.

———. 1981. "Proof and the Syllogism." In Berti 1981, 17–59.

———. 1984. *The Complete Works of Aristotle*. 2 vols. Princeton: Princeton University Press.

———. 1990. "Bits and Pieces." In Barnes and Mignucci 1990, 225–294.

Barnes, Jonathan, and M. Mignucci. 1990. *Matter and Metaphysics*. Bibliopolis.

Barnes, Jonathan, M. Schofield, and R. K. Sorabji, eds. 1975–79. *Articles on Aristotle*. 4 vols. London: Duckworth.

Bealer, George. 1982. *Quality and Concept*. Oxford: Clarendon Press.

Berti, E., ed. 1981. *Aristotle on Science*. Symposium Aristotelicum. Padua.

Blackwell, R. 1955. "Matter as a Subject of Predication in Aristotle." *Modern Schoolman* 19–30.

Block, Irving. 1964. "Three German Commentators on the Individual Senses and the Common Sense in Aristotle's Psychology." *Phronesis* 9:58–63.

———. 1978. "Substance in Aristotle." *Paideia: Special Aristotle Issue*, Second Special Issue: 59–64.

Blumenthal, H. J., and H. M. Robinson, eds. 1991. *Aristotle and the Later Tradition*. Oxford: Clarendon Press.

Bogen, James, and James E. McGuire, eds. 1985. *How Things Are*. Dordrecht: Reidel.

———. 1986–87. "Aristotle's Great Clock: Necessity, Possibility, and the Motion of the Cosmos in 'De Caelo' 1.12." *Philosophical Research Archives* 12:387–448.

Bolton, Robert. 1976. "Essentialism and Semantic Theory in Aristotle." *Philosophical Review* 85:514–544.

———. 1978. "Aristotle's Definitions of the Soul: *De Anima* 2.1–3." *Phronesis* 21:258–278.

———. 1994. "Aristotle's Conception of Metaphysics as a Science." In Scaltsas, Charles, and Gill 1994, 321–354.

Bostock, D. 1994. *Aristotle's Metaphysics Z and H*. Oxford: Clarendon Press.

Boudouris, Konstantine. 1985. *Language and Reality in Greek Philosophy*. Proceedings of the Second International Philosophy Symposium. Athens: Greek Philosophical Society.

Brody, B. A. 1980. *Identity and Essence*. Princeton: Princeton University Press.

Burnyeat, Myles. 1987. "Platonism and Mathematics: A Prelude to Discussion." In Graeser 1987, 213–240.

———. 1990. *The "Theaetetus" of Plato*. Indianapolis: Hackett.

———. 1992. "Is an Aristotelian Philosophy of Mind Still Credible?" In Nussbaum and Rorty 1992, 15–26.

Burnyeat, Myles, et al. 1979. *Notes on Zeta*. Oxford: Sub-Faculty of Philosophy, Oxford University.

Butler, R. J. 1965. *Analytical Philosophy. Second Series*. Oxford: Oxford University Press.

Campbell, Keith. 1990. *Abstract Particulars*. Oxford: Basil Blackwell.

Cartwright, Helen M. 1965. "Heraclitus and the Bath Water." *Philosophical Review* 74:466–485.

———. 1970. "Quantities." *Philosophical Review* 79:25–42.

———. 1972. "Chappell on Stuff and Things." *Nous* 6:369–377.

———. 1975. "Amounts and Measures of Amount." *Nous* 9:143–164.

Cartwright, Richard. 1968. "Some Remarks on Essentialism." *Journal of Philosophy* 65:615–626.

Cassam, Q. 1986. "Science and Essence." *Philosophy* 61:95–107.

Chappell, V. C. 1970–71. "Stuff and Things." *Proceedings of the Aristotelian Society* 71:61–76.

———. 1973. "Matter." *Journal of Philosophy* 70:679–696.

Charles, David. 1984. *Aristotle's Philosophy of Action*. London: Duckworth; Ithaca: Cornell University Press.

——. 1988. "Aristotle on Hypothetical Necessity and Irreducibility." *Pacific Philosophical Quarterly* 69:1–53.

——. 1993. "Aristotle on Substance, Essence, and Biological Kinds." In Cleary 1993, 227–261.

——. 1994. "Matter and Form: Unity, Persistence, and Identity." In Scaltsas, Charles, and Gill 1994, 75–105.

Charlton, William. 1970. *Aristotle's "Physics" I, II.* Oxford: Clarendon Press.

——. 1972. "Aristotle and the Principle of Individuation." *Phronesis* 17:239–249.

——. 1980. "Aristotle's Definition of Soul." *Phronesis* 25:170–186.

——. 1981. "Telling the Difference between Sweet and Pale." *Apeiron* 15:103–114.

——. 1983. "Causation and Change." *Philosophy* 58:143–160.

——. 1994. "Aristotle on Identity." In Scaltsas, Charles, and Gill 1994, 41–53.

Chen, C.-H. 1957. "On Aristotle's Two Expressions: $\kappa\alpha\theta$' $\dot{\upsilon}\pi o\kappa\epsilon\iota\mu\acute{\epsilon}\nu o\upsilon$ $\lambda\acute{\epsilon}\gamma\epsilon\sigma\theta\alpha\iota$ and $\dot{\epsilon}\nu$ $\dot{\upsilon}\pi o\kappa\epsilon\iota\mu\acute{\epsilon}\nu\omega$ $\epsilon\hat{\iota}\nu\alpha\iota$—Their Meaning in *Cat.* 2.1a20–b9 and the Extension of This Meaning." *Phronesis* 2:148–159.

——. 1961. "On Aristotle's "*Metaphysics*" K 7.1064a29: $\tau o\hat{\upsilon}$ $\ddot{o}\nu\tau o\varsigma$ $\hat{\eta}$ $\ddot{o}\nu$ $\kappa\alpha\grave{\iota}$ $\chi\omega\rho\iota\sigma\tau\acute{o}\nu$." *Phronesis* 6:53–58.

——. 1964. "The Universal Concrete. A Typical Aristotelian Duplication of Reality." *Phronesis* 9:48–57.

Chiba, Kei. 1991. "Aristotle on Explanation: Demonstrative Science and Scientific Inquiry." *The Annual Report on Cultural Science.* Parts 1, 2. Hokkaido University: The Faculty of Letters.

Clark, S. R. L. 1975. *Aristotle's Man.* Oxford: Clarendon Press.

Cleary, John J. 1985. "On the Terminology of 'Abstraction' in Aristotle. *Phronesis* 30:13–45.

——. 1988. *Aristotle on the Many Senses of Priority. Journal of the History of Philosophy,* Monograph Series. Carbondale: Southern Illinois University Press.

——, ed. 1993. *The Boston Area Colloquium in Ancient Philosophy.* Vols. 4 and 9. New York: University Press of America.

Cleary, John J., and D. C. Shartin, eds. 1988/1993. *The Boston Area Colloquium in Ancient Philosophy.* Vols. 4 and 9. New York: University Press of America.

Code, Alan. 1976. "The Persistence of Aristotelian Matter." *Philosophical Studies* 29: 357–367.

——. 1978. "No Universal Is a Substance—An Interpretation of the *Metaphysics* Z. 13.1038b8–15." *Paideia* 7:65–74.

——. 1985. "On the Origins of Some Aristotelian Theses about Predication." In Bogen and McGuire 1985, 101–131.

——. 1987. "Soul as Efficient Cause in Aristotle's Embryology." *Philosophical Topics* 15:51–59.

Cohen, S. Marc. 1978. "Individual and Essence in Aristotle's *Metaphysics*." *Paideia* 7:75–85.

——. 1981. "Proper Differentiae, the Unity of Definition, and Aristotle's Essentialism." *New Scholasticism* 229–240.

——. 1984. "Aristotle and Individuation." *Canadian Journal of Philosophy* 10:41–65.

Cohen, Sheldon M. 1984. "Aristotle's Doctrine of the Material Substrate." *Philosophical Review* 93:171–194.

Coll, F. 1974. "The Concept of Substance in the *Categories* and the *Physics*." *Danish Yearbook of Philosophy*, 72–119.

Cooper, J. M. 1975. *Reason and Human Good in Aristotle*. Cambridge: Harvard University Press.

——. 1982. "Aristotle on Natural Teleology." In Schofield and Nussbaum 1982, 197–222.

——. 1985. "Hypothetical Necessity." In Gotthelf 1985, 151–167.

Cresswell, M. J. 1971. "Essence and Existence in Plato and Aristotle." *Theoria* 91–113.

——. 1975. "What Is Aristotle's Theory of Universals." *Australasian Journal of Philosophy* 53: 238–247.

——. Forthcoming. "The Ontological Status of Matter in Aristotle." *Theoria*.

Dancy, Russell M. 1973. "Matter: Aristotle and Chappell." *Journal of Philosophy* 70: 696–698.

——. 1975a. "On Some of Aristotle's First Thoughts about Substance." *Philosophical Review* 84:338–373.

——. 1975b. *Sense and Contradiction: A Study in Aristotle*. Dordrecht: Reidel.

——. 1978. "On Some of Aristotle's Second Thoughts about Substances: Matter." *Philosophical Review* 87:372–413.

——. 1981. "Aristotle and the Priority of Actuality." Knuuttila 1981, 73–115.

——. 1983. "Aristotle and Existence." *Synthese* 54:409–442.

——. 1984. "The One, the Many, and the Forms: *Philebus* 15b1–8." *Ancient Philosophy* 4:160–193.

——. 1991. *Two Studies in the Early Academy*. Albany: State University of New York Press.

Davidson, Donald. 1980. *Essays on Actions and Events*. Oxford: Clarendon Press.

Devereux, D. T., and P. Pellegrin, eds. 1990. *Biologie, logique, et métaphysique chez Aristote*. Paris: Centre National de la Recherche Scientifique.

Driscoll, J. A. 1981. "Εἴδη in Aristotle's Earlier and Later Theories of Substance." In O'Meara 1981, 129–159.

Duerlinger, J. 1970. "Predication and Inherence in Aristotle's Categories." *Phronesis* 15:179–203.

Easterling, H. J. 1976. "The Unmoved Mover in Early Aristotle." *Phronesis* 21:252–265.

Edel, A. 1982. *Aristotle and His Philosophy*. Chapel Hill: University of North Carolina Press.

Ferejohn, Michael. 1980. "Aristotle on Focal Meaning and the Unity of Science." *Phronesis* 25:117–128.

——. 1991. *The Origins of Aristotelian Science*. New Haven: Yale University Press.

——. 1994. "The Definition of Generated Composites in Aristotle's *Metaphysics*." In Scaltsas, Charles, and Gill 1994, 291–318.

Fine, K. 1979. "A Defence of Arbitrary Objects." *Aristotelian Society*, Supp. Vol. 57:55–77.

——. 1985. *Reasoning with Arbitrary Objects*. Oxford: Basil Blackwell.

——. 1992. "Aristotle on Matter." *Mind* 101:35–57.

——. 1994a. "Compounds and Aggregates." *Noûs* 28.

——. 1994b. "A Puzzle Concerning Matter and Form." In Scaltsas, Charles, and Gill 1994, 13–40.

——. Forthcoming. "Senses of Essence." In Sinnott-Armstrong, Raffman, and Asher forthcoming.

——. Unpublished. 1979. "Aristotle on Substance."

Forbes, Graeme. 1980. "Origin and Identity." *Philosophical Studies* 37:353–362.

——. 1985. *The Metaphysics of Modality*. Oxford: Clarendon Press.

——. Unpublished. "The New Riddle of Existence."

Fortenbaugh, W. W., and R. W. Sharples, eds. 1988. *Theophrastean Studies: On Natural Science, Physics and Metaphysics, Ethics, Religion, and Rhetoric*. Vol. 3. New Brunswick, N.J.: Transaction Books.

Frede, Michael. 1985. "Substance in Aristotle's Metaphysics." In Gotthelf 1985, 17–26.

——. 1990. "The Definition of Sensible Substances in *Met. Z*." In Devereux and Pellegrin 1990, 113–129.

——. 1994. "Aristotle's Notion of Potentiality in *Metaphysics* Θ." In Scaltsas, Charles, and Gill 1994, 173–193.

Frede, Michael, and Patzig, G. 1988. *Aristoteles "Metaphysik Z."* 2 vols. Munich: C. H. Beck.

Freeland, Cynthia. 1987. "Aristotle on Bodies, Matter, and Potentiality." In Gotthelf and Lennox 1987, 392–406.

Furley, David. 1967. *Two Studies in the Greek Atomists: Study 1: Indivisible Magnitudes. Study 2: Aristotle and Epicurus on Voluntary Action*. Princeton: Princeton University Press.

——. 1978. "Self Movers." In Lloyd and Owen 1978, 165–179. Repr. in A. Rorty 1980, 55–67.

——. 1983. "The Mechanics of *Meteorologica* iv: A Prolegomenon to Biology." In Moraux and Wiesner 1983, 73–93.

——. 1985. "The Rainfall Example in *Physics* ii 8." In Gotthelf 1985, 177–182.

——. 1987. *The Greek Cosmologists I—The Formation of the Atomic Theory and Its Earliest Critics*. Cambridge: Cambridge University Press.

——. 1989. *Cosmic Problems—Essays on Greek and Roman Philosophy of Nature*. Cambridge: Cambridge University Press.

Furley, David, and Christian Wildberg, trans. 1991. *Place, Void, and Eternity*, by Philoponus and Simplicius. Ancient Commentators on Aristotle Series. Ithaca: Cornell University Press.

Furth, Montgomery. 1988. *Substance, Form, and Psyche: An Aristotelean Metaphysics*. Cambridge: Cambridge University Press.

Gallop, David. 1975. *Plato—"Phaedo."* Clarendon Plato Series. Oxford: Clarendon Press.

Gaukroger, Stephen. 1980. "Aristotle on Intelligible Matter." *Phronesis* 25:187–197.

——. 1982. "The One and the Many: Aristotle on the Individuation of Numbers." *Classical Quarterly* 32:312–322.

Gewidmet, P. M. 1985. *Aristoteles und Seine Schule.* Berlin: Walter de Gruyter.

Gill, Mary Louise. 1980. "Aristotle's Theory of Causal Action in *Physics* 3.3." *Phronesis* 129–147.

——. 1989. *Aristotle on Substance: The Paradox of Unity.* Princeton: Princeton University Press.

——. 1991. "Aristotle on Self-Motion." In Judson 1991, 243–265.

——. 1993. "Commentary on Charles: Aristotle on Substance, Essence and Biological Kinds." In Cleary 1993, 262–269.

——. 1994. "Individuals and Individuation in Aristotle." In Scaltsas, Charles, and Gill 1994, 55–71.

Gomez-Lobo, Alfonso. 1981. "Aristotle, *Metaphysics* H, 2." *Dialogos* 7–12.

Gotthelf, Allan. 1976. "Aristotle's Conception of Final Causality." *Review of Metaphysics* 30:226–254.

——. 1988. "The Place of the Good in Aristotle's Natural Teleology." Cleary and Shartin 1988:113–139.

——, ed. 1985. *Aristotle on Nature and Living Things.* Volume Presented to David Balme. Pittsburgh: Mathesis Publications.

Gotthelf, Allan, and J. G. Lennox, eds. 1987. *Philosophical Issues in Aristotle's Biology.* Cambridge: Cambridge University Press.

Graeser, A., ed. 1987. *Mathematik und Metaphysik bei Aristoteles.* Berne.

Granger, Herbert. 1980. "Aristotle and the Genus-Species Relation." *Southern Journal of Philosophy* 18:37–50.

Grene, Marjorie. 1974. "Is Genus to Species as Matter to Form? Aristotle and Taxonomy." 51–69.

Grossmann, Reinhardt. 1973. *Ontological Reduction.* Bloomington: Indiana University Press.

——. 1983. *The Categorial Structure of the World.* Bloomington: Indiana University Press.

——. 1990. *The Fourth Way: A Theory of Knowledge.* Bloomington: Indiana University Press.

——. 1992. *The Existence of the World: An Introduction to Ontology.* The Problems of Philosophy Series: Their Past and Present. London: Routledge.

Hale, Robert. 1987. *Abstract Objects.* Oxford: Basil Blackwell.

Halper, Edward. 1985. "*Metaphysics* Z.12 and H.6: The Unity of Form and Composite." *Ancient Philosophy* 4:146–159.

——. 1989. *One and Many in Aristotle's Metaphysics: The Central Books.* Columbus: Ohio State University Press.

Hamlyn, D. 1977. *Aristotle's "De Anima"—Books 2.12.* Clarendon Aristotle Series. Oxford: Clarendon Press.

——. 1984. *Metaphysics.* Cambridge: Cambridge University Press.

Hartman, Edwin. 1976. "Aristotle on the Identity of Substance and Essence." *Philosophical Review* 85:545–561.

——. 1977. *Substance, Body and Soul.* Princeton: Princeton University Press.

Haslanger, Sally. 1994. "Parts, Compounds, and Substantial Unity." In Scaltsas, Charles, and Gill 1994, 129–170.

Hayduck, M. 1888. *Asclepii in Metaphysicorum Libros A–Z Commentaria.* Vol. 6, Part 2 of *Commentaria in Aristotelem Graeca.* Berlin: Reimer.

——. 1891. *Alexandri Aphrodisiensis in Aristotelis Metaphysica Commentaria.* Berlin: Reimer.

——. 1897. *Ioannis Philopon—In Aristotelis De Anima Libros—Commentaria.* Berlin: Reimer.

Heinaman, Robert. 1979. "Aristotle's Tenth Aporia." *Archiv für Geschichte der Philosophie* 54:249–270.

——. 1981. "Non-substantial Individuals in the *Categories.*" *Phronesis* 26:295–307.

Hett, W. S. 1935. *De Anima.* London: Loeb Classical Library.

Hicks, R. D. 1907. *Aristotle—"De Anima."* Cambridge: Cambridge University Press.

Hirsch, E. 1978. "A Sense of Unity." *Journal of Philosophy* 75:470–494.

Hiz, H. 1978. *Questions.* Dordrecht: Reidel.

Hodges, W. 1981. *Logic.* London: Penguin.

Hughes, Gerald. 1979. "Universals as Potential Substances." In Burnyeat et al. 1979, 107–126.

Hull, D. L. 1964. "The Effect of Essentialism on Taxonomy: Two Thousand Years of Stasis, I." *British Journal for the Philosophy of Science* 15:314–366.

Hussey, Edward. 1983. *Aristotle's Physics.* Clarendon Aristotle Series. Oxford: Clarendon Press.

Jaeger, Werner. 1948. *Aristotle: Fundamentals of the History of His Development.* Transl. R. Robson. Oxford: Oxford University Press.

Jones, Barrington. 1972. "Individuals in Aristotle's *Categories.*" *Phronesis* 17:107–123.

——. 1974. "Aristotle's Introduction of Matter." *Philosophical Review* 83:474–500.

Kahn, C. H. 1966. "Sensation and Consciousness in Aristotle's Psychology." *Archiv für Geschichte der Philosophie* 41:43–81.

——. 1978. "Questions and Categories." In Hiz 1978, 227–278.

——. 1985. "On the Intended Interpretation of Aristotle's Metaphysics." In Gewidmet 1985, 311–338.

Kirwan, Christopher. 1970–71. "How Strong Are the Objections to Essence?" *Proceedings of the Aristotelian Society* 71:43–59.

——. 1971. *Aristotle's Metaphysics. Books Γ, Δ, E.* Clarendon Aristotle Series. Oxford: Clarendon Press.

Knuuttila, S., ed. 1981. *Reforging the Great Chain of Being: Studies in the History of Modal Theories.* Dordrecht: Reidel.

Kosman, L. A. 1969. "Aristotle's Definition of Motion." *Phronesis* 14:40–62.

——. 1975. "Perceiving That We Perceive: *On the Soul* III.2." *Philosophical Review* 84:499–519.

——. 1984. "Substance, Being, and *Energeia.*" *Oxford Studies in Ancient Philosophy* 2:121–149.

——. 1994. "The Activity of Being in Aristotle's *Metaphysics.*" In Scaltsas, Charles, and Gill 1994, 195–213.

Kripke, Saul. 1972. *Naming and Necessity*. Cambridge, Mass.: Harvard University Press.

Kullmann, W. 1977–78. "Ὁ Ρόλος της Τελολογίας στην Αριστοτελική Επιστήμη." Athens: ΕΕΦΣΠΑ, 136–156.

Judson, Lindsay. 1991. *Aristotle's Physics: A Collection of Essays*. Oxford: Clarendon Press.

Lacey, A. R. 1965. "Οὐσία and Form in Aristotle." *Phronesis* 10:54–69.

Laks, André. 1988. "Eurythus in Theophrastus' *Metaphysics*." In Fortenbaugh and Sharples 1988, 237–243.

Lang, H. 1981. "Aristotle's Immaterial Mover and the Problem of Location in *Physics* VIII." *Review of Metaphysics* 34:321–335.

Laycock, H. 1972. "Some Questions of Ontology." *Philosophical Review* 81:3–42.

Lear, Jonathan. 1988. *Aristotle: The Desire to Understand*. Cambridge: Cambridge University Press.

Lee, E. N., A. P. D. Mourelatos, and R. M. Rorty, eds. 1973. *Exegesis and Argument: Studies in Greek Philosophy Presented to Gregory Vlastos. Phronesis*, Supp. Vol. 1.

Lennox, James. 1982. "Teleology, Chance, and Aristotle's Theory of Spontaneous Generation." *Journal of the History of Philosophy* 20:219–238.

———. 1984. "Aristotle on Chance." *Archiv für Geschichte der Philosophie* 59:52–60.

———. 1985. "Are Aristotelian Species Eternal?" In Gotthelf 1985, 67–94.

———. 1987. "Kinds, Forms of Kinds, and the More and the Less in Aristotle's Biology." In Gotthelf and Lennox 1987, 339–359.

Lesher, J. 1971. "Aristotle on Form, Substance, and Universals: A Dilemma." *Phronesis* 16:169–178.

Lewis, David. 1986a. "Against Structural Universals." *Australasian Journal of Philosophy* 64:25–46.

———. 1986b. *On the Plurality of Worlds*. Oxford: Basil Blackwell.

———. 1991. *Parts of Classes*. Oxford: Basil Blackwell.

Lewis, F. A. 1984. "What Is Aristotle's Theory of Essence?" In Pelletier and King-Farlow 1984, 89–131.

———. 1985. "Form and Predication in Aristotle's *Metaphysics*." In Bogen and McGuire 1985, 59–83.

———. 1991. *Substance and Predication in Aristotle*. Cambridge: Cambridge University Press.

———. 1994. "Aristotle on the Relation between a Thing and Its Matter." In Scaltsas, Charles, and Gill 1994, 247–277.

Lloyd, A. C. 1962. "Genus, Species, and Ordered Series in Aristotle." *Phronesis* 7:67–90.

———. 1970. "Aristotle's Principle of Individuation." *Mind* 79:519–529.

———. 1981. *Form and Universal in Aristotle*. Liverpool: Francis Cairns.

Lloyd, G. E. R. 1964. "Hot and Cold, Dry and Wet in Early Greek Thought." *Journal of Hellenic Studies* 84:92–106.

———. 1969. *Aristotle: The Growth and Structure of His Thought*. Cambridge: Cambridge University Press.

——. 1983. *Science, Folklore and Ideology: Studies in the Life Sciences in Ancient Greece.* Cambridge: Cambridge University Press.

——. 1991. *Methods and Problems in Greek Science.* Cambridge: Cambridge University Press.

Lloyd, G. E. R., and G. E. L. Owen, eds. 1978. *Aristotle on Mind and the Senses: Proceedings of the Seventh Symposium Aristotelicum.* Cambridge: Cambridge University Press.

Long, A. A. 1981. "Aristotle and the History of Greek Scepticism." In O'Meara 1981, 79–106.

Loux, Michael J. 1970. *Universals and Particulars: Readings in Ontology.* Notre Dame: University of Notre Dame Press.

——. 1974. "Kinds and the Dilemma of Individuation." *Review of Metaphysics* 27:773–784.

——. 1978. *Substance and Attribute.* Dordrecht: Reidel.

——. 1979a. "Form, Species, and Predication in *Metaphysics* Z, H, Θ." *Mind* 88:1–23.

——. 1991. *Primary "Ousia": An Essay on Aristotle's "Metaphysics" Z and H.* Ithaca: Cornell University Press.

——, ed. 1979b. *The Possible and the Actual: Readings in the Metaphysics of Modality.* Ithaca: Cornell University Press.

Lukasiewicz, J. 1953. "Symposium: The Principle of Individuation." *Proceedings of the Aristotelian Society,* Supp. Vol. 27:69–82.

McCabe, Vicki. 1982. "The Direct Perception of Universals: A Theory of Knowledge Acquisition." *Synthese* 52:495–513.

McDowell, John. 1973. *Plato: "Theaetetus."* Oxford: Clarendon Press.

McKeon, Richard, ed. 1941. *The Basic Works of Aristotle.* New York: Random House.

Máté, András. Unpublished. "A Platonic Theory of Predication."

Matthen, Mohan. 1983. "Greek Ontology and the 'Is' of Truth." *Phronesis* 28:113–135.

——. 1984. "Forms and Participants in Plato's *Phaedo.*" *Noûs* 18:281–297.

——. 1986a. "Individual Substances as Hylomorphic Complexes." In Matthen 1986c, 151–176.

——. 1986b. "Introduction: The Structure of Aristotelian Science." In Matthen 1986c, 1–23.

——, ed. 1986c. *Aristotle Today: Essays on Aristotle's Ideal of Science.* Edmonton, Alberta: Academic Printing & Publishing.

Matthews, G. B. 1982. "Accidental Unities." In Schofield and Nussbaum 1982, 223–240.

Matthews, G. B., and S. Marc Cohen. 1968. "The One and the Many." *Review of Metaphysics* 21:630–655.

Maudlin, T. Unpublished. "Substances and Space-Time: What Aristotle Would Have Said to Einstein."

Mendell, Henry. 1987. "*Topoi* on *Topos*: The Development of Aristotle's Concept of Place." *Phronesis* 32:206–231.

Mignucci, Mario. 1972. *On a Controversial Demonstration of Aristotle's Modal Syllogistic: An Enquiry on "Prior Analytics" A 15.* Padova: Antenore.

——. Unpublished a. "Predication in the *Topics.*" Scottish Association for Classical Philosophy, 1992 Edinburgh.

——. Unpublished b. "Singular and General in Aristotle's Logic." Southern Universities Association for Classical Philosophy, 1991 Oxford.

Miller, F. D., Jr. 1978. "Aristotle's Use of Matter." *Paideia* 7:105–119.

Modrak, D. K. 1979. "Forms, Types, and Tokens in Aristotle's *Metaphysics.*" *Journal of the History of Philosophy* 17:371–381.

——. 1987. *Aristotle: The Power of Perception.* Chicago: University of Chicago Press.

Moraux, P., and J. Wiesner. 1983. *Zweifelhaftes in Corpus Aristotelicum: Studien zu Einigen Dubia.* Proceedings of the Ninth Symposium Aristotelicum, Berlin.

Moravcsik, J. M. E. 1967a. "Aristotle on Predication." *Philosophical Review* 76:80–96.

——. 1974. "Aristotle on Adequate Explanation." *Synthese* 28:3–17.

——. 1975. "*Aitia* as a Generative Factor in Aristotle's Philosophy." *Dialogue* 14:622–638.

——. 1994. "Essences, Powers, and Generic Propositions." In Scaltsas, Charles, and Gill 1994, 229–244.

——, ed. 1967b. *Aristotle: A Collection of Critical Essays.* New York: Anchor Books.

Mourelatos, A. P. D. 1967. "Aristotle's 'Powers' and Modern Empiricism." *Ratio* 9:97–104.

——. 1978. "Events, Processes, and States." *Linguistics and Philosophy* 2:415–434.

——. 1984a. "Aristotle's Rationalist Account of Qualitative Interaction." *Phronesis* 29:1–16.

——. 1984b. "Δημόκριτος: Φιλόσοφος τῆς Μορφῆς." *Proceedings of the 1st International Congress on Democritus* 109–119.

——. 1987. "Η Ανακάλυψη της Μορφῆς στην Πρώιμη Ελληνική Φιλοσοφία." *Παλίμψηστον* 5:95–114.

Nagel, Thomas. 1986. *The View from Nowhere.* New York: Oxford University Press.

Nehamas, Alexander. 1979. "Self-Predication and Plato's Theory of Forms." *American Philosophical Quarterly* 16:93–103.

Nussbaum, M. C. 1978. *Aristotle: "De Motu Animalium."* Princeton: Princeton University Press.

——. 1984. "Aristotelian Dualism." *Oxford Studies in Ancient Philosophy* 2:197–207.

——. 1986. *The Fragility of Goodness.* Cambridge: Cambridge University Press.

Nussbaum, M. C., and A. Rorty, eds. 1992. *Essays on Aristotle's "De Anima."* Oxford: Oxford University Press.

Olshewsky, T. M. 1976. "On the Relations of Soul to Body in Plato and Aristotle." *Journal of the History of Philosophy* 14:391–404.

O'Meara, D. J., ed. 1981. *Studies in Aristotle.* Washington: Catholic University of America Press.

Owen, G. E. L. 1965a. "Aristotle on the Snares of Ontology." In Bambrough 1965, 69–95.

——. 1965b. "The Platonism of Aristotle." British Academy Lecture. Repr. in Barnes, Schofield, and Sorabji 1975, 1:21–25.

——. 1978–79. "Particular and General." *Proceedings of the Aristotelian Society* 79:1–21.

Owens, Joseph. 1963. *The Doctrine of Being in the Aristotelian Metaphysics.* 2nd ed. Toronto: Pontifical Institute of Medieval Studies.

———. 1966. "The Grounds of Universality in Aristotle." *American Philosophical Quarterly* 3:162–169.

Page, C. 1985. "Predicating Forms of Matter in Aristotle's *Metaphysics.*" *Review of Metaphysics* 38:57–82.

Parfit, Derek. 1984. *Reasons and Persons.* Oxford: Clarendon Press.

Peacocke, C. 1986. *Thoughts: An Essay on Content.* Aristotelian Society Series, Vol. 4. Oxford: Basil Blackwell.

———. 1991. "The Metaphysics of Concepts." *Mind (and Content).* Centennial Issue:525–572.

Pelletier, F. J., and J. King-Farlow, eds. 1984. *New Essays on Aristotle.* Calgary: University of Calgary Press.

Penner, Terrence. 1970. "Verbs and the Identity of Actions—A Philosophical Exercise in the Interpretation of Aristotle." In Wood and Pitcher 1970, 393–460.

———. 1987. *The Ascent from Nominalism.* Dordrecht: Reidel Publishing Company.

Penrose, R. 1979. "Twisting Round Space-Time." *New Scientist,* 734–737.

Perry, John. 1970. "The Same *F.*" *Philosophical Review* 79:181–200.

Philoponus. 1897. *Aristotle's De Anima.* In Hayduck 1897.

Pitcher, G., and O. P. Wood, eds. 1970. *Ryle.* Garden City, N.Y.: Anchor Books.

Popper, K. R. 1953. "Symposium: The Principle of Individuation." *Proceedings of the Aristotelian Society,* Supp. Vol. 27:97–120.

Preus, Anthony. 1979. "*Eidos* as Norm in Aristotle's Biology." *Nature and System* 1:79–101.

Preus, Anthony, and John Anton, eds. 1992. *Aristotle's Ontology.* Albany: State University of New York Press.

Putnam, H. 1981. *Reason, Truth, and History.* Cambridge: Cambridge University Press.

———. 1987. *The Many Faces of Realism.* LaSalle, Ill.: Open Court.

———. 1993. "Ο Αριστοτέλης μετά τον Wittgenstein." In Scaltsas 1993c, 315–334.

Quilter, J. 1985. "What Has Properties?" *Proceedings of the Russelian Society.* Sydney: Philosophy Department, University of Sydney.

Quinton, A. 1973. *The Nature of Things.* London: Routledge & Kegan Paul.

Regis, E., Jr. 1976. "Aristotle's 'Principle of Individuation'." *Phronesis* 21:157–166.

Robinson, H. M. 1974. "Prime Matter in Aristotle." *Phronesis* 23:168–188.

———. 1978. "Mind and Body in Aristotle." *Classical Quarterly* 28:105–124.

Rorty, A., ed. 1980. *Essays on Aristotle's Ethics.* Berkeley: University of California Press.

Rorty, R. 1973. "Genus as Matter: A Reading of *Metaphysics* Z–H." In Lee, Mourelatos, and Rorty 1973, 393–420.

Ross, W. D. 1924. *Aristotle's "Metaphysics."* 2 vols. Oxford: Clarendon Press.

———. 1936. *Aristotle's "Physics."* Oxford: Clarendon Press.

———. 1961. *Aristotle: "De Anima."* Oxford: Clarendon Press.

———, ed. 1931. *The Works of Aristotle.* Oxford: Clarendon Press.

Sainsbury, R. M. 1989. *Paradoxes.* Cambridge: Cambridge University Press.

Sanford, D. H. 1970. "Locke, Leibniz, and Wiggins on Being in the Same Place at the Same Time." *Philosophical Review* 79:75–82.

Sauvé, S. 1987. "Unmoved Movers, Form, and Matter." *Philosophical Topics* 15:171–196.

Scaltsas, Theodore. 1980. "The Ship of Theseus." *Analysis* 40:152–157.

———. 1980–81. "Numerical versus Qualitative Identity on Aristotelian Properties." *ΦΙΛΟΣΟΦΙΑ.* 10–11:271–286.

———. 1981. "Identity, Origin, and Spatiotemporal Continuity." *Philosophy* 56:395–402.

———. 1983. "The Individuation of Substances in Aristotle." DPhil. diss., University of Oxford.

———. 1984. "The Uniqueness of Particulars." *Philosophia* 14:273–296.

———. 1985a. "A Defense of Aristotelian Realism." In Boudouris 1985, 210–219.

———. 1985b. "Substratum, Subject, and Substance." *Ancient Philosophy* 5:215–240. Rev. and repr. in Preus and Anton 1992:179–211.

———. 1989a. "The Logic of the Dilemma of Participation and the Third Man Argument." *Apeiron. Nature, Virtue and Knowledge.* Special volume dedicated to the memory of Joan Kung. 22:67–90.

———. 1989b. Review of Furth (1988). *Philosophical Books* 30:82–85.

———. 1990. "Is a Whole Identical to Its Parts?" *Mind* 99:583–598.

———. 1991. Review of Gill (1989). *Philosophical Books* 32:26–28.

———. 1992a. "A Necessary Falsehood in the Third Man Argument." *Phronesis* 37:216–232.

———. 1992b. Review of Loux (1991). *Philosophical Books* 33:139–142.

———. 1992c. "Substratum, Subject, and Substance." In Preus and Anton 1992:179–211.

———. 1993a. "Aristotle's 'Second Man' Argument." *Phronesis* 38:117–136.

———. 1993b. Ο Χρυσούς Αιών της Αρετής: Αριστοτελική Ηθική. Athens: Alexandria Press.

———. 1994. "Substantial Holism." In Scaltsas, Charles, and Gill 1994, 107–128.

———, ed. 1993c. Αριστοτελικός Ρεαλισμός. Δευκαλίων. Special Issue 11.3.

Scaltsas, Theodore, David Charles, and Mary Louise Gill, eds. 1994. *Unity, Identity, and Explanation in Aristotle's Metaphysics.* Oxford: Oxford University Press.

Schofield, Malcolm. 1972. "*Metaph.* Z 3: Some Suggestions." *Phronesis* 17:97–101.

Schofield, Malcolm, and Martha Nussbaum, eds. 1982. *Language and Logos: Studies in Ancient Greek Philosophy Presented to G. E. L. Owen.* Cambridge: Cambridge University Press.

Sedley, David. 1989. "Le critère d'identité chez les Stoïciens" *Revue de Métaphysique et de Morale,* 513–533.

Sellars, Wilfrid. 1955. "Vlastos and 'The Third Man.'" *The Philosophical Review* 64:405–437.

———. 1957. "Symposium: Substance and Form in Aristotle." *The Journal of Philosophy* 54:688–699.

Sharples, R. W. 1983a. *Alexander of Aphrodisias on Fate.* London: Duckworth.

———. 1983b. "The Unmoved Mover and the Motion of the Heavens in Alexander of Aphrodisias." *Apeiron* 16:62–66.

———. 1985. "Species, Form, and Inheritance: Aristotle and After." In Gotthelf 1985, 117–128.

Shields, Christopher. 1988. "Soul and Body in Aristotle." *Oxford Studies in Ancient Philosophy* 6:103–137.

———. 1990. "The Generation of Form in Aristotle." *History of Philosophy Quarterly* 7:367–390.

Silverman, A. 1992. "Timaean Particulars." *Classical Quarterly* 42:87–113.

Simmons, G. C. 1978. *Paideia: Special Aristotle Issue.* Brockport: State University of New York Press.

Sinnott-Armstrong, Walter, Diana Raffman, and Nicholas Asher, eds. Forthcoming. *Modality, Morality, and Belief: Essays in Honor of Ruth Barcan Marcus.* New York: Cambridge University Press.

Smart, B. 1972. "How to Reidentify the Ship of Theseus." *Analysis* 32:145–148.

———. 1973. "The Ship of Theseus, the Parthenon, and Disassembled Objects." *Analysis* 33:24–27.

Smart, J. J. C. 1989. *Our Place in the Universe: A Metaphysical Discussion.* Oxford: Basil Blackwell.

Solmsen, F. 1958. "Aristotle and Prime Matter." *Journal of the History of Ideas* 19:243–252.

Sorabji, R. 1971. "Aristotle on Demarcating the Five Senses." *Philosophical Review* 80:55–79. Repr. in Barnes, Schofield, and Sorabji 1979, vol. 4:76–92.

———. 1974. "Body and Soul in Aristotle." *Philosophy* 49:63–89.

———. 1980. *Necessity, Cause, and Blame: Perspectives on Aristotle's Theory.* London: Duckworth and Ithaca: Cornell University Press.

———. 1983. *Time, Creation, and the Continuum: Theories in Antiquity and the Early Middle Ages.* London: Duckworth; Ithaca: Cornell University Press.

———. 1988. *Matter, Space, and Motion: Theories in Antiquity and Their Sequel.* London: Duckworth; Ithaca: Cornell University Press.

———. 1991. "From Aristotle to Brentano: The Development of the Concept of Intentionality." In Blumenthal and Robinson 1991.

———. 1992. "Intentionality and Physiological Processes: Aristotle's Theory of Sense Perception." In Nussbaum and Rorty 1992, 195–225.

Sprigge, T. L. S. 1983. *The Vindication of Absolute Idealism.* Edinburgh: Edinburgh University Press.

———. 1987–88. "Intrinsic Connectedness." *Proceedings of the Aristotelian Society* 88:129–145.

———. 1988. "Personal and Impersonal Identity: A Reply to Oderberg." *Mind* 98:605–610.

Stahl, D. E. 1981. "Stripped Away: Some Contemporary Obscurities Surrounding *Metaphysics* Z 3 1029a10–26." *Phronesis* 26:177–179.

Stokes, Michael. 1971. *One and Many Presocratic Philosophy.* Cambridge, Mass.: Harvard University Press.

Stough, C. L. 1976. "Forms and Explanation in the *Phaedo.*" *Phronesis* 21:1–30.

Suppes, P. 1974. "Aristotle's Concept of Matter and Its Relation to Modern Conceptions of Matter." *Synthese* 28:27–50.

Sykes, R. D. 1975. "Form in Aristotle: Universal or Particular?" *Philosophy* 50:311–331.

Teloh, Henry. 1979a. "Aristotle's *Metaphysics* Z. 13." *Canadian Journal of Philosophy* 5:77–89.

———. 1979b. "The Universal in Aristotle." *Apeiron* 13:70–77.

Tennant, Neil. 1983. "A Defence of Arbitrary Objects." *The Aristotelian Society*, Supp. Vol. 57:79–89.

Van Fraassen, Bas. 1977. "Essence and Existence." Monograph Series. *American Philosophical Quarterly* 14:1–25.

Vlastos, Gregory. 1954. "The Third Man Argument in the *Parmenides*." *Philosophical Review* 63:319–349.

———. 1971a. *Plato: A Collection of Critical Essays 1: Metaphysics and Epistemology.* Garden City, N.Y.: Anchor Books.

———. 1971b. "Reasons and Causes in the *Phaedo*." In Vlastos 1971, 132–166.

Ward, J. K. 1988. "Perception and Λογος: *De anima* II.12." *Ancient Philosophy* 8:217–233.

Wardy, Robert. 1990. *The Chain of Change: A Study of Aristotle's "Physics" VII.* Cambridge: Cambridge University Press.

Waterlow (Broadie), Sarah. 1982a. *Nature, Change, and Agency in Aristotle's Physics—A Philosophical Study.* Oxford: Clarendon Press.

———. 1982b. *Passage and Possibility.* Oxford: Clarendon Press.

Wedin, Michael. 1973. "A Remark on *per se* Accidents and Properties" *Archiv für Geschichte der Philosophie* 55:30–35.

———. 1978. "Aristotle on the Existential Import of Singular Sentences." *Phronesis* 23:179–196.

———. 1984. "Singular Statements and Essentialism in Aristotle." In Pelletier and King-Farlow 1984, 67–88.

———. 1988. *Mind and Imagination in Aristotle.* New Haven: Yale University Press.

———. 1989. "Aristotle on the Mechanics of Thought." *Ancient Philosophy* 9:67–86.

———. 1991. "PARTisanship in *Metaphysics* Z." *Ancient Philosophy* 11:361–385.

White, M. J. 1974–75. "Substance and Essence in Aristotle." *Proceedings of the Aristotelian Society* 75:167–180.

———. 1980. "Aristotle's Concept of Θεωρία and the 'Ενέργεια-Κίνησις Distinction." *Journal of the History of Philosophy* 18:253–263.

White, N. P. 1971. "Aristotle on Sameness and Oneness." *Philosophical Review* 80:177–197.

———. 1972. "Origins of Aristotle's Essentialism." *Review of Metaphysics* 25:57–85.

Whiting, Jennifer. 1986. "Form and Individuation in Aristotle." *History of Philosophy Quarterly* 3:359–377.

Wiggins, David. 1963. "The Individuation of Things and Places." *Proceedings of the Aristotelian Society*, Supp. Vol. 37:177–203.

———. 1980. *Sameness and Substance.* Oxford: Basil Blackwell.

Williams, C. J. F. 1979–80. "Is Identity a Relation?" *Proceedings of the Aristotelian Society* 80:81–100.

———. 1982. *Aristotle's "De Generatione et Corruptione."* Oxford: Clarendon Press.

Witt, Charlotte. 1989. *Substance and Essence in Aristotle: An Interpretation of "Metaphysics" VII–IX.* Ithaca: Cornell University Press.

———. 1994. "The Priority of Actuality in Aristotle." In Scaltsas, Charles, and Gill 1994, 215–228.

Woods, M. J. 1963. "The Individuation of Things and Places." *Proceedings of the Aristotelian Society*, Supp. Vol. 37:203–216.

———. 1965. "Identity and Individuation." In Butler 1965:120–130.

———. 1967. "Problems in *Metaphysics* Z, Chapter 13." In Moravcsik 1967b, 215–238.

———. 1974–75. "Substance and Essence in Aristotle." *Proceedings of the Aristotelian Society* 75:167–180.

———. 1982. *Aristotle's Eudemian Ethics i, ii, viii.* Oxford: Clarendon Press.

———. 1991a. "Universal and Particular Forms in Aristotle's *Metaphysics*." *Oxford Studies in Ancient Philosophy* 9:41–56.

———. 1991b. "Particular Forms Revisited." *Phronesis* 36:75–87.

———. 1994. "The Essence of a Human Being and the Individual Soul in *Metaphysics* Z and H." In Scaltsas, Charles, and Gill 1994, 279–290.

Zeller, E. 1897. *Aristotle and the Earlier Peripatetics.* 2 vols. Trans. Costelloe and Muirhead. London: Longmans, Green.

# General Index

ability. *See* power
abstraction, 3, 4, 5, 11–14, 21, 31, 74, 77, 87, 97–113, 116–117, 142–143, 147, 151–152, 153n, 158, 160–161, 168, 175, 188, 190–194, 196–198, 223, 257
  defined, 117–118
  types of entity, 98–102, 116, 150n
  *See also* division
accidents, 65, 91, 95, 101n, 174, 247
  accidental compounds, 171–174, 179
  *See also* compound; essence
account. *See* definition; formula
Ackrill, John L., 202n
acting and being acted upon, 27, 217
activity. *See* actuality
actuality (*entelecheia, energeia*), 4, 86, 92, 103, 108, 114–115, 123–124, 136–137, 160, 168, 169n, 182, 186–187, 189–194, 196, 215–216, 218–219
  as ἐνέργεια/ἐνεργείᾳ, *an* actuality/*in* actuality, 4, 5, 123, 233
  defined by end, 232–234
  of nonsubstances, 4, 179
  of substances, 4, 5, 123, 233
  of substantial form, 4, 123, 191–194
  *See also* power
affection, 16, 174, 178, 203, 215–216, 218, 220–221
aggregate (*sōros*), 64, 66, 70–77, 82, 87–89, 109–110, 112, 151, 158, 160, 189, 256–258

Argument, 61–65, 72–73, 76, 82, 84, 110, 120, 187, 196, 256
  *See also* holism, substantial; whole: complex
air, 16, 201n, 211
Alexander of Aphrodisias, 50–51, 74n, 130n, 138n
Allen, R. E., 37n, 58n
alteration (*alloiōsis*), 8–16, 22, 30, 66n
analogy, 108
Anaxagoras, 36n
animal, 68, 85, 172–173, 176, 184–185, 213, 235
Annas, Julia, 252–256
*aporiai*, 1, 187, 249–251
Aquinas, Thomas, 51, 130n
arbitrary objects, 102–107, 117
argument, 31
  antinomy, 140–141
  dilemma, 113–115, 252–253
  existential, 6, 28–33, 109, 115, 224. *See also* aggregate: Argument; trope-overlap argument
  reductio ad absurdum, 59, 133n
  regress, 65, 111–113, 132–137, 139, 177n, 186, 244
  sorites, 242n
  *See also* aggregate: Argument; Second Man Argument (SMA); Third Man Argument (TMA); threshold argument; trope-overlap argument
Armstrong, David, 66, 74, 78–82, 87, 140–142

not composed of substances, 186–188, 258
and opposites, 19–20
particular, 1, 3, 79, 91, 102–107, 110, 166–167, 191, 195, 222, 229
peculiar, 182, 185
perishable. *See* substance: imperishable
*per se* (*kath' hauto*), 65, 132, 134–135, 139–140, 171, 178–179
Platonic, 47–50, 56, 76–77, 105, 119, 188
predicated of matter, 126, 224
primary, 90, 126, 134, 223
separate, 5, 14, 91, 98, 111, 126, 138–139, 143, 165, 167, 171, 182, 196, 252–255
similarity of, 5, 252–253
"this" (*tode ti*), 187n, 246
*See also* actuality; cause: of being; composite; essence; substantial form; individuation; inherence; subject; unity: substantial; wholes: unified
substantial form, 3, 5, 13, 20n, 54, 62, 65–78, 84–85, 87–96, 101–102, 106, 107, 111, 112, 115–117, 123, 125, 142, 152, 165–168, 172, 189, 198, 243, 258
actualization of, 4–5, 101, 114, 167–168, 192–193
identity criterion for, 118
particular, 93, 101, 121–122, 125, 126, 156, 166, 168, 191–193, 229–231, 235–251
not primitive, 235–244
potentiality of, 168
as substance *and* subject, 126, 167–168
universal, 5, 30, 35, 90–96, 127, 129–130, 132, 155, 168, 193, 197, 238, 246, 250, 253
*See also* definition; identity: criteria for substantial forms; knowledge; priority
substratum, 3, 9–22, 87–89, 99, 102, 107–110, 127, 173
characterless, 16, 18–19, 22, 121, 131, 141, 144, 153n, 159, 222–228
composition of, 226–228
Platonic, 40–41, 130–132
*See also* matter: substratum (*hupokeimenon*); predication
supervenience, 13. *See also* predication
Suppes, P., 222n

surface, 172–174, 213
syllables. *See* division: of syllables into letters

Tarski, A., 103n
teleology, 18, 84, 208, 230
Teloh, Henry, 182n
Tennant, Neil, 105
Theseus, ship of, 122, 238–243
Third Man Argument (TMA), 2, 29, 57, 131–133, 170n, 186, 191
thought, objects of, 32
threshold argument, 69–74, 76
thunder, 63, 77
time, 79–80, 110, 145, 148–149, 193. *See also* location, spatiotemporal
transformation, 8–12, 14–15, 22–27, 102, 120, 124, 158, 226–227
radical, 16–18, 23
tree, 2, 126, 134
trope-overlap argument, 74–77, 153n
tropes, 5, 75–76
truth conditions, 14, 113, 115–120

unity, 32, 44, 146
accidental, 171
of components, 61, 101–102, 107–120
of definition, 155n, 172, 176–179
emergent, 256–257
of form, 241–243
individual, 79
integration principles of, 84
by nomic connections, 78–79
numerical, 124–125, 144–146
in relation to time, 110
self-caused, 169–181
defined, 176–177
specific. *See* species
substantial, 1, 3–4, 63–69, 74–77, 82, 86–87, 101–102, 107–111, 186–187, 191–194, 196
of substantial form, 191–194
of wholes, 108
*See also* aggregate; form: as unifier; wholes
universal, 5, 14, 28, 30, 31, 91–96, 115, 148–149, 182, 195, 197, 198, 230, 247, 257–258
as component, 183–190, 254, 257
defined, 34–35, 143n, 182
dependent on individuals, 258

LaVergne, TN USA
18 November 2010
205393LV00001B/26/P